The Dropped Hand

The
Dropped
Hand

Terry Blackhawk

Lotus Press
Detroit

ISBN 978-0-9797509-4-6

Grateful acknowledgement to the editors in whose publications these poems, sometimes in altered versions, first appeared:

Borderlands:	"The Stone on the Island"
Comstock Review:	"Primer"
Driftwood Review:	"Peter Pan on Derby Day"
	"Here. There. Here."
Ekphrasis:	"Recalling 'The Diver'"
The Florida Review:	"Signaling Bridge"
	"Maundy Thursday"
The MacGuffin:	"Holding Hands with the Tin Man"
	"The Dropped Hand"
Nimrod:	"It Is"
	"Missing the Caves"
Performance Piece:	"A Blessing"
U. S. 1 Worksheets:	"A Puzzle"
Style!:	"Once" (as "Memorabilia")
Visions International:	"Everything About Elephants"

I send great gratitude to Peter Markus, good brother in work and words, for his thoughtful editorial care and advice. Thanks to the many friends who have shed light on these poems—especially Mitzi Alvin, Dan Minock, Mabelle Hsue, Robert Fanning, Bill Michaels and Elizabeth Socolow—and more thanks to Edward Haworth Hoeppner, Patricia Hooper, Jennifer MacPherson, and Judy Michaels for the laying on of hearts and minds over the manuscript. I am indebted to Naomi Long Madgett for her dedication, friendship and vision. Special thanks to Linda Gregerson and Jane Hirshfield—and gratitude, above and beyond all else, to my father for the words and my mother for the music.

Cover image: "Blue Space," by Sophia Rivkin, courtesy of the artist.

Cover design and typesetting by Ian Tadashi Moore. (http://onefullstop.net)

Second edition.
Printed and bound in the United States of America.
First published by Marick Press, 2007.

LOTUS PRESS
Post Office Box 21607
Detroit, Michigan 48221
www.lotuspress.org

For Julie

— and for Judy

i.

OVER THE STAGE

ii.

SIGNALING BRIDGE

iii.

MARKING THE FIRST

iv.

OPPOSITE SHORE

Let word be to absence
As color is to shadow…

Yves Bonnefoy

i.

OVER THE STAGE

Everything About Elephants

"This is not a joke," Metro Traffic explains,
but this herd of elephants slowing traffic
along I-275 makes news I'm glad to bring
to you in the Health and Living Center
where you lie, curled most days, your gaze
fixed below the sill. Why don't they make
these windows wider, deeper, let them stretch
from ceiling to floor, let in shrubbery, clouds,
road construction, teenagers waving cloths
to bring customers to their weekly carwash? I make
such a shallow window, bringing what little I can—
tales of self mostly, easy to relate and you
eager to hear. Of poems, friends, Fredrika
at the Cape on vacation. Before she returns, you
will be gone. Later she'll say she saw
a shadow over the sun, a passage
I try to deny, especially today as you
sit upright, tugging at the stocking cap
slipping over your brow. "Go on!" you scoff
at the pachyderm report, eyes bright
with the humor of it. These last few weeks, I,
slow to speak, have done most of the talking, while you,
always fluent, strain and wait for words.
Stir-fry, Kleenex, hope have eluded you.
So this quick laughter, set free from a cumbrous dark,
makes me grateful for everything
I know about elephants—their stately walk
to the grounds of their dead, the placid browse
of the great wide heads and their escape today
from the traveling circus into waist-high grasses.

Peter Pan on Derby Day

The Fairy and Human Relations Congress will hold
its annual meeting ... the first weekend in May.
Wireless Flash Weird News

Do **you** believe in fairies,
smudged sparrow—will you hang on to toeholds
of light, those pinpoints darting
                through the darkened hall?

These days you run through the green
mornings, each footfall a rebuttal
of cloud spots, liver spots, lung spots.

We missed War Emblem's victory today.
Next year, we'll get swept by the pound and gleam,
photo finishes and all the controversial dust.

We're planning to wear gaudy hats
and let horses make divinest sense.

Last Derby Day, just before they were Off!
we explained the race to our Bengali waiter
as we watched it from the counter in that Manhattan bar.

You bet your peanuts on Keats, who faded early.
I put mine on the colt whose trainer saved his life
with a mixture of milk, turpentine and faith.

I don't recall if he won or lost, but I'm shopping
for a comical hat, something bursting with spring
and belief, like the wires and pulleys I couldn't see

when I was five—supports that kept the actors
                flying out over the stage.

Fish Luck

Fact is, I owe my very life to fish,
"Fish Tales," Mary Jo Firth Gillett

High summer days
        it's almost enough
to let your gaze meander

across a lake's bright
        vacancy, and the blue-
green shore's a comfort

you motor out from
        to distance yourself
from words, or world—

as if one could ever be fully
        beyond the reach—of earth,
air—whatever element.

I like to think that yours
        is water and the fish
you caught flipped straight up

out of your wake—mind
        made manifest—
an instant's crystallization

of subject and will,
        current and dream.
It's how your *Chandeliers*

of Fish, for instance,
        (your homage to Breton)
capture and enact movement

or shine. I imagine them,
        chiming past
a deep sea reef, singular

connected, as if
       with wires, say—
eld in invisible linkage

as they wheel and turn.
       What makes these
creatures mark us

like totems or zodiacal signs
       but some tug between
the material and the real—sky,

shore, things that linger:
       your father's forearms
taut against the lunge

those long ago mornings
       he taught you the ways
of bait and be still,

to trust the translucent
       line. Yet no matter
how (or whether) the trout

chose you, you reeled it in
       and there it was,
not just word made flesh—

but fish, all flash and flicker,
       with its swivel
and flop of fin and tail

doing a dactylic dance
       on the floorboards,
eighteen inches (measure it!)

of pure surprise. Like Bishop,
      you opted not to
eat it but to let it go,

and what is left of that
      muscle and twist?
Picture carp teeming beneath

the surface of a pond—
      wave a hand
across them and they rise.

Ghost Turtle

The dream skims a shallow lagoon.
"See," I say, "he's like Joe Hill, never
died at all." Below its surface, gold
& turquoise spread like lichens, blossom
like anemones, while above them all,
not quite Christ on this water, you've come
walking. First you are the rare
Hook-beaked Ghost Turtle, and I want
to applaud your changeling nod.

Aha, I think, he's Jimmy Durante.
Then it's more clearly you,
despite the carapace & peculiar schnozz.
So white & transparent you are,
like moon on the water at night,
I think I could put my whole hand
through you, just as lately in sleep
I've resurrected lost friends, trolling
through moonlight & alpha rhythms.

After your funeral, folks would say,
"I've been dreaming of Larry..." scenes
bawdy, full of juice, just like you.
"This is how I monster-bate!" you sang
to Sara. But for me, you were mum, half
you, half turtle, until you faded
into a bony embrace & awkward cackle
that left me chilled & shaking
with laughter. Helpless, I watched

the cloud of your goodness
dissolve, yet awoke somehow glad—
glad to have felt what's left of your touch
(even if it was only your teeth
withdrawing from my neck)—glad
to survive the glimpse, through ground
freshly opened at my feet,
into the rag-draped pile of bones
that used to hold your heart.

Recalling "The Diver"

— after Jasper Johns

Tire tracks, beach glass, bird
scratch in the sand. Catch the grasses'
heavy heads responding to the wind, each
wavering stalk, each present clump
of soft gray-green, scumble of leaf and
twig, backwash of gravel and bark—
try to take in the whole beach, breeze, waves
and then this tern, holding to its one spot
in the air, an artist's eye, probing the shifting

surface. You came here riding on the artist's
raft, considering *the blue oneness*
of dreams. You came remembering *the blue*
oneness of the saturated grain
of the door without a frame, two blue
panels from a barn without a door.
Lake Michigan is many blues. You are
many blues. Where, how does one dive here?

When the docent said, "We are going to look
for the artist's hand"—you followed her
to the Kokoschka, with hands seemingly dipped
in blood, then to her "alchemy"
of Vuillard's hand pressed to a tilting wall,
but you were halted by the towering
blues of "The Diver," with its inverted life-
sized Calvary—two footprints at the top,
the curving slice of handprints, down and out
to each side—and the note about Crane drowning:
                              how a hand was seen
pushed up above the water as if waving from
the *fabulous shadow only the sea keeps.*

Fable   bell   toll   knell... Where
does the story end? Since *mortal*
makes a hollow sound, better Johns's *internal*
light that comes up from the brown paper

or his painted rough-hewn planks marked
by the actual, the living hand.
                        Half a moon, or less,
now sets in the west, half hidden by the day—
part memory, part reflection of how the artist dreamed
and then decided to grease palms and soles
before sprinkling each one with charcoal
in order to imprint them on the grain.

Holding Hands with the Tin Man

You get enough weight on your back, you twist
and turn and pop something loose.
TV football commentator

She was paring apples
when she learned the dangers of bearing too much
weight on artificial turf.

Sometimes you twist and turn—
yes, she thought, as she peeled a skin
and gouged a core. How many times

had she sliced apples? How many
Dorothys have landed in Oz?
She wouldn't mind holding hands

with the Tin Man, one video vision just now
seems as good as another. It's the weight
you worry about, she thought

hefting the usual images: block, tackle,
knock your enemy before he
knocks you. Run free.

Her peelings fell tangled in the sink
as the crowd let fly its inevitable roar—
all those throats straining, echoing

from the screen, or in barrooms
where guys hoot, slap hands and grab
bottle after bottle of beer.

She knows a man drinks alone
until his rage spends itself
in sleep. No matter his little son

who wets the bed or stands
in a corner waiting to don
pads and armor, crash about.

And her brothers, so far away now,
who cold autumn evenings would hurl themselves
against one another—

how gracefully their young heads
bobbed on slender stems.
Under the helmets she could see

the exposed place
below the crew-cut stubble, a soft dent,
like a kiss, an offering.

What's easy in leaving behind?
The vulnerable neck thickens
into meatiness. The knife

slips and cuts a thumb. And here
she yearns for that hollow man,
his heartfelt, heart-less grace.

A Puzzle

— *after Rene Magritte's "The Therapeutist"*

Maybe he lost his body
and they healed him
with a cage.

Maybe his questions dissolved
his brain.

Why is he called a survivor?

There is a brass drape
over the headless shoulder
and a bird who considers
        entering its cage.

How peacefully the breeze
must flow through him.

He has opened the cage
and that fuzzy bird, his heart,
sits on the ledge looking in.

The head has sunk below
his shoulders, while on the far wall
a weapon oozes blood.

He has left a space
for the answers to our questions.

He has left a space
for the whispers of children,
for belief in humanity,
for our chance to take a stand.

The hand rests calmly
on its walking stick.
The children still have questions.

Where do their gazes go?
Why doesn't he have a body?
How can he smell the air?

In a Flickering Circle

— for Anne-Marie, in Sweden

Morning light marks the distance
between your home and Tåkern,
its shallows a silver hint to the east,

mirage of marshes stretched beyond fields
where you and daughter Disa
collected flowers to turn into dyes

or hang from rafters in your weaving
cottage. You made me a bed there
among looms and drying racks

and I'd wake to seedlines filling the air
like clouds come to land. Twilights then
seemed never to end. Evenings

we'd row glass smooth streams
and you told how once, submerged and close
to drowning, you felt music and colors

so magical you resented the adult hands
pulling you to shore. It's dark now
but light's what you know to bring inside

this time of year, like that night
in our teacher's study, with candles brightening
walls and tabletops, when she told about

Krystallnacht—how she'd witnessed the terror,
then fled home to Sweden. As beeswax
melted down the sconces, I thought she held at bay

a sea we could drown in. What does it take
to truly see in the dark? Though *we are safe
in a flickering circle of winter festival,*

this year your Glädelig Jul tells of a niece
raped, race hate among the young and Tåkern:
a road to come between you and that horizon.

What's left unsaid deepens concern, for Disa
whose anxious eyes and broken sleep
spell an adolescent despair the same in both

our languages. Today I need new words
for summers, swans, and for Disa—her innocent
grief that day when she was five and you

threw away some old blooms to replace them
with the new. "Men de var ju levande!"
she cried. *They were still alive!*

A Blessing

— for Craig Foster, who loved the poems of children

David says *his soul*
is like lightning. It lights up the sky,
is gone in a flash.

Taryn, Grade 3, *is a tree*
wavering and swinging.

She *whirls and jumps*
in the sky at night.

Davetta's *a candle*
beginning to melt away.

These children write
a path to the clouds.

They wave to you, Craig,
from *a body with a hundred limbs,*

sing you onward from *a mouth*
with a hundred different voices.

May they make for you now
a bridge—a high walk across
to the other side.

ii.

SIGNALING BRIDGE

Signaling Bridge

i.

Aftermath

      My father
gropes for
     words, his hand
trembles, his eye can-
not connect
     the fork, the
fruit — melon,
word he tastes
but cannot
     say. Yet
the structure of sense
remains, cicada's shell,
a dry syntax.

     "Superfluity,"
he says. "There was a
superfluity of...."

       And
"What I mean
     to say is...."
"...get me to three no
trump, six spades..."

     And
oh dear heart, he is
signaling *bridge*
bridge we must
     build/lead
him across to where words
move leaves move air
moves over water we must
move him into the world
       of names.

ii.

Correct/Connect

Today, he puts his jacket
into the refrigerator. Then he
corrects himself. Coat closet, he says,
discovering a similarity of doors.

Coat, closet, cover, clothes,
close, open, open, close ...

What can we do but wait now
as we watch him gaze
at the anonymous leaves, listen into
the mute gradations of green.

Easy transposition, how now here
becomes nowhere. He has
now but he's lost know,
and we don't know where

he will land. I want to label
his world, tape signs to piano,
hearth, window, chair—but where to fix
surge, current, lift, breathe?

iii.

Toward the moon

Tonight I drive toward the moon
amber August melon moon
the road a line of lights
                    centered below
its rising. Creeping dragon,
red against black, trail of red eyes

so unlike the ribbon of moonlight
he recited for me when I was ten,
road whose disappearance
over the horizon I would draw then,
again and again, the moon
above it, the Highwayman's horse
rearing under that heartless moon.

I was three and he read to me
Goodnight Moon, Mother Raccoon.
The story said wait, wait till the moon
                    is full.

iv.

Riddle

Who writes the verse but does not know
Its name; who hums the tune
He cannot read. Does he or does he not belong

To the same leaves and lilies he knew
Before. These days he thinks chartreuse, perhaps—
Perhaps lavender, but can only signal "C" or "L."

At the wedding feast, who rose to the last
Minute request with grace, explicating
Our gratitude as *gracias*—origin of the name.

Who, as he gave welcome to our new daughter,
Let the memory of Grace, his mother, come
Filling him like prayer.

Who forgets the term but still follows
The form, repeating three five-seven-five lines
In "cautious small steps." Whose feet

Shuffle to the john; who later records his trip
In a measured hand that hasn't changed,
Though he no longer reads what it says.

Who makes his way with clues; who peed and sang
And crept back under the sheets. Who wanted to disturb
No one. Who put the time at the end of his line. 4:06 a.m.

Maundy Thursday

—April 9, 1998: 100th anniversary of Paul Robeson's birth

Forward from betrayal, my father writes,
his poem set to music and sung, finally,
by his congregation's choir. A year ago

they turned his offer down. The piece
was too dreary. And who betrayed whom?
What had he meant by that?

It's Maundy Thursday, the beginning
of the end for Christ, thirty pieces of silver
poised to fall into the traitor's palm.

Who betrays loses more, his song goes on.
For their next number the choir leads us
"By the Waters of Babylon"—a round this time,

the sopranos' *and wept, and wept* last to fade.
The pastor tells us to remember the darkness,
to light, then extinguish, six of seven candles,

the seventh carried out of the chapel to a secret
place as houselights dim. *...and wept, and wept*
was never Robeson's refrain, but we sing it again

while out of doors daffodils flout a wind-
driven rain we bundled in winter coats against.
Green is stubborn, rebellious, refuses

to lie down. *Forward from betrayal,* the voices ring,
easing pride and pain with melody as pure
and keen as the first thin greens of spring.

Missing the Caves

— in the south of France

At the hospital in Sarlat, we found him
struggling with what Roethke might have called
                    a loosening into the dark.

My mother wanted him to sluff off the vision
he'd set underway, but he insisted on incense
and candles, a cantor's song—and even,
or perhaps, some priestess—chanting.

                    My father dreamed for years
of epiphanies he'd find beneath the hills
of the Dordogne, and I guess he'd meant to turn
his "Homage to a Cromagnon Stone Carver"
into pilgrimage. But now there would be

no door opening in the side
of a hill, no torch-lit walls covered with lions,
mammoths or black hairy rhinos.
No ancient hands signaling from stone.

Instead, inner flickerings: a wild-eyed
woman with dangling breasts
and stretched wide mouth staring
him down through his dream.

                    As he swore she hovered,
luminous and laughing—there!—in a corner
of the air, I recalled his fling with art-wire
            sculpture—nudes, torsos, twisted
sinuous strands.
                    I was thirteen. His crucifix
showing Christ's penis stunned me, then.

                    Less startling, the mask
with flaming hair. Flimsy as it was,
I took it to my room, tacked it,
for the shadows it cast, upon my wall.

It Is

> *It is not down on any map. True places never are.*
> Herman Melville

...mid-September, days of dry
silent sky, and now this humid haze,
a fog my father shares as he sits
on the deck barely one week home
from the hospital, babbling less
but searching, more often staring
up at the maples and through them
to the school on the other side.
It is early yet, weeks before
he will be able to explain:
"Blasted. I was blasted," he'll say.
And later: "A great hand went through
and swept everything away."
Within a year, he will have tried
and given up, tried and given up
and finally declined cards or books
on tape or any more well-meaning
notions of change.
         But this is the day when
the prompt is egg and he writes *shirred*—
amazing, we agree, so much language
still intact, but how laborious to un-
cover, how hit-or-miss to probe.
An hour and he's still at work
on twelve short items, the slow
pen laboring over the speech
therapist's worksheet, the Palmer hand
with its discipline and rhythm
but the elegant slant is shaky now,
so frail and lacy anything might slip
through—*cloud puff, sign bubble...*

"Coffeestone!" he proclaimed,
when the intake nurse with her clip-
board form asked him for his name.
Call me...

In his eyes at the time
I saw Lear on the heath—or was it Ahab,
his internet bridge handle, password
to the game? Today that bridge stands empty,
all decks cleared, the virtual waves
he loved to travel break on a receding shore—

          and what's his memory now but sea-
wrack, beach glass, spindrift bits of legend
              dissolved from ink and paper
into air—like those long ago annotations
              in shoeboxes
filled with index cards: his own hand-
made concordance to the metaphors
in *Moby Dick.*
                Then he'd been
an eager grad student, awash in the symbolic
ropes and lines, light, dark and all the watery
wild—netting every nuance,
writing each one of them down,
and what shall we call him now—
Ahab or Ishmael?
                  wanderer or scribe?

          His hand wavers
off any map we know. I hope he is
finding some true place
but for now he must write the first
word that comes to mind.   *It is ...*

Here. There. Here.

—at the International Traveler's Club Restaurant

In order to order a beer, my father
conjures a map. The menu—international—
displays the world he traveled once so well.
We play a game of narrowing questions
following zigzagging global directions.
Despite the stroke, his will's still there.
Cerveza? I ask. No. Nothing Mexican.
He waves, points east. How about Lebanon?
No. But closer. Almost. Another gesture.
Europe? Yes. West? No. East? Well, yes,
German? North of there. Czech? Let me guess.
...we're closing in, but we're not quite there.
There, not here, although now it's an earlier year,
and I AM HERE, reading my first lines, first
captions beneath the cartoon stick figure
pointing its finger at the triangular chest
where the heart should be. No phonics.
Just I AM HERE. Look. See. Picture first. Self
in space, until THEY (bears, up to their tricks)
move in from the next square and, oh help
THEY ARE HERE! Picture by picture, and square
by square, the world evolves at Father's side.
The page turns. The menu turns. The child
reads on past bears, couch, the apartment, past Taipei,
Ankara, Singapore. Hop-stepping countries, we play
at clues and questions. Again I ask: Where?
Amsterdam? Yes! Order, please. We've arrived. Here.
We're pulling in at Heineken. Dutch beer.

Sunday Drive

Still...he has
his inner weather of pure meaning.
"Aphasia," Vijay Seshadri

Synaptic, synoptic, the searched-for
bit of the story—three Sundays in a row
he's told it—flickers and is gone,
just as the quick, low swath
of the Cooper's Hawk nearly sends me
swerving off the road—while my father
in the passenger's side laughs at my surprise.

Last autumn, lost in grief, he'd look up, sharp,
askance, startled. "Where did you go?" he'd ask
the air. What lies between the screen and the story,
the mother and the screen? In the early Thirties
when she still could spare a dime, Saturdays,
for the double feature, his mother would stand
inside the parlor to listen through their screen.

Mother I never knew, I give her a smile, a plump cross-
hatched shadow, make her lean a bit back so as not to
disturb. Call it training for the teller, surely my father
learned his trademark ease during the Depression,
those sessions on the porch where—among cousins,
playmates, friends, and basking in a grace he'd always carry —
he retold the movies, held sway with the tales.

Primer

These were the words
You put in your pocket—
Hearth table window chair.
These were the lifelines
I wanted to give you
In order to help you read.

You taught me to read
The music of words.
I felt so grown up beside you.
I found tobacco in your pocket.
I loved reading the lines
As I sat with you in your chair.

Today you sit in your chair
No longer expecting to read.
The doctor said: Try headlines.
You creased and caressed the words
Before putting them in your pocket,
The ones I prepared for you,

Each word a sign for you
Taped to table or chair.
How precious they felt in your pocket,
Even if you could not read
Them—those fat, large-font words
With their unfamiliar lines.

Now Mother says the lines
Of your own poems for you.
Sometimes you recall the words.
Hearth window chair—
Find other ways to read
Them. Put them in the pocket

Of your pajamas, pocket
Of sleep and dreams. Line
Them up heart-wise to read

However you can. I know you
Disdain the utility of chair
Without the magic of words,

So I say to you, Father, read the moon. Tonight
She pulls songs from the lining of her pocket
And sings them for you, rocking in a chair of words.

iii.

MARKING THE FIRST

Scallop: In Memoriam

Listen, ear, to the house, its abundant
emptiness. Hear now the forever chime
of children and the evergreen brushing
in the night against the glass. No window
shall mar her view as long as whelks, mussels,
cones and clams cover, overflow its frame,
and if all that remains is what the tides
brought and she carried home, even a scallop
may serve to improvise a fugue upon.
Heart, attend to the two quiet hands drawn
beside her door. Recall how camouflage
can blush at love's attention, and open—
yes, open—to the undeniable
light that still spills, refracted, through her panes.

F. W. (1941-2006)

Once

Once at a glacier's foot, I found
a clam, or so it seemed, turned to stone.

I wondered at its journey and kept it
all these years.

My dresser top is detritus
and dust, dried grasses, glass

tumbled and ground in oceans.
Odd corners turn up odd

fragments as I paw, searching
a poem lost among them.

A bud vase, coyly painted—
my mother's—a feather in that one.

Her hand held firm in mine
the week before she died.

The Stone on the Island

In the middle of Lake Erie is an island,
and in the middle of the island is a stone.
Mornings, as air moves with the warming
of the water, a cabin on the eastern shore
receives the sun. Curtains sway in the new day's
breeze beside a wooden table, with two chairs,
where a man sits by the window watching.
By now Lake Erie water snakes will have cast
countless shadows in the shallows over the ledge
below the cabin, where he'd look for fossilized
crustaceans scribbled in hardened ooze. Dozens
of warbler waves will have come and gone,
but the two-ton Indian grinding stone will not
have been moved from its spot in the grass between
the playing field and the road. The man will not
test again the granite wheel with his palms, feeling
corncob-sized grooves worn into its surface. He will not
waken again to the sun's path widening toward him
across those waves, those mornings the watery east
pulled him west into the dry landscape of home—
she so newly gone, it was as if he dwelt again
in the story of his birth: the brush hut and how
the women who built it for her washed and wrapped him
and sprinkled on his face drops of cold water
so he might endure *many things*. He will not
inhale again the lake-laden air, but he will keep
and carry the story hereafter, safe as a light-
filled cabin and solid as a grinding stone
intended for the work of women's hands.

The Dropped Hand

i.

Marking the first

Beneath a waning moon I follow smooth
asphalt, the setting sun. Past lighted windows,
the harvest dusk allows a tender seeing in:
families gathered and framed speed by.

To the waitress at the roadhouse
who wants to know about my journal
(curious, a woman, eating and writing alone)
I simply say I am on my way

to my mother's house.
I don't say that my mother is dead,
that my journey marks the first
birthday she will never see.

ii.

Already dark

Little Ash Girl passes the tree
her mother sings from.
tree = mother, bird = singing = mother
I wanted to get there in time for the
sun to set,

I wanted to say goodbye
to the leaves, but it was already dark
when I stopped to eat.

No more than four
hours of the rest of her day. I will
stay up until midnight,
keeping watch.

iii.

Something she said

The last words I heard her say
came to me in a dream
as the afternoon sun fell
slantwise through the slats.

"Don't you just *love* it?"

Perhaps I will dream her
tonight. Tonight I will put
my portion of her ashes

in the wooden apple she gave me.
"I wanted to give you
something," she said.

iv.

Interval

The night she died
I heard her voice, rising at intervals
from her kitchen below.

"You've reached Ben and Marie.
At the sound of the tone..."

Three times, ten minutes
apart. Half awake, unable
to imagine a nurse's urgent call

I believed it was my brother,
sleepless, playing the message, just to hear her
say her name.

v.

Three corners, four

Here, at her front door, I inhale the night.
The birch does not tremble.
The facade of the house is smooth and calm.

On the dining room wall, a sheaf of wheat she placed there.
Nearby, the Buddha's up-reached arms, as if his palms
carry the tray of the sky.

At the table, I write by the light of four flames.
Not the tension of threes. Four is static,
corners. Coroners. Four-square. Dug in.

vi.

Bell tower

       Mother, your house
has become your grave. I visit you here,
sit at the table with your ashes before me
in a thick clear plastic bag.

I heft the bag, surprised by the weight.
The hollow of your going is a bell, echoing;
it is the bell tower I never climbed with you,
your hands on the keyboard, the carillon

sending out its stream of sound.

vii.

Light figures

Spirit matter, spirit mater.

This is the puzzle, the light wood
holding the dark inside
the hollowed, blackened core
where the ashes reside.

Around the apple's sides,
jig-sawed clovers dance upward
to where the shoulder arcs out,
then pulls back toward the stem.

Puzzle of light
figures against a darker ground.
The ground unites them,
but they do not touch.

viii.

The page

       is such a small filter
for this rush, this static. Dried
tears on my cheeks dissolve
to white paper, furnace hum.
Outside stars circle us, fixing.

ix.

Pool

Flame
       licks brass.

       A slim
       ethereal appears
             between
       the curved
       side and the diminishing
flame.

The flame
clings to the side,
burns itself away.

The wax pools
       as the candle
       dies   down.

x.

Say she

Say she laughed and suddenly stopped
laughing
Say she decided and then could not
decide
Say there was a rustling in the cards
an opening of the mouth
Say there was a fixed stare
an abrupt and final
silence

Say she sat east
and looked west
or north and looked south

Say there was a number and a suit
a plan and a course
of action of course a bid

There would have to have been
a bid

Say she had trumped
or passed or overbid or doubled
her opponent who would have been
her friend doubled
her breath doubled
until the friend knew
the last   then

And then other   numbers that   began
to be dialed   calling
for the engine that began

And then there was the stunned husband
staring at the dropped hand

xi.

Letter

Mother,

I wanted to be there when they set you
to the flames.
I imagine the iron doors closing
after the casket on its trolley
rolled inside.
I hope they sent you clothed
into that fire, wearing the dress
I selected for you
with its soft dark blue folds,
the scarf around your neck
adorned with spades, clubs, diamonds
hearts.

xii.

Last tongue

Wick speck. Pin point.

As it dies, a flame
turns blue.

      Every moment
mattered to you, mother.

I am watching
the last tongue

burn itself   out.

iv.

OPPOSITE SHORE

October Letter

—after the anthrax scare, 2001

Some days to look
    into the sky
        is to ask *why*

not be endless
    especially when crows
        signal coded

warnings the under-
    sides of their wings
        catch rays setting

from some other time
    zone   bright
        patches of light

outlined in black
    against the un-
        forgiving blue.

Yesterday I found
    yellow jackets   off
        and on   all day

I watched them fly
    out and return
        fly out and re-

turn to and from their
    slit in the ground they'd
        hover over

the rhubarb's tent-
    like leaves as if
        held up by strings

always at least one
    sentry   soil still warm
        early autumn

something more frantic
		in their aggression
				this time of year.

Perhaps I could
		have waited them
				out waited for

the wilt the frost-
		shot leaves but I
				crept out past dark

with my sweet
		white foam firmly
				cast the flashlight's

eye   then held oh
		held my breath my
				hand and arm with-

out moving sprayed
		the aerosol
				deep soaked the earth

and mulch and pushed
		a stone hard
				upon it sealed

it like a bargain
		to protect us
				here above ground.

Today I dug
		up the comb in-
				spected the whole

papery nest
		flat as a basket
				bottom then shook

off the dirt pulled
		apart its hex-
				agonal cells

found just a few
      throbbing abdomens
            the rest corpses

handfuls of them
      the soaked bees'
            unmoving swarm.

Another year
      and I've kept
            my beloved

safe again from
      collapse   the shock
            near   lethal   sting

but now the mail
      that just thunked through
            its metal slot

bears a perilous mark
      almost too heavy to lift
            and   then ever

so slightly   tap the
      envelope tear
            the narrow edge

gingerly fearing
      the swish the buzz
            the unleashing

of god knows what
      minuscule sting
            some numb limbic

logic   that echoes leaves
      soon to rattle hard
            down our empty

street   even as it sets
      contagion   prickling
            across my skin.

The Wooden Heart, #1

I see smoke where there is
               no smoke
I wait for leaves to flame
               and fall
to shiver and crack
this unremitting blue
wall of sky

I want gray   I want
               mist hanging
low   I want to smell rain rising
      from street
             to air

**

Oh to dismiss the sun
the parched heart to undo
this fruit's interlocking lines

**

What resembles a heart   but has
      no core?
Without fire   how did the wood
come to char? How did its batik pattern
come to be?

My mother
loved batik   the inter–
weaving the wax
       resist   design

**

All day I have walked
with her without
her walked with without
grief's companion

I want to return to the one-room
cabin on stilts beside the lake I want moon path
at night over water the march of clouds
across the southern shore

Not these high dry days

Letter from Bornholm, Halloween Eve

From the radio, a thin wavering—
like a musical saw or chorus
of ghosts, a high pitched hovering
smoke this late autumn morning.
Elsewhere, nuclear news, and the hour
seeming to hold its breath
                    as I open the letter and enter
again that Baltic summer day
with Lene and Knut guiding us, after herring
and schnapps in their pink-washed house,
to a grove in a field near the sea. Here,
as the sun rises farther to the south,
we walk through dwindling
warmth, step into pockets of colder air.
Tomorrow we stop saving our daylight.

Tonight, I'll set my clock and think again
of that grove on Bornholm, its beeches
dappling a ring of monoliths settled
into the earth. We moved quietly there
through silence and a slow shade broken
only by the linnet's song and waves
of yellow rape blooms shining between the trunks.
More ancient than the ruined castle
on the island's opposite shore, the granite plinths
dwarfed, baffled us. All that came to us
were calls of birds, the speculations of the breeze,
and whatever our fingertips gathered from lichens,
nubbled runes, a plexiglass plaque translating:
Ole raised this stone according to magic rules.

The Wooden Heart, #2

So this is how wood
becomes an apple how apple
becomes a heart
a heart made of pieces jig-sawed
                whipsawed
oh jig-sawed whipsawed heart
the smooth wood the round the wooden heart

Is there a pulse to it?   Is there?
Even as the spirit falls away?

**

The wood winds the grief
the woodwinds wind her
notes entwine her hair she
wore it long pulled back severe
bun classic profile darkly strong

As heart empties sorrow
finds channels fits
in with the dark stems
the light figures
in the background fitting

**

I would infuse you wooden apple-heart
let the candle's flame play across
your surface enlivening it
like a zebra's flank rippling

Are you dark against light or light against dark?

Amortization

Inventory   Crystal
glasses the table the plants
pulled away from
it across the wooden floor
sunlight on the wooden floor
the shutters yanked
off so there is some glare
you must be careful now the floors
are not what you are
used to   your carpets
are gone the piles
the books piled on them
heavy smell nothing left over
the hearth the pictures pulled down

Death benefits   How
does death benefit
Death sends tendrils
into the living room   its traces
slip along the vine   The pulse
is not the heart   no   not
heart

Assessment   What price
to assign this space without her
touch her voice lighting
the glass the branches
in the yard lifting
the child's first music like ice
melting into flowers a shower
of petals she forgot to scatter
while all the while
trees stretched fierce fingers
over the astonishing
blinding snow

Maintenance   There is something
wrong with your bushes the jeep
will pull them out   There is something
wrong with your teeth   your breath
leaves a gap we will not
be able to fill   Don't think you might
fall   don't fall you might
be exposed   Where did you ever think you would
put this phone

Closing   Cold
blasts the house
plant   the cells' structures
dissolve   the basket
holds a pile of sodden leaves
collapsed and indistinguishable
from one another   far too
tender even to turn
brittle or shatter
like crystal   like ice

Closing costs   Impossible
to reckon the times
she climbed to bed and back
down again the comfort
of each good night or
the almost infinite
gestures the clean energy of her
hands   working   plucking   playing
the short nails   the working hands

How many   flicks   breaths   scratches   sneezes
pats   sighs   swipes   movements inseparable really
from the active flesh but if you could
simply calculate the times
her hands (each finger) touched the keys
(each one!) what portion would you claim
what divisor what dividend

and how would you space them
time   over   time

Set Me Gently

We are sitting at a table. There are windows near the table. It is my mother's dining room table beside the window looking up into the high trees. My mother is laughing. Her voice is clear, her speech is joyful but somehow without words. Now she is gesturing toward the window, pointing out branches, trees. At each move of her hands, branches fill with birds. The birds are making her happy. The branches are making her happy. She is gesturing, pointing to the branches and the birds, and I know she is not merely pointing them out. She is bestowing them, giving me what belongs to her. I will wake to the certainty that my mother has given me the green of the leaves and the movement of the birds.

**

In the foggy dream—the first dog, Softy, at the corner of a doorway I walk through. This is not the dream where I hear her voice. This is the faded dream where human figures dissolve into odd vertical shadows. A warm hello to an old dog I haven't seen in a long time.

**

I sit in the back of the church trying to sing along.
The children's choir is performing a poem that
I have written. My mother is accompanying the
choir. It comes as a surprise to me that she has
set my poem to music. But then I understand—
somehow, from the front of the church and
without any words, she tells me this—that she has
set all the other children's poems to music, too.

**

The next dream with dogs is also the dream of
clothes. In this dream, my mother has a rack of
clothes she wants to give me—an unattached rack, a
rolling rack, a freestanding rack, on wheels. I have
somewhere to go and I am badly dressed for the
occasion. I am wearing two orange shirts and the
collars conflict with one another. My mother is
helping me adjust my collar. Leo, my second dog,
is on the floor in this dream. Something is wrong
with one of his eyes. He needs tending. I must
care for him.

**

If I were to paint this dream, it would have no
horizon. Water fills the frame of the dream, but at
the very top, above the crests of the waves, the sky is
clear. The dream carries me on its waves. I think
the waves will drown me but I let them carry me on.
Do I decide, or do I have no choice? They take me,
these towering, jagged, white-capped waves. They
are what I need to get where I am going. But even if I
know this, first comes the fear, then acceptance, then
a wild, amazing ride, and I feel the maternal power
surge before the wave sets me gently down. It puts
me down in a new neighborhood, with an old house
that I need to add onto. Somewhat crumbling, but
full of possibility.

**

In the dream of the ocean her wave sets me gently
on another shore. In the dream of the blanket we
sit together on the couch. She covers me with the
blanket she is using. Two of us, together, under this
blanket: one fabric, two heads. We sit there side by
side, facing forward, but when I turn my head again,
she is gone.

In Just

Fog today and a new green
memory   yesterday's leaves pierced
by sun

**

How bright and fierce
the spring   the penetrating
chill of air and light

**

I am learning to lose
without losing   to count without
counting on

**

Now rain pelts the just–
opened buds   bounces
from the metal roof

Soon petals will coat
this asphalt   releasing
fragrance to our feet

Early Evening on the Eastern Shore

Breathe in thank-you; breathe out good-bye.
Li-young Lee

Here, on the cusp between
gratitude and good-bye,

I note the waning
waves seem louder than

before. Down the shore
a kingfisher pierces

the water. A minor feat,
repeated hundreds of times

a day, hundreds of days.
On his low-lying rock

he hops back and forth
facing east, then west.

Too far to tell what
he found, maybe a clam,

the way it separates
his beak like pincers.

East, then west. West,
then east. How is it

memoriam in-
fuses every sky?

This morning, as I stepped
from the forest onto a beach,

hundreds of cormorants,
an entire nesting colony,

flew up, all at once,
and it seemed to me a sign—

a gigantic fabric flapping
sorrow   loosened

at last   her voice rippling
like light on the water

as lake breezes lift
the locust's delicate leaves.

Notes and Dedications

"Everything about Elephants" (p. 15)
is in memory of Elsie Mayer.

"Peter Pan on Derby Day" (p. 16)
is dedicated to Judy Rowe Michaels.

"Fish Luck" (p. 17)
is for Mary Jo Firth Gillett,
with gratitude for its title.

"Ghost Turtle" (p. 20)
is in memory of Larry Pike.

"Recalling 'The Diver'" (p. 21)
is dedicated to Dan Malski and Karen Mulvahill.
"The blue oneness of dreams" is from Sekou
Sundiata's poem and spoken word album of the
same name. "The fabulous shadow only the sea
keeps" is from "At Melville's Tomb" by Hart Crane.
"...the internal light that comes up from the brown
paper" is found in "Jasper Johns: 'The Examined
Life,'" *Art in America*, April 1997.

"In a Flickering Circle" (p. 27)
"...we are safe in a flickering circle/ of winter
festival" is from Denise Levertov's
"Christmas 1944."

In "A Blessing" (p. 29),
the italicized phrases were written by Detroit
children in classrooms led by poets-in-residence
from InsideOut Literary Arts Project.

"Scallop: In Memoriam" (p. 47)
was written for the funeral service of Fredrika
Weisenthal.

In "October Letter" (p. 65)
"...why not be endless?" is from Mark Doty's
"Nocturne in Black and Gold."

Terry Blackhawk is the founder and director of Detroit's acclaimed InsideOut Literary Arts Project (www.insideoutdetroit.org) a poets-in-schools program serving over 5,000 youth per year. She began teaching English in Detroit schools 1968 after graduating from Antioch College and took up writing poetry herself, twenty years later, when she began teaching creative writing at Detroit's Mumford High School.

Blackhawk's poetry collections include *Body & Field* (Michigan State University Press, 1999), *Escape Artist* (BkMk Press, 2003), selected by Molly Peacock for the John Ciardi Prize; and *The Light Between* (Wayne State University Press, 2012) as well as two chapbooks. Her poems have appeared in numerous anthologies and journals, including *Marlboro Review*, *Michigan Quarterly Review*, *Florida Review*, *Borderlands*, *Artful Dodge*, and elsewhere. Her essays have been published in *An Emily Dickinson Encyclopedia*, *Language Arts Journal of Michigan* and three anthologies from the Teachers & Writers Collaborative. Recognitions for her teaching include Creative Writing Teacher of the Year from the Michigan Youth Arts Festival (1990 and 2008), Humanities Award from Wayne County Arts, History and Humanities Council, the Michigan Governors Award for Arts Education, Detroit Bookwoman of the Year from the Women's National Book Association and a Detroit Metro Times Progressive Hero Award. Terry is the recipient of five Pushcart Prize nominations as well as the 2010 Pablo Neruda Poetry Prize from *Nimrod International* and the Foley Poetry Award.

Kristina Carter

Introduction

BY RICHARD A. HOEHN

A person who has food
has many problems.
A person who has no food
has only one problem.

Chinese saying

During the fall of 2000, a gaunt figure haunted the hearts and hallways of the U.S. Congress. The Rev. David Duncombe, appearing frail and emaciated from his 45-day, water-only fast, was calling on members of Congress. He wanted them to hear a starving person ask for help, to come face to face with hunger.

"When I walk into a congressional office, it is not only my words that I carry, but my body," Duncombe said. His goal was to embody hunger, so that legislators would understand how the burden of unpayable debt was crushing poor people in developing countries. His commitment stems from religious values.

Congress and the president did commit $435 million toward debt relief. The effort was successful because Rev. Duncombe and thousands of other grassroots activists, many of them Bread for the World members, mobilized Jubilee letter writing campaigns; because people in the developing world raised their voices in protest; because President Clinton, Rep. Spencer Bachus (R-AL), Rep. Maxine Waters (D-CA), and Rep. Nancy Pelosi (D-CA) and others pushed for passage of debt relief, a critical component of a comprehensive program to eliminate hunger. This bipartisan congressional action on debt relief is a major step in the right direction.

Rev. David Duncombe (right) after completing his fast, with Rep. Spencer Bachus.

Tackling Rural Poverty

BY JOHN WESTLEY

It can be discouraging that there are still so many poor people in the world when there is so much prosperity around us. [More than 1.2 billion people live in poverty.] About three-fourths of them, or more than 900 million people, live in rural areas.

Yet there are encouraging signs as well. For the first time, the international community has agreed on a specific objective for poverty reduction. The target is to cut in half the number of poor people, and to do it by the year 2015. That would mean helping perhaps 450 million people in the world's rural areas move above the poverty line in the next 15 years.

Although IFAD is one of the smallest...agencies [of the United Nations], the projects we approved in 1999 will reach an estimated 11.9 million rural people during the course of their implementation. Over a 15-year period, IFAD could reach nearly 180 million people at that rate. Of course, not all of these people will be below the poverty line at the beginning of the project, although IFAD does try to target its assistance on the rural poor. And not all of the people reached will actually live above the poverty line at the end of the project, although we try to monitor that carefully.

Nevertheless, the fact that we can reach 180 million rural poor over the next 15 years (which is over one-third of the total 2015 target of 450 million) indicates the potential there is in carefully targeted rural development programs. It is not merely a question of numbers. IFAD's experience of the past 20 years has shown how much we now know about tackling the problem of rural poverty.

We have the know-how. Given adequate financial resources, the target can be reached.

Mr. Westley is a vice president of the International Fund for Agricultural Development.

Bread for the World Institute's *A Program to End Hunger: Hunger 2000* says that hunger can be cut in half by 2015. The world has already made significant progress against hunger because individuals, governments, and international organizations have tackled the task with vigor and intelligence.

The U.S. government teamed with the Rockefeller and Ford foundations to create the Green Revolution that has had a major impact on reducing hunger and poverty in Asia for the past 30 years. The International Fund for Agricultural Development (IFAD) has been particularly effective in reducing rural poverty.

Cutting Hunger in Half

The 1996 World Food Summit recommended cutting hunger in half by 2015. The Food and Agriculture Organization of the United Nations (FAO), which tracks hunger worldwide (Table I.1), projects that the incidence of hunger could decline from 792 to 576 million people between 1998 and 2015, a drop of 216 million.

According to a study commissioned by the U.S. government, a relatively modest increase in effort could cut more than twice that many (512 million) people from the ranks of hungry people by 2015 (Table I.2).[1]

BFW Institute emphasizes that cutting hunger in half is a first step toward ending hunger and poverty. Hunger is a clear indicator of severe poverty and can be documented. Reducing hunger by half is a doable goal. Success can be measured in calories, nutrients, weight, and physical growth. If people can see proof that programs to end hunger work, they will be inspired and empowered to push for ending mass hunger and poverty.

Table I.1: Incidence of Undernourishment (in millions and % of total population)

	1969/71		1979/81		1990/92		1995/97		1996/98		Projections 2015		2030	
	#	%	#	%	#	%	#	%	#	%	#	%	#	%
Developing countries	959	37	937	29	828	20	792	18	792	18	576	10	401	6
Sub-Saharan Africa	88	34	125	36	162	34	180	33	186	34	184	22	165	15
Near East/North Africa	45	25	22	9	25	8	33	9	36	10	38	8	35	6
Latin America & Caribbean	54	19	46	13	59	13	53	11	55	11	45	7	32	5
South Asia	267	37	337	38	299	26	284	23	294	23	165	10	82	4
East and Southeast Asia	504	43	406	29	283	17	242	14	221	12	144	7	86	4

Source: All figures from FAO. All 95/97 numbers from *The State of Food Insecurity 1999*; all 96/98 numbers from *The State of Food Insecurity 2000*; all numbers before 1995 and projections from *Agriculture: Towards 2015/30, Technical Interim Report*, 2000.

Table I.2: Cutting Hunger in Half Scenario

	Reduction in Number of Undernourished People (in millions)	Total Cost (in millions of $U.S.)
Sub-Saharan Africa	80	10,886
Latin America	14*	186
South Asia	316	27,826
East and Southeast Asia	51	4,040
Rest of the World	50*	396
Total	512	43,335

* In this scenario Latin America and the "rest of the world" would largely reduce undernourishment out of their own resources.

Source: J. Dirck Stryker and Jeffrey C. Metzel, *Meeting the Food Summit Target: The United States Contribution — Global Strategy*, Agricultural Policy Analysis Project, Phase III, Research Report No. 1039, Prepared for the Office of Economic Growth and Agricultural Development, Global Bureau, U.S. Agency for International Development, Cambridge, MA: Associates for International Resources and Development, September 1998, 22.

Strategies for Change

A Program to End Hunger: Hunger 2000 recommends three strategies to end hunger – livelihood (income), social investment (health, education), and empowerment. While people in developing countries themselves will do the hardest work, industrialized countries can do their part with debt forgiveness, poverty-focused development assistance, and democratic practices in global institutions such as the International Monetary Fund. Table I.3 summarizes what these three strategies mean for developing countries, for industrialized countries, and for the United States in relation to domestic hunger.

Critics claim that foreign aid has been ineffective and has even harmed people. "Money down a rat hole," they say. "Food rotting on the docks." The logistical nightmare of shipping and delivering tons of emergency grain did lead to at least one instance of food rotting on the docks. But one instance became a legend that defines how millions of people view the whole foreign aid program.

Less remembered are the success stories achieved in foreign aid's early years. The two foremost aims of the U.S. foreign aid program

Nepalese students line up for school lunch.

after World War II were to resist the spread of communism and to help Europe and Japan recover from the devastation of the war. The Marshall Plan achieved both goals. During the Cold War, U.S. funds were often used to prop up dictators who stole large sums. Some foreign aid was spent on projects that did not work, partly because there was little consultation with local people. But most developing countries have moved toward democratic structures in which both leaders and new projects are subject to public scrutiny.

People in developing countries are investing huge efforts to build democratic institutions, implement poverty- and gender-focused policies, and create jobs that pay – the steps to end hunger. Foreign assistance can help developing country governments strengthen education, agricultural production, job creation, public

> **Hunger – a condition resulting from inadequate consumption of calories, protein, and nutrients to meet the basic physical requirements for an active and healthy life.**

Table I.3: Strategies to End Hunger

	Livelihood	Social Investment	Empowerment
Developing countries	Economic growth that creates jobs and assets for poor people	Poverty and gender-focused policies	Participatory Governance
Industrialized countries and international agencies	Debt cancellation for poorest countries	Poverty-focused aid	Democratic global institutions
United States	Jobs with livable incomes	Nutrition, education, and health care	Campaign finance reform and grassroots organizing

Source: *A Program to End Hunger: Hunger 2000*, Bread for the World Institute, Silver Spring, MD, 3.

health, and other people-centered programs. When people are educated, when they have secure access to land and other productive resources, when they are not dragged down by poor health or the costs of health care, then they are more able to provide food for their families.

Official development assistance (ODA) of the U.S. government is deployed directly to developing country governments, but also to private voluntary organizations (PVOs) and universities. PVOs often experiment with innovative pilot programs that government agencies then implement on a larger scale. A portion of poverty-focused development assistance would be administered by PVOs such as those listed in Table I.4.

To cite a specific example of how U.S. aid works, in the 1960s the U.S. Agency for International Development (USAID) began funding a collaboration between Oklahoma State University (OSU) and Alamaya Agricultural College in Ethiopia. OSU trained the first generation of faculty and students at Alamaya, who in turn set up and staffed other agricultural schools throughout Ethiopia. OSU-trained experts were hired by PVOs in 1984-86 to help farmers recover from famine and they were the backbone of the successful Jimmy Carter-Norman Borlaug effort to double food production in Ethiopia between the mid-80s and mid-90s. (And, they may be the people who staff the agricultural rehabilitation program mentioned in *The Unforgettable Face of Famine*.)

Senegalese women survey their newly irrigated crops.

Funds Are Needed

Debt relief and increased development assistance from industrialized countries can make the difference between achieving the World Food Summit goal (fewer than 400 million hungry people) and the FAO projection of 576 million hungry people by 2015 (Table I.1). These funds would also help developing countries reallocate some of their own resources to achieve the same goal.

Hunger 2001 says little about most of the money that comprises the official $14.9 billion foreign aid budget, which includes funds for U.S. strategic interests (especially Israel and Egypt), and support for transition economies such as the Commonwealth of Independent States (formerly

Table I.4: U.S. Government Funding via Selected PVOs

Agency	Total Budget	U.S. Government Funds	Percent of Funds from U.S. Government
	(in millions of $U.S.)		
Academy for Educational Development	112	102	91
CARE	411	349	83
Catholic Relief Services	233	144	52
Save the Children (U.S.)	133	74	56
The United Methodist Committee on Relief	46	24	52
World Vision (U.S.)	358	55	15

Source: Shanta M. Bryant and Tienne McKenzie, eds. With Robert Layng, *InterAction Member Profiles 2000-2001*, Washington, DC. www.interaction.org.

The Unforgettable Face of Famine

BY JOHN F. SCHULTZ

The face of famine is always hard to look at, even for seasoned relief workers. But on a tour of Ethiopia in the spring of 2000, I came upon a scene I wasn't prepared for. As my Christian Children's Fund (CCF) colleagues and I entered the remote village of Jello Dida, we saw 10- or 12-year-olds preparing the fields in case rain might come. The adults were not strong enough to plow.

The village was hushed, like a hospital ward. Many of the people were in the last stages of starvation. They had received no international aid. In one home, a widow whose daughter had died the week before was cradling another daughter in her arms. Her son was lying on the floor wrapped in what would likely become his burial shroud. They had had nothing to eat for days and were on the brink of death. We immediately dispatched a truck from the nearest village, where CCF was running a feeding program, funded in part by a USAID child survival grant. By the next morning, 500 families were receiving food.

The horrific situation I saw in Jello Dida village did not happen overnight. Famine, occasional or endemic, doesn't result from lack of rainfall alone. Easy access to weapons along Ethiopia's border with Kenya, Uganda, and Somalia perpetuates violence, one long-term cause of hunger in the region. Food distribution systems also need a complete overhaul, from building better roads to streamlining government agencies that deal with food commodities.

Yet even if these factors can be addressed, a basic environmental issue remains. Balance must be restored between the small-scale farmers who depend on the land and the carrying capacity of the land itself. Land degradation, caused by overgrazing, soil erosion, planting on hillsides, and deforestation, is a major problem.

Agricultural practices that lead to crop failure can be changed. To tackle these long-term issues in six districts of Ethiopia, CCF launched community-based agricultural development projects to help farmers adopt drought-resistant crops, conservation-based farming systems, and limited grazing practices to preserve the land. In cooperation with the Ethiopian government's agriculture office, CCF is training farmers to diversify their cropping system.

The program in Fantale and Basona Worena helps farmers to use simple irrigation — also a tool to combat hunger — to raise fruits and vegetables as cash crops to increase family income. About 3,000 Ethiopian farmers are taking part in these agricultural training programs. In addition to learning new agricultural practices, most of the farmers are participating in a loan program that provides improved seeds, cultivation equipment, fertilizer, and draft oxen.

Drought is part of life in the Horn of Africa and will remain so. But how people prepare for it can make all the difference. In the meantime, what we saw in Jello Dida will make us all work even harder to prevent famine. I'll always keep this blessing sent to me by the recovering people of Jello Dida: "With previously unseen and unbelievable speed, CCF has fed us with hope and food at the same time, preventing the death that loomed upon us. We have thus named CCF our father. Let God protect even the vehicle CCF uses from thorns."

Dr. Schultz is president of the Christian Children's Fund.

---

the Soviet Union). Nor does this book analyze humanitarian assistance in response to natural and civil disasters, although that is clearly important to some very hungry people.

We focus instead on the $4.4 billion that goes for long-term development assistance, referred to as pro-poor aid, poverty-focused development assistance, or aid for sustainable development.

In *A Program to End Hunger*, BFW Institute calculates that the cost of cutting hunger in half by 2015 would be an additional $60 billion in pro-poor aid, or $4 billion a year for the next 15 years. The $60 billion includes the $43 billion shown in Table I.2, funds for debt relief, and a margin for imperfect targeting of programs.[2] A U.S. contribution of $1 billion annually could leverage $3 billion a year from other industrialized countries and from developing countries themselves.

Governments and individual citizens choose every day how to spend their money. A single bridge over the Potomac River will cost $2 billion, the same amount as the cost overrun on Boston's "big dig" transportation project. Individuals in the U.S. spend $7 billion a year on videotape rentals, $20 billion at jewelry stores, and $24 billion at liquor stores. Compared to these expenditures, $1 billion a year is a modest sum. It is morally unimaginable that we wouldn't respond generously to the needs of our global neighbors.

Instead of growing, the development assistance pot has been shrinking. The high point of U.S. foreign aid, in constant dollars adjusted for

One African's Perspective on Foreign Aid

BY HENRY W. MAINGI

Although much criticism has been leveled at foreign aid, many people have benefited from it directly. I am one of those people. I was born in a typical African family of eight children in a small, poor, dusty village 32 miles southwest of Nairobi, Kenya. My parents were farmers with no formal education. Our family wealth consisted of a small piece of land on which we grew crops and grazed one cow and four goats.

After completing high school, I wanted to study medicine. I could not get medical training through the Kenyan Ministry of Health because of budget cuts. The country's health centers and hospitals were under-staffed, under-equipped, and short of medications. Not surprisingly, health practitioners were demoralized. Many doctors, nurses, and pharmacists left government service for state-of-the-art medical facilities within Kenya and abroad.

Patients were discouraged by the poor services. They turned instead to self-treatment with traditional medicines. Patients who could afford modern medicines purchased drugs of dubious quality from local venders, or traveled long distances to pharmacies, which were often expensive. At times, it was difficult to find medicines from any source.

Then, the Kenyan government, supported by the government of the Netherlands, began to revamp rural heath-care service delivery. The Dutch foreign aid was used to train registered clinical officers to serve the rural health centers and sub-district hospitals. I participated in this program. Without foreign aid, neither the Kenyan government nor I could have afforded this training, which included prevention and treatment skills: vaccinations, maternal and child health, family planning, and health education.

I learned to diagnose diseases, prescribe drugs, and treat patients, referring complicated cases to provincial doctors. As a clinical officer with the Ministry of Health, I managed a health-care center from 1974 to 1979 in Kakamega, a rural district in western Kenya.

Both the government and the public hailed the training program a success for its capacity to graduate well-trained clinical officers in a short period of time. Public use of health care services increased, which led to more health centers being built. The program left a lasting model of quality medical care for the Kenyan health sector and beyond.

Dr. Maingi is program associate at Bread for the World Institute.

inflation, was in 1949.[3] We need to go back to the high goals of U.S. development assistance immediately after World War II and the funding that realized those goals.

A Moral Calling

Values count. Ending hunger is a moral calling. The most important arguments for increasing poverty-focused development assistance are moral. A sense of moral obligation provides the push (ought) and a vision of happy, healthy people (the common good) provides the pull.

Moral sentiment rises partly from the realization that other people are just like us. When impoverished people get up in the morning they go through the same routines as people in the industrialized world – washing, eating, working, loving, and struggling. At night when they lie down, they too hope for a safe and secure tomorrow. In spite of cultural differences, we are all, ultimately, one human race.

The world is shrinking. More than one in 10 people in the U.S. traveled abroad last year, and

Justice for Poor People

In Germany, Bread for the World (Brot für die Welt)* has become widely known as a quality seal and token of Protestant development work. It has brought about a lasting change in church consciousness relating to worldwide development. It conveys to church people and the secular public the causes and consequences of conditions that are unjust and destructive of human dignity and sustainability. Bread for the World intends to bring home to the wider public — particularly to younger people — the complementary nature of specific aid to combat poverty, projects and programs for sustainable improvements in health and education...and commitment to changing the underlying social, ecological, political, and economic conditions in the interest of the poor....

* Brot für die Welt is the international assistance program of German Protestant churches. Bread for the World in the United States has the same name, but is entirely separate.

Source: adapted from Brot für die Welt, *Justice for the Poor — 2000*, Stuttgart, Germany, November 1999, 20.

"about 10 percent of all bachelor's degree candidates in the United States have studied abroad. Small towns in the Midwest are aware that their local economies depend on foreign trade; imports and exports total a quarter of the U.S. gross national product."[4]

We are increasingly bound together by common ties ranging from shared values to diseases without borders. Cholera bacteria found in the Chesapeake Bay probably traveled in ship wastewater from far away.

And the Internet is wiring us together on one huge grid. Mali, with a population of 11 million people, has only 30,000 telephone lines and it takes three months to get a line. Yet, "the number of people with Internet access has gone from 500 to 5,000 over two years."[5] In the past four years the number of countries with Internet access in Africa has jumped from 11 to 54. China has nearly 17 million users, and that figure is predicted to double every six months. There is still a serious

© Clugy-Soto

True freedom is attainable only through relations with others, since in an interconnected world I can never be safe until you are secure; nor can one person be whole unless others are fulfilled. That is only possible in a cooperative world. Is that the kind of world we want to live in and bequeath to those we love? If so, our responsibilities are clear.

Michael Edwards, *Future Positive*: Earthscan Publications, London; quoted in "Foreign aid: Does it harm or help?" by David Sogge, *The Christian Century*, Feb. 23, 2000, 209.

digital divide. But much of the world is being knit together at a phenomenal rate. In a globalizing world, everyone is your neighbor.

Concerned people know what it means to love individuals. But how is it possible to show love to a group? Theologian Paul Tillich said that justice is the form that love takes when dealing with groups, and politics is the dynamic through which love moves to accomplish justice. We love people in groups by creating a just society and we create a just society by working through politics. Changing the politics of hunger is the best way to end hunger.

Chapter 1 of this report calls on the president, Congress, and citizens across the nation to lead the race against hunger.

Chapter 2 points out that when people learn what it would take to cut hunger in half in Africa and to end hunger worldwide, they show strong support. The U.S. public consistently overestimates how much our government spends on foreign aid, but favors spending much more than we do. The public must become more vocal, otherwise lawmakers and the media will continue to underestimate public support for foreign aid.

Chapter 3 zeroes in on U.S. development assistance – history, rationale, trends. It also describes the leadership that other countries have shown. The U.S. is last among industrialized countries in the percentage of development assistance contributed.

Chapter 4 describes achievements, lessons learned, and proposals to reform development assistance. It outlines a program to cut hunger in half by 2015.

Chapter 5 says that trade alone will not meet development needs. There is a continuing role for development assistance in helping poor countries become full participants in globalization.

Spotlight on Children

On November 20, 1989, the United Nations General Assembly unanimously adopted the Convention of the Rights of the Child (CRC), the most widely ratified human rights treaty in history. It recognized, for the first time, the unique rights and needs of children as distinct from those of adults, and represented an unprecedented global commitment to protecting and caring for children everywhere.

At the 1990 World Summit for Children (WSC), leaders from more than 150 countries endorsed a global plan of action that included specific steps in the areas of health and nutrition, safe water and sanitation, basic quality education, child protection, and gender equity. A total of 27 goals were identified and targeted for completion by the year 2000.

To mark the 10th anniversary of the WSC, the U.N. is holding a three-day Special Session of the General Assembly in September 2001. CRC signatory nations will review implementation of the 1990 goals and establish strategies for improving living conditions and opportunities for children by the year 2010.

Village children in Angoche, Mozambique.

IFAD photo by Robert Maass

Chapter 6 applies the program to reduce hunger in sub-Saharan Africa. Poverty-focused development assistance can contribute to economic growth in Africa. Africa must not be left out of the emerging global economic system.

Chapter 7 describes hunger crises and publishes a new hunger index for 49 countries.

Chapter 8 suggests what individuals and groups can do to make a difference. One important option is to support campaigns to increase effective assistance to Africa. How Congress responds will depend on vocal grassroots support generated by moral commitments.

Rep. John Lewis, noted civil rights activist and current member of the U.S. Congress, describes a formative event when he was four years old. As he was playing with his cousins, a terrible thunderstorm came up. His Aunt Seneva hustled the children inside the house but when the storm hit, "the house [began] to sway. The wood plank flooring. . .began to bend. And then, a corner of the room started lifting."

His aunt had the children "line up and hold hands." Then they walked "as a group toward the corner of the room that was rising." The weight of the fifteen children was enough to keep the corner down. But the wind shifted. And so they "walked back in the other direction, as another end of the house began to lift.

"And so it went, back and forth, fifteen children walking with the wind, holding that trembling house down with the weight of our small bodies."

Lewis comments that through the crises of recent history, "our society was not unlike the children in that house, rocked again and again by the winds of one storm or another. . .But people of conscience never left the house. They stayed. They came together and they did the best they could, clasping hands and moving toward the corner of the house that was the weakest. . . And we still do, all of us. You and I. Children holding hands, walking with the wind."[6]

Bread for the World, its 45,000 members and churches, and BFW Institute are committed to joining hands with other individuals and groups to prevent the storm of hunger from consuming the lives of vulnerable people. We invite you to join us in this high calling.

Dr. Hoehn is director of Bread for the World Institute.

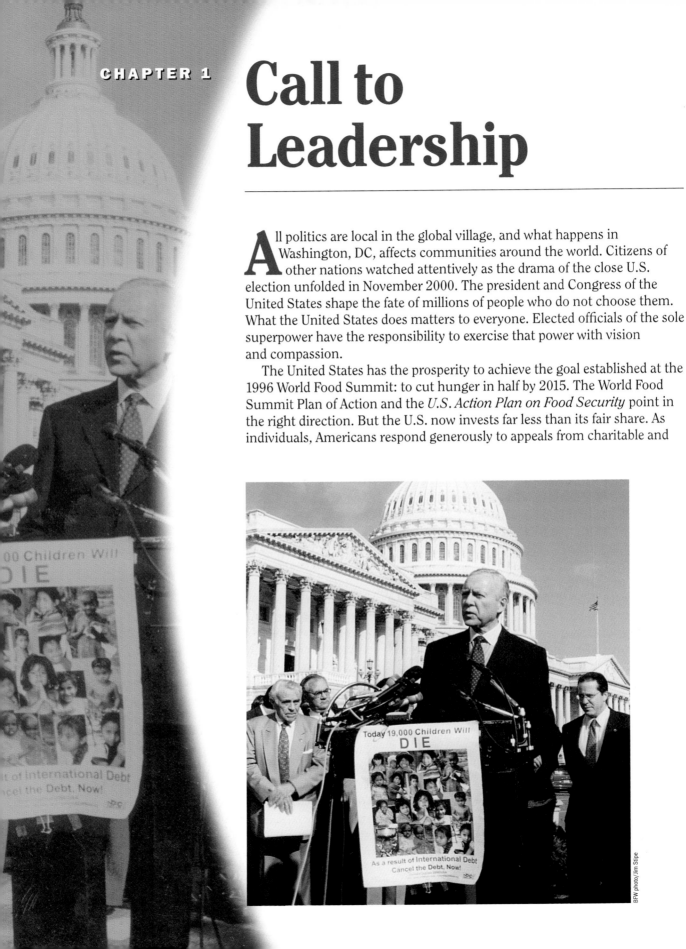

CHAPTER 1

Call to Leadership

All politics are local in the global village, and what happens in Washington, DC, affects communities around the world. Citizens of other nations watched attentively as the drama of the close U.S. election unfolded in November 2000. The president and Congress of the United States shape the fate of millions of people who do not choose them. What the United States does matters to everyone. Elected officials of the sole superpower have the responsibility to exercise that power with vision and compassion.

The United States has the prosperity to achieve the goal established at the 1996 World Food Summit: to cut hunger in half by 2015. The World Food Summit Plan of Action and the *U.S. Action Plan on Food Security* point in the right direction. But the U.S. now invests far less than its fair share. As individuals, Americans respond generously to appeals from charitable and

Today 19,000 Children Will DIE

As a result of International Debt Cancel the Debt, Now!

BFW photo/Jim Stipe

relief organizations. But as a nation, the U.S. has a stingy, mixed record on poverty-focused foreign aid. Only tenacious leadership by the U.S. president and Congress can turn the nation's pledge to join the world community's efforts against hunger from rhetoric to reality. Without a visible, serious commitment to this objective by the administration and Congress, millions of hungry families will continue to suffer and die.

If the United States, whose economic primacy underpins the global economy, does not rise to the challenge to end world hunger, who will? There are few areas of international affairs in which U.S. leadership is not critical. U.S. leadership to end hunger could change the terms of the current debate about globalization and poverty and improve the lives of millions.

Negative Leadership

The United States, which once set the standard for long-term development assistance, no longer leads the industrialized nations in foreign aid or in support for eliminating hunger (Chapter 3). In fact, the U.S. is dead last on the roster of country-to-country foreign aid donors. Congress has withheld assessed contributions to U.N. organizations, shirking U.S. responsibilities. The U.S. continues to have large arrears with several U.N. agencies for which contributions are voluntary, hindering important U.N. activities and leaving other countries to pick up the slack.

The European Union, Canada, and Japan allocate more than the United States for poverty-reduction foreign aid programs, measured as a percentage of their gross national income. Even so, all industrialized nations are giving less than they used to.

The United States not only spends much less than is commensurate with the nation's wealth. It invests only a fraction of the amount the American people believe is being spent for foreign aid and far less than the public believes the United States should spend for hungry people (Chapter 2). The United States allocates only a small percentage of its foreign aid to development assistance for poor countries and regions. If this continues, planned foreign assistance levels by all donors will not be enough to halve world hunger by the year 2015.[1] The world's 800 million hungry people cannot wait.

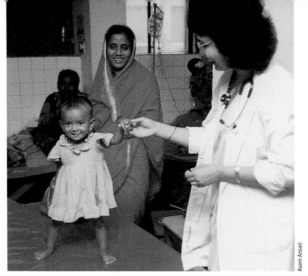

A healthy baby at the International Centre for Diarrheal Disease Research, Bangladesh.

The end of the Cold War led to the hope that there would be an increase in funds for hunger alleviation. But it led instead to a lower level of U.S. interest in progress in developing countries.

Increase Anti-Hunger Allocation

The time is right to increase foreign aid for pro-poor policies and programs that help hungry people. Economic growth and expanded world trade have lifted the industrialized nations to new levels of affluence. But the poorest regions of the world have not shared the wealth. Populations that lack the resources, training, or education to gain access to the new technology and knowledge economy of the 21st century are being left out.[2] Direct actions to extend the benefits of globalization to developing countries must complement free market policies (Chapter 5).

World hunger can be ended. Bread for the World (BFW) Institute estimates that the cost of meeting the World Food Summit goal would be an additional $60 billion over 15 years, or $4 billion per year until 2015, of which $1 billion per year would be the U.S. portion. This additional money should support sustainable development programs that enable poor people to help themselves. Fifty years of experience have demonstrated what works: economic growth and market-oriented trade that benefit everyone, investments in agricultural research, focus on smallholder farmers, building human capital through health care and education, women's empowerment, and environmental sustainability.

Foreign Aid Primer

Foreign Aid to End Hunger focuses on long-term development assistance, which has been proven to help hungry people move from poverty to self-sufficiency. BFW Institute understands sustainable development to include the following mutually reinforcing objectives:

- Expanding economic opportunity to poor people.
- Meeting basic human needs for food, clean water, health care, shelter, and education.
- Protecting and enhancing the environment by managing natural resources.
- Promoting democratic participation by poor women and men in economic and political decisions that affect their lives.[3]

Long-term development assistance constitutes about 40 percent of U.S. foreign aid. The largest amount of foreign aid goes not to food or development programs, but to military and security programs, international narcotics control, and trade promotion.

There are two types of foreign aid: bilateral and multilateral.[4] Bilateral assistance is given directly from one country to another (government to government) and includes:

- Military aid – grants and loans, administered by the U.S. Departments of Defense and State, to allow other countries to buy military equipment from the United States, bring foreign military officers to the United States for training, and send U.S. military advisors in country to give technical assistance.
- Security aid – to achieve political and security ends of the United States. The overwhelming majority of funds in this category go to Egypt and Israel.
- Export aid – administered by organizations such as the Export-Import Bank and the Trade and Development Agency, these programs include direct lending to exporters, insurance guarantees for credit that companies extend to foreign customers, feasibility studies for prospective exports, and trade-related training.
- Development aid – programs for poor countries, including sustainable development, population and reproductive health, child survival, environment, and agriculture, administered through governments, NGOs and PVOs.
- Humanitarian aid – international disaster assistance programs and refugee aid.
- Food aid – the U.S. Department of Agriculture administers programs under three titles. Title I supplies food aid in the form of loans to promote U.S. food exports. Title II funds emergency and humanitarian relief, much of it administered by private voluntary organizations (e.g., CARE, Catholic Relief Services, World Vision), and the United Nations World Food Program. Title III is given in the form of commodities to governments that agree to long-term market reforms. The recipient governments may use the commodities to feed people or create food reserves, or they may sell the commodities and use the proceeds to promote development projects.
- Other aid – includes assistance to the newly independent states of the former Soviet Union, refugee assistance, anti-terrorism, and narcotics control.

Ugandan farmer picks coffee beans on her farm in Masaka.

In addition to bilateral programs, the United States contributes to multilateral institutions such as the World Bank, the International Monetary Fund, the regional development banks, the United Nations and its agencies, and other international programs.

U.S. foreign assistance began in 1947 with the Marshall Plan to help rebuild the war-damaged economies of Western Europe, Greece, and Turkey and to prevent the spread of communism. The United States Agency for International Development (USAID) is the executive branch agency that administers most of the bilateral programs related to development. Its goals as outlined by Congress are to:

- Alleviate the worst physical manifestations of poverty, i.e., hunger.
- Promote conditions enabling developing countries to achieve self-sustaining economic growth with equitable distribution of benefits.
- Encourage respect for individual civil and economic rights.
- Integrate developing countries into an open, equitable international economic system.[5]

Redefining U.S. National Security Interests

To some, the U.S. national interest in reducing hunger and poverty seems less compelling than it did during the Cold War, when fighting hunger in poor countries was a means to make communism less appealing to populations yearning for better lives. For these critics, the rationale for foreign aid evaporated with the end of the Cold War. But reducing poverty and hunger overseas is in the United States' best interests from security, humanitarian, and economic perspectives.

The United States no longer faces a showdown with the Soviet Union. Today, a multitude of smaller, less easily identifiable threats confront the nation. These range from environmental degradation to terrorism, rogue states, civil wars, weapons of mass destruction, chemical warfare, and political instability. Persistent poverty and hunger cause conflict and instability in developing countries. Seventy-five percent of state failure, civil war, insurgency, and instability since the Cold War has occurred in the world's poorest countries. "These new conflicts do not follow the model of the Cold War era. . . [They] are being fought over poverty and food security issues."[6] While environmental stress and ethnicity explain these crises in part, hunger, poverty, and economic stress are underlying causes.

Emergencies that require humanitarian assistance and food aid reflect longer-term, chronic problems. Therefore, confronting the causes of humanitarian crisis would better serve U.S. interests than spending billions per year to address symptoms only. The need for emergency relief has skyrocketed. From 1985 to 1989, there were on average five humanitarian emergencies overseas each year whose cause was politics or war rather than natural disaster. In the 1990s, the occurrence of such crises increased by a factor of four or five, ranging between 20 and 26 per year from 1990 through 1999.[7] From the mid-1980s through the 1990s, the number of people in need of emergency humanitarian assistance tripled.[8]

The proliferation of internal conflicts and civil wars is "concentrated in the poorest parts of the world."[9] Widespread poverty and hunger can bring down governments. Governments collapse in countries that benefit least from global economic expansion, especially in Africa.[10]

The Role of the Military in Humanitarian Assistance

In the age of CNN and instant communication, crises often impel U.S. military engagement in countries where we may have no apparent interest.[11] The Somali experience made the international community increasingly reluctant to engage in other complex emergencies when it meant a military involvement. But the genocide in Rwanda two years later and the subsequent evaluations of that tragedy caused donors and aid agencies to review their mandates, their capacities, and their management of resources. The decade ended with the Kosovo crisis and the first-ever intervention by NATO outside its boundaries in the cause of humanitarianism.

The cost of U.S. military operations in support of humanitarian crises in the mid-1990s averaged $2 billion a year. The U.S. military intervention in Somalia in 1992-93, with its costs in loss of life and in U.S. credibility, was driven by a humanitarian concern for victims of famine.[12] The Somali intervention was the first of several costly

Indonesian woman makes pottery to sell in the village market in Banyumulek, Lombok.

military actions in the 1990s to prevent starvation and suffering in poor countries. Overall costs for total military and humanitarian response to crises such as those in Rwanda, Bosnia-Herzegovina, and Kosovo are approaching several billion dollars per operation.[13]

It is likely that the costs of development aid that creates long-term solutions would be far lower and the results far better for poor and hungry people than short-term rescue and peacekeeping missions. Long-term development strategies could help prevent crises and hence eliminate the expenditure of billions of dollars per crisis or per year on peacekeeping and humanitarian missions.

But the most significant cost of U.S. intervention in these crises has not been financial. Rather, it has been the increasing rate at which U.S. military forces were deployed, which has tripled since the end of the Cold War. The president and the Joint Chiefs of Staff advised the Congress in 1999 that these deployments had led to a decline in the readiness of the U.S. military to defend the national interest in war. Addressing hunger and poverty as underlying causes of conflict could enhance U.S. national security by reducing deployment of the nation's military defense capability.

Pro-Poor Foreign Aid Is Sound Economics

World poverty and hunger threaten U.S. prosperity as well as its security. The mature economies of the world are no longer growth markets for many U.S. exports. Markets in developing countries have grown much faster than those in the developed world during the past two decades, accounting for a substantial percentage of U.S. exports. Foreign aid can help bring poor developing countries into the mainstream of global trade and increase the incomes of poor people. Higher incomes in developing countries increase U.S. exports.[14] Prosperity in developing countries benefits U.S. trade and poor people abroad.

It is important not to overstate the growth possibilities of the developing countries. U.S. business has spent the last 100 years expecting the imminent transformation of China into a nation of hundreds of millions of consumers seeking U.S. products. That hasn't happened yet. Nevertheless, major U.S. trading partners such as Japan, Korea, Thailand, and Taiwan were poor countries with poor consumers one or two generations ago. Foreign aid helped transform these countries. With very few exceptions, foreign aid also played a crucial role in educating and training leaders and technocrats in those countries, providing models of economic management and policy that laid the groundwork for solid economic growth.

U.S. businesses investing in developing countries recognize that there is an essential role for development assistance as part of U.S. global engagement. Even small-to-medium-size companies, which traditionally would not have seen federal activities overseas as of even indirect interest to them, share some of these views, as demonstrated during 1996 hearings on foreign aid before a subcommittee of the House Appropriations Committee.[15] The Business Alliance for International Economic Development stated unequivocally that "there is a strong self-interest case for foreign assistance in the new world of globalization, [where we are competing for the markets of the future]. Development programs assisted by the U.S. government create the essential first steps in this growth process."[16]

Local Food Mavericks Avert Malnutrition

BY CHARLES MACCORMACK

Although malnutrition in Than Hoa, Vietnam, affected more than 70 percent of all children under age 3, a surprising number of families — equally poor — were raising well-nourished children. In 1990, Save the Children trained local villagers to identify those families and find out what they were doing right. In other words, we looked for "positive deviance."

In every poor family with a well-nourished child, the mother or caretaker collected tiny shrimp and crabs from the rice paddies and added these protein-rich foods to the child's diet, along with green sweet potato tops. Although readily available and free for the taking, these foods were ignored by the other villagers, who believed they were inappropriate or even dangerous for young children. Families with well-nourished children differed from their neighbors in other practices, such as frequency of feeding and quality of child care.

As a result of this study, Save the Children developed a Nutrition Education and Rehabilitation Program (NERP). All mothers and caretakers of malnourished children were invited to attend a two-week session, where they practiced "positive deviant" ways of feeding and caring for their children. NERP provided "food as medicine," using locally produced rice, tofu, fish, and oil. However, in order to reach the more difficult goal of sustaining their children's enhanced nutritional status, all caretakers were required to bring a handful of shrimp, crabs, and greens as their "price of admission" to the NERP session.

After the first two years of the program, 93 percent of children in participating families had been rehabilitated. Save the Children has since used the positive deviance approach in Bangladesh, Bhutan, Egypt, Mali, Mozambique, and Nepal.

Dr. MacCormack is president of Save the Children.

The Asian economic crisis exposed how closely tied the U.S. economy is to developing country markets. The U.S. private sector recognizes that functioning legal and financial systems in developing countries improve the business climate. The investments upon which business depends, but which it cannot make – in health, education, agriculture, and other areas needed to ensure stability and a strong workforce – need financing from somewhere. That somewhere is foreign aid that helps developing countries strengthen the public institutions and infrastructure essential to sustained economic and social development.

Agriculture and Business

For many years the U.S. agricultural sector did not support foreign aid. Significant portions of the farm lobby in the 1970s and 1980s turned against foreign aid for fear that it would make the agricultural exports of developing countries more competitive in markets where the U.S. had traditionally maintained an advantage. U.S. oilseed and vegetable oil interests, for example, opposed technical and financial assistance to East Asian and Latin American producers of these products. The U.S. Congress even prohibited U.S. agricultural assistance for commodities that might lead to competition with U.S. exports.

Gambian children.

These views have changed significantly. The long-term interests of farm and agribusiness groups are best served by expanding the economies of developing countries. Because agricultural growth raises incomes, and therefore demand, developing countries that have successfully transformed their agricultural sector have also increased agricultural imports, often from the United States.

Families that struggle with hunger in developing countries often spend up to 80 percent of their income on food. When their incomes rise, most of the added income is spent on an expanded and diversified diet, including some food imports. That is why reductions in hunger in East Asia have resulted in a dynamic market for U.S. agriculture.

In addition, much of the scientific research that led to the breakthroughs of the Green Revolution in Asia also benefited U.S. agriculture by making new genetic material available. U.S. government investments of $134 million in wheat and rice research to benefit developing countries returned $14.7 billion, roughly 100 times the investment cost.

Increased Funding for Development Aid

The foreign operations portion of the federal budget is influenced by a set of interest groups. Fifteen years of declining budgets created a very competitive environment within the foreign aid constituency. Interest groups stopped working together to increase overall foreign aid allocations because relentless budget deficit pressures made that goal impossible. Instead of working together, each interest group sought to maximize its slice of an ever-shrinking pie.

The budget process drove interest groups to narrow advocacy for particular aspects of development. Turf issues discouraged coalition building just as consensus was growing that simultaneous approaches on many different fronts promote economic development and reduce hunger (Chapter 4).

The deficit budget environment created incentives for interest groups to seek congressional earmarks (requirements that a specified budget amount be dedicated to a particular program) to ensure that at least some of the foreign aid funds were spent to help poor people. U.S. bilateral support for the child survival revolution began with an earmark in the mid-1980s, and the Development Fund for Africa was created by an earmark.

While the negative budget environment made interest group attention to earmarks a rational objective, the proliferation of earmarks had some unfortunate consequences. It created competition rather than cooperation among groups with laudable objectives, all of whose programs taken together constitute the multifaceted approach needed to end hunger and poverty. A strong sense of winners and losers pervaded the interest group community, making it difficult to create common vision and common cause for an overall foreign assistance effort to address poverty and hunger. For example, when effective lobby groups generated sufficient congressional support for expanding child survival and microenterprise programs, the other interest groups were left with a sense that increasing these programs reduced their own efforts to help poor people.

The budget surplus fundamentally changes the overall climate and calls for building a very strong coalition to increase development assistance, including a substantial increase to fight poverty and hunger. The budget surplus is conducive to broad vision, cooperation, and coalition building for foreign assistance. Interest groups should seize the opportunity for strategic collaboration to advance sustainable development.

Gambian man weaves items for his children to sell.

A Call for U.S. Leadership

The incidence of hunger and poverty in the world is morally unacceptable, contrary to U.S. economic interests, and dangerous to national security. It is past time for the United States to return to a position of leadership in the fight to eliminate poverty and hunger. The goals of the World Food Summit can be achieved. But only if the United States accepts its responsibilities and provides its fair share of the intellectual and financial resources that are needed.

Leading by example would return rich dividends. The United States would reap material benefits through sales to new trading partners and could look forward to the day when less spending for military security, peacekeeping, and responding to manmade emergencies would be needed.

Activists against hunger call upon the administration and Congress to fight hunger and poverty, here and everywhere. Without a visible and credible commitment to this objective at the highest levels of government and at the grassroots, hundreds of millions of hungry and poor people will suffer. U.S. elected officials should:

- Reaffirm the commitment of the United States to reduce hunger and poverty by half before the year 2015.
- Request and approve an increase of at least $1 billion in annual funding to implement national plans of action to cut hunger in half by 2015.
- Prepare and approve a realistic plan to pay accumulated arrears to the international organizations.
- Approve increases to the budgets of the voluntary contribution international organizations involved in the fight against poverty and hunger.
- Adopt the principle of capacity to pay, measured by national income, as the fundamental guide in determining our fair share of the budgets of international organizations and official development assistance.

Putting Our Money Where Our Mouth Is

To reap the large future net benefits of an accelerated attack on hunger and poverty, a substantial increase in the budget for international affairs is needed.

Gambian woman transports water.

BFW Institute suggests that the first $1 billion increase be focused on Africa, since it is there that the trends are most ominous. Highest priority should be granted to the agriculture and food security component of USAID. Programs should improve the nutritional status of hungry people, help small-scale farmers increase productivity, and improve transportation systems so that surplus food produced within sub-Saharan Africa can be transported to food-deficit areas.

Additional funds from the United States could be used to augment and extend programs in other regions where hunger is severe. If the United States were to embrace and apply the principle of ability to pay there would be additional funds for improving health, education, safe water, adequate sanitation, governance, and the environment in low-income developing and transition countries where the incidence of hunger and poverty is high (Chapter 6). The United States could do all this and continue to be a major source of humanitarian emergency assistance, as well as support Middle East countries in their struggle for peace.

Such U.S. leadership requires political commitment from the executive and legislative branches of government that has not been seen in many years. Of particular importance for foreign aid are the Office of the President; the Departments of State, Treasury, and Agriculture; USAID; the majority and minority leadership in Congress and the chairs of the relevant legislative and appropriations committees. To lead, the United States must allocate a convincing level of resources to do what works to improve the lives of hungry people. But it will take top-level political muscle to reinvest in foreign aid and continued grassroots activism to make real the vision of a world free from hunger.[17]

Leadership from the Grassroots

Several distinct, sometimes overlapping, groups comprise the constituency for foreign affairs and foreign aid:

- The humanitarian community, which includes human rights, health, and charitable organizations, is directly concerned about relieving poverty, hunger, and hardship for people in developing countries.

- The religious community is concerned about justice for poor and marginalized people.

- The development community, including many nongovernmental organizations, is concerned about improving stability, sustainability, and democracy in developing countries through foreign aid.

- The private sector, which includes foundations, businesses, agricultural concerns, and other diverse interest groups supporting overall U.S. foreign affairs spending and international engagement, is concerned with expanding opportunity and prosperity.

These groups must form a strong coalition for a renewed attack on hunger and poverty. Together, the leaders of the coalition could convince their colleagues in the Executive Branch, in Congress, and in the business, foundation, development, and human rights communities to restore U.S. leadership in poverty- and hunger-focused foreign aid. Unless they do so, the historic opportunity to direct additional resources to pro-poor development assistance will be squandered.

Millions of children are alive today because a strong coalition formed to support the Child Survival Initiative, a major worldwide effort to save lives through simple health interventions, such as immunization and oral rehydration therapy. So powerful was the momentum of this leadership that presidents, prime ministers, ministers of health, and even some guerrilla army commanders (who agreed to stop fighting to permit national vaccination campaigns to take place)

Bread for the World staffers support debt relief.

cooperated. Similarly, when the private foundations, with assistance from the U.S. government, committed resources to double rice production in Asia in the 1960s and 1970s, most developing countries in Asia were impelled to address the needs of their rural areas.

The coalition at the national level must be replicated at the community level in order to ensure success. Elections are not won or lost on questions of foreign aid. Often, Congress will address foreign aid for reducing poverty and hunger only if representatives perceive an immediate crisis or high voter interest. The essential task therefore is to make certain that members of Congress understand that reaching poverty and hunger goals is the right thing to do, will return benefits to the United States, and is important to constituents. Grassroots groups have made a difference in the past. They can do so in the future.

The challenge is to convince our leaders that a share of the surplus should be allocated to reducing poverty and hunger. That relatively small investment would return high dividends economically, morally, and spiritually.

This chapter has been excerpted and adapted with permission from David Atwood, *Cutting Hunger and Poverty in Half: Interest Groups and a Renewed U.S. Commitment in the Post-Cold War World*, unpublished paper submitted July 28, 2000 to the Industrial College of the Armed Forces, National Defense University, in fulfillment of a research program. Howard Hjort, former Deputy Director-General of FAO, also contributed to this chapter.

Where Miracles Happen

BY JOEL UNDERWOOD

Last summer, I spent two weeks in Bangladesh at a remarkable institution partly funded since 1978 by USAID through the Child Survival Initiative. Founded as the International Centre for Diarrheal Disease Research, Bangladesh (ICDDR,B), and now called the Centre for Health and Population Research, this facility in Dhaka is the scene of daily miracles. I saw children admitted in the morning dehydrated to the point of death from persistent diarrhea. By the end of the day these same children were literally sitting up and taking food.

With the severest cases, recovery takes longer. Sheema, the little girl pictured below at four stages of recovery over five weeks, was brought to the hospital suffering from severe diarrhea, pneumonia, and malnutrition. Using the oral rehydration therapy (ORT) that the Centre developed and a low-cost, high-nutrient diet based on its nutrition research, doctors sent Sheema home healthy and happy.

Sheema's story is one of more than 2,000 miracles wrought at the Centre's two hospitals, which treat 120,000 patients each year — with a 99.5 percent recovery rate. State-of-the-art laboratories with rapid diagnostic techniques provide immediate results.

Patients pay no fees. Most cannot afford to. But many patients contribute as research subjects to help develop innovative treatments such as ORT. ORT is credited with saving more than a million children every year throughout the developing world.

Health research is often best done where the problems are greatest. Bangladesh is densely populated, with high rates of infectious disease, malnutrition, and maternal mortality. Scientists and health professionals from all over the world come to the Centre to study, then return home to apply what they have learned.

The miracle of Sheema's recovery is more than a poignant illustration of the Centre's effectiveness. It is also a symbol of a nation's recovery. Bangladesh, once among those nations with the highest birth and child mortality rates, has seen a significant drop in both, primarily due to Centre initiatives. The government of Bangladesh has adopted the Centre's program of urban and rural community-based health services as the standard for the whole country. The Centre's program of village-based training in women's reproductive health has already reduced the nation's fertility rate by 50 percent.

In addition to development assistance funding from the U.S. government, more than 50 nations, U.N. agencies, medical research groups, universities, foundations, and corporations support the Centre. In 1982, Bread for the World's Offering of Letters, *A Chance to Survive*, spurred the establishment of the Child Survival Fund, which channeled significant USAID support to the Centre.

A subsequent BFW campaign convinced Congress to mandate the use of the Child Survival Fund to underwrite immunizations in developing nations. A World Health Organization initiative proposed and tested by the Centre in Dhaka has been responsible for cutting the death rate from childhood diseases in the developing world by more than a third. An estimated 70 percent of the world's children have been now immunized against the major childhood diseases. Bread for the World members and friends can be proud of the link they have forged with poor people in Bangladesh and around the world through the Child Survival Fund and the Centre for Health and Population Research in Dhaka.

Rev. Underwood has been on staff at Bread for the World since 1974.

Asem Ansari

From Hunger to Health: ORT restored Sheema to life.

CHAPTER 2

Hearing the Constituency to End Hunger

BY DAVID DEVLIN-FOLTZ

The constituency to cut hunger in half by 2015 exists. The American public supports a U.S. role in the world that promotes more cooperative, just, and sustainable outcomes for everyone. Americans want to do the right thing. We want to be good neighbors: doing our part, respectful and respected, ready to help when needed. Americans believe that this position is consistent with our long-term responsibilities to our own families and communities and necessary for our self-preservation. Substantial majorities, especially among women, are persuaded by moral arguments in favor of foreign aid and of addressing hunger wherever it occurs.

At the same time, large majorities mistakenly believe that we are already doing more than we are. They reject or are unaware of evidence to the contrary. Nevertheless, most Americans support continued foreign aid. But they are not vocal about it.

Policymakers and the media, hearing little, assume that the public is unconcerned, even opposed to foreign aid spending. Moving systemic hunger higher on the political priority list requires strategies to reach policymakers and other opinion elites directly. Closing this gap between public opinion and public policy will also require a more vocal, more engaged citizenry. This, in turn, demands a different approach to communicating about hunger, one that encourages the public to be more articulate and policymakers to be better listeners.

Recent research tells us how the public views the United States' role in the world and what might be done to build a broader constituency for global engagement. Some key findings:

- Policymakers and media are talking to each other in language that excludes average Americans.

- The public supports international engagement in principle but rejects its expansion because people believe that the United States is already doing too much.

- The public resists long-term engagement because our concept of the "good neighbor" includes minding our own business except in emergency.

- The public is confused about who is responsible for doing what in response to global challenges.

The public wants the United States to play a positive role in a troubled world. A study conducted for A Women's Lens on Global Issues found that "women and men share a vision of the United States as that of a good neighbor, not a policeman. . ."[1] The Program on International Policy Attitudes (PIPA) found that 78 percent of the public agreed that "because the world is so interconnected today, the U.S. should participate in efforts to maintain peace, protect human rights, and promote economic development."[2]

The public believes that working through the United Nations is one way to do our part. According to the PIPA study, 67 percent of the public supports strengthening the United Nations.[3] This is not an isolated finding. A November 1998 poll by the Chicago Council on Foreign Relations also found that 84 percent of Americans felt that strengthening the United Nations should be a very important (45 percent) or somewhat important (39 percent) foreign policy goal.[4] A September 1997 poll sponsored by the Pew Research Center for the People and the Press found that 83 percent believed that strengthening the United Nations should be a priority in U.S. foreign policy, with 30 percent saying that it should be a top priority.[5]

Americans believe we are more generous in our country-to-country aid than we actually are. When PIPA, the *Washington Post*/Kaiser, and other researchers asked a sample of Americans what percentage of the federal budget is spent on foreign aid, their responses were 15 to 20 times the actual percentage. Respondents were often shocked to learn that barely 1 percent of the budget goes to foreign assistance.[6] Overwhelming majorities believe that the United States is the most generous nation, as measured by the percentage of a country's gross national product (GNP) that foreign aid represents. In fact, the United States ranks dead last among wealthy industrialized nations.

Sixty-eight percent of the public believes that the U.S. should give about the same, proportionally, as other wealthy nations.[7] Even when asked to compare domestic and international priorities, the general public supports far more spending on global hunger and poverty than the government allocates. PIPA's June 1996 poll found, for example, that the public wants the government to spend $1 to fight poverty internationally for every $4 it spends to fight poverty domestically. The actual ratio at the time was roughly $1 spent to help the poor abroad for every $32 spent to address domestic poverty.[8]

These sentiments are not confined to liberals and progressives. In 1997, PIPA compared attitudes from national polls with reactions in congressional districts that, "based on the representatives' positions, were most likely to show public support for international disengagement."

These districts elected the late Sonny Bono (R-CA), Joe Scarborough (R-FL), Helen Chenoweth (R-ID), and David Funderburk (R-NC), who co-sponsored a bill to have the U.S. withdraw from the United Nations.

PIPA surveyed 500 residents in each of the four districts. In response to the question, "Do you favor or oppose legislation that would have the United States withdraw completely from the United Nations?" 18 to 21 percent said they favored such legislation, while 74 to 77 percent was opposed. Only 22 percent said they were more inclined to vote for a candidate if the candidate favored withdrawing from the United Nations. These responses tracked national polls very closely; one district was actually more supportive of the United Nations than the national sample. Responses from the districts represented by the four anti-engagement members of Congress matched almost precisely the national sample on support for U.S. foreign aid.[9]

A favorable view of globalization and of global engagement by the United States cuts across lines of race, class, and gender. Just over half the public sees globalization positively. Women recognize and accept global interdependence. Younger women are particularly at ease with globalization: two-thirds of women aged 18 to 29 see more advantages to globalization than problems for themselves personally "as the world becomes more interconnected."[10]

Bread for the World and other faith-based organizations believe that our moral obligation to the poorest among us is the strongest possible argument for American engagement beyond our shores. But the public is pragmatic as well as moral. The study done for A Women's Lens on Global Issues found that support for cooperative forms of engagement is rooted in two core values: "a desire to leave the world a better place. . .for the next generation" and "self-preservation and protection of what is dear to us. This includes taking pride in being a world leader and protecting our economic interests and national security."[11]

Moral or religious obligations appeared less important in this study than responsibility to future generations, safety, and self-preservation as reasons to support U.S. foreign aid. Recent polling data on foreign policy issues revealed concerns about terrorism, nuclear safety, and biological weapons. People worry about these issues and believe that government needs to make them a priority. Such concerns tap into the desire for self-preservation, rather than more selfless values, according to researcher Margaret Bostrom.[12]

But PIPA's study of attitudes toward globalization concluded that in some instances moral arguments were even more powerful than those based on self-interest. Asked to compare two arguments in favor of requiring compliance with international labor standards as part of world trade agreements, 83 percent supported the argument based on moral concern for foreign workers. A robust but smaller 74 percent of the public agreed with an argument based on preventing nations from having an unfair trade advantage because they exploit workers. That is, the moral argument trumped the self-interest argument. A similar pattern held for the inclusion of environmental standards in trade agreements, with self-interest rationales faring less well.[13]

Researchers Axel Aubrun and Joseph Grady interviewed average Americans and concluded that "the public is much more concerned with social and moral values" than are foreign policy experts.[14] Perhaps most important for policy-oriented NGOs and anti-hunger activists, combating world hunger is the only altruistic goal for government that ranks among the top 10 priorities for government action in Bostrom's poll.[15]

How can we account for the apparently contradictory evidence concerning the public's responsiveness to altruistic concerns? The difference may lie in the distinction that the public makes between international relations in general and foreign aid in particular. The public's top goal for U.S. foreign policy generally is to address global challenges to our collective security. The top goals for foreign assistance appear highly altruistic. When asked to rate the priority of several goals for U.S. government assistance programs, relieving human suffering was most important, while military support to friendly governments was least important.[16]

Whether couched in terms of securing a brighter future for our children or doing what we are called to do by secular morality or religious values, broad and diverse majorities support a significant U.S. role in addressing hunger and poverty. But because policymakers do not hear from their constituents on issues of international engagement they – and the media – assume that the public is indifferent.

Let us not overstate the case. Politically, domestic concerns far outweigh international issues. Elections are rarely won and lost on the basis of international issues. If the choice is between domestic and international issues, Bostrom found, "Americans continue to want to put energy into domestic problems over international problems." She cited a *Washington Post*/ABC News poll from September 1999 that ranks foreign affairs 13th out of 15 issues determining the 2000 presidential vote.[17]

It should come as no surprise that when presented with a choice most people will focus on issues close to home rather than international questions. Nevertheless, people in this country care about the world and our role in it. Presented in isolation, international development elicits a strong altruistic response.

So why do policymakers persist in believing that the public favors withdrawal from the United Nations and reducing foreign aid, even when presented with contrary evidence from polls conducted in their own districts? Aides to members of Congress consistently reported in interviews and workshops with PIPA researchers that constituents who telephoned, wrote letters, and spoke at public meetings were predominantly in favor of U.S. disengagement.

Steven Kull and his colleagues note that "this was reported across the political spectrum . . . by congressional representatives who favored engagement as well as those who opposed it. Apparently, the vocal public that opposes foreign aid has convinced legislators that their views represent the majority.[18] But Kull's follow-up work demonstrated that in many cases congressional staff could not point to much evidence of vocal opposition to U.S. engagement abroad. Opponents of international engagement, in other words, are squeaky wheels; at least as important, they appear to be on a wavelength that congressional staff hear well. They easily prevail over a silent majority.

Hothouse and Mirrors

The majority of the public is with us. Why is that public not heard? A metaphor may help: Foreign policy is created in a hothouse lined with mirrors. The hothouse is small, the conditions conducive to a handful of species rarely found outside its walls: academics, staff of relevant congressional committees, veteran specialists in the State Department and intelligence services, lobbyists for major exporters, and a handful of reporters and commentators. The involvement of nongovernmental organizations in foreign policy issues, from Bread for the World to the National Wildlife Federation to Human Rights Watch, has introduced some new varieties into the hothouse. But the scale and salience of NGO lobbying and public participation in support of international engagement remains relatively low.[19] The absence of new faces in the hothouse mirror means that the foreign policy community speaks mainly to itself.

Those in the hothouse work diligently, nurturing strategies and cultivating opinion. These experts communicate through journal and magazine articles, in academic seminars and congressional hearings, and through Sunday morning talk shows and op-eds. The Center for Media and Public Affairs' (CMPA) study of television news coverage of global issues found that about three-quarters of the nongovernmental sources cited on network news reports "came from various elite foreign policy experts, academics, and think tank scholars."[20]

Increasingly, members of the media also see themselves as experts and as legitimate players in the policymaking process. What they cover and how they cover it influences policymakers. Susan Bales, a strategic communications expert who directs the FrameWorks Institute, wrote in her recent review of the literature on the media and foreign policy that "while policymakers may pay little attention to the public as represented in polls, they pay an inordinate amount of attention to the public's surrogate, the media."[21] Former investigative journalist and arms control negotiator Richard Burt concurs: "U.S. officials spend far more time worrying about what the news media are saying about them and their decisions than is commonly understood by either the public or the media. Early morning staff meetings in government departments focus as much on press problems as 'real' problems, as much on how to depict a policy to the press as on what policy should be in the first place."[22]

Media and policymakers believe that members of the other group reflect public opinion. Each makes a reasonable assumption. The media are supposed to react to readers and viewers; and elected policymakers are supposed to respond to the public. But, in fact, many journalists and foreign policy officials see only each other and hear only each other's opinions.

Interviews with congressional staff and journalists underscore the confidence each group has in the other's grasp of public attitudes. One reporter said that Congress is the best reflection of the public's views, while another stated that Congress reflects the public mood. At the same time, policymakers believe that the media have their finger on the public pulse. Daily press coverage is assumed to reflect the public's interests and attitudes.[23]

When media and policy elites look across the hothouse they see one another: "Congress and the media each get cues from the other, creating a closed, self-reinforcing information loop."[24] This small cadre of specialists may believe that the public is in the room. But the mirrors block their view of the people outside, whose firm but quiet opinions are represented by neither their elected officials nor the commercial media.

Not all disregard for public opinion is inadvertent, however. Some policymakers deliberately ignore public opinion. For them, "the public has little 'standing' on international issues. Americans are viewed by policymakers as woefully naïve and uninformed, and their participation in foreign policy debates is often discounted as limiting diplomatic options and threatening security."[25]

Journalist and historian Eric Alterman summarizes the relationship between the public and policymakers in the international domain: "The modern day foreign policy establishment is less concerned with its own ability to conceal or disclose selectively than with the public's ability to muck up its work with inconvenient interference and ignorant objection. . .Its members contribute to the shielding of foreign policy from democratic scrutiny by treating foreign policy as if it occurred without significant domestic ramifications."[26]

How can the public get the attention of media and policymakers busy in the hothouse? How can we move hunger and its systemic causes high on the list of priorities for policymakers? A more vocal public would help. What prevents the public from being more involved in debates on issues that apparently tap such deeply held values? In part, it's a question of language.

Jargon vs. Plain Talk

Communications strategist Ethel Klein, in a recent study for Oxfam America, blamed policymakers and the media for failing to connect global issues to the realities on the minds of citizens. Klein found that: "The public and the nation's opinion leaders have very different agendas when it comes to globalization. The language barrier between them, and the differing perspectives implied by that policy language, are clear: elites talk about GATT/WTO, IMF, Kyoto, and WHO, while the public worries about losing jobs, dramatic changes in weather conditions, and cures for deadly diseases. As opinion leaders debate global economic, environmental, and health issues as foreign policy concerns, they fail to reach an American public that is concerned about the domestic implications of these problems."[27]

Language, however, is only one obstacle to public engagement in support of cooperative international relations. A second issue, ironically, is the public's conviction that we are already more generous than we actually are.

What Do You Mean We're Not #1?

The public's unshakable belief that the United States gives more foreign aid than any other country is related to the media's portrayal of our role on the world stage. But it is also consistent with the deep pride U.S. citizens feel in our real (and perceived) leadership in the world. According to Susan Bales, "The problem arises because Americans only see their own efforts, while those of other countries are virtually invisible. As a consequence, Americans believe the U.S. is shouldering the majority, if not all, of the responsibility for world peace. Both experts and ordinary Americans reflected this view."[28]

Joseph Grady and Axel Aubrun call attention to the tendency of the print media to exaggerate

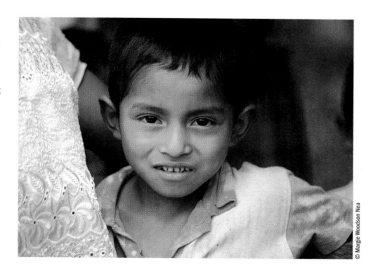

© Margie Woodson Nea

U.S. contributions, even in multilateral efforts. For example, they note, the headline of a *Washington Post* story in July 1998 stated "U.S., Japan, Other Nations Pledge $7.9 Billion in Food Subsidies."[29] The headline lumps the U.S. contribution of $300 million with Japan's pledge of $1.3 billion and other countries' pledges totaling $6.3 billion, misleadingly suggesting that the U.S. contribution is on a par with the most generous foreign aid donors.[30]

The resilience of the erroneous belief in high levels of U.S. foreign aid is reflected in a range of polls summarized by Steven Kull and I.M. Destler,[31] and by Margaret Bostrom in her 1999 study of earlier opinion research.[32] The deeply held "frame" or mental model shaping public beliefs about the generosity of the United States creates public resistance to hearing the truth about U.S. contributions to foreign countries. Susan Bales remarks that "the conventional wisdom would be to attack the misperception with a 'public education' campaign designed to get the fact in front of Americans that U.S. foreign aid spending accounts for a minute percentage of our total budget. This tactic is likely to end in failure. When informants were confronted with such information, they showed momentary surprise, and then reverted to their old patterns of reasoning. . .If the facts don't fit the frame, it is the facts that are rejected, not the frame."[33]

Good Fences Make Good Neighbors

Americans may remain silent on foreign aid because of our definition of the good neighbor. "Americans, like other people, try to understand international engagement by reference to their experience with parents, children, and neighbors . . .Given the American emphasis on individualism, the village model is not always a positive factor in Americans' thinking about international relations. The broad but passive support for greater international cooperation reported by Steven Kull and other researchers reflects the fact that Americans understand the idea of social bonds (e.g., between neighbors), but have a much weaker model than people from other cultures. The emphasis on self-sufficiency, which is a strong organizing principle even within American families, poses a challenge to any enterprise aimed at increasing engagement. The model of the American loner has an impact on every relationship in American life, from the one between mother and child to the one between the U.S. and the Third World."[34]

Aubrun and Grady describe the model that they claim dominates American thinking about the meaning of neighborliness and its implications for understanding our international relations: ". . .[I]n current American culture, the neighbor model refers mainly to casual and episodic interactions, or to unwanted ties and intrusions. . .Most of the time, Americans tend to feel and act as though they have no neighbors. An important exception is that Americans like to feel they can trust their neighbors in times of crisis. In effect there are two understandings at work: The good neighbor is invisible day-to-day but on the scene when urgently needed."[35]

Aubrun and Grady relate this notion of the "invisible neighbor" directly to the public's rejection of the facts concerning the low levels of U.S. foreign aid. "Interviews with the public reveal that in their day-to-day lives ordinary Americans have little awareness of other countries and have an especially hard time thinking of foreign countries as actors on the world stage. For example, they tend to hold fast to the belief that the United States provides a disproportionate share of development aid to needy countries, even when confronted with facts that contradict this understanding."[36]

The U.S. concept of the good neighbor is paradoxical. It may increase support for aid during a crisis. But it is also likely to dampen American interest in international affairs; no one likes a nosy neighbor. In fact, the Women's Lens poll found that 73 percent of Americans agree with the statement that "the U.S. should not try to change what goes on in other countries, because it is inappropriate for us to impose our values on others." The nosy neighbor quickly devolves into the neighborhood bully, the least desirable role for the United States to play.[37]

Who's Responsible?

Public engagement requires a clear sense of who is responsible and what they need to do. But "the public lacks an understanding of cause and effect or even a strong image of effective international solutions. They do not know whom to hold accountable for global issues, or what role government and private groups should play."[38] Organizations that seek to address the systemic causes of hunger and poverty need to describe complex problems clearly while offering understandable – and meaningful – solutions.

In the foreign affairs arena, some Americans acknowledge their ignorance and prefer to leave policy to experts. Yet on issues such as taxation and abortion that touch individual lives directly, people speak out without the benefit of expert knowledge. Something else is at work in the domain of foreign policy. Because Americans hear little about international issues from policymakers and the media, people believe that foreign affairs are not relevant to their busy lives and thus not worth making a fuss about. It is difficult to hold themselves or others accountable without a clear sense of what is at stake, who is responsible, why they should care, and what they should do. Television news portrayals of global issues, including poverty and hunger, project a sense of global mayhem that exacerbates the public's sense of confusion about what needs to be done.

Dan Amundson and his CMPA colleagues analyzed television news about international affairs. Both national and local network news programs consistently present hunger and other evidence of poverty overseas as a series of episodes – individual stories of individual distress – rather than as symptoms of systemic problems. CMPA concluded that the news "focus[ed] on discrete events and short-term crises rather than broader trends and processes or long-term problems."[39] The figures were dismal: "Out of over 1,000 local and national television news stories, only 84 took a thematic approach to international news."[40]

The 1999 demonstrations against the World Trade Organization in Seattle occurred during CMPA's study. The event offered an excellent opportunity for television to present and analyze complex issues. Instead, network news covered the protests as a media event rather than explaining the reasons for the demonstrations. The reports included almost no context for the images of colorfully costumed protesters, heavily armed police, and brooding trade ministers. As Susan Bales observed, we saw nothing but "turtle suits versus business suits."

Unfortunately, both the quality and the quantity of American TV reporting on international news are insufficient to provide a knowledge and conceptual base for furthering public interest in global interdependence. The good news is that, as superficial and episodic as this coverage is, its impact on core American beliefs is not as corro-sive as one might expect. It is puzzling to consider how Americans can continue to hold positive international views and to support policies of engagement when the nightly news is so filled with footage of disaster rather than more comprehensive information about the world.

But "public understandings are not closely based on media representations, even though those representations are a major source of information for the public."[41] In fact, the dominant media frame tends to quicken public concern, to motivate people to want to exert some control on an out-of-control arena and to provide relief to victims.[42]

The Whole World is Watching

Not everyone believes the "experts" know best. U.S. and some foreign activists "do not accept the foreign policy establishment's definition of the nation's priorities in the world. . ."[43] These skeptics include the thousands who demonstrated outside recent meetings of the international financial institutions in an attempt to force policy reassessment.

The media and policy elites were surprised by the intensity of protests in Seattle against the WTO, and in Washington, DC, and Prague against the World Bank and International Monetary Fund. Trapped in the hothouse, watching themselves in the mirror instead of the public, the "experts" missed the depth of feeling that animated the demonstrators.

"When thousands of protesters took Seattle by storm and disrupted the meetings of the. . . WTO in 1999, decisionmakers and opinion leaders were taken aback," according to Ethel Klein's Oxfam study.[44] "The very fact that they were surprised reflects the problem. The concerns raised by the Seattle protesters over the WTO tap into public fears. The public is more likely (77 percent) to place protecting jobs of American workers on their list of top priorities for long-range foreign policy goals than are media elites (31 percent), business and financial leaders (40 percent), or Capitol Hill policy staff (30 percent)."[45] The public, in other words, perceives a threat that invokes the instinct for self-preservation. Policymakers are likely to dismiss these fears as irrational or shortsighted.

Costumed activists in Seattle protest WTO policies.

Ted Grudowski

F2F: Face-to-Face Networking Still Vital in the Internet Age

BY DAVID DEVLIN-FOLTZ

The power and speed of e-mail networking helped Jody Williams lead a worldwide education and advocacy effort to ban landmines. From her home in a small Vermont town, Williams used electronic communications to mobilize the International Campaign to Ban Landmines (ICBL). In less than five years, she and colleagues around the world persuaded 122 countries to sign an international treaty, despite strong opposition from major powers. In 1997, Williams shared the Nobel Peace Prize for her work.

Significant international campaigns now routinely rely on e-mail and the Web. The Internet contributed to the successful 1998 derailment of the Multilateral Agreement on Investment by 600 electronically linked NGOs. The size and agility of the mass demonstrations in Seattle against the World Trade Organization in 1999 and against the World Bank and International Monetary Fund in Washington, DC, and Prague in 2000 were also attributed to the Internet.

E-mail offers instantaneous communication at minimal cost. A study of "transnational civil society organizations" like the ICBL, Human Rights Watch, and Transparency International highlighted the growing potential for Web use as its reach becomes truly global.[1] According to estimates by the Computer Industry Almanac, over 31 million of the 44 million people online weekly in 1995 lived in North America. By 2005, 765 million people will be online: 200 million each in North America and Western Europe, nearly 200 million in the Asia-Pacific region..., and [up to] 60 million in each of the remaining regions of the world."[2]

Despite the impact of the Internet, face-to-face organizing remains the foundation for social change. Abolitionists and advocates of women's suffrage developed sophisticated strategies and tactics for "information politics" in the 19th century with nothing more than sailing ships and trains to carry their letters across the Atlantic and around Europe. Later generations of

activists credited changes in ship design and postal reform with speeding their work and facilitating international cooperation. As one British antislavery activist put it, "We can no longer ignore what is going on in America—it is only two weeks away."[3]

The telegraph and photography figured heavily in the success of the campaign that pressured Belgium's King Leopold to halt the brutal system of rubber extraction

> ### Never doubt that a small group of thoughtful committed citizens can change the world: Indeed it's the only thing that ever has.
>
> Margaret Mead

that caused millions of deaths in the Congo.[4] The Chilean human rights diaspora coordinated its efforts through weekly telephone calls in the early 1970s. Then came faxes and the information and communication technologies we rely on today.

Jessica Mathews, president of the Carnegie Endowment for International Peace, credits contemporary technologies in part for the "power shift" from governments to businesses, international organizations, and the citizen groups constituting global civil society. "Information technologies disrupt hierarchies," she says, "spreading power among more people and groups. In drastically lowering the costs of communication, consultation, and coordination, [electronic technologies] favor decentralized networks. . .[that link] individuals or groups. . .for joint action without building a physical or formal institutional presence. Networks have no person at the top and no center. Instead, they have multiple nodes where collections of individuals or groups interact for different purposes. . .Governments, on the other hand, are quintessential hierarchies, wedded to an organizational form incompatible with all that the new technologies make possible."[5]

Political scientist Kathryn Sikkink believes that changes in technology have not altered a simple truth: At the heart of every transnational advocacy network is a small core of people and their mutual trust. "Once they have established this trust, often through face-to-face meetings, then the networks can go on to sustain themselves. . .through e-mail or modern communications technology." But no networks she studied "have been initiated solely via the Internet."[6]

Even in recent cases such as the ICBL, the importance of e-mail may be overstated: "Face-to-face meetings between activists and Canadian diplomats, traditional lobbying of American politicians, and other personal contacts between individuals were just as essential for the movement's success."[7]

Activists know that personal contact lays the basis for political success. Juliette Beck of Global Exchange gets "tired of the Internet and e-mail. We couldn't do this work without it, but, really, it's not organizing. There's nothing like face to face."[8] Lori Wallach, an organizer of the Seattle protests for Public Citizen's Global Trade Watch project, believes the Internet is "a tool like anything else. The real organizing. . .was face to face [with] people I've been meeting. . .three to four times a year, from around the world, since 1992."[9]

Margaret Mead's famous maxim is as fresh as when she penned it long before there was an Internet. But there is little doubt that the Internet gives today's activists a speed and ubiquity that make the world smaller, and changing it a more possible dream.

[1] Ann Florini ed., *The Third Force: The Rise of Transnational Civil Society* (Tokyo and Washington: Japan Center for International Exchange and the Carnegie Endowment for International Peace, 2000), 22.

[2] Computer Industry Almanac, December 1999, http://www.c-i-a.com/199908iu.htm.

[3] Kathryn Sikkink, "From Santiago to Seattle: Transnational Advocacy Networks in the Information Age," lecture May 16, 2000, at the Carnegie Endowment for International Peace, 2.

[4] Adam Hochschild, *King Leopold's Ghost* (Boston and New York: Houghton Mifflin, 1999).

[5] Jessica Mathews, "Power Shift." *Foreign Affairs*. January/February 1997, 50-66.

[6] Sikkink, "From Santiago to Seattle," 2.

[7] Ibid.

[8] William Finnegan, "After Seattle: Anarchists Get Organized." *The New Yorker*. April 17, 2000, 40-51.

[9] Moises Naim, "Lori's War: The FP Interview," *Foreign Policy*. Spring 2000, 28-54.

Activists protest globalization.

Closing the gap between the public and policymakers will require a different approach to communicating about poverty-focused foreign aid, one that encourages the public to be more vocal and policymakers to be better listeners. How can organizations like Bread for the World unlock the latent support that pollsters find in survey after survey? The key lies in finding ways to invoke, or "prime," the supportive attitudes the public already holds and to frame issues in terms that maintain those attitudes. A nascent constituency exists. Evidence of public support may embolden leaders to lead, and with that the foreign policy gap may begin to close.

Closing the Foreign Policy Gap

For elected officials and appointed policymakers to respect the public's views, credible sources must first articulate those views in ways that officials can hear. It requires effort to become the kind of squeaky wheel that members of Congress and their staff cannot ignore.

The Global Interdependence Initiative commissioned research to test different ways to prime the public in order to engage as strongly as possible the latent support for international engagement. Researchers also investigated possible differences in the ways that policymakers and the public might understand global problems and potential solutions.

Margaret Bostrom posed a series of questions to gauge public support for U.S. engagement in general and for foreign aid. Using the initial results as a baseline, she then tested responses to the same questions by similar Americans *after* they had been primed by hearing four different introductions:

- One mimicked the chaotic, dangerous view of the world portrayed by television news.

- A second portrayed the world as a place where internationally accepted social norms are developed and respected and where the United States joins other nations to defend those norms.

- A third called for the United States to be a partner with other countries in addressing international problems.

- A fourth included a series of questions about environmental issues before posing the standard questions about foreign policy and global issues.

- A fifth began with a series of similar priming questions about infectious diseases.

It seems reasonable to assume that Americans will respond most readily if we link global issues to their domestic counterparts. To test that hypothesis, Bostrom split the groups that heard priming questions about the environment, giving one half a series of questions about global environmental issues, and the other half a list of questions about domestic environmental issues. She used the same technique with the priming questions about infectious diseases.

The goal was to see which of these primes would help make audiences most receptive to global interdependence, as measured by the standard battery of questions about foreign policy and foreign aid. In addition, Bostrom sought to learn which primes would increase the importance the public attached to specific global issues. In each group, the interviewer asked people to rank a series of priorities, including hunger and poverty, for international activity.

When the question was asked without any priming, 49 percent of the public gave the highest possible priority to hunger and poverty. When the interviewer reminded the public of the world as portrayed through television news – a place of global mayhem – the priority the public accorded hunger and poverty jumped by 14 percent. Priming the audience with the kind of negative portrayals typical in the news media appeared to create a strong humanitarian response, a desire to help rather than to disengage.

The Bostrom study found that priming the public with questions about the global environment increased support for addressing hunger and poverty by 7 percent and produced a surge of 15 percent in support for foreign assistance in general. Domestic environmental questions produced no such boost. More important to those who would build a constituency for long-term development assistance, priming the audience to think about the global environment was also associated with increased support for long-term humanitarian and social justice concerns: promoting human rights, combating sweatshops and child labor, and providing equal education for girls.[46]

Bostrom's research suggests that warming up an audience by discussing global environmental issues would make people more receptive. Why? We have grown accustomed to thinking of the environment as something global, and this habit of mind apparently carries over into a sympathetic mindset as we consider other international issues. Perhaps we understand that self-reliance is no answer to environmental issues and that collective action is required; this inclines us to think the same way as we turn to long-term social justice and economic development. However the priming process works, it appears to increase the importance of development issues in the public mind, and our willingness to consider cooperative, long-term assistance.

Is all this talk of priming and framing just another technique for spinning the public, a sophisticated variety of manipulation? If so, advocates risk deepening what pundit Jack Rosenthal calls "spinicism." But it is not manipulative to help the public understand reality by replacing one metaphor with another it already uses to make sense of the world. And if we do not change frames, vital facts about the world will go unseen. The public will remain sympathetic, but disengaged. Policy will remain the province of those in the hothouse. If we leave things as they are, we will abandon the goal of building a constituency for global interdependence and for addressing hunger and poverty wherever it occurs. And that truly would be an act of cynicism with tragic global consequences. The U.S. public has not given up on the world. It is vital, if hunger and poverty are to be cut in half worldwide by 2015, that anti-hunger advocates not give up on the public.

Mr. Devlin-Foltz directs the Global Interdependence Initiative and the Faith and Public Policy program at the Aspen Institute's Democracy and Citizenship Program.

U.S. Public Attitudes on Foreign Aid and Hunger Relief

BY STEVEN KULL

The U.S. public strongly supports foreign aid to reduce hunger worldwide and would likely support an international program to cut hunger in half in Africa by the year 2015, according to a nationwide Rockefeller Foundation-funded poll conducted by the Program on International Policy Attitudes (PIPA)[1] in November 2000. At the same time, Americans have reservations about U.S. aid programs based on extreme overestimations of the amount the U.S. spends on foreign aid. Americans also doubt that aid gets to the people who really need it. However, these reservations do not undermine support for aid for hunger relief worldwide or in Africa.

Public Supports Aid for Hunger Relief

The poll found strong support for efforts to alleviate world hunger, stronger than for foreign aid in general. Eighty-seven percent said they favored giving "food and medical assistance to people in needy countries." Seventy-seven percent said that "alleviating hunger" was a good reason for giving aid. Seventy-six percent had a positive view of child survival programs.

Seventy-three percent favored "aid that helps needy countries develop their economies." When presented with pairs of arguments for and against development assistance, including the arguments that it is ineffective and simply ends up in the pockets of corrupt officials, a strong majority still favored it.

Americans feel better about giving aid to help poor countries than for strategic purposes. A strong majority (63 percent) agreed that "when hunger is a major problem in some part of the world we should send aid whether or not the U.S. has a security interest in that region." Only 23 percent thought that increasing U.S. influence was a good reason to give aid. Asked to choose which countries should get U.S. aid, only 23 percent said "countries important to U.S. security" and 13 percent said "countries needed by the U.S. as trade partners." However, 59 percent said "countries with the poorest economies."

The PIPA poll asked about the World Food Summit goal of cutting world hunger in half by the year 2015. The arguments in favor of doing so were much more convincing than those against, and an overwhelming 83 percent supported it.

Perhaps most significant is how Americans feel about paying for an international initiative to cut hunger in half. Asked how much they thought the average taxpayer in the industrialized world would have to pay to support that goal, the median response was $50 a year. An overwhelming 75 percent said that they would be willing to pay that amount.

Support for a Program to Cut Hunger in Half in Africa

Many Americans would likely support a specific international initiative to cut hunger in Africa by 2015. Seventy-two percent agreed that Africa should get special attention because it is the continent with the highest percentage of undernourished people and where hunger is growing the fastest. Seventy percent rejected the argument that aid to Africa should be a low priority because the U.S. has no vital interests there. Only 12 percent thought that too much aid goes to Africa.

Reservations About Aid

Americans support efforts to alleviate hunger, but they have reservations about foreign aid. Sixty-two percent said that the U.S. spends too much on foreign aid, though only 40 percent said they wanted to cut it — down from the 1995 PIPA poll, when 75 percent said too much was being spent on foreign aid and 62 percent wanted to cut it. The median estimate of how much of the federal budget goes to foreign aid was 20 percent — more than 20 times the actual amount. Asked how much would be appropriate, the median response was 10 percent — still 10 times the actual amount.

Another widespread concern about aid stems from the belief that a huge amount is wasted, primarily due to corruption. Asked how much reaches the people who really need it, the median estimate was a shockingly low 10 percent. While there are problems with some aid programs, even the sharpest informed critic would not make such a dire estimate of their effectiveness.

This perception might be mitigated if the public understood that much aid is not given to foreign governments, but rather is channeled through private charitable organizations that help needy people directly. A majority of respondents had a positive view of giving aid in this way because they believed that much more of it would reach people in need.

Even with these reservations about foreign aid, Americans' support for aid to reduce hunger is strong. An overwhelming 79 percent agreed that "the United States should be willing to share at least a small portion of its wealth with those in the world who are in great need."

Dr. Kull directs the Program on International Policy Attitudes and is on the faculty at the University of Maryland School of Public Affairs.

[1] The poll was conducted with a nationwide sample of 901 randomly selected Americans. The margin of error was plus or minus 3-4 percent.

Arguments For and Against a Program to Cut Hunger in Half

For	Percent who found the argument:	
	Convincing	**Unconvincing**
Given the high level of wealth in the industrialized countries, we have a moral responsibility to share some of this wealth to reduce hunger in the world.	69%	29%
Because the world is so interconnected today, reducing hunger in the world ultimately serves U.S. interests. It creates more political stability, and by promoting economic growth helps create more markets for U.S. exports.	64%	33%
The industrialized countries have huge economies and tremendous resources. If they would all chip in, hunger could be cut in half at an affordable cost.	75%	23%
Against		
It is not the responsibility of countries like the U.S. to take care of the hungry in other parts of the world; that is the responsibility of *their* governments.	45%	52%
It is unrealistic to try to cut world hunger in half. It would cost more money than people in the industrialized countries would be willing to pay.	42%	53%
The causes of hunger in other countries are complex and poorly understood. It is naive to think that outsiders can really make a serious difference by throwing money at the problem.	41%	55%
Conclusion	**Should**	**Should Not**
So, having heard all these points of view, do you think that, if the other industrialized countries are willing to do their share, the U.S. should or should not be willing to commit to a joint plan for cutting world hunger in half by the year 2015?	83%	13%

CHAPTER 3

U.S. Development Assistance

BY ASMA LATEEF*

At one time, the U.S. was an active player in the area of international development, often leading efforts to feed, educate, and empower poor people. But the U.S. role in international development assistance has sharply diminished along with budgetary funds allocated for foreign aid. This trend reflects a lack of recognition on the part of the nation's leaders that international hunger and poverty reduction are directly relevant to U.S. economic and political interests. U.S. commitment to reducing hunger and poverty, however, should not be based solely on these interests. There is a moral imperative. Experience shows that when U.S. foreign aid has been used for development purposes, it has been instrumental in lifting people out of poverty.

FAO/P. Cenini

*Two sections of this chapter were excerpted and adapted with permission from Isaac Shapiro, *Trends in U.S. Development Aid and the Current Budget Debate*. Center on Budget and Policy Priorities, Washington, DC, April 25, 2000.

A Bit of History

Since the end of World War II, Americans have supported the idea of helping countries develop. The Marshall Plan was the first coherent attempt to involve the United States in the economic development of other nations. It set the tone for future development assistance goals, as support for the reconstruction of Europe and Japan after the war was closely linked with other foreign policy objectives, namely containing communism. A desire to avoid the mistakes made following World War I, which created the conditions that led to Hitler's rise, was one motivation. Rebuilding Europe and Japan to balance the power of the Soviet Union and China was another.

In the 1950s, foreign policy objectives ran parallel to development objectives. While development assistance gained political support for foreign policy reasons, it was sometimes used to help the poorest countries meet basic human needs. The goals of the realists and the idealists among policymakers overlapped.

> Realists saw poverty and hunger as a breeding ground for communism; they saw economic development – increasing food production, incomes, and opportunities for poor people – as an important part of the overall containment strategy. They saw growing prosperity and the alleviation of hunger and poverty as ways to make the promises of communism unattractive to poor countries and people. These arguments provided a compelling rationale for U.S. assistance to reduce poverty and hunger, and increase prosperity in poor countries. . .The idealists, by contrast, saw U.S. help to poor countries and people as a moral imperative resting on earlier efforts by U.S. religious groups and private foundations to reduce overseas poverty and hunger . . .Indeed much of the overt rationale for foreign aid in the post-World War II period was couched in humanitarian as well as security rationales.[1]

A Senegalese woman irrigates community-owned crops.

During this time, not only was the United States the largest provider of development assistance but it took the lead in innovating ways to help the poorest people around the world out of their poverty. In 1960,

> with the United States taking the initiative, a group of [World] Bank member countries decided to set up an agency that could lend to very poor developing nations on highly concessional terms. They called it the International Development Association (IDA). Its founders saw IDA as a way for the "haves" of the world to help the "have-nots." But they also wanted IDA to be imbued with the discipline of a bank. For this reason, President Dwight Eisenhower proposed, and other countries agreed, that IDA should be a part of the World Bank.[2]

In 1961, Congress passed the Foreign Assistance Act, which formalized U.S. policy on development assistance and established the U.S. Agency for International Development (USAID). USAID is the primary vehicle through which

U.S. development assistance is distributed. Its purpose: "to promote socioeconomic development in the Third World."[3] The creation of the Peace Corps and the U.S. role in spearheading agricultural advances, known as the Green Revolution, are examples of U.S. engagement in international development.

In the early 1980s, the raison d'être of U.S. foreign assistance changed. It aimed less at economic development and more toward political ends. The Reagan administration saw foreign aid as a way to achieve short-term political goals, using it to win allies in the standoff with the Soviet Union.

> The goal of foreign aid to increase prosperity long term in developing countries shifted to the goal of minimizing Soviet influence over a very short time period. For several years in the 1980s, the four largest recipients of aid in Africa were Liberia, Somalia, Sudan, and Zaire. Within Africa, these countries have had the worst record of economic growth, poverty reduction, stability, human rights, and contributions to U.S. security. This was not because of a failure in foreign aid, but because the choice of recipient countries was made without regard to the ability of those countries to use foreign aid to help poor, hungry people.[4]

The separation of foreign policy goals and economic development goals had a surprisingly negative impact on the United States' role in alleviating hunger and poverty worldwide. The political reasons for foreign aid so overshadowed humanitarian concerns that by the time the Cold War ended the international development constituency in the U.S. had been considerably undermined. In the 1990s, the political gains from foreign aid further diminished. With Soviet communism out of the way and China opening itself to foreign investment and trade, foreign policy objectives in the post-Cold War era became less clear. The disappearance of a communist threat has not led to a return to the objectives of poverty reduction and expanding economic opportunities for developing countries as a mobilizing motive for foreign aid.

During the 1990s, support for transition economies, reconstruction after the war in the Balkans, and the ongoing support for Mideast peace were primary concerns of foreign assistance. National security interests have become defined more in terms of transnational issues such as global warming, HIV/AIDS, and immigration. Economic issues and trade agendas have become equal in importance to concerns such as peacemaking and combating international crime and terrorism.[5]

Missing from the current thinking on foreign assistance is the link between development and U.S. interests. Economic development provides poor people in poor countries with skills, tools, and opportunities. These elements create the conditions for economic growth, increased trade,

What Is Development Assistance?

The Organisation for Economic Co-operation and Development's (OECD) Development Assistance Committee (DAC) oversees the foreign aid allocations and programs of member countries.[1] The DAC uses the term official development assistance (ODA) to measure aid to developing countries and the term official assistance (OA) to measure aid to countries in transition, such as the republics of the former Soviet Union and more advanced developing countries. ODA and OA include "grants or loans that are undertaken by the official sector; promote economic development and welfare as the main objective; and given at concessional financial terms (if a loan, having a grant element of at least 25 percent)."[2] Technical cooperation is included while aid for military purposes is excluded.

The U.S. government calculates ODA differently.[3] Therefore, what constitutes development aid and the amount of aid varies depending on the source of information. For the purposes of this report, the DAC definition of ODA is used when comparing countries. To analyze the most recent U.S. figures, the Foreign Operations budget is used to approximate ODA and OA. It includes international development and humanitarian assistance and the Economic Support Fund.

---

[1] Members of DAC: Australia, Austria, Belgium, Canada, Denmark, Finland, France, Germany, Greece, Ireland, Italy, Japan, Luxembourg, the Netherlands, New Zealand, Norway, Portugal, Spain, Sweden, Switzerland, the United Kingdom, the United States, and the Commission of the European Communities

[2] OECD, *Development Co-operation, 1998 Report* (Paris: OECD, 1999), 131.

[3] J. Tony German Randel and Deborah Ewing (eds). *The Reality of Aid 2000: An Independent Review of Poverty Reduction and Development Assistance* (London: Earthscan Publications, 2000).

peace, and stability. How can a world with increased trading opportunities, more countries at peace, and greater numbers of healthy and productive people *not* serve U.S. interests?

The Decline in U.S. Development Assistance

The share of development assistance, as a percentage of the gross national product and budget, began to slide in the early 1960s but it was not until the early 1990s that the slide became precipitous.

In the 1980s, the average ODA for the U.S. as a percentage of gross national product (GNP) ranged from 0.25 percent at the beginning of the decade to 0.19 percent at the end. However, since 1992, U.S. ODA as a percentage of GNP has fallen from 0.17 percent averaged over 1992-93 to 0.09 percent over 1997-98. The annual average drop in the volume of U.S. ODA between 1992-93 and 1997-98 was 8.3 percent.[6] Furthermore, data collected by the U.S. Office of Management and Budget (OMB) suggest that aid as a percentage of the U.S. budget also declined (Figure 3.1).[7]

On a more positive note, between 1997 and 1998, there was a 27.7 percent increase in ODA, totaling one-tenth of 1 percent of the country's $10 trillion GNP. According to preliminary estimates, U.S. assistance to developing countries rose again in 1999 to $9.1 billion, a 2.5 percent increase over the previous year.[8]

How Aid Is Disbursed

The Foreign Operations budget is often considered to be the foreign aid budget of the U.S. government. Much of what is budgeted under Foreign Operations, however, does not address the particular needs of the poorest people. The total foreign operations appropriation for FY 2001 is $14.9 billion. Of this, only about $4.4 billion goes to programs and organizations that work directly with poor and hungry people (Table 3.1).[9]

Various government agencies and departments, including USAID, the State Department, the Department of Treasury, and the Department of Agriculture provide forms of foreign assistance. These agencies deal with many concerns other than international development and poverty reduction.

Figure 3.1: U.S. Foreign Aid as a Percentage of Budget Outlays

Source: Data presented in Isaac Shapiro, *Trends in U.S. Development Aid and the Current Budget Debate,* Washington, DC: Center on Budget and Policy Priorities, April 25, 2000, 12.

Foreign aid is given in a number of forms. Bilateral assistance goes directly from the U.S. government to recipient countries. Multilateral assistance is given through international organizations, such as the United Nations Development Programme (UNDP) or the World Bank. Most aid supports development efforts of developing country governments, but about 40 percent of USAID's development assistance goes through private voluntary organizations (PVOs).

The Foreign Operations appropriations are divided among U.S. economic, political, and national security interests. These include export and investment promotion through the Export-Import Bank and the Overseas Private Investment Corporation (OPIC), allocations of over $1.5 billion for Israel and Egypt, funds for Eastern Europe and the states of the former Soviet Union, international narcotics control, anti-terrorism activities, peacekeeping, and military assistance.

USAID

USAID's mission has been redefined over the years depending on the ideological bent and political agendas of the administration and Congress at a given time. In FY 2001, USAID is operating under a budget of about $7.6 billion. Of the programs that fall under USAID's purview, only Child Survival and Diseases (CSD), and Development Assistance (DA) have a strong anti-poverty focus. Using CSD funds, USAID improves maternal and child health through immunization and nutrition programs. It also helps countries develop public

Table 3.1: Foreign Operations Appropriations for FY 2001[1]

Program	(in millions of $U.S.)
Title I — Export and Investment Assistance	**741.0**
Export-Import Bank	865.0
Overseas Private Investment Corporation	62.0
Trade and Development Agency	50.0
Title II — Bilateral Economic Assistance	**9,062.0**
Development Assistance	2,268.0
Child Survival and Diseases Fund	963.0
Development Assistance Fund	1,305.0
Peace Corps	265.0
Transition Initiatives	50.0
Debt reduction	448.0
International Disaster Assistance	165.0
Development Credit Programs	1.5
USAID Operating Expenses and Inspector General	547.0
Economic Support Fund	2,295.0
International Fund for Ireland	25.0
Support for Eastern European Democracy	600.0
Kosovo/Balkans Supplemental	75.8
Assistance for the Former Soviet Union	810.0
Treasury Department Technical Assistance	6.0
International Narcotics	325.0
Migration and Refugee Assistance	700.0
Emergency Refugee Fund	15.0
Non-proliferation/Anti-terrorism	312.0
Title III — Military Assistance	**3,761.0**
International Military Education and Training	55.0
Foreign Military Financing	3,545.0
Peacekeeping Operations	127.0
Title IV — Multilateral Economic Aid	**1,332.0**
World Bank	
International Development Association	775.0
Global Environment Facility	108.0
Multilateral Investment Guarantee Agency	10.0
Inter-American Development Bank	35.0
Asian Development Bank	72.0
African Development Fund	100.0
African Development Bank	6.1
European Bank for Reconstruction and Development	35.8
International Organizations and Programs	186.0
Total	**14,896.0**

[1] The shaded areas represent programs that could be considered development assistance

Source: House of Representatives. *Report of the 106th Congress: Making Appropriations for Foreign Operations, Export Financing, and Related Programs for the Fiscal Year Ending September 30, 2001, and for Other Purposes.* http://thomas.loc.gov/cgi-bin/ [Accessed October 26, 2000].

Formula for Success: Seedlings, Training, and Hard Work

BY LAURA WHITE

Seventy-year-old Amalia Moncada Ponce's long gray braid swings as she moves from row to row, plucking the stubborn weeds from the soil of her farm in north-west Nicaragua. Amalia's 10 children, 58 grandchildren, and eight great-grandchildren are her co-laborers.

The family's property was not always so productive. "This used to be a stark area with steep slopes," says Yamilet Alvarez, an agricultural promoter for World Relief, who trained Amalia to diminish erosion by erecting natural barriers of rocks and fruit trees to hold the soil.

Basic grains alone are not very profitable, so Amalia has diversified. She grows beans, squash, papaya, grapes, plantains, and bananas, and has started to produce high-income crops such as coffee, cacao, pineapples, coconuts, and avocados. World Relief's agriculture program in Nicaragua, which is partially funded by USAID, provided the seedlings.

"When I look out at this farm I feel very good and am encouraged," Amalia says, surveying the lush green slopes. "We have been working in a different way for only two years and already we see the results."

With technical assistance and "starter" livestock, Amalia has transformed her farm into a profitable enterprise. With World Relief loans, she purchased two metal silos for $48 each. The silos keep the corn dry and insect-free, safely stored for sale in the dry season, when prices are higher. Amalia repays World Relief for the pigs and hens, one for one, as the animals reproduce.

"She always pays when accounts are due," Yamilet says. "I admire how she keeps her farm running well.

Amalia and her husband, Visitación.

She is the hardest-working, best-producing woman in the entire community. While all the women are good, Amalia is outstanding."

When Hurricane Mitch struck Nicaragua, the land-conservation techniques Amalia learned protected most of her plants and prevented erosion of the steep hillside. The rainfall rotted most of the growing corn, but the family had six months' worth of corn stored in their silos to sustain them. "Our life is inside that silo," Amalia's husband says. "Without that, we are finished."

Ms. White is a communications associate at World Relief, the international assistance arm of the National Association of Evangelicals.

---

health systems to address infectious diseases and HIV/AIDS. Funding for HIV/AIDS has almost doubled from $175 million in 2000 to $300 million in 2001. Through DA, USAID focuses on economic growth, human capacity building, democratic participation, sustainable development, the environment, and population and family planning.

The Economic Support Fund (ESF), assistance for Eastern Europe and the Baltic States authorized under the Support for Eastern European Democracy (SEED) Act of 1989, and assistance for the states of the former Soviet Union authorized under the Freedom Support Act (FSA) are the most political of the programs and are aimed primarily at middle-income countries. ESF provides economic and political support for U.S.

allies, for countries important for national security interests, and for countries in transition to democracy. ESF finances the U.S. contribution to the peace processes in the Middle East, Ireland, and Cyprus. It has been used to assist countries transitioning to democracy such as Nigeria, Indonesia, Guatemala, and Haiti.[10] SEED and FSA provide funds for countries in Eastern Europe and the former Soviet Union to develop market-oriented policies and institutions. Support for post-conflict reconstruction and development in the former Yugoslavia comes under SEED.

USAID has suffered from the superimposition of other goals on its original development mission. Development assistance was used primarily

Foreign Aid Supports Individual Initiative

BY LORI METCALF

For 10 years, Nguyen Thanh Hien worked on the formula for BioGro, a low-cost, bio-engineered fertilizer. The Vietnamese scientist received no funding from the private sector, so she used a cooking pot with three holes punched in the lid to carry out her work. Hien culled select strains of bacteria from the roots of rice plants and mixed them with peat and sugar. The resulting compound helps crops absorb essential nitrogen from the soil and the atmosphere.

Then the United Nations Development Programme funded Hien. She established a workshop for farmers to produce 20 tons of fertilizer locally. Without this infusion of foreign aid, Hien might not be teaching farmers how to mix the fertilizer and sell it to their neighbors, creating employment for themselves and increasing their income.

For the 500 households that use BioGro, rice yields have increased by an average of 15 percent. Local people also report tastier fruit and more robust tea leaves. Farmers use up to 50 percent less chemical fertilizer, reducing their costs and producing healthier crops in an environmentally sound way.

Ms. Metcalf is a research assistant with BFW Institute.

Source: Adapted from Margot Cohen, Fertile Mind. *Far Eastern Economic Review*, Sept. 28, 2000, 38-39.

---

to promote political and strategic objectives. Congress and the president have also complicated USAID's work with myriad earmarks and specific instructions. Thus USAID has achieved mixed results. Mixed results and weak political support for foreign aid in general have made USAID vulnerable to continual attack. USAID has been threatened with closure on a number of occasions and has been repeatedly reorganized. Attacks and reorganizations have further weakened the agency.

One recent response to congressional criticism has been an attempt to measure all USAID activities in terms of short-term results. This is meant to improve performance and political support, but some crucial development work is intrinsically long term and some results may not be evident in short time frames.[11]

USAID works with private voluntary organizations (PVOs), universities, and businesses to engage them in international development and to increase political support. USAID and the State Department have also made some effort to explain and justify foreign aid to the public, but with limited effectiveness:

> To revive public interest in aid, USAID must reexamine the value bases of the agency's humanitarian and development assistance missions. Both remediative and preventative aid missions draw on Americans' sense of moral obligation and desire to secure and enhance human well-being. USAID's challenge is to enliven these motivating impulses and to persuade average Americans that their participation is not only desirable, but indispensible.[12]

© Jim Stipe

A Guatemalan man harvests coffee.

Dialogue on Development Finance

BY LORI HENINGER AND DON REEVES

For the first time, finance ministers from all countries will gather as equals to take a global look at the methods, strategies, and foundations of development finance. The United Nations Development Programme (UNDP) will sponsor the meeting in late 2001 or early 2002 to give developing countries a greater voice in decisions that affect them. Voting at UNDP is one country/one vote, which gives developing countries greater influence on UNDP policies than on those of the World Bank, the International Monetary Fund, and the regional development banks.

These international financial institutions lend money to poor countries for development and set the standards for investment and lending by governments and private businesses. Voting is proportional to the shares of capital stock held by each country. Wealthy countries, notably the United States, dominate the discussions and policy decisions. For this reason, developing countries lack influence. Gender, environment, labor, and social concerns often get short shrift.

The UNDP-sponsored United Nations High-Level Event on Financing for Development (FfD) calls for participation by all relevant stakeholders in the preparatory meetings and the final event. In addition to the IMF and World Bank, the World Trade Organization and the International Labor Organization will take part. The UNDP has invited nongovernmental organizations and the private sector to participate.

Six working groups are developing concrete, action-oriented policy proposals around the following tentative agenda items:

- Mobilizing *domestic* financial resources for development
- Mobilizing *international* resources for development: foreign private investment and other private flows
- Trade
- Increasing international financial cooperation for official development assistance
- Debt
- Enhancing the coherence and consistency of the international monetary, financial, and trading systems in support of development.

The FfD event is an unparalleled opportunity to shine a light on development financing from the grassroots as well as the policy level, and can be the beginning of a longer dialogue on international equity and standards. Contact: U.N. Coordinating Secretariat for Financing for Development, www.un.org/esa/ffd/ or the Quaker United Nations Office, www.quno.org.

Lori Heninger co-directs the Quaker United Nations Office in New York. **Don Reeves**, a former Bread for the World Institute policy analyst, is a consultant on development issues.

What is really needed is presidential leadership and congressional support for development assistance. If President George W. Bush decides that expanding opportunity for poor and hungry people around the world is important – in its own right, and for the security of the United States – he could win bipartisan backing from Congress and tap into widespread public support for effective aid. A clear mandate from the president and Congress would do more than anything else to improve the effectiveness of USAID.

Funding for Multilateral Agencies

About 10 percent of U.S. development assistance is disbursed through multilateral agencies, which includes the United Nations agencies and the international financial institutions.

The United States is the largest shareholder at the World Bank and the IMF. Both organizations give member countries a number of votes proportionate to their contribution. The United States controls 16.5 percent of the votes at the World Bank, and 17.6 percent at the IMF, about 10 percent more than the next largest shareholder, Japan.[13] This means that the United States heavily influences and can veto the policies of these organizations.

USAID administers U.S. contributions to UNICEF. The State Department administers funds appropriated for some of the U.N. agencies, including the U.N. Development Programme (UNDP), and the U.N. Fund for Population Activities (UNFPA). The Food and Agriculture Organization (FAO) comes under the auspices of the Department of Agriculture, while contributions to the World Health Organization (WHO) are administered by the Department of Health and Human Services. The Foreign Operations appropriations for UNICEF in FY 2001 were $110 million. Other international organizations and programs received $186 million.

The Department of Treasury is responsible for disbursing funds for bilateral debt relief and for monitoring the Highly Indebted Poor Countries (HIPC) Initiative. It also disburses the funds allocated for the international financial institutions, the World Bank's International Development Association (IDA), the Global Environment Facility (GEF), the Multilateral Investment Guarantee Agency (MIGA), the regional development banks, and the International Fund for Agriculture and Development (IFAD). The budget allocation for IDA in FY 2001 is $775 million; $448 million goes to the HIPC trust fund and IFAD receives $5 million.

Treasury's role in international development reflects recognition of the importance of developing countries to U.S. interests. Its goals with regard to its work through international organizations includes the promotion of international monetary stability, sustainable economic growth and development, poverty reduction, private sector development, and good governance.[14]

Food Aid

The U.S. gives more food aid than any other nation. This comes under Public Law (PL) 480 through the Department of Agriculture. The budget for FY 2001 was $837 million. "The landmarks in U.S. food aid are the intensively negotiated Farm Bills, which reflect lobbying that effectively ties all food aid to U.S. exportable surpluses, requires 75 percent of commodities (including that for relief purposes) to be shipped in U.S. registered vessels, but also allows NGOs to monetize over one-third of commodities and use the proceeds for development projects."[15] The next Farm Bill is scheduled for 2002. Title II of PL 480 is administered through USAID but is included in the agriculture appropriations bill.

Senator George McGovern, now U.S. ambassador to the FAO, is proposing that the United States lead a global food aid initiative to establish school-lunch and child-feeding programs worldwide. Such programs have helped to reduce hunger in the United States and they can attract political support from U.S. agriculture that would not be available for cash development assistance. Senator McGovern argues that free school lunches would be an incentive for poor families to send their children, particularly their daughters, to school. Senator Bob Dole worked with Senator McGovern to expand domestic nutrition programs in the 1970s and is now joining the global school-lunch initiative. The Clinton administration launched a pilot school-lunch program in Africa in 1999.

The U.S. agricultural surpluses of the last few years have led to a sharp increase in food aid, particularly to the former Soviet Union. Some of it helped avert famine in Ethiopia in 2000. One problem is that poor countries may invest in systems that use food aid and then face a sudden

WFP/E. Espaillat

Children eating at school in the Dominican Republic.

decline in aid when U.S. agricultural markets shift. The McGovern proposal is a good idea, but should be only one part of the U.S. response to hunger worldwide.

Is U.S. Aid Misdirected?

There are two ways of analyzing how U.S. aid has been spent over the years. One looks at the geographical distribution of aid and the other assesses which sectors the aid has supported. The geographic distribution of U.S. ODA over time reflects the strategic priorities of foreign aid policy. In the early 1970s, when the Vietnam War and national security concerns in Asia were high priorities, India, Vietnam, Indonesia, and Pakistan were the top four recipients. South and East Asia received over 61 percent of U.S. ODA. Sub-Saharan Africa received only 7 percent of ODA.

In 1977-78, following the Camp David Peace Accords, Israel and Egypt topped the list, receiving almost 25 percent of total ODA (Table 3.2). India followed, receiving 2.6 percent of the total. By 1997-98, Israel had graduated from the DAC list of developing countries, leaving Egypt as by far the largest recipient of ODA. The reclassification of U.S. aid to Israel accounts for the huge

Figure 3.2: Major U.S. Aid Uses in 1997-98

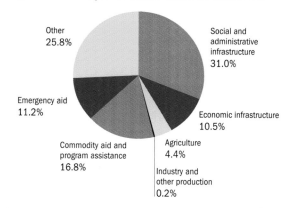

Other 25.8%
Social and administrative infrastructure 31.0%
Emergency aid 11.2%
Economic infrastructure 10.5%
Commodity aid and program assistance 16.8%
Agriculture 4.4%
Industry and other production 0.2%

Source: OECD, 2000, *Development Co-operation*, 204-205.

drop in the percentage of ODA received by the top 15 recipients to 24.8 percent and the sudden increase in OA by almost $1 billion dollars. Sub-Saharan Africa has gained in gross disbursements of U.S. aid, rising from 8.6 percent in 1977-78 to 20.6 percent by 1997-98.[16]

A sectoral analysis of U.S. ODA flows between 1977-78 and 1997-98 reveals a fivefold increase in ODA for social and administrative infrastructure, which includes education, health and population, water supply and sanitation, and institution

Table 3.2: Major Recipients of U.S. Aid
(Gross Disbursements as a Percent of Total ODA)

1977-78		1987-88		1997-98	
Israel	14.7	Israel	11.9	Egypt	8.5
Egypt	10.0	Egypt	9.3	Bosnia-Herzegovina	2.3
India	2.6	El Salvador	3.3	Peru	2.0
Indonesia	2.4	Pakistan	2.7	India	1.7
Pakistan	2.0	Philippines	2.7	Jordan	1.5
Bangladesh	1.9	India	1.7	Bolivia	1.5
Northern Marianas	1.7	Northern Marianas	1.6	South Africa	1.1
Rep. of Korea	1.4	Honduras	1.5	Haiti	1.0
Jordan	1.4	Guatemala	1.4	Vietnam	0.8
Philippines	1.4	Costa Rica	1.3	Palestinian Adm. Areas	0.8
Sri Lanka	0.7	Bangladesh	1.3	Mozambique	0.8
Bolivia	0.6	Sudan	1.0	El Salvador	0.8
Morocco	0.6	Jordan	0.9	Micronesia, Fed. States	0.8
Syria	0.6	Indonesia	0.9	Philippines	0.7
Peru	0.6	Morocco	0.9	Ethiopia	0.6
Total	**42.7**		**41.4**		**24.8**

Source: OECD, 2000, *Development Co-operation*, 243.

Foreign Aid to Israel and Egypt

Egypt and Israel are not poor countries. Egypt has a per capita income of $1,400, which puts it in the middle-income category. Israel is estimated to have a per capita income of $9,266, qualifying it as a high-income country. Yet these countries have figured highest on the list of recipients for U.S. foreign aid. Together they get over 20 percent of U.S. foreign assistance. Ensuring peace in the Middle East and Israel's security have been the primary motives. Consider aid per capita in 1998: Israel and Egypt received $179 and $31, respectively, while Uganda received a mere $22, Peru $20, and India $2 per capita.

Source: World Bank. 2000. *World Development Report 2000/2001: Attacking Poverty*. New York: Oxford University Press, 314-315.

building (Figure 3.2). This suggests a positive trend towards spending the much-diminished aid budget on investments in people. Emergency aid, however, grew from 0.8 to 11.2 percent of total ODA, reflecting the growing need to respond to crises. In addition, ODA doubled for economic infrastructure, including transport, communications, and energy. The level of development assistance to agriculture, industry and production, commodity aid, and program assistance fell. The decline in ODA for agriculture is troubling. The importance of agriculture to the lives of poor and hungry people cannot be overstated. Chapter 4 will expand on this point.

Other Countries Pick Up the Slack

According to the OECD's Development Assistance Committee, foreign aid remained fairly steady during the 1980s, averaging between 0.3 and 0.35 percent of the national income (GNP) of the industrialized countries. In the early 1990s, some of the richest countries in the world made huge cuts in their foreign aid budgets. The end of the Cold War weakened political support for aid. Economic slowdown and ensuing budget crises in the OECD countries also contributed to the decline in foreign aid. From 1992-1997, ODA dropped significantly, reaching a low 0.22 percent of the total GNP of the industrialized countries in 1997 (Figure 3.3).

The cumulative drop in foreign aid between 1992 and 1998 amounted to $88 billion, of which the U.S. share was $22 billion. The U.S., Japan, Italy, France, and Germany accounted for nearly three-quarters of the drop in ODA during that period. The decline in development assistance can be partly explained by large cuts in industrialized-country government budgets in the early 1990s, but it was greater than the decline in other public expenditures.[17]

By the end of the decade, the rich countries were once again enjoying sustained prosperity. Although the world's wealthy nations increased their levels of foreign aid in 1998-99, it did not rebound to pre-1992 levels. ODA in 1999 was still much lower in relation to national income than in the 1980s.

Figure 3.3: U.S. and Total DAC ODA as a Percentage of GNP

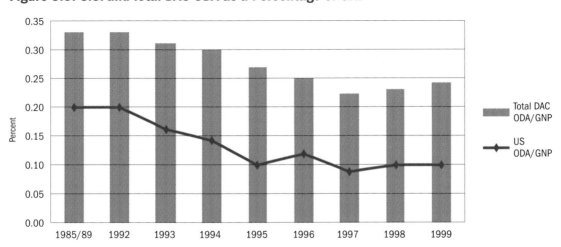

Source: OECD DAC Reports 1995, 1997, 1999, and Press Statement from May 12, 2000.

Japan Is #1 in Foreign Aid

BY RICHARD FORREST

Japan has been the largest provider of official development assistance (ODA) for 10 consecutive years. At the July 2000 Group of Eight Summit in Okinawa, Japan pledged to continue its generous support for the world's poorest countries, including $3 billion for research and dissemination of vaccines for infectious diseases and $15 billion over five years for information technology to overcome the global "digital divide." With the Okinawa pledge, Japan topped its 1999 foreign assistance total of $15.3 billion, which represented an increase of 43.8 percent over previous years. ODA in 1998 accounted for 0.28 percent of Japan's gross national product, more than twice the U.S. allocation level.

Japan advocates a comprehensive approach to poverty alleviation. "Fighting poverty is both a moral imperative and a necessity for a stable world," the Japanese Ministry of Foreign Affairs' *Global Poverty Report* (2000) asserted, and countries such as Japan should ensure market access for developing country imports, including agricultural and labor-intensive products. The report acknowledged that poverty includes economic, social, and governance dimensions that can be addressed only by overcoming deficiencies in education, nutrition, and access to information and markets, and by promoting local participation in planning.

Japanese ODA supports improved agriculture and fisheries. Approximately 60 countries receive food production assistance, which distributes fertilizers and promotes irrigation, transportation, and the infrastructure to access markets. Japan seeks to maximize food security, targeting staple food crops such as rice, wheat, soybeans, and maize. Aid priorities and projects clearly reflect Japan's national interests in maintaining good economic and diplomatic relations with key geopolitical and resource-rich nations, such as China, Indonesia, and the Middle East.

Asia receives more than 60 percent of Japanese ODA. Indeed, Japan's extraordinary 1999 ODA increase was a response to the Asian economic crisis. However, Japan's current economic doldrums will not sustain continued high foreign aid budgets. Annual ODA outlays are expected to drop to about $10 billion over the coming years. But since foreign aid is so important a component of Japan's foreign policy, Japan will likely remain the top donor for some time.

Africa received the second highest amount over the past decade: Ghana got the most, followed by Kenya, Tanzania, and Zambia. In addition, Japan has hosted two meetings of the Tokyo International Conference on African Development, which resulted in the *Tokyo Agenda for Action*. This plan called for prioritizing social and economic development and for creating the conditions that foster poverty reduction: good governance, conflict prevention, and post-conflict development.

Japan provides 30 percent of its country-to-country ODA in the form of loans. This stems from Japan's own experience with World Bank loans for reconstruction after World War II. Japan is proud of its aid program, which is an important diplomatic tool for a country strictly limited in its ability to wield military influence. Japan has used foreign assistance to reinforce its stated values of promoting democracy and international security, cutting off aid to countries that tested nuclear weapons, for example.

The Japanese public is keenly interested in the effectiveness of their country's foreign aid, due in part to national budgetary constraints, but also to NGO and press reports of wasteful or destructive aid projects. In 1999, the Japanese government included ordinary citizens in the oversight of its foreign aid efforts to engage the public and gain support for its programs.

In its first year, the ODA Civilian Monitor System offered one citizen from each of Japan's 47 prefectures the chance to inspect project sites in developing countries. To qualify, applicants must be Japanese citizens, at least 18 years old, in good health, and able to complete an orientation, the evaluation itself, and a debriefing following travel to the developing country. Civilian monitors are expected to participate in ODA-related events such as the annual International Cooperation Festival, and to share with the public their experiences in the field. No special achievement or technical knowledge is required to become a civilian monitor. Candidates must pass an international cooperation quiz attached to the application form and write a short essay. The ODA Civilian Monitor System has been so successful that the number of inspectors increased in 2000.

Mr. Forrest coordinates the U.S.-Japan Common Agenda Public-Private Partnership, a project hosted by InterAction. E-mail: rforrest@interaction.org.

The U.S. share of ODA worldwide has dropped dramatically over the past four decades.[18]

- Between 1950 (the earliest year for which this information is readily available) and 1968, the United States contributed more than half of the ODA provided by DAC countries. By 1977-78, the U.S. was contributing less than one-third of ODA; in 1987-88, the U.S. contributed less than one-fourth of ODA; by the 1997-98, the U.S. contributed less than one-sixth of ODA.[19]

- In absolute dollars, the U.S. is no longer the largest source of ODA. Japan, with an economy less than half the size of ours, is now a bigger contributor. The United States is the second largest contributor in total dollars.

The United Nations has established an ODA target for donor countries of 0.7 percent of GNP.[20] In 1998 and 1999, four of the 21 countries that the OECD examined – Denmark, Netherlands, Norway, and Sweden – met or exceeded this goal. In contrast, a mere 0.10 percent of the U.S. GNP went to ODA in 1998-99, one-seventh of the U.N. goal. The share of GNP the United States contributed to ODA declined by more than half between the late 1980s and the late 1990s.[21]

- In 1997-98, the typical or median country examined contributed 0.3 percent of GNP to ODA. In other words, half of all countries contributed a larger share than this amount, while half contributed a smaller share. The U.S. contribution level was less than one-third of the median level (Figure 3.3).

- In 1997-98, the United States contributed a smaller share of its national income to ODA than any other OECD country. Italy was the second lowest, contributing 0.15 percent of GNP. Spain was third lowest, with a contribution of 0.24 percent of GNP (Figure 3.4).

- In 1998, the U.S. gave only 12 percent of its net aid disbursements to sub-Saharan Africa, compared with an average of 24 percent for all the DAC countries. Fifteen percent of U.S. ODA in 1998 went to the least developed countries, compared with an average of 21 percent for all the DAC countries and the European Union average of 24 percent (Figure 3.5).

Another way to measure national commitment is to compare assistance per capita. For each person in the United States, the U.S. contributed $29 per year in ODA during 1997-98. The median contribution among the 21 nations the OECD examined was $70 per capita. On the high side, Denmark contributed $316 per capita to ODA. Of the 21 OECD countries, only Portugal – a far poorer country than the United States – contributed a smaller amount per capita than the U.S.

Figure 3.4: ODA of DAC Members as a Percentage of GNP in 1998 and 1999

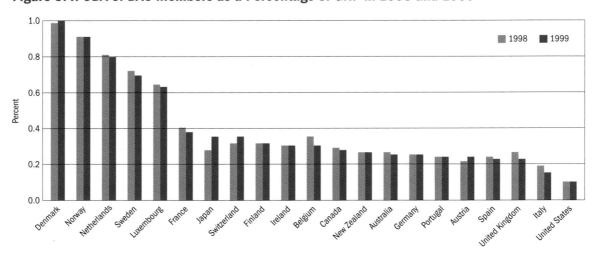

Source: OECD, 2000, *Development Co-operation*, 169; DAC Press Statement from May 12, 2000.

Figure 3.5: Aid from DAC members to Least Developed Countries in 1998

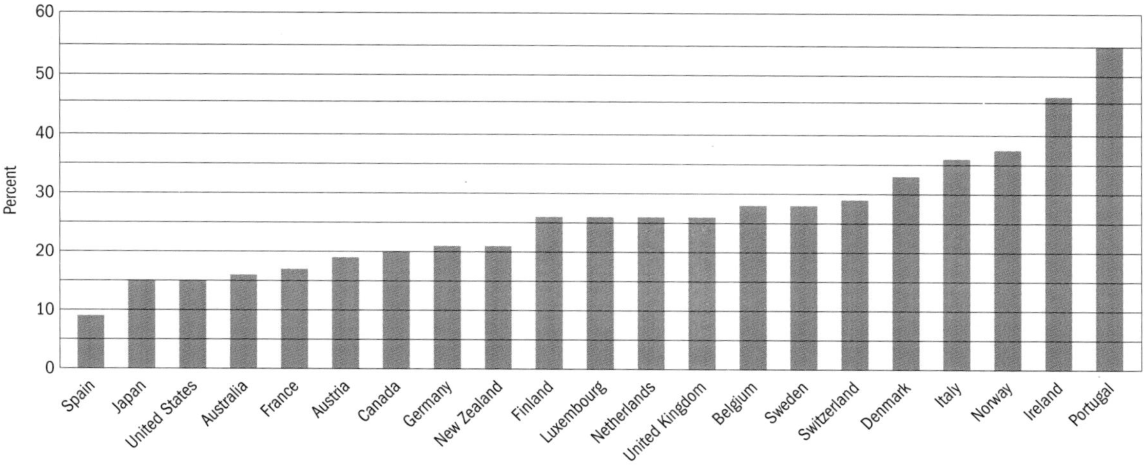

Source: OECD, 2000, *Development Co-operation*, 227.

The amount of OA extended worldwide is much lower than the amount of ODA. The difference is that ODA goes to developing countries, OA to better-off countries. Partly because U.S. economic aid is less focused on poor countries, the United States ranks above average in the amount of OA it provides, measured as a share of the economy.

When OA and ODA are combined, however, the United States continues to compare unfavorably. In 1997-98, approximately 0.13 percent of U.S. GNP went to OA and ODA. This was the lowest share of any of the 21 countries. In fact, it was well below half of the average share of GNP (0.33 percent) that other countries contributed in OA and ODA combined.

OECD Country Rationales for Foreign Aid

The difference in aid spending patterns between the United States and other donors can be explained by why countries give aid. While funding for foreign policy objectives is important, particularly to ensure peace and stability, these objectives are distinct from poverty reduction objectives. Foreign aid has often been used to prop up sympathetic governments or allies, even if these governments were known to be corrupt or to follow policies that were detrimental to their

Scandinavia and the Netherlands Set the Standard

The Netherlands, Denmark, Norway, and Sweden stand out in their commitment to eradicating hunger and poverty. All four nations spend a much higher percentage of their national incomes on development assistance than other industrialized countries, far exceeding the U.N. target of 0.7 percent. Denmark's ODA accounted for 1 percent of its GNP in 1999. Norway gives 0.91 percent and intends to reach 1 percent.

The three Scandinavian countries direct more than 70 percent of their ODA to countries where the need is greatest, to the least developed and other low-income countries (as classified by the U.N. and the World Bank). Less than half of U.S. ODA finds its way to the poorest countries.

Poverty reduction is at the center of these countries' aid programs. Norway directs ODA "to poor countries with good policies...to help to foster economic growth, contribute to social development programs, and target aid on vulnerable groups."[1] In addition, international development features prominently in how the governments of these countries are organized. For instance, Norway has a minister of international development and the Netherlands has a minister for development cooperation. In the United States, the administrator of USAID is not a cabinet-level position.

[1] OECD, 2000, *Development Co-operation*, 97.

A kitchen in rural Rajasthan, India.

populations. Historic and cultural ties have also been a reason for giving foreign aid. Former colonies are favorite destinations for foreign aid; the top 15 recipients of British and French foreign assistance are former colonies.[22] Common language and religion have also been a motivation.[23]

Many donors use foreign aid to pursue commercial goals. This helps explain the geographic distribution of ODA, which is often directed at regions that are or have the potential to become large markets, such as Eastern Europe, Central and South America, and the Pacific Rim countries.

According to DAC, overarching poverty reduction goals are a feature of Belgium, Canada, Denmark, Finland, the Netherlands, Norway, Sweden, the United Kingdom (strengthened in 1997), and the World Bank.[24]

Lifestyles of the Rich and Stingy[25]

In assessing the relative level of resources the United States devotes to development aid, it is useful to examine the wealth and living standards of the United States relative to other countries. World Bank data are particularly useful in this regard.[26]

- Each person in the United States has 56 times the average annual income of each person in the world's low-income countries.

- The U.S. economy is 27 percent of the world economy, although the United States makes up just 5 percent of the world's people.

- In 1998, there were an estimated 1.2 billion people in developing or transitional countries who lived on less than $1 a day. These individuals accounted for nearly one in every four people in these countries. In South Asia alone (which includes India), an estimated 522 million people (40 percent of the population) lived on less than $1 a day in 1998. In sub-Saharan Africa, 291 million people (46 percent of the population), more than the entire U.S. population of 276 million, lived on less than $1 a day.

United Nations data provide some sense of the living conditions associated with such low levels of income.[27]

- In the United States, 13 percent of the population is not expected to survive to age 60. In South Asia, 30 percent of the population is not expected to live this long. In sub-Saharan Africa, 56 percent of the population is not expected to reach age 60.

- In the United States, there are eight cases of tuberculosis (TB) per 100,000 people. In both South Asia and sub-Saharan Africa, there are more than 100 TB cases per 100,000 people.

- The United States has 245 medical doctors for every 100,000 people. South Asia has 44. Sub-Saharan Africa has 16.

A Nigerian woman winnows millet.

- The adult literacy rate is 99 percent in the United States. By comparison, only 52 percent of South Asian adults and 59 percent of sub-Saharan African adults are literate.

- The FAO estimates that nearly 800 million people in the developing world are undernourished – that is, their "food intake does not provide enough calories to meet their basic energy requirements."

- In the developing world, an estimated two of every five children are stunted (i.e., have significantly low height for their age), and one in three is underweight.

Helping Ourselves by Helping Others

Many opponents of foreign aid in the U.S. argue that foreign aid has not helped poor people. These arguments are not based on the reality of U.S. foreign aid policy in the last two decades. The primary purpose of U.S. foreign assistance has never been development or poverty reduction. Whether U.S. assistance achieved its true objectives is another question altogether.

With the opportunities and pressures created by globalization, there is a vital role for foreign aid. However, to cut hunger in half by 2015, the U.S. and other OECD countries must both increase funding and make sure the money is used directly for eradicating hunger and poverty. Committing sufficient resources to poverty reduction, hunger alleviation, and long-term development assistance and improving the nature and quality of that development assistance are the keys to success.

Ms. Lateef is a policy analyst at BFW Institute.

CHAPTER 4

Foreign Aid that Works for Hungry People

BY ASMA LATEEF

When hungry people have opportunities and the freedom to think about more than where their next meal is coming from, their creativity flourishes. Foreign aid can help produce those opportunities. But foreign aid is underfunded. Foreign aid's success stories have been dwarfed by the perception of failure, skewing opinion in Congress and the executive branch. Many do not believe that foreign aid works. This tarnished reputation is a legacy of Cold War decisions and the implementation of foreign aid, not an inherent defect of foreign aid itself.

Foreign aid has contributed to the great strides made against hunger and poverty worldwide. Many lessons have been learned about how to target the structural causes of poverty. But without concerted assistance from the international community, the problem of hunger, which is the most severe manifestation of poverty, will continue well into the 21st century.

FAO/M. Marzot

In 1996, representatives to the World Food Summit from 186 countries pledged themselves to the goal of cutting hunger in half by 2015. The good intentions of the signatory countries remain unfulfilled. The latest Food and Agriculture Organization (FAO) data place the number of undernourished during 1996-98 at 826 million, 792 million in developing countries and 34 million in developed countries. The number of people going hungry declined by 8 million a year throughout the 1990s – until 1999, when there was no decline. To meet the World Food Summit's 2015 goal requires a collaborative campaign against hunger. The traditional relationship between donors and recipients must give way to building true partnerships among the many stakeholders: governments, civil society, and the private sector in developing and industrialized countries. Everyone stands to benefit from the eradication of hunger and poverty. Adequate funds and improved poverty-focused policies and programs are essential.

Evaluating Foreign Aid

Studies on the effectiveness of foreign aid have concluded that it has significantly increased economic growth and reduced poverty.[1] The right mix of market-oriented policies and good governance enhances aid's usefulness.[2] In countries with poor policies, aid can fund technical assistance to improve government processes and administration, build human capacity, and expand access to information and technology. In Vietnam, donors contributed to widespread reforms by nonfinancial interventions such as technical assistance, training, and policy workshops to help local decisionmakers learn how other countries have attracted investment.[3]

Complex Problems

Foreign aid has produced impressive results, even in countries with poorly managed or unstable governments. In low-risk environments, the private sector can be expected to finance most endeavors. But private capital is unlikely to fund basic needs such as primary education, public health, and infrastructure, particularly in remote or agricultural areas. This is where governments must take an active role. Development assistance is the public capital that fills the financing void in poor countries and in neglected sectors.

Development assistance has helped improve the status of many developing countries (Table 4.1). "Overall, developing countries have made tremendous progress: more babies are surviving, more food is on the table, more children are in school, and there are fewer deaths from easily preventable diseases. There has been more global improvement in life expectancy in the past 40 years than in the previous 4,000."[4] Since 1960, adult literacy in sub-Saharan Africa has increased by over 280 percent; infant mortality has declined in East Asia by more than 70 percent; the under-5 mortality rate has declined by over 75 percent in Latin America and the Caribbean; and life expectancy has risen by 46 percent in South Asia.

Achievements of Foreign Aid

Don't mistake tales of the worst excesses of Cold War foreign aid for the whole story. In fact, at its best, foreign assistance works for poor people.

Child Survival

"In the mid-1980s, James P. Grant, an American serving as head of the United Nations Children's Fund (UNICEF), set out a straightforward but ambitious goal: to reduce early childhood death rates worldwide."[5] Thanks partly to grassroots lobbying by Bread for the World, RESULTS, and other groups, congressional funding for child survival has grown. A measure of success: 4 million children under age 5 have been saved each year in poor countries.[6]

River Blindness

Coordinated action against onchocerciasis (river blindness) in Africa is another development assistance triumph. River blindness affects 20 million people. A further 120 million people in 30 African countries are at risk. In 1974, the Onchocerciasis Control Program was set up to eliminate the black fly, which transmits the disease. The program brought 11 West African governments together with international organizations, bilateral donors, NGOs, foundations, and the private sector. The Merck Corporation donated medicines. In 1996, the African Program

Table 4.1: Social Indicators of Development

	1960	1970	1980	1990	1998
Infant Mortality Rate (per 1,000 live births)[a]					
Sub-Saharan Africa	156	137	115	107	107
South Asia	146	139	119	92	76
East Asia	133	78	55	34	38
Latin America and the Caribbean	102	84	60	47	32
Under–5 Mortality Rate (per 1,000 live births)[a]				(1991)	
Sub-Saharan Africa	261	222	189	180	173
South Asia	239	209	180	131	114
East Asia	201	126	81	42	50
Latin America and the Caribbean	154	123	..	57	39
Life Expectancy (in years)[b]				(1991)	
Sub-Saharan Africa	39.6	44	..	51	48
South Asia	42.5	48	..	59	62
East Asia	52.8	58	..	68	69
Latin America and the Caribbean	56.1	60	..	68	69
Adult Literacy (in percent)[c]					(1995)
Sub-Saharan Africa	14.7	19.4	40.2	51.3	56
South Asia	..	..	39.1	46.6	48
East Asia	65.3	77.2	69.3	80.3	82
Latin America and the Caribbean	69.2	75.8	79.7	84.9	86

[a] 1960/1998 Infant mortality/under-5 mortality – *State of the World's Children 2000*; 1970 Infant mortality/under-5 mortality – *World Development Indicators 2000*; 1980 Infant mortality rate/under-5 mortality rate – *World Development Report 2000*; 1990 Infant mortality rate – *Social Indicators of Development 1991-92*.

[b] 1960 – World Bank, *World Tables 1980*; 1970/1998 – *State of the World's Children 2000*; 1990 – *World Development Report 1993*.

[c] 1960/1970 – World Bank, World Tables 1980; 1980/1990 – *The UN Report on the World Social Situation 1997*; 1995 – *State of the World's Children 2000*.

for Onchocerciasis brought the 19 other African countries affected by the disease into the alliance. By 2002, when the program ends, 34 million Africans will have been spared, 600,000 cases of blindness will have been prevented, and 5 million labor years, otherwise lost, will have been saved.[7]

Agricultural Research and the Green Revolution

One of the most notable achievements of foreign assistance in reducing hunger has been agricultural research that developed high-yield varieties of wheat, maize, and rice. In the 1960s, research at the International Rice Research Center in the Philippines and the International Maize and Wheat Improvement Center in Mexico resulted in the Green Revolution. Recognizing that without major improvements in food production, Asia's growing population would starve, governments and the Rockefeller and Ford Foundations joined forces to increase crop yields per acre. Asian rice productivity doubled in 10 years. Hunger in Asia dropped from 38 percent of the population in 1969-71 to 18 percent in 1990-92.[8]

In 1971, the Consultative Group on International Agricultural Research (CGIAR) was established to promote food security through sustainable agriculture and to formalize the international network that had been growing around these issues and research centers. Thirty years later, 58 public and private sector members support 16 international agricultural research centers (including four each in Asia and Africa and two in South America).[9] In the 1980s, the U.S. Agency for International Development (USAID) was very active in supporting agricultural research.

New varieties of wheat, maize, and rice "have led to greater production:. . .they result in yield increases over traditional varieties, typically of 40 percent or more and, especially with more recent high-yielding varieties, have disease and

Child Survival

BY LORI METCALF

The child mortality rate in developing countries has decreased by more than half since 1960, thanks to child survival programs implemented by USAID, UNICEF, WHO, UNDP, and the World Bank. These programs receive less than 0.5 percent of the U.S. federal budget each year.[1]

The Child Survival Initiative authorized by the U.S. Congress in 1984 consists of these simple health measures:

- Immunization: More than 80 percent of the world's children are protected against measles, diphtheria, pertussis, polio, and tuberculosis. In the least developed countries, about 60 percent of children have been vaccinated.

- Vitamin A: An estimated 100 million children a year are affected by vitamin A deficiency. USAID launched a program to provide vitamin A supplements to young children and mothers, increase the consumption of vitamin A-rich foods through dietary diversification, and fortify common foods such as sugar, flour, and cooking oil with vitamin A.

- Oral rehydration therapy (ORT): One of the most important medical advances of the century, ORT is an inexpensive sugar-salt solution to treat dehydration from diarrhea. ORT can be made at home and saves more than 1 million children annually.

- Breastfeeding: USAID has helped establish "baby-friendly" hospitals in more than 40 countries. New mothers are encouraged to breastfeed infants from birth to improve infant and child health.

- New health technologies: USAID has invested in health-care products for use in the developing world. SoloSHOT, a single-use, auto-destruct syringe prevents reuse of needles. Vaccine vial monitors indicate whether a serum should be discarded because of heat overexposure. For prenatal care and safer home births, a variety of tools have been developed, including strips to detect protein in urine, low-cost delivery kits, and color-coded scales to identify low-birthweight infants. New chemotherapies for drug-resistant malaria and insecticide-impregnated mosquito nets are under development in Africa, where 85 percent of all malaria cases occur.

- Displaced Children and Orphans Fund: USAID has helped thousands of children orphaned by AIDS or wars in Ethiopia, Liberia, Mozambique, Angola, Rwanda, and the former Yugoslavia. The USAID War Victims Fund provides prostheses and rehabilitation assistance to more than 20,000 injured civilians.[2]

Ms. Metcalf is a research assistant with BFW Institute.

[1] USAID Population, Health & Nutrition-Child Survival. Information posted at: www.usaid.gov/pop_health/cs/csoverview.htm. [accessed December 6, 2000.]

[2] Ibid.

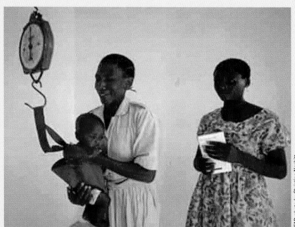

A Tanzanian midwife weighs a baby at the Maternal Child Health unit in Isangha village.

pest resistance."[10] Larger farms that could buy increased amounts of fertilizer and water, profited immediately. "Owing to the persistent difficulties small farmers face in getting access to. . .credit, water, and other inputs," small farmers benefited less.[11] CGIAR is working in areas where the Green Revolution was weak – small farms, diverse cropping patterns, dryland farming, and environmental sustainability. The International Fund for Agricultural Development (IFAD) has backed research on crops such as millet and sorghum that are important for rural poor people. The Convention to Combat Desertification and IFAD are focusing on issues important for dryland farmers and those affected by desertification.[12]

How to Improve Foreign Aid

Through trial and error, development practitioners have gained an understanding of what works. Aid policies and programs can employ best practices to meet the needs and realities of recipient countries. To achieve results for poor and hungry people, donor and recipient governments must reexamine their approach in light of these lessons.

Lessons for Donor Countries

Foreign assistance should be demand driven.[13] A top-down, donor-driven approach undermines the very purpose of foreign aid. Recipient governments and civil society must be actively involved in decisions regarding their own development. In the past, donors often formulated and implemented aid programs that reflected their own, not recipient country, priorities. Frequently, the programs did not fit local conditions and needs. Consequently, some recipient governments did not take initiative and felt no "ownership" or involvement in the programs that purported to help them.

Many development assistance projects import foreign experts because there are no local people with required skills. Once foreign assistance runs out, these projects are simply too expensive, technically complicated, and impossible to staff.[14] Development assistance should train local technicians and administrators so that progress can be sustained.

Thanks to an IFAD loan, villagers in Niger use a diesel motor to pump water.

Foreign assistance has traditionally been disbursed through central governments. Local or provincial governments and nongovernmental organizations (NGOs) representing the interests of poor people rarely shared in decisions about how aid should be used or allocated. This has changed in recent years, with much greater emphasis on collaboration to identify and address the needs of poor people.

Foreign assistance should flow to the poorest countries. For political reasons, only 20 percent of total bilateral aid has gone to the countries that need it the most, the poorest 12 percent. Furthermore, there is a donor bias against large countries.[15] India and China, where approximately 655 million people live on less than $1 a day,[16] received $2 of aid per capita in 1998, while much smaller countries received up to $50 per capita. Middle-income countries received an average of $12 of aid per capita.[17]

Development strategies take time. Short-term emergency assistance to alleviate hunger crises is essential. But to reduce hunger permanently, donors need to take a long-term, multi-sectoral approach to development. Health and education

Figure 4.1: People Living on Less than $1 a Day

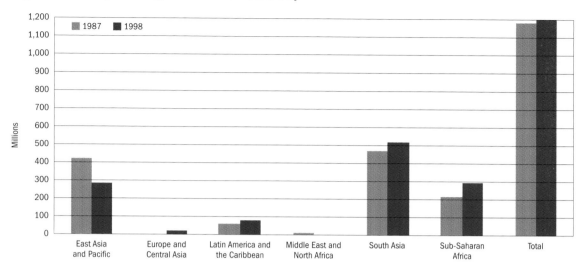

Source: World Bank. 2000. *World Development Report 2000/2001: Attacking Poverty*. New York: Oxford University Press, 23.

must go hand in hand with economic growth, access to credit, rural development, and support for smallholder agriculture. All of these efforts must be made within the context of macroeconomic stability, good governance, and solid institutions, without which progress will not be sustained. Donors and recipients must think in terms of broader outcomes. (See Development and Empowerment Outcomes, in the Appendices).

It takes time to train teachers and health-care workers; build schools, hospitals and roads; and establish institutions, policies, and laws. It takes even longer for attitudes and behaviors to change. To allow for this complicated process, donors and recipients need to establish appropriate time horizons when planning and evaluating projects.

Aid should be untied. A quarter of all foreign aid requires the purchase of goods and services from the donor.[18] "Donors often pay for inappropriate schemes which require their exports and expertise, whereas smaller, locally run projects would serve better. When donors favor their own contractors over those from other countries, rivals who might do the job more effectively are excluded. The practice is also sometimes used as a way of subsidizing donors' own industries in

Cotton farmers and the Agricultural Finance Corporation credit agent calculate expected income in Musenge, Zimbabwe.

order to protect jobs."[19] Although recipient countries gain from the net transfer of resources, tied aid prevents the proper functioning of markets, since it results in trade and transactions that may not have occurred otherwise.[20] As a result, it reduces the effectiveness of the aid by between 15 and 30 percent.[21] The British government's recent decision to abandon the policy of tying its development assistance to the purchase of British goods and services is promising.[22]

Conditionality must be mutual. Donors set criteria for and conditions on the development assistance they provide. International financial institutions have insisted that recipient governments adopt structural adjustment policies. But the imposition of such outside conditionality has not been successful in changing policy in recipient countries. Recipient countries may agree to changes they will not make in order to get desperately needed funds. This pattern of noncompliance starts with nonmutual conditions. The sheer number of conditions has also been a problem.[23]

> The conditionality and project proliferation . . .have fallen short in advancing development goals. They have been too intrusive and burdensome on the developing country's capacity, and they have not encouraged the crucial component of recipient ownership of the development process at either the government or local level.[24]

IFAD photo by Robert Maass

Bore holes and nine water pumps were installed by an IFAD project in Larde village, Mozambique. An abundance of clean drinking water has improved health conditions.

Of course, donor agencies want to make sure that money is well spent, which implies conditions for aid. When recipients actively engage in designing programs and conditions, both donors and recipients set more realistic goals, targets, and deadlines. Mutually agreed upon conditions are more likely to be met.

Effectiveness depends on policy coordination among donors. U.S. and other donor nations need to coordinate their foreign assistance activities, so that recipients do not receive conflicting advice and need not fulfill different reporting and accounting requirements. In some African countries, governments and local institutions have limited capacity to monitor progress or adhere to donor terms. Tending to the administration of multitudes of foreign aid projects has become a full-time occupation for some African government officials, who could otherwise contribute their expertise to their country's development.

Foreign aid must add to existing resources, not replace them. When donors provide aid for public health services, water and sanitation, or other poverty reduction measures, recipient governments can shift funds they would have allocated to these programs to other purposes, such as military expenditures. This is known as the fungibility of aid. Donor agencies need to monitor their aid so that it results in more funding for poverty reduction. If a poor country government is strongly committed to development and poverty reduction, unrestricted financial support may make more sense than funding specific projects.[25]

Debt must be cancelled. Many developing countries are burdened by public debt. Lack of economic growth, falling commodity prices, mismanaged economies, and poor governance account for the inability of highly indebted poor countries (HIPCs) to repay. Much foreign aid in the 1990s was spent on interest payments, not poverty reduction. Recent HIPC II initiatives to provide debt relief are important first steps in freeing poor countries of the burden of repayment.

The secretary of her microfinance group makes payments on the UWESO loans of group members at the bank in Masaka, Uganda.

Industrial countries should open their markets. Protectionist trade policies in the industrialized countries have lessened or negated the benefits of foreign aid. Donors have given poor countries money, policy advice, and technical assistance to develop their export sectors. Simultaneously, donor trade policies have made it difficult for developing countries to access international markets, particularly in the agriculture and textile industries. This lack of policy coherence contradicts the very intentions of aid and has cost developing countries dearly.[26]

Food aid is only one part of a broader development assistance program. Food aid supplies commodities to feed hungry people during famines or through routine child-feeding programs, to replace food imports, or to be monetized in order to finance development projects. Over the years, donors have learned how to use food aid so that the distribution of free food doesn't become a disincentive for domestic food production. Driven more by agricultural surpluses in rich countries than by development concerns in poor countries, food aid is less reliable and less effective in reducing hunger than cash assistance.[27] Creating employment opportunities for poor people addresses long-term hunger by increasing their ability to purchase food.

Lessons for Recipient Countries

Recipient governments must commit themselves to poverty reduction and to the welfare of their citizens. Sub-Saharan Africa receives about a quarter of all official development assistance (ODA) from the member countries of the Organization of Economic Co-operation and Development (OECD). But foreign assistance has been far less effective in Africa than in India and China because of how aid was used. For reasons related to Cold War politics, donors provided ODA even if recipient governments mismanaged those funds. Donors tolerated corruption, inept leadership, and poor economic policies because development goals were subordinated to national security interests. This terrible disservice to the poorest segments of the population in recipient countries actually worsened inequalities and living conditions.

Recent analysis suggests that foreign aid works best at reducing poverty in countries that have macroeconomic stability, openness, rule of law, and little corruption.[28] In some cases, foreign aid can be used to encourage reform in poor policy environments. "Aid agencies can provide ideas about how to improve services and finance innovative approaches. Learning from these innovations generates knowledge about what works and what does not."[29] Even in countries that have ignored the needs of their citizens through mismanagement, corruption, or repression, foreign aid can reach poor people if they are the focus of programs that work through civil society and local NGOs.

An Indian farmer makes cane sugar.

Civil conflict and war destroy development.
Many foreign aid recipients have suffered reversals or setbacks due to internal political crises that have halted normal activities. There are many examples of this in Africa, notably Rwanda, Burundi, Ethiopia, and Sierra Leone, and in Asia, Sri Lanka and Indonesia. Donors can contribute to a return to normalcy once the conflict dies down. "Rwanda is now in a full phase of post-conflict reconstruction, for which short-term assistance can be essential. But aided rehabilitation must lead to an early restoration of normal development processes and encourage a mentality of self-sufficiency rather than dependence. . ."[30] One of the root causes of conflict is poverty. By acting quickly, donors may prevent struggling countries from slipping back into civil war.[31]

Equitable growth reaches poor people.
Countries with higher growth rates and policies that equalize income distribution have succeeded in raising the incomes of poor people. In East Asia, the number of poor people dropped – from 452 million in 1990 to 278 million in 1998 (Table 4.2). A stable macro-economic environment, low inflation, an open economy, free exchange rates, and an active private sector have led to increased investment and sustained economic growth rates in East Asia. Because these policies were also accompanied by income redistribution, land reform, and effective social policies, East Asia has had great success in reducing poverty.

Table 4.2 Regional Poverty Indicators

Region	Number of Poor People (in millions)	
	1990	**1998**
East Asia	452	278
Latin America	74	78
South Asia	495	522
Sub-Saharan Africa	242	290
Total	1,263	1,168

Source: Oxfam. 2000. *Growth With Equity is Good for the Poor.*

According to Oxfam, "[E]very percentage point of growth in East Asia reduces the incidence of poverty at four times the rate achieved in Latin America. . .If Latin America had achieved East Asia's rate of conversion from growth to poverty reduction, there would be 3 million fewer people living below the poverty line."[32]

Democracy reduces poverty. In the last decade, more countries have had elections than ever before, a profound change that makes development assistance more effective. Foreign assistance can strengthen democratic governance by training developing country administrators, policymakers, lawmakers, and enforcers. Donors can work with recipient governments to create mechanisms by which NGOs, the private sector, trade associations, and civil society are involved in decisions that affect them and the people they represent. The active participation of nongovernmental actors makes governments more accountable, transparent, and responsive to the needs of disadvantaged groups that would otherwise not have a voice.

Gender equality must be at the heart of all development programs. Improving the legal, health, nutrition, and human rights status of women is urgent. Recognizing women's contribution to agricultural productivity and economic development is long overdue. It is not sufficient to target one or two projects at women. "Small-

Nepalese women attend literacy classes in Dumre, Nepal.

IFAD photo by Anwar Hossain

scale interventions tend to be the preferred option for tackling women's poverty – downgrading it, in effect, to a minor problem."[33]

Key Measures

Economic growth, good governance, efficient institutions, peace, and stability are necessary conditions for poverty reduction. However, specific policies and projects are required to reach poor people. There is growing consensus among donor and recipient governments about what needs to be done and how to do it: focus foreign aid on agriculture and rural development, public health, education, poor women, and institutions (Table 4.3). These long-term investments address the structural causes of hunger and poverty.

Invest in Agriculture

A productive agricultural sector is key to reducing hunger. Agriculture not only provides nutrition and food security, it is also a vital source of income and economic growth. Currently, about 70 percent of people in developing countries live in rural areas. Therefore, investment in agriculture and agricultural research that emphasizes smallholder farming and environmentally sustainable practices ensures long-term benefits

Women harvest millet in the Kayes region of Mali.

Table 4.3 Interventions to Reduce Undernutrition

What is Needed	How to Achieve It
Global	
Secure access to world markets	International agreements
Peace and physical security	Conflict prevention and recovery
National	
Promote democracy in rural areas	Civil participation and advocacy
Enabling environment	Macroeconomic, trade, and legal reform
Sectoral	
Rural production and marketing	Public investment in roads
Infrastructure	Private technology transfer
Increase farm productivity	Public agricultural research
Household	
Raise entitlement to food	Target food aid
Empower women	Educate women and girls
Improve rural health conditions	Safe water and sanitation

Source: J. Dirck Stryker and Jeffrey C. Metzel. 1998. Meeting the Food Summit Target: The United States Contribution.

and creates livelihoods in rural areas. If people cannot make a living in the countryside, rapid urbanization will continue, bringing its own set of hunger issues. The International Food Policy Research Institute estimates that by 2020, the urban population in developing countries will account for 52 percent of the total.[34] Bolstering the agricultural sector will foster food security, and provide the impetus for economic growth in the countryside.

Land Reform [35]

Without access to land, rural dwellers have no way to raise food for family consumption or grow commercial agricultural products. Land is an asset and therefore a form of savings and collateral. Improving access to land has been very successful in increasing the productivity of small farms in East Asia and elsewhere.

> ## A community without roads does not have a way out.
>
> — A MAN IN JUNCAL, ECUADOR [36]

Rural Development [37]

Rural areas in developing countries have been neglected for decades. In many countries, farmers cannot get their crops to market because there are no roads. The lack of public transportation infrastructure, such as railroads and highways connecting rural areas to urban centers, makes shipping expensive and time consuming. Even within rural areas, road infrastructure is so poor that selling produce to neighboring villages can be as much of a problem as reaching urban markets.[38] Poor transportation infrastructure prevents small farmers from selling what they grow and reduces income to buy food and farm inputs such as fertilizers, tools, and seeds.

In order to move out of poverty, smallholders have to grow cash crops. This requires improved access to land, labor, capital, and livestock. Farmers also need help understanding and complying with the complex rules and regulations that govern the international trading system.

Foreign aid can help governments create institutions and farmer capacity to access markets, information, training, and credit.

Policies must target the special conditions of rural poverty. Most hungry people in rural areas are either smallholder or landless farmers. Both groups are vulnerable to falling world commodity prices, drought, flood, and civil strife. Foreign aid should provide income-earning opportunities for smallholder farmers and protect the labor rights of landless workers. Tenant farmers are the most vulnerable. When they can find employment, they work as seasonal farm laborers. When they can't find work, they go hungry. Income-generating activities for smallholder farmers raises incomes, increases savings, and renders poor households less vulnerable to changes in the weather or in the national or global economy.

Agriculture-related industries in rural areas would mean that landless workers would not have to migrate in search of income. Furthermore, during a drought or during the off-season, smallholder farmers could supplement their incomes with temporary employment while tending their land and livestock. Food processing and other businesses are willing to invest in an area if roads, electricity, a safe water supply, and a healthy, trainable work force are available.

Public Health Infrastructure

Disease destroys or impairs the productive capacity of poor people. Investing in public health systems that reach poor people where they live makes prevention and treatment feasible and reduces the spread of disease. Clean drinking water dramatically reduces rural poverty. Safe water and sanitation are central to good health and hygiene, reducing or eliminating the risk of debilitating water-borne diseases such as cholera. Only 24 percent of the population in low-income

> ## We face a calamity when my husband gets ill. Our life comes to a halt until he recovers and goes back to work.
>
> — A WOMAN IN ZAWYET SULTAN, EGYPT [39]

Girls attend school in Mexico.

countries and only 16 percent in South Asia are served by sanitation infrastructures such as sewage pipes and treatment methods.[40]

Educate Women and Girls

Universal primary education gives poor people the skills and confidence to create their own opportunities. A special effort must be made to ensure that girls are included in "universal" education. The important economic and social roles that women play keep families and communities alive. Yet most countries consistently ignore the contributions of women, keep traditions punitive to women in place, and underinvest in women. Aid agencies are beginning to recognize the importance of investing in women, but much more needs to be done.

Educating girls unlocks the door to social and economic opportunity. "Gender equality and economic development are mutually reinforcing. Female education is a good investment that raises national income and higher income in turn leads to more gender equality in education and in other areas."[41] Educated girls become women who earn a better living, understand their rights within society and within their own families, make

decisions about their own health and well-being, and improve their communities and nations.

Schooling for girls is the most powerful way to slow population growth. Educated women plan their families, space their children, and protect their own health and that of their children. Educated women are knowledgeable about the nutritional needs of their children and ensure that their children receive what they need. Women's education accounted for 43 percent of the improvement in child malnutrition rates between 1970 and 1995.[42] Improvement in the status of women in developing countries accounted for more than half of the reduction in child malnutrition. The "best hope" for tackling . . .child malnutrition lies in educating girls.[43]

Reforming Foreign Aid to Help Hungry People

The bulk of U.S. foreign aid simply has not reached poor and hungry people. This must change, beginning with a commitment to use development assistance to address the root causes of hunger and poverty. There are many positive signs that more donors are indeed beginning to focus on reaching poor people. The 1995 United Nations Social Summit in Copenhagen formulated seven goals for international development assistance. If these goals, combined with the World Food Summit target, were the core of all development assistance programs, hunger and poverty could be eradicated.

A new consensus has emerged that is predicated on the importance of building partnerships between donors and recipients. Sectorwide approaches have become increasingly popular. Developing country governments plan a strategy for a sector and create the necessary conditions under which it could be implemented. Donors then decide which aspect of the strategy they would like to fund. This approach has been tried in Bangladesh, Pakistan, Tanzania, and Zambia. The Zambian experience in the early 1990s in developing a health sector strategy was particularly successful. The Ministry of Health conceived and managed the plan, then delegated implementation to the districts. Donors were asked to give funds directly to the Ministry of Health, which

Girls' Education in Guinea

BY JOYCE SAMPSON

When a Guinean canning company promoted girls' education on soup can labels, it confirmed May Rihani's theory that empowered people produce powerful results. Rihani is the director of Strategies for Advancing Girls Education (SAGE), a USAID-funded project whose mission is putting girls' education at the forefront of the national consciousness.

Though educating young girls is vital to a country's development, SAGE had to convince the Guinean people themselves that girls' education is an engine for economic growth. Educated girls have the skills to earn a decent living. They marry later and bear fewer children. Their children are healthier, better nourished, and more likely to succeed in school.

SAGE's strategy is to establish a national alliance of government and industry leaders; ministers of finance, planning, and health; religious leaders of all sects; women's groups; and other nongovernmental organizations. SAGE formed 18 local alliances to make girls' education a national priority. The goal: to develop remedies and action plans that overcome the obstacles to girls' education.

When Rihani first spoke to people in Guinea, they asked, "Who is going to do this for us?"

"You will learn to do it for yourselves," she replied.

Two years later, the Guineans are producing results. They have pooled resources, bartered for goods and services, pinpointed problems, and devised their own novel solutions, such as providing housing as an incentive to attract new teachers. In Lelouma, residents created an educational fund, added classrooms, and raised more than $5,000 to build their own secondary school. In Dougountouny, the local alliance constructed a new secondary school using its own resources and labor.

In Kaback, the local alliance built five new classrooms. By agreeing to purchase notebooks and other school supplies exclusively from one vendor, Kaback parents negotiated a discount that reduced school costs. Since the alliance started, the community has built three schools and is paying the salaries of eight teachers.

In Guendembou, the citizens mandated that girls make up one-half of all new students enrolled in school. Residents partnered with a local radio station and organized an awareness campaign in local languages that included a music contest among schools.

"Education empowers individuals and communities to identify their needs and to find the resources to meet those needs," Rihani said. In addition to the local focus, "it was important to engage the religious and media sectors, government, nonprofits, and businesses simultaneously at the national and community levels."

There has been significant progress. Girls' enrollment has risen. In 1990, 17 percent of girls attended school. Today, 40 percent do. But sustaining change requires a deep sense of ownership and commitment from public and private sectors. With 60 percent of Guinean girls still not in the classroom, there is much more to be done.

The SAGE program, which operates in Guinea and Mali, is implemented by the Academy for Educational Development (AED) and Plan International. The project provides technical and training assistance in girls' primary education to USAID missions.

Ms. Sampson is a media relations specialist at the Academy for Educational Development.

Table 4.4: Gender Differences[1]

	Female population	Labor force participation	Adult illiteracy rate	Net primary enrollment ratio	Life expectancy at birth
	Percent of total, 1998	Ratio of female to male, 1998	Female-male difference, 1998	Female-male difference, 1997	Female-male difference, 1998
East Asia and the Pacific	48.9	0.8	14	0	4
Europe and Central Asia	51.9	0.9	4	0	9
Latin America and Caribbean	50.4	0.5	2	–2	6
Middle East and North Africa	49	0.4	22	–7	3
South Asia	48.5	0.5	24	–12	1
Sub-Saharan Africa	50.5	0.7	17	–9	3

Source: World Bank. 2000. *World Development Indicators 2000*. Washington, DC: The World Bank, 20-21.

[1] "A labor force participation ratio of 1.0 indicates gender equality in labor force participation in the formal sector, while a lower ratio indicates that women's participation is lower than men's. For net primary enrollment, a positive value means that the enrollment ratio for girls is higher than that for boys, and a negative value means that girls are falling behind. Conversely for adult illiteracy, a positive value indicates a female disadvantage...A positive value for life expectancy represents a female advantage." *World Development Indicators 2000*, 21.

applied funds as needed. Although these reforms are still underway, the strategy has already yielded a far-reaching public health system that involves the private sector.[44]

The World Bank is exploring how to apply a partnership approach to development assistance. One way would be for developing countries to assess their own needs and design development strategies. Donors would evolve their own interventions based on the national strategy of the recipient government and coordinate their activities with other donors. This way, each donor country can maximize its own strengths at the country level.[45]

To encourage donor coordination, the World Bank has proposed the *Comprehensive Development Framework*, which matches the various facets of a recipient country's development strategy with the activities of all development partners, from the country's own government to donors, civil society, and the private sector.[46] The framework provides a "visual representation of the state of development assistance in any given country."[47]

Members of a women's co-operative in Mitkay, Mauritania fertilize their garden.

The *Common Pools Approach* takes these reforms a step further. The recipient country creates its own development strategy reflecting the demands and needs of its citizens, to which all participants agree. Donors' financial commitments would depend on their assessment of the plan and the country's ability to implement it. The financial contributions of all donors would go into a common pool, which the recipient country would control and disburse. Donors would continue to finance the strategy as long as they believed in it, forcing recipient governments to be realistic and accountable.[48] But donors would not be able to micromanage because they give up control over their contribution.

The broad tendencies are clear – a stronger focus on poverty reduction, a joint commitment to measurable reductions in hunger and poverty, and partnerships between developing countries and donor agencies that allow local people more initiative and control.

Ms. Lateef is a policy analyst at BFW Institute.

International Development Goals

- Reduce the proportion of people living in extreme poverty by half between 1990 and 2015.

- Enroll all children in primary school by 2015.

- Make progress towards gender equality and empower women by eliminating gender disparities in primary and secondary education by 2005.

- Reduce infant and child mortality rates by two-thirds between 1990 and 2015.

- Reduce maternal mortality ratios by three-quarters 2015.

- Provide access for all who need reproductive health services by 2015.

- Implement national strategies for sustainable development by 2005 so as to reverse the loss of environmental resources by 2015.

Source: IMF, OECD, UN, World Bank Group. 2000. *2000: A Better World For All*, 5.

Poverty Reduction in Uganda

BY EUGENE D. MCCARTHY

Uganda, afflicted by severe internal strife in the 1970s and 1980s, is the first low-income country in Africa to prepare a comprehensive, participatory national strategy for poverty reduction. Uganda's experience inspired the design of the World Bank's Highly Indebted Poor Countries (HIPC) Initiative. Since 1996, when the Ugandan government made a serious commitment to its poverty eradication action plan, social indicators for infant mortality, malnutrition, literacy, and school enrollment have all improved, though life expectancy is still low, mainly due to AIDS.

Uganda's early lessons on how to fight poverty are relevant to other low-income countries about to embark on poverty reduction strategies of their own. Uganda's top political leadership used existing data on poverty to refocus public policies to benefit poor people directly. A participatory, 24-month planning process involved central government, local communities, civil society, nongovernmental organizations (NGOs), universities, and donor communities. Firm budget allocations transformed the plan into action.

Civil society shared in policy making, public spending decisions, and monitoring progress toward the plan's goal. Ugandans openly debated the impact of macroeconomic policies on poverty, the damaging impact of inflation on the poor, and the low level of public expenditure on basic services such as primary health care and education, water, sanitation, agricultural extension, and maintenance of rural feeder roads.

The participatory process involved a series of conferences and workshops, followed by discussions of specific poverty reduction strategies. The Ministries of Finance and Planning took the lead in preparing the poverty action plan. Working groups on specific topics brought government officials, NGOs, and representatives from civil society and the universities together to formulate the plan's goal of lowering poverty to 10 percent of the population by 2017.

Reduction in the number of people living in poverty has been substantial, especially given the relatively short interval of five years. Recent surveys show that 56 percent of Ugandans were poor in 1992, while 44 percent were poor in 1997-98. Poverty declined in every region of the country, with households involved in cash crop farming, manufacturing, and trade faring best. Only subsistence farmers and households headed by the elderly, children, or the disabled were not better off. Average household consumption rose by 17 percent over five years and the expenditures of the poorest 20 percent rose even more.

Improvements in Education

Perhaps the most dramatic progress has been in education. The number of children enrolled in primary schools increased from 3.1 million in 1996 to 5.2 million in 1997 to an estimated 6.8 million in 2000. Between 1990 and 1995, as little as 20 percent of each dollar budgeted for school expenditures ever reached the schools. Surveys found that 40 percent of the users of public services had to pay bribes. Since the action plan was implemented, 90 percent of funding now reaches most schools.

Progress in Health and Education

	1988/89	1995
Infant Mortality (per 1000)	119	97
Immunization (% 12-23 months)	31	49
Malnutrition (% stunting)	43	39
Net School Enrollment (% age 6-10)	47	64
Literacy (%)	54	61

Source: John MacKinnon and Ritva Reinikke. Lessons from Uganda on Strategies to Fight Poverty. Working paper #2440, (World Bank: Washington, DC), September, 2000.

The Ugandan government's social expenditures target the very poor. These expenditures are and will continue to be monitored by NGOs and civil society. Greater transparency and accountability ensure that money reaches the intended beneficiaries. For example, monthly transfers of public funds to districts are now reported in major newspapers and on the radio. This approach confirms that information can be a powerful tool for change, even in a weak institutional setting.

While military expenditures have continued, including the purchase of a presidential jet, these have not affected the budget allocations for health, education, and related public service sectors. Uganda's experience shows how successful a coherent program of poverty reduction can be. But preparation of the plan must be grounded in a careful assessment of poverty conditions and must involve all stakeholders. Uganda offers hope that poverty can be reduced significantly.

Dr. McCarthy was an officer of the World Bank for 27 years.

Beyond Jubilee 2000: National Plans to Fight Poverty

BY ELENA MCCOLLIM

Bread for the World and many other groups campaigned for years to win debt relief for the poorest countries. International public mobilization for a lasting solution to the debt crisis reached a turning point at the 1999 Group of Seven (G-7) summit in Cologne, Germany, when 70,000 Jubilee 2000 activists peacefully surrounded the building where the meetings took place. The G-7 heads of state agreed on a scheme to write off $90 billion in poor-country debts. At the annual meetings of the World Bank and International Monetary Fund (IMF) three months later, the nations of the world approved an implementation plan for the Cologne debt relief initiative.

April Jubilee 2000 rally in Washington, DC.

The original HIPC initiative, begun jointly by the World Bank and IMF in 1996, was designed to reduce debt just to the point where a poor country could continue to make the payments. Under HIPC II, debt relief applies to more countries and should result in bigger cuts in debt payments, more quickly. The borrowing country must prepare a Poverty Reduction Strategy Paper (PRSP) describing its plan to reduce poverty and its programs to help poor people. Funds that would have gone to debt repayment must be used instead to finance implementation of this plan. The borrowing-country government is required to consult citizens' groups through a democratic process that is to exemplify partnership among governments, creditors, and people at the community level.[1]

The degree to which a country possesses an organized and vibrant civil society with the capacity to participate in a national process of this kind will help determine the success of the PRSP. Uganda, the first country to actually receive debt relief under HIPC II, is a successful example (see *Poverty Reduction in Uganda*). Uganda had previously formulated a poverty eradication action plan with substantial participation from civil society and from donors. That plan established the Poverty Action Fund to be jointly managed by the Ugandan government, representatives of donor countries, and representatives of civil society. The government focused on reducing poverty by increasing spending for basic education. Within two years, primary school enrollment doubled.

Zambian civil society had to organize itself quickly to participate in the government-led PRSP consultation process. The Jesuit Center for Theological Reflection (JCTR) held regional meetings throughout Zambia, building on the Jubilee movement's earlier popular education on the debt. The meetings were meant to build civil society capacity to participate in the government-organized consultation once that begins.[2] JCTR and colleague organizations sit on government-organized working groups charged with gathering public input for a poverty reduction strategy to be completed in the first half of 2001.[3] It is too soon to report outcomes, although the new process of consultation and participation is producing changes in both the government and the international institutions. After decades of corruption, the Zambian government is being pushed to show clearly how it proposes to use the savings from debt relief for the benefit of ordinary citizens. And the World Bank and IMF, long known for their imperious ways, are becoming more flexible and responsive to country concerns about the impact of their policies and prescriptions.

Civil society's capacity to get involved in a participatory process varies widely across countries. As many civil society organizations will be the first to acknowledge, they lack the technical capacity to engage meaningfully in consultations. Much needs to be done to promote participation: raise economic literacy broadly among the population, educate the public about the external debt burden and relief initiatives, and organize broad-based consultations that include religious organizations, trade unions, peasants' federations, professional associations, indigenous and women's groups, and others. The World Bank is pouring substantial resources into PRSP. In addition, the United Nations Development Programme is pooling and coordinating donor funds for capacity building in the borrowing countries.

All of this takes time. Under pressure to implement debt relief more quickly, the World Bank and IMF now allow an interim poverty reduction strategy, with lower standards of participation than for the final PRSP. So far, interim strategies seem to have been drafted almost exclusively by finance ministry officials, without public participation. The process cannot be both fast and participatory. Thus some organizations, such as Oxfam, advocate that HIPC governments channel debt-relief funds into an account to be used only for social spending; spend no more than 10 percent of revenues on debt service; and not tie debt relief to the PRSP timetable.

BFW Institute is working with civil society organizations, including JCTR, to monitor the PRSP process. Relating PRSP to existing national plans is important, so as not to undermine previous work. For example, in Mozambique the government had already produced a national poverty strategy for the years 2000-2004. But the initial strategy was too broad and needed a clear set of priorities. As Mozambique creates the new strategy, it will have to respond effectively to the existing plan.

Civil society groups are especially focused on the macroeconomic policies of PRSPs. In Honduras, the IMF and the World Bank made privatization of the electricity sector a condition for debt relief. But the national legislature had not approved privatization before Honduras was due for debt relief in September 2000. The IMF and World Bank therefore waived the requirement, granting debt relief for Honduras without privatizing the electricity sector. But Honduras received only a temporary reprieve, since the bank and fund are still requiring privatization as a condition of receiving full debt relief.[4] In Uganda, civil society organizations were aware that important issues of macroeconomic policy were left off the table. Still, they recognized that participation is a continuous process whereby objectives not achieved initially could be addressed by future participation.

The Jubilee campaign drew new constituencies into the international network of NGOs, which can monitor debt relief and hold the World Bank and IMF to their ambitious new reforms. Entrenched interests in the HIPC countries and a tendency of the international financial institutions to revert to business-as-usual policy prescriptions will exert powerful pressure against democratic participation in decisionmaking and investment in poor people. Church groups and NGOs in the industrialized countries will keep their legislatures (upon which the World Bank and IMF depend for funds) and the public (which elects legislators) informed on how debt relief is working in practice. This will influence public support for foreign aid more generally.

A Sustainable Exit from Debt?

Achieving genuine public participation in national policymaking is just one challenge facing the developing countries as they seek to benefit from the HIPC II initiative. Getting out from under the burden of unpayable debt is another. Current debt relief initiatives leave many countries deeply in debt and unable to devote sufficient resources to the programs that will overcome poverty and hunger.[5]

The internationally agreed goals of cutting both world poverty and hunger in half by 2015 are feasible, but will require increased development assistance from rich countries and effective, accountable governance in poor countries. Those low-income countries that use debt relief to launch sound and democratic poverty reduction strategies could clearly make good use of additional poverty-focused aid.

Debt cancellation alone is insufficient to put poor countries on the path to sustainable development. But it is a necessary first step. For this reason, Bread for the World has made debt cancellation one of its legislative priorities over the past 15 years. BFW Institute will continue to monitor the progress of debt relief. In 2001, Bread for the World will urge Congress to continue funding for debt relief and provide a substantial increase in poverty-focused foreign aid to Africa.

Ms. McCollim coordinates BFW Institute's Debt and Development Project.

1 There is an ever-expanding body of literature on PRSP. For an introduction to the topic, see "The IMF and World Bank Initiate a New Reform Package — The Poverty Reduction Strategy Papers: An Initial NGO Assessment," Sara Grusky, *Debt and Development Dossier*, Issue # 3, Bread for the World Institute: Silver Spring, MD, April 2000. For more information on PRSP, contact the European Network for Debt and Development (Eurodad), at eurodad@eurodad.ngonet.be.

2 For JCTR and others, "consultation" connotes informing civil society of government plans, rather than actively engaging it in the construction of those plans. Thus, they maintain, "participation," rather than "consultation," should be the goal.

3 For more on Zambia's PRSP process, see the *Debt and Development Dossier Issue #5*, forthcoming. Bread for the World Institute, Washington, DC.

4 Under the HIPC II, countries typically receive relief in their debt service payments upon completing an Interim PRSP. However it is only upon completion of a PRSP that the debt stock is reduced. At that point, debt relief becomes irrevocable.

5 For an extensive discussion of this dilemma, see *Debt Relief Initiative for Poor Countries Faces Challenges*, General Accounting Office, Washington, DC, June 2000. The GAO study concludes that to achieve a sustainable exit from debt, countries will have to maintain growth rates at 7-9 percent, and that these projections are based on unrealistic assumptions about the growth of exports. For example, for Honduras, Nicaragua, Tanzania, and Uganda, growth would have to average at least 9.1 percent per year over 20 years. While these projections are based on historical performance, the fact remains that export earnings for these countries tend to derive from a few key primary commodities, whose prices fluctuate.

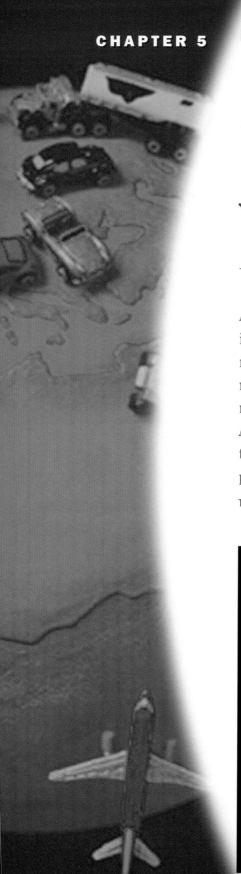

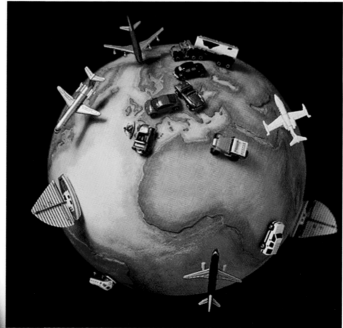

CHAPTER 5

Trade + Aid: Making Globalization Work for Everyone

As the country that benefits most from global economic integration...America can be, and should be, the world's role model...We have the tools to make a difference. We have the responsibility to make a difference. And we have a huge interest in making a difference. Managing globalization is a role from which America dare not shrink. It is our overarching national interest today, and the political party that understands that first...is the party that will own the real bridge to the future.[1]

Thomas L. Friedman, *The Lexus and the Olive Tree*

Some opponents of foreign assistance use globalization to justify a reduction in foreign aid budgets. They argue that the tremendous increase in trade, foreign direct investment, and private capital flows to developing countries in the last decade eliminates the need for development assistance. The "trade not aid" view is based on some indisputable and positive facts. Between 1990 and 1998, private capital flows to developing countries jumped from $44 billion to $227 billion. The level of private capital flows was lower than the level of official development assistance (ODA) in 1990, but by the end of the decade, private capital flows were 4.5 times greater than ODA.[2] These striking trends, and the fact that many developing countries are much more concerned about attracting private investment than about foreign aid, have led some people to conclude that economic growth and increased trade are sufficient to lift developing countries out of poverty.

This view does not acknowledge that an overwhelming 93 percent of foreign direct investment to developing countries goes to middle-income countries.[3] The poorest countries are not benefiting equally. In fact, inequalities between regions and countries are growing because some areas are unable to attract private investment.

The world is changing more rapidly than ever. Advances in telecommunications, transport, and computer technology have facilitated the surge in international trade, private capital flows, and foreign direct investment (Tables 5.1 and 5.2). The global economy is increasingly integrated. The term "globalization" implies:

> a stretching of social, political, and economic activities across frontiers such that events, decisions, and activities in one region of the world can come to have significance for individuals and communities in distant regions of the globe. In this sense, it embodies transregional interconnectedness, the widening reach of networks of social activity and power, and the possibility of action at a distance.[4]

New and exciting opportunities abound. But not for everyone. Globalization transcends boundaries, both geographical and attitudinal. But the boundaries and limitations imposed on people by hunger and poverty are difficult to cross.

Globalization is inexorable, and a force without conscience. Foreign assistance can be a tool to mitigate the negative effects of globalization on poor populations. Foreign aid can help developing nations take advantage of the opportunities globalization creates. Donor countries can use their foreign aid programs to bolster developing countries as they adapt to the ever-changing global economy. Donor government commitment to global inclusion would appeal to those elements of the NGO and grassroots community that distrust globalization.

Without additional foreign assistance, the poorest countries and people are likely to fall by the wayside as the rest of the world speeds on. This is morally unacceptable. And strengthening poor countries economically develops future markets for U.S. exports. Now more than ever, what happens half way around the world affects us, where we live.

Persistent poverty and worsening inequalities in developing countries can cause or exacerbate a host of problems, including the spread of disease, environmental degradation, pollution, war and conflict, and international crime and terrorism. While these problems are not new, technological advances have increased the speed with which they cross borders.[5]

Development assistance that addresses hunger and poverty gets at the root of these transnational challenges. Poor and hungry people are vulnerable to disease. Poor countries do not have adequate health and sanitation infrastructure that could prevent and contain epidemics. Given their limited resources, developing country governments must make difficult choices. Environmental considerations are often sacrificed for more pressing short-term goals. Desperation and frustration caused by poverty can lead to crime and terrorism. Foreign aid can directly ameliorate transnational problems.

Table 5.1: Net Long-term Resource Flows to Developing Countries (in billions of $U.S.)

Year	Official Flows	Private Flows		
		International Capital Markets	Foreign Direct Investment	Total Private Flows
1990	56.9	19.4	24.5	43.9
1991	62.6	26.2	34.4	60.5
1992	54.0	52.2	46.1	98.3
1993	53.3	100.0	67.0	167.0
1994	45.5	89.6	88.5	178.1
1995	53.4	96.1	105.4	201.5
1996	32.2	149.5	126.4	275.9
1997	39.1	135.5	163.4	299.0
1998	47.9	72.1	155.0	227.1

Source: World Bank. 1999. *Global Development Finance 1999*. Washington, D.C.: The World Bank, 24.

Some Countries Are More Equal Than Others

Globalization is "global" in the sense that everyone is affected, either by participating in it or by being excluded from it. Foreign direct investment (FDI) is highly concentrated in North America, Europe, and Japan.[6] Developing countries receive a very limited share of FDI, and that, too, is directed to only a few countries (Table 5.2). At least half of the world's population is not benefiting from the process of economic integration.[7]

While some developing countries, especially in East Asia, have successfully attracted private capital flows at unprecedented levels, many have had mixed experiences. A large number of nations has been entirely bypassed, especially in sub-Saharan Africa. Even countries that benefited from foreign investment and private capital are vulnerable to sudden shocks. The Asian financial crisis clearly showed the risks associated with global capital flows. Almost overnight, families in Indonesia were thrown into poverty after years of prosperity.

Within countries, rich or poor, the fruits of globalization are not evenly distributed. Only the wealthiest segments of society have benefited, leading to increased inequality. For example, the impact of globalization in developing countries is felt predominantly in urban, coastal areas and in certain value-added industries.[8] In India, foreign direct investment has sought computer-programming skills. The software industry in India is growing at a phenomenal rate, but its benefits are felt largely by the middle class.[9] Global trends have an uneven impact in industrialized countries too, leading to social exclusion. "The United States is vastly richer than China and India, but the life expectancy of African Americans is about the same as that in China and in some states in India."[10]

Some groups are harmed by globalization. Competition with developing countries is one reason that wages for unskilled workers have not kept up with inflation in the U.S. In developing countries, some industries and some aspects of agricultural production are depressed because of international competition.

Demonstrations in Seattle in 1999 against the World Trade Organization (WTO) and in Washington, DC, and Prague in 2000 against the International Monetary Fund (IMF) and the World Bank dramatized fears about globalization, world trade rules, new information technology, and biotechnology. Many of those who have been left behind, in industrialized nations and in developing countries, do not see, understand, and experience the benefits of expanding world trade. Some express their distress in organized demonstrations like Seattle.

© Ted Grudowski

But protests against the worst aspects of uncurbed capitalism have taken many forms. In the past, "communism, fascism, and socialism. . . emerged in response to the brutality of capitalism," according to *New York Times* columnist Thomas Friedman. He believes that

> those who can't keep up are not going to bother with an alternative ideology. [Rather], their backlash will take a different form. In Indonesia, they will eat the Chinese merchants by ransacking their stores. In Russia, they will sell weapons to Iran or turn to crime. In Brazil, they will log the rest of the rain forest or simply steal [or kidnap to get] what they need. . . They have no flag,

no manifesto. They have only their unmet needs and aspirations. That's why what we have been seeing in many countries, instead of popular mass opposition to globalization, is wave after wave of crime – people just grabbing what they need, weaving their own social safety nets and not worrying about the theory or ideology.[11]

Why Are So Many Left Out?

Economic growth, and the public policies and private investments that make it happen, are necessary to reduce hunger and poverty.[12] Openness to trade, macroeconomic policies that contain inflation, low budget deficits, incentives for investment and savings, and a strong financial sector set the stage for economic growth and successful participation in it. However, such policies alone will not pull the majority of people out of poverty. Without publicly funded investments in the health and education of poor people and in the labor-intensive economic activities upon which they depend, such as agriculture, economic growth does not benefit poor people. In addition, foreign direct investment and private capital seek countries that have market potential, the necessary infrastructure, a trainable and healthy labor force, and political stability.

Countries that have established these preconditions for investment in their development programs have been able to participate in the expanding opportunities afforded by globalization

Table 5.2: Foreign Direct Investment (in billions of $U.S.)

Region	1990	1998
Low-Income Countries	2.2	10.7
Middle-Income Countries	21.9	160.3
High-Income Countries	169.3	448.3
East Asia and the Pacific	11.1	64.2
Europe and Central Asia	1.1	24.4
Latin America and the Caribbean	8.2	69.3
Middle East and North Africa	2.5	5.1
South Asia	0.5	3.6
Sub-Saharan Africa	0.8	4.4

Source: World Bank. 2000. *World Development Report 2000/2001: Attacking Poverty*. New York: Oxford University Press, 315.

Hunger for Land

BY RICARDO REZENDE FIGUEIRA

Brazil exemplifies the huge and growing gap between the very rich and the very poor that is worsening everywhere as a function of globalization. Brazil's economy ranks eighth in the world. Yet out of a total population of 170 million, 21 million Brazilians are indigent and 50 million are poor. According to Brazil's Institute of Economic Research (Instituto de Pesquisa Econômica), "poverty in Brazil should not be associated primarily with a scarcity of resources, but rather with poor distribution of those resources."[1]

To confront inequitable income distribution, Brazilians launched the grassroots Campaign Against Hunger in 1993. More than 6,000 local volunteer committees throughout the country distributed food to hungry people. This helped. But it did nothing to alter the structural causes of hunger. Subsequently, the campaign identified two solutions to the problem of extreme social inequality: creating employment for poor people and democratizing access to land. Most of Brazil's 8,520 million square kilometers are arable, but idle and concentrated in large estates.

In 1995, the Landless Rural Workers Movement (MST) joined the grassroots effort to end hunger. Through demonstrations in the public square, occupations of unused public and private land, conflicts over land in which many landless rural workers were killed, media coverage of those events, and academic seminars, the movement succeeded in putting the question of agrarian reform on the national agenda. Organized civil society forced state and federal authorities to rethink land policy.

Economies of scale are supposed to make industrialized agricultural conglomerates more productive than small family farms, which are assumed to be uneconomical, backward, and unproductive. When it comes to land use in Brazil, however, the opposite is true. Globalization concentrates wealth and power in the hands of fewer and fewer transnational corporations and individuals. This does not fulfill the social function of property as defined by the Brazilian Constitution.[2]

According to a 1996 survey by Brazil's National Institute of Colonization and Agrarian Reform (INCRA),[3] 35,083 rural properties of more than 1,000 hectares each include 153 million unproductive hectares, an area equal to the combined territories of France, Spain, Germany, Austria, and Switzerland. Seventeen national and foreign nonagricultural economic entities with landholdings totaling 10,991,211 hectares used scarcely 1,991,396 hectares. Eleven financial groups held 2,106,539 hectares, of which only 788,605 hectares were used. In other words, only 21.2 percent of the 13 million hectares held by large businesses is under cultivation. Data from the Brazilian Institute of Geography and Statistics (FIBGE) show that less than 14 percent of corporate-owned land is being farmed. The largest land-holders cultivate less than 3 percent of arable land. In contrast, small farmers cultivate an average of 65 percent.

In the 1970s and 80s, the Brazilian government promoted a policy to develop the Amazon region. The government's priority was to establish large national and international agricultural and cattle businesses. These deals were subsidized by taxpayer money. The policy failed in many ways. Brazil's poorest people lost their livelihoods. The majority of projects proved inefficient and, officially, did not turn a profit. Environmental destruction was and continues to be astronomical. Even if the large landowners were to use more of their land, however, there would still be a serious problem. These enterprises cannot absorb an adequate number of permanent workers, which creates massive unemployment. As Pope John Paul II affirmed on his 1980 trip to Brazil, "every private property carries the weight of a social debt."

That debt can be repaid through the redistribution of land whose use does not comply with Brazilian law, under which idle land can be legally expropriated and distributed to landless people. There are millions of landless, jobless rural workers who cannot feed their families. The best investment is the one that would create work for them: settling farmers on small plots of land.

The policy to distribute land in large parcels was also a moral failure. It resulted in violations of human rights, including slave labor and violence against residents of the Amazon. From 1990 to 1997, 3,636 conflicts over land erupted throughout Brazil, affecting 2,354,759 people; 365 were killed.

The Brazilian government claims it doesn't have the resources to deal with the problem of social inequality and hunger. According to the Central Bank, between the end of 1994 and 1998 the country's foreign debt grew from $148 billion to $243 billion. Brazil paid $126 billion to creditors, with interest. With these same dollars, the government could have resettled 5,833,000 poor farm families, ending the problem of landless agriculturalists and stimulating economic activity.[4]

Father Ricardo received the Chico Mendes Resistance Prize (Brazil) and the Anti-Slavery International Prize (Britain) in 1992. Translated by Joanna Berkman.

[1] O Globo, 04.07.2000.

[2] Article 186 of Brazil's 1988 Federal Constitution states: "the social function is accomplished when a rural property meets the following criteria...established by law: 1. Rational and appropriate utilization; 2. Utilization appropriate to the available natural resources and to environmental preservation; 3. Observance of the clauses that regulate work; and 4. Management that favors the well-being of land owners and workers."

[3] Instituto Nacional de Colonização e Reforma Agrária (INCRA) is a federal agency. The data cited here on production and size of properties were gathered in *The Brazilian Choice* (*A Opção Brasileira*), a book with multiple authors (Rio de Janeiro, Contraponto Editora, 1998: 184-188).

[4] Jornal do Plebiscito–órgão de divulgação do Plebiscito da Dívida Externa. Número 1, abril/maio 2000.

and have translated these opportunities into social progress. In East and Southeast Asia, the percentage of the population that is undernourished declined by two-thirds to only 16 percent between 1961 and 1992.[13] This happened first as a result of the Green Revolution, which gave poor rural people higher farm wages or income, more and cheaper food, and more employment in most of the developing Asian economies.[14]

Subsequently, strong business climates and educated workforces attracted investment (including foreign investment) that broadened and deepened economic development, carried it well beyond the rural areas, and provided an engine of growth that increased the incomes of large numbers of people. The Asian economic crisis temporarily reversed many of these gains and revealed that strong institutions and good governance are also important to investors, who can withdraw capital from a country with the press of a button.

Sub-Saharan Africa has been unable to attract the kind of investment that would bring jobs, technology, and access to international markets (Chapter 6). Much of this has to do with how sub-Saharan Africa has been engaged in global geopolitics over the last few decades and its dependence on commodity-based exports. Caught up in Cold War politics, continuing civil conflict, poor management, and falling commodity prices, African leaders have been unable or unwilling to devote precious resources to building their infrastructure, labor force, and markets. Foreign assistance to Africa in the past failed to overcome these problems. South Asia has also had limited success in attracting private capital flows, but its prospects are somewhat better given the sheer size of its market and middle class. Again, poor policies and infrastructure, and political instability are to blame.

Trade Not Aid

Many "trade not aid" devotees on Capitol Hill and in the private sector assume that if countries put into place sound economic policies they will acquire the investment capital they need, leading to an eventual "convergence" between the incomes of poor and rich countries.[15] "Trade not aid" advocates reason that when poor countries make the right policy decisions, they can attract very high private investment flows because their untapped economies offer high rates of return.

A Senegalese man irrigates crops.

They also assume that high investment levels with high rates of return will help developing countries grow fast enough to catch up with richer countries and that fast growth will rapidly reduce poverty and hunger.

Getting policies right is a first step, but good policies are not enough to attract investment. Peace and stability, healthy and educated workers, well-maintained roads, an uninterrupted supply of electricity, and access to water are all factors that investors consider when making location decisions.

Foreign aid can help develop these preconditions for private investment. Developed countries can also help by opening their markets to imports from developing countries. Market access for agricultural products from developing countries is still limited.

> [W]hile world trade in manufacturing expanded at 5.8 percent a year from 1985 to 1994, agricultural trade grew at only 1.8 percent. One reason for this slow growth is the continuing protection of agricultural products by developed countries. . . The tariffs that high-income countries impose on agricultural goods from developing countries, especially such staples as meat, sugar, and dairy products, are almost five times those on manufactures. . . These barriers are a huge obstacle for developing countries striving to break into export markets. . . [and] a serious setback to development efforts in poor countries.[16]

The Tchoda Trade Tales

BY DUNCAN SAMIKWA

The market in Tchoda, a poor rural district in Malawi, is a microcosm of the effects of globalization on local people. Some smallholder farmers are better off now because they produce tobacco for export. Many traders and vendors have increased their incomes by selling cheap imported goods. But in general, Malawi's cost of living has risen and the number of poor people has increased.

Tchoda is located about 15 kilometers from Blantyre, Malawi's commercial capital. Tchoda's main road is in such bad shape that even the state-owned bus company suspended regular service. On market day, Tchoda swarms with buyers and sellers. Merchants display their goods in wooden stalls or on the bare ground: imported second-hand clothes, plastic wares, meats, vegetables, and fruits. The market serves the most densely populated and perhaps the poorest district in Malawi.

Discussion is lively. The topic: globalization. At the taxi stand, Mbewe is seated on the back of a beat-up Toyota truck chewing a sugarcane stem. A small crowd has assembled to listen. From his clothes and mannerisms, it is easy to see that he is not just another entrepreneur.

Mbewe was a tenant farmer before the government liberalized tobacco production. Then, like many other men, he left in search of employment on a large tobacco estate. At the beginning of the growing season, he sold his crop to the estate owner at a predetermined price. The estate owner deducted Mbewe's expenses, then gave him the balance.

After he learned to farm tobacco, Mbewe returned to Tchoda to grow his own crop. He broke even for the first few years, then began to turn a profit. As an intermediate tobacco buyer and seller, Mbewe participates directly in the global auctions and is paid in U.S. dollars.

Mbewe now owns three pick-up trucks, which he bought second-hand in Dubai. They are the taxis on the Blantyre-Tchoda road. Mbewe plans to buy a van at the end of this tobacco season to serve his customers better.

Elsewhere in the Tchoda market, serious bargaining takes place over chickens. A man and a woman claim that the Tchoda chickens are more expensive than the imported ones sold at a larger town's supermarket. The butcher feebly defends the quality and flavor of the local chickens, but the couple decides not to buy and moves on.

The chicken vendor complains that the townspeople are "sell-outs who don't help their country. They always want to buy cheaply even though they are aware of rising production costs." Politics enters the discussion when another vendor loudly proclaims that the previous regime controlled prices and made things affordable for most people. The assertion is quickly dismissed because the area is controlled by the current ruling party and blame shifts back to the townspeople.

Two others speak their minds, one a former poultry farm hand and the other an ex-soap-factory worker. Both lost their jobs when their former employers could not compete against cheaper imports. "The real problem in this country is that it has opened up too much," declares the farm hand. "Not only that, the authorities are weak and accept anything donors say," adds the factory worker. "Just imagine consumer prices rising daily. Who benefits from the so-called liberalization? Only foreigners and the rich!"

A last voice from the crowd argues that liberalization has improved some things, like transport. He is quickly silenced by a chorus of "sell-out" from the crowd and the debate takes on the tone of an opposition campaign meeting. How good is globalization for Malawi? Perhaps it depends on who has the last word.

Mr. Samikwa is the European Food Security Network's representative in Malawi and a participant in BFW Institute's African Writers Project.

Prophets of Doom

The gap between the countries and populations that are integrated into the global market and those that are not is widening. Some believe that the persistence of poverty and hunger in some parts of the world is inevitable. Poor countries are cut off from the benefits of global knowledge and technology, while in developed countries, "highly capitalized, knowledge-based technology will take over many tasks now done by the cheaper-labor countries and actually do them faster, better, and more cheaply."[17] Already, mechanization has displaced thousands of workers in the United States.

As globalization progresses, replacing many manual repetitive jobs with machines and requiring more skills to do the jobs that are left, the good jobs. . .become fewer and

Guatemalan girl grinds corn.

fewer. A *Washington Post* article from June 1998 reported that in the past 20 years, General Motors (GM) has cut employment in Flint to 35,000 workers from 76,000 and it says 11,000 more jobs could be eliminated over the next few years. . .Among its total U.S. workforce, GM has trimmed jobs to 223,000. . .Some of the jobs were moved to Canada and Mexico, where plants were either more efficient or less costly, but the bulk of the people were simply replaced by machines.[18]

Private sector investment in developing countries that replicates these concepts of efficiency and economies of scale will have the same results for poor and working people elsewhere as they have in the United States.

Allen Hammond presents a grim scenario of the near future in "Which World? Scenarios for the 21st Century." Those countries and groups that have benefited from globalization, information technology, biotechnology, and other changes may wall themselves off from the rest of the world, which increasingly falls behind and is left to war, destitution, and ecological disaster. The difference, however, is that Hammond explicitly posits this

prediction as the consequence of policy choices. Different choices would lead to different, and more positive, outcomes. Pro-poor approaches that keep many people employed on farms, in factories, or in micro-businesses where they live will help decrease poverty and hunger. A preferential policy for the poor is needed to keep them from sinking deeper into misery and despair.[19]

Thomas Friedman is widely seen as a proponent of globalization. Nevertheless, he devotes considerable attention to the possible negative effects of globalization on countries and people who can't keep up with the new world of rapid information transfer and trade. Like Hammond, Friedman believes U.S. policy choices are a key determinant of what happens to those countries and groups. Increasing and improving development assistance is one of those policy choices.

Foreign Assistance in a Global Economy

Two main roles have emerged for foreign assistance as a result of globalization. First, help the poorest and most marginalized countries and communities get to the point where they can exploit the opportunities of globalization. Second, address transnational challenges by making sure that developing countries have access to information and technologies.

Funding Development

Here's the Catch 22 of "trade not aid": there's no money in poverty. Hungry people with no income are not consumers. Very poor developing countries do not have the basic infrastructure or political stability that private investors seek. Foreign assistance and philanthropic aid from countries like the United States can help people in these countries gain the skills, information, knowledge, and technologies needed to succeed in the global economy. Aid can also support investment by developing country governments in services and sectors important to poor people and where private sector presence is weak.

The private sector recognizes that investments in social and human capital undergird creation of new markets for American firms in developing countries. Healthy, educated people will produce, earn, and buy more. But social investment is a lengthy process and does not yield the short-term payoffs that the private sector demands. The U.S.

A woman makes clothes to sell in Masaka, Uganda. She purchased the sewing machine with the help of microcredit.

government can invest public funds in agricultural research, public health, safe water supply, education, and transportation infrastructure. Development assistance is the means by which the U.S. government makes such investments. This role is explained in Chapter 4.

Providing International Public Goods

"A public good is a commodity, service, or resource whose consumption by one user does not reduce its availability to the next...Public goods are also 'nonexcludable,' that is if the good is provided, the provider is unable to prevent anyone from consuming it whether that user pays for it or not."[20] Clean air is an example. Efforts to eliminate air pollution benefit everyone. Clean air cannot be withheld. But public goods are vulnerable to what economists call the "free-rider problem." "This characteristic means that if production of public goods were left to the market, there would be an undersupply unless the government stepped in to produce the good or to provide incentives (such as subsidies) for their production."[21]

International public goods are just public goods that are transnational in nature, and that require collective action and a multinational approach. Examples of international public goods include vaccinations for infectious diseases, technologies that reduce environmental pollution, and the creation of and support for international institutions that coordinate policies to address transboundary issues. Disease often travels from poor to rich countries. Pollution anywhere affects the entire atmosphere. International agreements help find solutions to these problems and monitor progress. All countries benefit from the results.

The rapid growth of private capital flows to developing countries should not obscure what motivates and guides private investment decisions. The profit motive makes "trade not aid" a false promise at best. The private sector will not make philanthropic investments in developing countries. No savvy venture capitalist would knowingly make what appears to be a bad investment, no matter how noble. Losing propositions run counter to the very tenets of capitalism. It will be some time before many developing countries are capable of floating bonds for investments in health care or education. Private agribusiness corporations are unlikely to increase costly scientific research on the food crops upon which most of the world's poor people rely. Corporations do not see a solid rate of return for that kind of research.

The Green Revolution showed that governments and foundations could collaborate to conduct research to improve rice and wheat yields. Similar international cooperation and intervention will be required to deal with water scarcity, global warming, desertification, and other urgent problems such as HIV/AIDS; 90 percent of those infected are in developing countries and cannot afford treatment. The same is true for research on other infectious diseases, such as malaria, that are found predominantly in developing countries. The market incentives simply do not exist.

Foreign assistance can help create a market for private sector companies by supporting research and development.[22] The Global Alliance for Vaccines and Immunization (GAVI) brings together the resources of national governments, UNICEF, the World Health Organization, the World Bank, private foundations, and public health and research institutions. GAVI's aim is to inoculate children in poor countries and to encourage research on diseases that affect the poorest regions. GAVI procures vaccines from pharmaceutical companies on behalf of developing countries. Because GAVI represents a very large number of poor people, it is able to reach more favorable deals with vaccine suppliers than could individual countries.[23]

Fishermen Organize to Preserve Their Livelihood

By Joanna Berkman

When industrial fishing fleets began casting nets just one mile off the coast of central Mozambique, they threatened the livelihoods of 9,000 small independent fishermen in the region. What the Mozambican and foreign companies were doing was perfectly legal. The foreign companies had signed an agreement with the Mozambican government that allowed them to trawl for shrimp close to the shore.

But the results were a disaster for local people. The huge nets of the industrial fishing ships destroyed the hand-made nets of the small-scale fishermen. For every kilo of shrimp the large boats caught, they also captured five kilos of other marine fauna. Since only the shrimp were processed, the rest of the region's fish were simply wasted, depleting the environment, diminishing the food supply, and lowering the incomes of local families.

With funding from the International Fund for Agricultural Development (IFAD), the government of Mozambique's Institute for the Development of Small-scale Fisheries (IDPPE) took action to help fishing communities. In 1998, the IDPPE helped organize 103 local fishermen to file a grievance with the government, one of many efforts to empower fishing communities. In 1999, a new law extended the offshore limit from one to three miles as an experiment in the Nampula region only. The area was supposed to have been monitored by satellite. But when limited government funds prevented surveillance from space, the local fishermen themselves served as watchdogs. Their aim was to preserve the number of fish species in the area and to mediate conflicts between themselves and the large foreign companies. Already, the waste of fish has diminished.

IFAD support helped the fishermen address other serious problems. IFAD funding enabled local fishermen to build a private-sector system to buy and sell supplies at nearby retail outlets. Road rehabilitation made the development of local markets possible. When entrepreneurs researched local, regional, and national markets, they learned that the supply of fish was much too large for local demand. Larger cities in the region were more promising as markets, but only if the fish could be preserved properly. One local family business was capable of freezing the fish quickly enough to retain quality, but it could not meet the potential demand. The firm's freezer was tiny, its available transportation was inadequate, and the roads, though under improvement, were still precarious.

With IFAD's help and the support of the IDPPE, local people continue to seek ways to expand the market for their catch. Keeping track of the daily market price for fish in the project office has already yielded results. Consumer prices are broadcast daily by amateur radio. Informed fishermen now throw fish of low market value back in the ocean, an economic choice with favorable environmental impact. By observing price quotations, fishermen have become aware of exactly how much profit remains in the hands of middlemen, and are discussing how to increase their own share.

IDPPE has also facilitated exchanges between the fishermen's cooperative associations and their counterparts in Sri Lanka and India. The Mozambicans learned better techniques to smoke fish and to make fishing nets.

The IFAD-funded project has created great interest among the fishermen in changing the international rules that affect them. They have begun collaborating with fishermen in the Zambezia region to extend the experimental three-mile limit to the entire nation. And they are studying WTO market rules for food products, which have a strong impact on the informal economy and on the food security of low-income people in Mozambique.

Ms. Berkman is the editor of *Foreign Aid to End Hunger.*

Source: Translated and summarized from Filippo Dibari, *Relatório da Visita ao Projeto IFAD (Moçambique) de Pesca Artesanal em Nampula,* versão preliminar, 2000.

If developing countries become partners in development with industrialized country governments and private sector investors, a viable new approach to foreign assistance would put new technologies and trade opportunities at the service of poor countries and poor populations. If developing countries benefited from public-private sector partnerships for agricultural research, biotechnology could serve the world's poor and hungry people.

Enlightened Self-Interest

The future of U.S. foreign aid policy has been much debated in recent years, reflecting the end of Cold War imperatives. A popular emerging theory[24] suggests that in the 21st century, U.S. foreign aid will focus on peacemaking, transnational issues, humane concerns, particularly issues that affect women and children, and disaster relief, through humanitarian aid. These four purposes reflect American values and interests, the current mood in Congress, and changing goals due to globalization (see box).

According to this view, economic and social development will be less important in future foreign aid policy because most developing countries will be at a point where they can access private capital and fund such interventions themselves. But countries not at this point will still need development assistance. If U.S. foreign aid policy does go this route, a substantial reduction in an already meager long-term development assistance budget will follow.

In this chapter, BFW Institute has argued that most developing countries are not attracting the level and type of private investment that can reduce widespread poverty. Many are being further marginalized. It is entirely within the means of the industrialized countries to prevent this from happening and to overcome hunger and poverty worldwide. Well-planned, long-term development assistance is essential if people are to pull themselves out of poverty. This is an American value. It is an end in itself, and a reachable goal.

It would be unwise to let hunger and poverty continue. To do so would affect prospects for long-term U.S. economic growth. Addressing the root causes of transnational challenges is far more efficient and effective than simply applying stopgap solutions as problems arise.

The exact same conditions that underlie economic growth and a healthy world economy are preconditions for cutting hunger and poverty.

Market vendor in Nepal.

Therefore, the interests of the business community overlap those of the faith community. Both must care about reducing hunger and poverty. Peace, stability, predictable and fair rules of world trade, and transparency in financial transactions favor U.S. business, economic growth, and the reduction of hunger and poverty. Most of these preconditions require that the U.S. provide the leadership, spend the money, and dedicate the personnel required to maintain that leadership.

Chapter 4 describes the specific program and policy reforms that empower poor people. BFW Institute recognizes that funds allocated to the following foreign affairs functions also contribute to the fight against hunger:

- Making Peace: U.S. involvement in international agreements and military action if necessary reduces armed conflict, which devastates economies, creates refugees, and disrupts agricultural production.

- Negotiating World Trade Agreements: Fair, predictable trade rules expand economic opportunities for poor countries.

- Setting Health Standards: Agreement on sanitary and health guidelines for food will help expand world agricultural trade, create new opportunities for farmers from poor countries, and protect U.S. farmers and consumers.

- Establishing Sound Financial Practices: Banks and markets need consistent, transparent financial procedures that are not prone to corruption.

Fundamental National Interests of the U.S. State Department

- Economic prosperity and freer trade
- Protection of U.S. borders and U.S. citizens abroad
- Fighting international terrorism, crime, and drug trafficking
- Establishing and consolidating democracies; upholding human rights
- Providing humanitarian assistance to victims of crisis and disaster
- Improving the global environment, stabilizing world population growth, and protecting human health

Source: Richard Gardner, "The One Percent Solution: Shirking the Cost of World Leadership," *Foreign Affairs* (July/August 2000), 3.

Can Cash Croppers Compete?

BY JERONIMO TOVELA

The global isolation of Mozambique used to allow smallholder farmers to sell cash crops easily. Limited product diversity and supply meant limited competition. A successful harvest could bring in the cash needed to meet a household's daily needs. Cash cropping provided rural employment and helped minimize poverty.

But the transition to a market economy overseen by international financial institutions changed conditions for farmers like Helena. With her husband away in the gold mines of South Africa, Helena worked her two hectares of land with her seven children. She planted cash crops and hired three laborers until 1995, when she could no longer keep up. Liberalization had increased the number of businesses and intensified competition, especially from foreign investors with stronger assets.

Market liberalization brought opportunities to some smallholders. The price of seeds and fertilizers dropped as supplies increased and the demand for cash crops rose. But Helena felt the constraints of liberalization. "The government could have given us credits or subsidies, or taxes could have been raised on imported products, to help us compete," Helena said.

Perhaps most damaging has been the lack of credit to smallholders, who face lengthy and often unmanageable bank procedures and conditions. Limiting governmental subsidies, as prescribed by the World Bank and International Monetary Fund, made credit scarce and expensive. The smaller "agricultural funds" didn't reach many smallholders due to lack of information and bureaucratic burdens.

"Land was the only thing I had in 1995, but I could not use it as a guarantee. I worked hard to follow the requirements of the bank, but the interest rates made it

© Michael Kuchinsky

impossible to get the credit I needed when I needed it," Helena reported. Even when credit is obtainable, the small cash-cropping farmer faces obstacles. Rural Mozambique remains isolated due to very poor roads. Vehicles cannot travel into some areas. Local people commonly say that maize travels to Maputo from Europe or the United States easier than it does from the center Mozambique to Maputo. And when small farmers finally get their goods to market, they must compete with large importers, who in some cases have benefited from economies of scale and their own country's subsidies.

"With such competitors," Helena asks, "where will the buyers be for us?"

Mr. Tovela works for the National Union of Peasant Farmers, BFW Institute's partner in Mozambique.

■ Sponsoring Education and Exchange Programs: Knowledge of how the U.S government and businesses operate by citizens of the developing world and of how other countries function by U.S. citizens fosters understanding.

Profit, not public welfare, drives private investment, locally and internationally. Therefore, investment is not a substitute for foreign aid. Without foreign assistance, developing countries unable to attract foreign investment will be forced to choose between important and complementary policy goals, for example between health care and safe water. With foreign assistance, developing countries can improve and increase their investment in their own people.

When people are secure – when they have food, health, and peace – they can focus on sustainable, productive activities that protect the environment and invest in the future. Everyone would benefit.

This chapter has been excerpted and adapted with permission from David Atwood, *Cutting Hunger and Poverty in Half: Interest Groups and a Renewed U.S. Commitment in the Post-Cold War World*, unpublished paper submitted July 28, 2000 to the Industrial College of the Armed Forces, National Defense University, in fulfillment of a research program.

CHAPTER 6

Realizing Africa's Potential

There is good news from parts of Africa. Apartheid has ended in South Africa. Dictatorships are giving way to democracy. Many countries are experiencing economic revival. Women are expanding their roles in the economic and political life of most countries. The private sector is growing and diversifying. In Uganda and Senegal, aggressive campaigns to halt the spread of HIV/AIDS are showing signs of success.

Many nongovernmental organizations are emerging to articulate grassroots concerns, participate in planning and decisions, and connect poor people in Africa to their neighbors and to the international community. While missionary churches had a checkered history in Africa during the colonial period, these same churches now bring education, better health, and hope to people. Today, churches are profoundly respected as a vital force for democratization and development in many African countries, especially in rural areas.

© Celia Escudero-Espadas

Across the continent, public officials, professionals, businesspeople, academics, journalists, religious leaders, trade unionists, and small farmers, as well as human rights, women's movement, and environmental activists are organizing with new dynamism, new demands, and new expectations. The current generation is determined to achieve prosperity, democratic rights, and lasting security. Although enormous obstacles remain, Africa has clearly entered a new phase of social and economic change.

And yet, in the midst of these hopeful signs, hunger persists, threatening the continent's fragile and uneven recovery. While the number of malnourished people is higher in Asia than in Africa, the depth of hunger is greater in Africa. The average per capita intake of calories is lower in Africa and the percent of people who are hungry is higher (Tables 1.1, 1.2).[1] The Food and Agriculture Organization (FAO) of the United Nations predicts that in 2015, 22 percent of Africans will still be malnourished, compared with 10 percent of people in South Asia. However, "the successes achieved in other parts of the world demonstrate [that] a concerted, focused effort can make a difference and prove the projections wrong."[2]

Pro-poor development assistance is necessary to achieve a substantial reduction in hunger in Africa, and would be the single most important step in achieving the World Food Summit goal. Development assistance can also help African countries become fuller participants in the global economy, a critical step toward achieving long-term food security.

A Diverse Continent

Africa, the second largest continent in the world, includes 54 countries, 48 of which comprise sub-Saharan Africa. Africa's 600 million people speak hundreds of languages and live in every type of climate, from desert to rainforest. Muslims shop next to Christians, Hindus, secularists, and those who adhere to traditional spiritual beliefs. Africa's cultures are as diverse as the colors and patterns of its fabrics.

The political and economic situation of African countries varies widely. African states rich in minerals, oil, gems, and other natural resources, such

A Nigerian man and woman grind cassava at a roadside market.

Principles of Development Assistance to Africa

- **Truly sustainable development in Africa can only be achieved by Africans.** The primary objective of industrialized nations should be to facilitate African initiatives to strengthen their institutions and capabilities to manage long-term development. Africans must be agents for change in their own countries.

- **U.S.-Africa policies must focus on poverty reduction.** The success of U.S. support for Africa should be measured by the ability of policies and programs to promote broad-based economic growth and social and political programs that actually reach and help the poorest, most marginalized people in Africa. The policies should create opportunities for people both individually and collectively to achieve economic advancement and sustainable human development.

- **U.S.-Africa policies must grow out of participatory consultation.** African perspectives, drawn from a broad range of social and economic sectors, must be the foundation for all development policies and programs. Governments, multilateral organizations, educational institutions, nongovernmental organizations, village-level grassroots organizations, and businesses are essential in the search for solutions.

Cecilia Makota Advocates for Women

BY SAMUEL KASANKHA

Cecilia Makota, an elderly South African-born woman, has lived in Zambia much of her life. Her energy and vision drive Zambian Women in Agriculture, a nongovernmental organization (NGO) with a mission to develop affordable, sustainable agriculture for rural women.

"We have 500 women at Lukanga, where the local chief donated 50 hectares of land," Makota says. "We till 30 hectares collectively and divide the rest among the women for private cultivation."

The Lukanga women's story typifies problems plaguing peasant farmers across Zambia. They must fall back on over-used and infertile land. And because maize is their staple food and cash crop, the women constantly need costly seed and fertilizer.

"We approach the problem in two ways," Makota says. "We try to put back into the land what the land has produced. We use compost manure where possible, but this does not eliminate the need for chemical fertilizer."

There were no credit facilities serving the women until Zambian Women in Agriculture provided soft loans for seed and fertilizers so that the women could borrow with little or no collateral. The NGO borrows the inputs from producer companies like Omnia and Zambia Seed Company (Zamseed).

Makota's NGO has taught the women to depend on animal power rather than tractors and has introduced crop management days where the women learn more effective techniques. Some women now generate additional income through their livestock or by making grass mats and baskets.

Women confront other problems. Poor roads inhibit transportation. The ruling party either dismantled or discouraged district-level cooperative unions, the former agricultural marketing boards. The women now complain that private marketing agents want to purchase produce at prices that do not cover their costs. Rather than being saddled with unsold produce, the women barter their harvest for second-hand clothes and pots or sell at lower rates.

"These conditions make it impossible for some women to repay their loans," Makota discloses rather sadly. "Also, there are women who do well but are influenced by their husbands not to repay the loans. It's a big problem because as an NGO, we have to repay our creditors, too."

Mr. Kasanhka, a student at the University of Zambia, participated in the BFW Institute African Writers' Project on Food Security.

---

as South Africa and Nigeria, have attracted large amounts of foreign private investment, while the Central African Republic and Mali have received little. Botswana and Mauritius enjoy political and social stability, with per capita incomes higher than most sub-Saharan African nations. Mozambique remains one of the world's poorest countries, despite the impressive progress it has made since the end of its civil war less than a decade ago. Recognizing that the circumstances of each nation are different, *Foreign Aid to End Hunger* paints solutions in broad strokes. Policies to reduce hunger must be tailored to each country's needs.

Obstacles Africans Face

In the past, Africa's human and natural resources have been exploited by foreign colonial and industrial powers. Only 50 years ago, most of Africa remained under the control of European powers, which established national boundaries and ordered economic production primarily for the benefit of their own people and industries.

Even after African countries won independence, local conflicts were frequently proxies for confrontation between the United States and the Soviet Union. The U.S. propped up venal dictators, such as Mobutu Sese Seku in Zaire and Samuel Doe in Liberia, collaborated with South Africa's apartheid regime, and supported other unpopular governments – as "friends" in the fight against communism. By backing ill-conceived and costly development projects, encouraging heavy financial borrowing, fueling civil conflict, and dispensing sometimes inappropriate economic prescriptions, the United States, the international financial institutions, and others have impeded Africa's development. The interests of ordinary people often took a back seat to other concerns.

Africans face many obstacles as they struggle to achieve sustained and broad-based development. Thirty-two of the world's 48 least developed countries are in sub-Saharan Africa;[3] 250 million people live on less than $1 per day. Of these, about 200 million live in rural areas.

- 186 million Africans are malnourished.[4]
- 19 of the 24 countries with an average daily deficit of more than 300 calories are in sub-Saharan Africa.[5]
- 26 million African children (30 percent) are undernourished, and over half of all deaths among preschool children are linked to malnutrition.

Bad health and inadequate education undermine poor people. HIV/AIDS is destroying the family and other social and economic structures upon which poor people depend. Poor roads inhibit their activities. The absence of peace and stability, good governance, and reliable institutions isolates poor people and increases their vulnerability. Desertification, soil degradation, and deforestation caused by population pressure, land-use practices, and climate change further reduce food security. These problems have made it very difficult for most countries in sub-Saharan Africa to attract private investment and reap the benefits of globalization.

Civil strife and HIV/AIDS exacerbate hunger and poverty, which in turn aggravate civil conflict and increase people's vulnerability to disease. This circular causality illustrates the need to act on many fronts simultaneously to achieve results. Foreign assistance can help Africans overcome obstacles and rebuild their institutions. In much of Africa, governments have been weakened by civil conflict and must be strengthened. A stable political environment and functioning governmental institutions reassure investors and make sustainable development possible. While NGOs provide much needed funding at the micro-level to communities and projects, their efforts must be complemented by change at the macro-level. This necessarily involves national governments. Therefore, foreign assistance must also support pro-poor governmental initiatives, including policies that encourage private sector development.

African Initiatives

Development assistance supports what individuals, communities, and nations are already doing for themselves. Strong government leadership has been vital in attacking malnutrition in many countries. The Madagascar Food Security and Nutrition Project enjoyed political support and adopted a multisectoral approach to the problem of hunger. The project financed income-generating activities, initiated a food-for-work program, and established a nutrition program supported by community groups and NGOs. It also legislated the universal iodization of salt, a simple technology with widespread benefits. Malnutrition in the project's catchment areas fell by 50 percent. Similar projects in Senegal, Benin, and Mali have been equally successful.[6] Supporting governments that are taking initiatives to help poor people ensures long-term commitment to such activities in the face of difficult budgetary choices.

Democracy is taking hold, but is still fragile. People in Africa are attempting to build transparent, accountable, and participatory democratic processes. Organizations such as the Human Rights Lawyers' Committee in Cameroon monitor elections to ensure fairness. Some African elections draw up to 90 percent of voters, in spite of the transportation difficulties many people face getting to the polls and long lines once they arrive. Throughout Africa, civil society organizations that lobby to express the views of the people and build consensus are burgeoning.

African countries are working in regional alliances and in partnership with industrial countries to take a proactive role in their own

U.S., Not Africa, Owes the Greater Debt

BY CORETTA SCOTT KING

Fifty years ago, the United States made a commitment to rebuild a devastated Europe, endorsing the idea that a society must have hope, opportunity, and stability to meet the needs of its people and prosper.

Today, we are richer and better off as a result. The Marshall Plan, which expanded the market for U.S. products and services, proved to be one of our most cost-effective investments. But we lack the political will to make that kind of commitment again, when and where it is needed most: in Africa, the continent to which we owe our greatest debt.

African countries face more than $370 billion in foreign debts, which consume much of their budgets. Canceling these debts is the morally right thing to do — partial reparation for the tragic history of slavery, colonialism, and exploitation that brought fabulous wealth to the United States and Europe on the backs of the African people.

No amount of money can right the injustices of slavery. But even a conservative estimate of the fair-market value of the unpaid labor of slaves and the ruthless exploitation of Africa's resources would put the U.S. several hundred billion dollars in debt to Africa.

Misery marks many lives in the 42 most heavily indebted African nations, where one in five children dies before age 5, one in three children is malnourished, and more than half the adults are illiterate. Each of these countries spends more on debt service than on primary health care or education. It is unconscionable for the United States, with its wealth, to force severely impoverished countries to spend more on interest payments to us than on the basic needs of their citizens.

African leaders also must put their citizens' health and education needs first. Merely wiping away the debt without constructive programs that reach the most needy would be myopic and counterproductive.

Debt relief should be part of a larger initiative to improve the lives of Africans and help their nations build more secure and prosperous futures. In so doing, we would be making a cost-effective investment in developing a vibrant new market for America as well.

In his 1964 Nobel Peace Prize lecture, my husband, Martin Luther King Jr., challenged Europe and the United States: "The rich nations must use their vast resources of wealth to develop the underdeveloped, school the unschooled, and feed the unfed. Ultimately, a great nation is a compassionate nation."

We can accept this responsibility by canceling Africa's oppressive debts. It is the right thing to do — morally, economically, and politically.

Mrs. King founded the Martin Luther King Jr. Center for Nonviolent Social Change. Reprinted with permission.

development. The Southern African Development Community (SADC), the Central African Customs and Economic Union (UDEAC), and the Common Market for Eastern and Southern Africa (COMESA) are addressing shared problems, harmonizing policies, and creating common markets.[7] Developing countries are urging rule changes that would make international financial institutions and trade regimes fairer and more favorable towards them. People in the industrialized nations can support African initiatives by making sure that international institutions respond to developing country needs.

The movement for debt relief illustrates the interplay between African countries and industrialized nations. African people have articulated the severity of their debt burden and its adverse effects on investment in education, health care, and infrastructure. The All-Africa Conference of Churches may have been the first institution to propose debt cancellation in 2000, and African Catholic bishops consistently asked the Vatican to focus on this issue. Within the Anglican Communion, African bishops brought the idea of Jubilee 2000 to the worldwide Lambeth Conference in 1998. Churches and other non-governmental organizations in the industrialized countries have taken up the cause of debt relief with their governments and the international financial institutions.

Until recently, the debt stock of the countries in sub-Saharan Africa was growing much faster than countries could repay it. Between 1980 and 1998, Africa's debt as a percentage of its GNP nearly tripled, from 24.1 percent to 68.3 percent. In country after country, Africa's debt burdens skyrocketed. Mozambique, for example, added $570 million to its debt stock between 1990 and

1993 because it could not even make 10 percent of its scheduled payments. Thirty-three of the 41 countries classified as Heavily Indebted Poor Countries (HIPC) by the World Bank and IMF in 1996 were in sub-Saharan Africa. All told, by 1998 sub-Saharan African countries owed foreign creditors more than $226 billion.

The heavy burden of growing, unpayable debt meant that African governments were diverting scarce resources from education and health to meet debt service obligations. Sub-Saharan Africa was paying more than $12 billion in debt service annually, while owing about $8 billion more that it could not pay. Some governments were devoting as much as 50 percent of their country's budget to debt service payments. International financial institutions and African governments became locked in a costly and debilitating charade of reschedulings, with lengthy, complex conditionality attached.

Donor governments often gave "foreign aid" grants to debtor governments, knowing full well they would be used to pay off old loans rather than for new programs. Debt became a huge obstacle to development because countries were unable to attract foreign investment.

In June 1999, the G-7 nations meeting in Cologne agreed to an international debt relief plan. This was a significant first step in the effort to halt the crippling effects of debt. Uganda, the first country to qualify under the new plan, has received more than $7 billion in debt relief. In just two years, Uganda's primary school enrollment doubled. For Mozambique, debt relief meant a reduction in annual debt service payments from $127 million a year to $52 million, with much of the savings going for hospitals and housing.

After the economic decline of the 1980s and early 1990s, Africa has experienced growth of 2 to 4 percent a year since 1995. However, given that the region's population is doubling every 25 years, at current growth rates, African economies would have to grow by 5 percent a year simply to maintain current standards of living. To begin moving out of poverty, 7 percent growth in annual gross domestic product (GDP) would be required, with its benefits distributed widely.[8]

Foreign Aid to End Hunger focuses on how the United States can help. An infusion of foreign aid for development programs proven to get results for poor people can speed the economic recovery of African nations, reducing the poverty that condemns so many millions of people. A 1998 study commissioned by the U.S. government (Table 6.1) suggests that the number of undernourished people in Africa can be cut by over 80 million people.[9] Though the situation has changed somewhat since this study was done, the numbers represent orders of magnitude and possible directions for public action.

In *A Program to End Hunger: Hunger 2000*, Bread for the World Institute calculated that an additional $1 billion annually in U.S. funding for development assistance, plus commensurate increases by other donor nations, would make it possible to meet the World Food Summit goal worldwide, beginning with Africa.

U.S. Development Assistance Flows to Africa

Sub-Saharan Africa gets only 20.6 percent of U.S. official development assistance (ODA) (Chapter 3). Aid appropriations for Africa, including economic and military assistance, food aid, and the Peace Corps, peaked in FY 1985 at $2.4 billion, declining to $1.2 billion in FY 1990 (in constant 1997 dollars).[10] The decline reflected the

Table 6.1: Reduction in Undernourishment in Sub-Saharan Africa by 2015

Program	Total number of people (in millions)	Intervention Costs (in millions of $U.S.)
Reduce war and increase democracy	–16	887
Open trade and reduce tariffs	–7	660
Rural roads	–7	1,172
Agricultural research	–27	4,092
Targeted food aid	–4	1,633
Female literacy	–21	1,634
Total reduction in undernourished	**–82**	**10,078**

Source: J. Dirck Stryker and Jeffrey Metzel. 1998. *Meeting the Food Summit Target: The United States Contribution* (Washington, DC: Prepared for USAID), 22 and 26.

Sex for Food

BY JOSEPH KALUNGU SAMPA

Pemba, a town in the southern Monze region of Zambia, has fewer than 5,000 inhabitants. Many farmers lost their cattle and crops in the drought of 1997-98, the year that I visited Pemba to research the effects of structural reforms on Zambian households.

As I was having a drink at a grocery near the main road, I saw two boys and a girl between 6 and 13 years old picking up kernels of maize. The children told me that their mother sent them to pick the grain so that they could grind it into "mealie meal" and make *nsima* (a thick local porridge). The children did this often.

I asked them to show me where their mother was. We found her at home lying on a reed mat. After I explained who I was, she agreed to have a conversation. When I asked her what she did for a living, she looked at me for some time then looked down and sighed.

"My husband was discharged in 1994," she began. "He was our sole bread winner. I was a full-time housewife and mother. I thought I would never have to earn an income. Food was never a problem and everything was well with us. We managed well with my husband's income.

"Things changed after my husband left the army. He did not receive his benefits for two years, which meant the family had no income. My husband couldn't cope and died of depression in 1997. Though his benefits came before he died, most of the money went to repay the debts we had accumulated. We experienced serious food shortages. We often went without a good meal for several days. My children always wore hungry and sad faces. I tried to sell vegetables but everyone else sold vegetables, too. Whatever I sold didn't bring in much.

"I had no choice but to send my children to beg in town and glean the maize that dropped from trucks passing along the road. But this was no solution. I had to find food for my family."

She paused, looked down with a clenched fist, hit her chest, and said, "Against my own will, against my faith, I became a walker. I slept with men for money. At first it tormented me and I found it extremely hard to understand. Today I do it with less difficulty.

"Do not ask me about sexually transmitted diseases," she said. "I may or may not be a carrier. But as long as I can afford a meal for my family, I am happy. I know that one day sooner or later I will die of AIDS," she said, on the verge of tears. "But I can tell you that I find hunger more deadly than AIDS. AIDS kills in years. But hunger kills within days."

I had few words to say except to thank her for her time. She never mentioned school, health, entertainment, or clothing. . .only food. I realized that when you have no food, you have no choice.

Mr. Sampa is assistant coordinator of the Structural Adjustment Policy Monitoring Project in Lusaka and a participant in BFW Institute's African Writers' Project.

Tanzanian mothers and newborns wait for well-baby check-ups at the Maternal Child Health unit in Bahi Sokoni village.

end of the Cold War imperatives of U.S. foreign aid to the region. Cuts were made predominantly in military assistance and the Economic Support Fund (ESF) allocations to Africa.

In light of falling foreign assistance to sub-Saharan Africa, the Development Fund for Africa (DFA) was designated by Congress in 1990. The DFA earmarked funds from USAID's Development Assistance (DA) Fund for sub-Saharan Africa. Its purpose was to promote long-term development through economic growth, emphasizing policy reform, agricultural production, health care, primary education, and income-generating programs. Bread for the World helped win a special legislative mandate for the DFA, including flexibility regarding procurement from the United States and a strong emphasis on grassroots development.

In the mid-1990s, Congress reduced funding for many anti-poverty programs, including aid to Africa. In 1995, Bread for the World helped to moderate the cut and maintain the DFA as a separate account. In 1996, the DFA was eliminated. Development assistance to Africa declined from $802 million to $665 million in FY 1996. It rose again in the late 1990s but has yet to reach the 1995 level. FY 2000 saw an appropriation of $737.8 million for the region.[11]

In the FY 2001 foreign operations appropriations, there was no specific mention of sub-Saharan Africa in the Development Assistance Fund, the Child Survival and Diseases Fund (CSD), or the Economic Support Fund. However, DA and CSD appropriations were greater than the administration's request. The exact allocations to sub-Saharan Africa will be determined in early 2001. The CSD HIV/AIDS earmark of $300 million will benefit Africa. The budget requests for FY 2001 suggest how the allocations will be made: $211 million for economic growth and agricultural development, $36 million for human capacity development, $73 million for democracy building, $103 million for population programs, and $107 million for protecting the environment.[12]

Under FY 2001 appropriations, the African Development Foundation (ADF) received $16 million, the African Development Bank $6.1 million, and the African Development Fund $100 million.[13] Africa will receive $161 million in food aid from the PL 480 Title II account. The African Development Bank makes concessional loans for projects in African countries. The African Development Fund is the African Development Bank's grant or low-interest loan facility. The African Development Foundation is a U.S. government agency that gives small grants to create revenue and employment and to support sustainable pro-poor growth strategies and local initiatives. For example, in Cape Verde, where 38 percent of the people are unemployed, the ADF funded a sewing cooperative, which grew from eight individuals to become the country's leading clothing manufacturer in just three years. In Botswana, an ADF-sponsored project to harvest the cochineal insects that produce red dyes increased the household incomes of nearly 200 families to $1,250, well above the national average.[14] In Zimbabwe, a furniture-making cooperative begun by 12 laid-off workers now employs over 270 people.

© Celia Escudero-Espadas

Key Measures for Africa

Chapter 4 describes programs and policies that can eradicate chronic hunger. These measures are urgently needed in Africa.

Invest in Agriculture

Investing in agriculture is the surest strategy to help cut hunger in half. Per capita food production in Africa has fallen by 23 percent in the last 25 years. Drought, floods, variable rainfall, poor soils, disease, and pests have taken their toll. Costs of inputs like fertilizer, which are often controlled by state monopolies, are two to four times higher in Africa than in Asia. Table 6.2 illustrates some of the differences in productivity experienced by farmers in Africa, compared to other developing regions.

African agriculture suffers from low productivity due to lack of investment, bad roads, insufficient irrigation, poor policies, and weak institutions. The largest share of new foreign assistance in Africa should strengthen agriculture and rural development. Over 70 percent of the people in many sub-Saharan African countries work in agriculture. The majority of these are smallholder farmers. Most are rural women, who produce 80 percent of food in sub-Saharan Africa.

New investments in agricultural research and extension for Africa are critical. The international

Table 6.2: Indicators of Agricultural Productivity

	Africa	Asia	South America
Cereal production/capita (metric tons)	0.17	0.28	0.29
Fertilizer use (kg/hectare)	18	129	60
Avg. cereal yields (kg/hectare)	1220	2895	2547
Irrigate cropland (percent)	6.0	25.1	7.7

Source: World Resources, *A Guide to the Global Environment, 1998-99.*

network of agricultural research institutes that spearheaded the Green Revolution is now working on improved varieties and techniques for the small-scale, rain-dependent farming systems of Africa. Productivity has improved in maize, wheat, cotton, and bananas. The cassava mealy bug was eliminated in the 1980s. Agricultural research and extension systems should be tailored to the needs of farmers, with emphasis on women. African governments, scientists, and farmers are weighing the risks and benefits of biotechnology, which needs to focus on African agriculture in order to be useful there.

To address the growing problem of desertification in sub-Saharan Africa, the International Fund for Agricultural Development (IFAD) sponsors a program on drylands agriculture. Working with farmer organizations, NGOs, PVOs, and the private sector, IFAD has focused research on water and soil conservation techniques, rain-fed agriculture, small-scale irrigation, and rehabilitation and recovery of drought-affected land. In Niger, IFAD supported a project to dig pits or *tassas* in which millet could be planted, transforming 5,800 hectares of nonarable land. In Burkina Faso, stone bunds reduced water runoff on 30,000 hectares of sorghum and millet fields. In Senegal, village irrigation schemes raised rice production from 2 to 3 tons to 5.5 tons per hectare.[15] All of these projects used traditional methods and materials that were easily accessible to smallholder farmers.

Producer organizations and farmer associations provide new information and improve farmers' bargaining skills. Farmers' organizations in Mozambique and Malawi improve farmers' skills, incomes, access to credit, and local empowerment.

The Potential of Biotechnology in Africa

BY HENRY W. MAINGI

The Green Revolution of the 1960s and 1970s doubled yields of rice, wheat, and maize and fed millions of hungry people in Asia and Latin America. But the Green Revolution bypassed Africa. Roots and tubers such as cassava and yams, and grains such as sorghum and millet are Africa's staple crops, not rice and wheat. Higher yielding varieties of wheat and rice require irrigation, which is rare in the dryland agriculture of sub-Saharan Africa, where drought is a recurrent problem. In addition, the crossbred grain crops of the Green Revolution require fertilizers, insecticides, and herbicides that African farmers cannot afford.

A second Green Revolution, one that includes Africa, is long overdue.[1] Genetically modified (GM) seeds that resist insects and diseases and grow in hostile conditions hold great promise for Africa.[2] GM products, in addition to reducing the need for chemical sprays, may also increase yields and contribute to land conservation and environmental protection. GM foods such as rice enriched with vitamin A, sweet potatoes enriched with protein, and maize fortified with high quality iron, could provide essential nutrients lacking in hungry people's diets. Kenyan scientists, working with Monsanto, the United States Agency for International Development (USAID), and Kenya's International Service for the Acquisition of Agri-Biotech Applications have developed a virus-resistant sweet potato that could increase yields by 20 to 80 percent.[3]

But genetically modified crops are controversial and worldwide criticism has limited research. Some European countries have banned GM foods and consumers have boycotted them. In the U.S., taco shells that contained GM corn approved only for animal consumption were pulled from the supermarkets.[4] GM foods might raise resistance to antibiotics, transfer allergens, and produce as yet unknown long-term human health consequences. Yet respected organizations, including WHO, FAO, OECD, the Nutritional Research Council, and the American Medical Association have determined that GM technology can be safe.

Africans have an additional set of concerns. Who owns the native plant genes? Who owns modified plant genes and can these genes be patented? Can GM seeds be reused or are they purposely bred to be sterile? How will poor farmers benefit? Will seeds be made available only to those who can afford them? Whose commercial interests are being served? How will sustainability be ensured? And how will the threats to biodiversity be handled?

While researchers at agribusinesses such as Novartis and Dupont extract biological resources from indigenous African plants for purposes of genetic modification, African farmers are being left out of the equation. Africans are wary about the appropriation and transfer of genetic material from local plants by the multinationals. We fear losing the continent's biodiversity and suspect that products developed from African plants will be sold back to us at a higher cost. African farmers want local policymakers to slow the introduction of biotech products and to encourage local communities to use, save, and exchange seeds to ensure that the new GM varieties do not replace native varieties.[5] Africans want more research and testing conducted under closely controlled conditions in Africa.[6]

Both African and non-African environmentalists worry that genes from modified varieties will transfer to wild relatives, introducing the risk of mutant superbugs and superweeds. Reliance on GM varieties might also lead to the abandonment of the central principles of sustainable agriculture, such as biologically integrated pest management, monitoring field trials, and indigenous cultivation practices.[7]

Africans want to decide for themselves whether to adopt GM crops. As Hassan Adamu, Nigeria's Minister of Agricultural and Rural Development, said in a *Washington Post* op-ed: "We want to come to the table as stakeholders. We know the conditions of our fields. We know the threats, the insects, and the diseases. We can work as partners to develop the seeds that could build peoples and nations. We will proceed carefully and thoughtfully, but we want to have the opportunity to save the lives of millions of people in many nations. That is our right, and we should not be denied by those with a mistaken idea that they know best how everyone should live or that they have the right to impose their values on us."[8]

Dr. Maingi, a Kenyan, has a Ph.D. in agricultural sciences.

[1] Gordon Conway, "Crop Biotechnology, Benefits, Risks, and Ownership." speech delivered March 28, 2000 in Edinburgh, Scotland at: GM Food Safety: Facts, Uncertainties, and Assessments, The Organisation for Economic Cooperation and Development (OECD) Edinburgh Conference on the Scientific and Health Aspects of Genetically Modified Foods.

[2] Gordon Conway, Remarks to Monsanto Board of Directors Meeting, Washington, DC, June 24, 1999; Hassam Adamu, "We'll Feed Our People as We See Fit," *Washington Post*, September 11, 2000, A23.

[3] C.S. Parakash, "Must Tap Biotech's Potential" *San Francisco Chronicle*, March 30, 2000; Florence Wambugu, "Why Africa Needs Agricultural Biotech." *Nature* 400 (July 1, 1999): 16.

[4] Marc Kaufman, "Biotech Critics Cite Unapproved Corn in Taco Shells," *Washington Post*, Monday, September 18, 2000, A02.

[5] Rachel Wynberg, "Privatising the Means for Survival: The Commercialization of Africa's Biodiversity, Global Trade and Biodiversity in Conflict," *Biowatch* 5 (April 2000), 1.

[6] Wambugu, "Why Africa Needs Agricultural Biotech," 16.

[7] Conway, Remarks to Monsanto Board of Directors Meeting.

[8] Adamu, "We'll Feed Our People as We See Fit," A23.

© Michael Kuchinsky

The National Smallholder Farmers' Association of Malawi (NASFAM) has benefited farmers and earned their respect. Ten years ago, smallholders were absent from the market. But NASFAM members now bring over 40 percent of burley tobacco, the country's chief cash export product, to market. These farmers have come to "believe that they are agricultural entrepreneurs."[16] At the regional training centers, activities focus on building production and marketing capacity. NASFAM also acts as a mediator, negotiating prices to lower fertilizer, seed, and transportation costs. Foreign assistance can help strengthen these organizations.

Inheritance and Land Tenure

Land is both an asset that can be used as collateral and a means of earning an income. But 70 percent of smallholder farmers in Africa are barred from land ownership and inheritance because they are women. Women own only 1 percent of the land, receive only 7 percent of extension services, and get less than 1 percent of the credit provided to farmers and less than 10 percent of the credit targeted to small-scale farmers.

Improving access to land by smallholder farmers is important in reducing food insecurity. Mozambique has begun to reform land tenure. In 1999, grassroots organizations of peasant farmers in Mozambique such as the União Nacional de Camponeses and Associacão Rural de Ajuda Mutua took the lead.

© Celia Escudero-Espadas

I used to never worry about my illiteracy and the fact that I was not able to send my children to school, as long as we had something to eat. But now I realize that my children are in trouble for life because they cannot get any decent job if they don't know how to read and write.[17]

— WOMAN IN SWAZILAND

Invest in Female Literacy

When African nations first gained their independence, they invested heavily in education. But economic pressures have cut into education budgets. The enrollment of sub-Saharan African children in primary school lags behind other developing regions. More boys attend primary school (61 percent) than girls (57 percent).[18] Only seven sub-Saharan countries report primary school age attendance at 90 percent or above. The gap between males and females dramatically increases as one moves from secondary to higher education.

USAID has had much success with primary and secondary education programs in Botswana. USAID supported teacher training by establishing degree programs in primary education at the University of Botswana and improving the management skills of education professionals. The collaborative approach taken in developing the programs ensured their relevance to local needs.[19]

Invest in Health

A child in sub-Saharan Africa dies every three seconds, usually from an infectious disease. The infant mortality rate, a key indicator of public health, is 107 per 1,000 in sub-Saharan Africa, compared with 76 per 1,000 in South Asia and 64 per 1,000 for all developing countries.[20] Eighty percent of malaria cases worldwide occur in Africa

Organizing Benefits Malawi Farmers

BY MICHAEL KUCHINSKY

Over the past two years, Bread for the World Institute and the National Association of Smallholder Farmers of Malawi (NASFAM) have assessed the impact of U.S., World Bank, and International Monetary Fund policies on farmers and food security. The goal of this Ford Foundation-funded research was to learn how farmers were affected by policy changes. In the liberalized market environment, some farmers gained access to new resources and were able to take advantage of opportunities. Others suffered from decreased purchasing power, unstable prices, and lack of inputs. More than 300 Malawi farmers participated in the study, including male- and female-headed households working land parcels of all sizes. Some belonged to farmers' organizations, some did not.

Farmers responded to the liberalization of tobacco markets by increasing production of burley tobacco. The distribution of starter seed packs helped them diversify their cash crops. And when farmers were able to acquire land, they increased the area under cultivation.

Household food security results were mixed. Sixty-one percent of interviewees said their food security had either stayed the same (19 percent) or improved (42 percent); 39 percent said it had worsened. Nearly 70 percent of the farmers said they still suffered from food insecurity during the dry season. Food insecurity was worse for female-headed households and small landholders. Farmers who belonged to producer organizations suffered less chronic hunger than those who did not.

Twenty percent of the farmers indicated that access to cash or growing cash crops made a big difference in their ability to achieve food security. To increase income, they produced different crops, did piece work for others, or sold their assets. The smaller their plot of land, the more likely they were to resort to nonagricultural sources of income.

> **Before I joined a club for farmers, I was facing difficulties attaining food security. Since joining, I have access to credit, which allowed me to expand my food production and income through tobacco sales. The problem I face now is that during times of heavy rains, leaching of fertilizer reduces my yields.[1]**
>
> — MALAWI FARMER

As part of the study, NASFAM hosted a food security forum for farmers, donors, Malawi government officials, and NGOs. Farmers said that access to information about market cycles, price fluctuations, and cash crop production techniques would boost their productivity. Above all, farmers said they needed access to information and credit.

Farmers joined associations to benefit from shared marketing and to learn new techniques. The farmers agreed that when they organized, they could lower costs and become more competitive. Membership in a producer organization raised incomes and provided new training and social benefits. The farmers said they needed crop diversification, more land, and alternative forms of agricultural research and extension services. They also stated that:

- Additional education and small business opportunities would aid the most vulnerable rural populations.

- Producer clubs should reach out to women and smaller landholders, provide more diverse training opportunities, and become more involved in the public policy dialogues that affect members.

- NGOs could do a better job of providing the information and skills needed by vulnerable populations.

- Government should facilitate development opportunities for women and vulnerable smallholders in general, support producer organizations, stabilize markets and prices, and provide reliable information to help farmers choose what to produce.

Dr. Kuchinsky coordinates BFW Institute's Africa Food Security Project.

[1] Jennifer Peterson and Chigomezgo-Lizzie Mtehga. *Smallholder Farmer Household Food Security in Malawi*, April 2000, a report to BFW Institute's Africa Food Security Project.

© Michael Kuchinsky

and account for 11 percent of the disease burden.[21] Maternal mortality rates in sub-Saharan Africa range between 600 and 1,500 per 100,000 women, the highest in the world.

Increased investments in public primary health care will also improve nutrition and food security. Africans have less access to safe water and sanitation facilities than people anywhere in the world, and the worst conditions are in rural villages. Improving public sanitation could save millions of lives.

HIV/AIDS Epidemic

AIDS has been a huge setback for Africa. By the end of 1999, 24 million of the world's 34 million adults and children living with HIV/AIDS were in sub-Saharan Africa – over 70 percent of the world's infected persons. AIDS is killing millions of people in their prime (2.2 million in 1999), and crippling economic development. As teachers, managers, and trained health personnel die of AIDS, the education, business, and health sectors lose the talents of the very people whose creativity, commitment, and labor keep countries dynamic.

The impact of HIV/AIDS on agriculture and household food security is especially alarming. In Africa, the majority of AIDS victims have been people between 20 and 50 years of age. As these caregivers and providers die, they leave a huge generation gap. AIDS orphans and the elderly are left without the support of the middle generation, a dynamic that has dire implications for household food security and human development. Currently, there are 12 million AIDS orphans in sub-Saharan Africa.[22]

> **The U.S. is panicking over the AIDS crisis in Africa, but the basic problem in Africa is malnutrition. If we want to build a healthy, peaceful, and prosperous Africa, we must guarantee its people the fundamental right to an adequate diet.**
> —FORMER U.N. AMBASSADOR ANDREW YOUNG
> CHAIRMAN, GOODWORKS INTERNATIONAL

> **When a lion comes into your village, you must raise the alarm loudly. This is what we did in Uganda; we took [AIDS] seriously and we achieved good results. AIDS. . .is not like smallpox or ebola. AIDS can be prevented, as it is transmitted in a few known ways. If we raise awareness sufficiently, it will stop.[24]**
> —UGANDAN PRESIDENT YOWERI MUSEVENI

Recognizing the damaging impact of the AIDS pandemic on national development, the government of Uganda was the first in Africa to tackle HIV/AIDS. Following strong presidential leadership, political, religious, and community leaders launched a public education campaign in local languages through churches, mosques, schools, radio, and television. The empowerment of women has been highly effective in fighting the AIDS epidemic. Uganda has brought its estimated prevalence rate down from 14 percent to 8 percent.[23]

Botswana's HIV/AIDS policy includes house-to-house counseling to reach all families; raising awareness through the school curriculum; and providing voluntary testing, counseling, and drugs for the treatment of AIDS-related illnesses.

Improve Infrastructure

Colonial administrations invested in roads, rail lines, and other infrastructure designed to serve extractive industries and commodity exports to Europe, not to facilitate commerce within and between countries in Africa. Natural disasters like the recent flood in Mozambique have washed away bridges, twisted and relocated train tracks, and destroyed paved roads. Economic constraints and war have hindered the development and maintenance of the continent's limited, antiquated transportation infrastructure.

Yet good roads, transportation, and communications can make the difference between life and

Microcredit Helps Uganda's AIDS Orphans

BY ANTHONY MATTHEWS

One in every four families in Uganda cares for a child orphaned by AIDS. With per capita income in Uganda at roughly $300 a year, new mouths to feed and minds to educate put tremendous strain on household resources.

With the technical expertise of the International Fund for Agricultural Development (IFAD) and financial support from the Belgian Survival Fund, the Ugandan Women's Effort to Save Orphans (UWESO) has pioneered the use of microcredit to help Uganda take care of its children.

UWESO was founded in 1986 by First Lady Janet Kataha Museveni to provide food, clothing, blankets, and other necessities to children orphaned by Uganda's civil conflict. By 1990, UWESO realized that its original relief approach was no longer working. The AIDS epidemic was shattering Ugandan families and the support system they once offered. So UWESO began working with IFAD to transform itself into a development organization.

By linking AIDS with microfinance, UWESO's Savings and Credit Scheme has enabled adoptive families of AIDS orphans to provide for them since 1996. UWESO provides microcredit only to rural AIDS-affected families caring for orphans. It has provided loans to 6,447 clients who care for more than 30,000 AIDS orphans. All clients who receive loans from UWESO live below the poverty line.

UWESO uses a "solidarity group lending" approach. It gathers clients, 90 percent of whom are women, into small groups, then gathers 10 of these groups into "clusters" that meet for about an hour a week. Clients learn principles of business and loan management. After 10 weeks clients can access their first loan. The interest rate is 3 percent per month. Payments are made weekly over four months. UWESO has a 90 percent repayment rate.

Sixty-five year old Namayanja Paulina can testify to the success of UWESO's microcredit program. Six of her sons have died from AIDS. This left Namayanja struggling to provide for the 16 young children they left behind. The safety net once provided by her extended family had vanished.

© IFAD photo by Denise Hughes

Then, Namayanja learned about UWESO's microcredit program from one of its local volunteers. She joined UWESO's Savings and Credit Scheme last April, and took out two loans. The first was for $55 and the second for $100. With this money, she expanded her business selling bananas. From her home, Namayanja also sells soap, cooking oil, matches, kerosene, and other basic goods to villagers who would otherwise have to walk many miles into town.

"Now I give my children three meals a day, I can afford their school fees, and people ask me for money," she says with pride.

Namayanja has never been late making payments on her loans. Each week, she earns up to $5.50. She plans to continue borrowing from UWESO to build a small shop for her growing business. That way, her grandchildren will be able support themselves when she dies.

Mr. Matthews is the media and NGO liaison officer at IFAD/Washington, DC.

HIV/AIDS and Hunger in Sub-Saharan Africa

BY EILEEN STILLWAGGON

"The microbe is nothing, the terrain everything."
— Louis Pasteur

Eradicating hunger is one way to help stop the AIDS catastrophe that now engulfs sub-Saharan Africa. In Zimbabwe, life expectancy has fallen from 59 to 39 years in less than a decade, and South Africa, Zambia, and Botswana face similar declines. More than one-third of people in sub-Saharan Africa will not reach age 40. HIV prevalence among adults exceeds 5 percent in 24 African countries; 20 percent of adults are HIV-positive in Zambia, Namibia, and South Africa; and more than 25 percent of adults are infected with HIV in Zimbabwe and Botswana.

Chronic poverty and hunger play a role in every health crisis in Africa, and AIDS is no exception. HIV/AIDS shares with other infectious diseases the opportunist tendency to prey on people with weakened immune systems. Host factors (Pasteur's terrain) are important determinants of infectious disease transmission. For people who are malnourished, each sexual contact is more likely to transmit HIV, regardless of the number of contacts.

Although HIV is transmitted sexually, differences in sexual behavior cannot explain the extremely high rate of HIV transmission in Africa or its more rapid progression to AIDS and death. Western assumptions about African sexuality are not supported by comparative data on rates of partner change or other aspects of sexual behavior. A narrow focus on sexual behavior diverts attention from conditions in Africa that contribute to higher rates of illness and death.

Malnutrition undermines immunity and fuels the AIDS pandemic. One-third of African children under the age of 5 are underweight and suffer from various degrees of protein and calorie deficit. Protein-energy malnutrition (PEM) and deficiencies in iron, zinc, and vitamins increase susceptibility to infectious and parasitic diseases. Even moderate PEM weakens the skin and mucous membranes, which are the body's first line of defense against infection because they impede the entry of pathogens.

Micronutrient deficiencies significantly weaken every component of the immune system. Iron is essential for resistance to infection, promoting production of B cells, T cells, and Natural Killer (NK) cells. Vitamin A, a super-vitamin for the immune system, is important to healthy skin and mucous membranes and to production of NK and T cells. Protein-energy malnutrition, vitamin-A deficiency, iron-deficiency anemia — especially common in women and children — are widespread in sub-Saharan Africa.

Parasitic diseases such as malaria, schistosomiasis, and hookworm are transmitted by insects or in water or food, and are endemic in tropical and subtropical Africa. Parasite infestation is almost universal among poor people in the developing world. It aggravates anemia and decreases resistance to other diseases because it chronically activates the immune system, impairing its ability to fight infection from other pathogens.

From 1988 to 1998, when nascent or concentrated AIDS epidemics escalated in sub-Saharan Africa, 30 percent of the population was malnourished. Of 19 famines worldwide from 1975 to 1998, 18 were in Africa. Sub-Saharan Africa was the only region to experience a decrease in calorie supply from 1970 to 1997. In Zimbabwe, per capita daily supply of calories fell by 4 percent; Zambia, Kenya, and Uganda all had decreases of around 10 percent. In Malawi, calorie supply fell by more than 13 percent, and in the Central African Republic, the decrease was 16 percent.

Sub-Saharan Africa was also the only region to suffer a decrease in daily protein supply per capita — a drop of more than 4 percent — with supply falling in 25 countries. In 10 countries (including Zimbabwe, Kenya, Uganda, Zambia, and Malawi), protein supply fell by more than 15 percent from 1970 to 1997. Among all low- and middle-income countries, HIV prevalence correlates strongly with falling protein and calorie consumption, unequal distribution of national income, and labor migration.

Like any other infectious disease, HIV is most easily transmitted to a host whose immune system is weakened by malnutrition and by the negative synergistic effects of other infectious and parasitic diseases. Nutrition is certainly not the only factor influencing the course of the HIV pandemic, nor is HIV a nutritional disease like pellagra or scurvy. But the same health and hygiene factors that contribute to morbidity and mortality from other infectious diseases fuel the HIV/AIDS epidemic in sub-Saharan Africa.

Because of malnutrition, parasite infection, and the lack of health care for other sexually transmitted diseases, poor people are at greater risk of HIV infection. An effective strategy for AIDS prevention, therefore, must end hunger and be part of a comprehensive campaign for good health. That is not as expensive or as hopeless as it might seem. A year's vitamin-A supplementation sufficient to prevent blindness and strengthen the immune system for one person costs less than one condom. Fortifying foods with iron to prevent anemia and increase disease resistance costs about 20 cents per person per year. Hunger claims its victims in many ways; people who do not die outright of starvation provide fertile terrain for disease.

Dr. Stillwaggon is Assistant Professor of Economics at Gettysburg College. E-mail: estillwa@gettysburg.edu.

death. During floods and drought, food, medicines, and vital equipment must reach those affected. Adequate infrastructure also makes it possible to access new markets, to buy needed inputs, to attend school, and to get to the doctor.

Infrastructure is essential to African women, who work 65 percent more hours than men in Kenya and twice as many hours as men in Cameroon and Guinea Bissau. "In Uganda, women produce 80 percent of the food and 70 percent of the agricultural labor. Similarly, village surveys in Burkina Faso, Uganda, and Zambia have found that women move, on average, 26 metric ton-kilometers a year (especially water and firewood) compared with less than 7 metric ton-kilometers for men."[25] For many, water scarcity means daily hardships. "We have to spend more than an hour to fetch and bring a pot of water," say villagers of Dibdibe Wajtu, Ethiopia. In Netarhat, India, women trek two kilometers to fetch water and face many risks along the way. . .[26]

Transportation infrastructure would reduce the time women spend on their chores, freeing them to go to school, increase agricultural productivity, improve market opportunities, access social services, and engage in nonagricultural employment.[27]

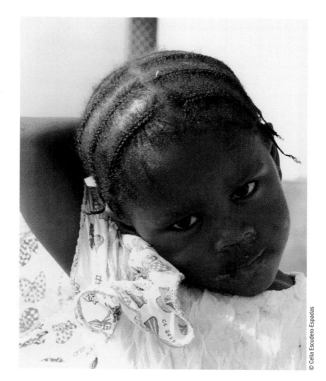

© Celia Escudero-Espadas

Credit and Microenterprise

The U.S. government has played a key role in promoting microcredit over the past decade. It works. Repayment rates average over 90 percent. From the Grameen Bank's small beginnings in Bangladesh, microcredit has expanded to improve the lives of millions throughout the world. In the past, rural and agricultural communities have had little access to loans. Potential lenders claimed there was too much risk due to uncertain weather and harvest yields.

Many large international NGOs provide microcredit either directly, through their indigenous partner NGOs, or through informal women's groups. These small, informal, community-based organizations remain one of the most effective and trusted institutions for the rural poor. ACDI/VOCA and the Cooperative Leagues of the U.S.A.

provide rural credit to farmers belonging to producer organizations, particularly in Zambia and Mozambique. USAID's microenterprise development office brings new credit to underserved regions. But funding remains limited. Additional resources can expand these efforts and target the most vulnerable groups and locations.

With the *Africa: Seeds of Hope* legislation, Congress urged the Overseas Private Investment Corporation (OPIC) to support and encourage U.S. businesses and PVOs investing in small and middle-sized businesses, particularly in rural Africa. OPIC's People's Investment Fund for Africa provided matching funds for microenterprise. OPIC also lent $1.8 million to a California company to invest in Ugandan chrysanthemum farmers, many of whom were women. However, there is still some uncertainty about the logistics of how OPIC will work with PVOs and their African partners.[28]

Strengthen Institutional Capacity

Government institutions give poor people access to information, public services, and protection under the law. Where inadequate infrastructure and distribution networks, unresponsive bureaucracies, or other factors cause interruptions in the supply of goods and services, bribery is often the most effective way to meet essential needs. This has contributed to widespread corruption in many countries.

The private sector is weak in most sub-Saharan African countries. Foreigners dominated business in the pre-independence era and many African governments overregulated economic life in the 1960s and 1970s. They launched a host of state-owned enterprises, most of which never turned a profit. In the 1980s and 1990s, most African governments relied on markets and the private sector. The transition has sometimes caused hardship. The precise balance between the private sector and the government is a matter for debate in each country, but both governmental institutions and businesses need to be strengthened.

The Constituency to Cut Hunger in Africa

Three broad interest groups are coalescing to push for U.S. leadership to cut hunger in Africa. The first is composed of religious and humanitarian groups – the Roman Catholic Church, Protestant church bodies, and humanitarian agencies like Catholic Relief Services, Lutheran World Relief, Oxfam, World Vision, and

Gambians participate in a women's health seminar organized by Peace Corps volunteers.

InterAction. Many of these groups worked together to win U.S. support for debt relief.

They could now join forces with African-American groups, such as the Constituency for Africa, which helped pass the *Africa Trade Bill* in 2000. African ambassadors, African-American members of Congress, and corporations that do business in Africa, such as Coca Cola, Chevron, and Cargill, worked hard to pass the *Africa Trade Bill*.

The Jubilee and trade bill constituencies for Africa have distinct emphases. The religious groups focus on reducing poverty and hunger, and are sensitive to the negative social impact that unchecked pro-market, pro-trade reforms can have. The *Africa Trade Bill* constituency focuses more on the overall progress of Africa. But these differences should not keep them from joining forces. The two constituencies could now work together to increase poverty-focused aid to Africa.

The U.S. agricultural community is a third emerging constituency. Some researchers at U.S. universities work on African agriculture, but U.S. government support for international agricultural research is much less than it once was. Researchers have organized to revive U.S. aid to African agriculture and are enlisting support from the U.S. agricultural community more generally. As East Asia reduced hunger over the last generation, that region became an important market for U.S. agriculture. In the same way, reducing hunger in Africa would provide a growing market for U.S. farmers and agribusiness.

In early 2000, Peter McPherson, former administrator of USAID under President Reagan and current president of Michigan State University, started the Partnership to Cut Hunger in Africa. Leaders from the three constituencies have committed themselves to this partnership. The goals are to develop a proposal for U.S. assistance to help cut hunger in Africa and a broad constituency to promote the proposal. The partnership began by consulting African leaders of government, agriculture, religion, and development agencies and continues as a series of activities to promote support for a U.S. initiative to help reduce hunger in Africa.

Meanwhile, a number of African governments are developing their own proposals for a new

Bread for the World Takes Action for Africa

BY RAY ALMEIDA

Bread for the World's commitment to justice and development in Africa goes back many years and will continue until current trends are reversed.

1983–1985: Bread for the World (BFW) joined with church and community organizations to publicize the horror of the famine across the Sahel region. BFW lobbied the U.S. government to create the Development Fund for Africa and to increase funding levels to support grassroots activities.

1986–1990: BFW participated in the anti-apartheid movement. Acting in concert with TransAfrica, the Washington Office on Africa, and the church-led Southern Africa Working Group, BFW won $800 million in emergency assistance for the Horn of Africa.

1991–1992: BFW led the fight to pass the *Horn of Africa Recovery and Food Security Act*, which conditioned aid to the war-torn region on peace, human rights, democracy, and grassroots development.

1995: BFW led the *Africa: Crisis to Opportunity* campaign to maintain resources for self-help development, conflict resolution, and debt relief.

1998: BFW activists lobbied their members of Congress to pass the *Africa: Seeds of Hope Act* to help small-scale farmers. With this legislative victory, Congress and the American people reinforced U.S. commitment to African agriculture for broad-based, equitable development.

1999–2000: BFW members worked with the international Jubilee 2000 movement to cancel the debt of the world's poorest countries, most of which are in Africa. With support from the Ford Foundation, BFW Institute launched a two-year study of the effects of economic liberalization policies on smallholder farmers in Malawi and Mozambique.

BFW photo

2001: BFW has joined with a broad coalition of universities and agriculture groups in the *Partnership to Cut Hunger in Africa*. The partnership aims to win new resources for poverty-focused development assistance. BFW's 2001 Offering of Letters campaign, *Africa: Hunger to Harvest*, seeks a strengthened U.S. commitment to reducing hunger in Africa, including continued funding for debt relief and an increase of $1 billion in poverty-focused assistance.

Mr. Almeida is Bread for the World's Senior Policy Analyst for Africa.

global compact for Africa. They are stressing what Africans themselves have to do and calling on the industrialized countries to increase development assistance, debt reduction, and trade opportunities. U.N. Secretary General Kofi Annan has also been proposing a special effort by the international community to keep Africa from falling behind the rest of the world. British Prime Minister Tony Blair is initiating discussions among European governments and intends to bring an Africa proposal to the G-8 summit in July 2001.

Bread for the World has launched a campaign to get Congress to commit the United States to reduce hunger in Africa and increase poverty-focused assistance to Africa by $1 billion a year. This campaign is called *Africa: Hunger to Harvest*. Bread for the World is calling on President George W. Bush to lead a global effort to reduce hunger in Africa. A modest shift in the priorities of the United States could significantly improve the prospects of tens of millions of people in Africa who are struggling to escape abject poverty and hunger.

CHAPTER 7

Hunger Hotspots 2000

BY MARGARET ZEIGLER

Hunger hotspots emerge when large numbers of people in a region can no longer employ their usual coping mechanisms to obtain food. They are "hot" because the number of hungry people quickly increases or because hunger grows more severe. Households may not have the income to purchase enough food for survival or they may have neither the resources nor the ability to produce their own food. The triggers that ignite hunger hotspots may be economic upheavals, environmental disasters, political strife, or some combination of these events.

Very poor countries are most likely to become hotspots partly because many of their citizens live near the edge and struggle with hunger even in normal times. Any change for the worse can push vulnerable families into complete destitution. Very poor countries are also more likely to spawn violent conflict, which disrupts agriculture and can completely destroy development efforts.

© WARDA

During the Cold War, the West and the Soviet bloc were quick to get involved in situations of instability in an effort to keep the other side from using crises to gain influence. But since the late 1980s, the big powers have left developing countries in crisis to cope on their own. To keep pace with these post-Cold War shocks, emergency food aid to the developing world has increased dramatically from a low of 1.7 million tons in 1989 to almost 5 million tons in 1999.[1]

Increased development aid could curb the proliferation of hunger hotspots, but food aid and emergency assistance are vital in the short term.

Economic Shocks

Countries that have little connection to the global economy tend to be poorer and less able to draw on imports or international borrowing to cushion themselves against domestic economic crises. Countries that have shared in globalization face different vulnerabilities. Foreign markets for their goods can decline. Foreign investors may suddenly remove their capital from a fragile economy and precipitate economic collapse in a country or region within weeks.

The Asian financial crisis of the late 1990s pushed millions in the region out of an emerging middle class into poverty levels not seen since the 1960s. In 1999, the Republic of Korea stabilized with some promising signs of economic growth. The Philippines and Thailand are slowly recovering. However, Indonesia is still struggling with the aftermath of the financial crisis and has become more dependent on outside emergency food assistance.

Environmental Shocks

Environmental disruptions affect millions of people each year, destroying homes and killing livestock and crops. In 1999 and 2000, the United Nations humanitarian agencies declared 17 major drought-related emergencies and 55 major flood-related disasters.[2]

In poor countries, population growth has pushed increasing numbers of people into environmentally precarious situations, such as drylands prone to drought and hillsides vulnerable to mudslides. Environmental disasters are on the increase and often strike the poorest people hardest.

The Famine That Never Happened

Climate variations known as the El Niño and Southern Oscillation (ENSO) occur when unusually warm water temperatures prevail over large areas of the Pacific Ocean, which then create irregular patterns of drought across Indonesia, India, and Southern Africa, and flooding in Peru, Ecuador, Bolivia, and Chile.

Food shortages caused by ENSO can be prevented. In 1991-92, early warning mechanisms that monitored the ENSO alerted African nations to the threat of drought. In response, humanitarian organizations and the national governments of Lesotho, Malawi, Mozambique, Namibia, South Africa, Swaziland, Zambia, and Zimbabwe worked together to mount a comprehensive food-aid operation that forestalled large-scale loss of life. Donors such as the United States and the European Union provided funds and emergency cereals for transport and distribution directly or via the United Nations World Food Program (WFP) and NGOs.

Climatologists recognized the same patterns of rain failure in 1994/95 and again in 1997/98, making prevention and preparedness strategies possible throughout southern Africa. Farmers and poor households now monitor climatic indicators to reduce the risk of crop loss and stockpile grain in the event of crop failure.

Two regional droughts during the year 2000 affected over 80 million people. Media sources have been covering the two-year drought in East Africa and the Horn of Africa, where 20 million pastoralists and small shareholders in Kenya, Ethiopia, Eritrea, and Somalia have lost harvests and herds. But the media have virtually ignored the drought spreading across northern India, Tajikistan, Pakistan, Afghanistan, and Iran, despite the fact that some 60 million people are affected. Humanitarian organizations have sounded the alarm, but immediate action will be necessary to prevent food shortages and mass migration during 2001.

Political Shocks

In the second half of 2000, some 21 countries and the Great Lakes region of Africa suffered the ravages of complex humanitarian emergencies (CHEs).[3] The number of countries across the globe impacted by CHEs in the wake of the Cold War hovers between 15 and 22 per year, down slightly from a record high of 26 in 1994. While Kosovo and East Timor have attracted major media coverage and relatively rapid response,

School feeding program in Malawi.

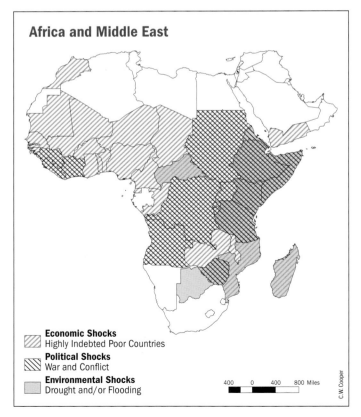

Africa and Middle East

Economic Shocks
Highly Indebted Poor Countries

Political Shocks
War and Conflict

Environmental Shocks
Drought and/or Flooding

400   0   400   800 Miles

C.W. Cooper

long-running conflicts in Sudan and Angola have faded into the background. CHEs represent the most difficult type of hunger hotspot to manage, with some civilian populations remaining dependent on outside food assistance for many years.

Other hunger hotspots emerged due to sanctions against countries such as Iraq and Cuba. The blockade on importing food and medicines into these countries caused health problems for children and the elderly. Due to starvation in North Korea, the United States relaxed 50 years of restrictions on imports of most consumer goods and food products. Ending sanctions has not ended hunger for North Korea, but has alleviated the worst deprivation for innocent civilians.

Hunger Status by Region[4]

Africa: The Triple Threat of Climate, Conflict, and Debt

Economic, environmental, and political shocks have combined in many African countries to produce hunger hotspots that will remain with us for years. Chronic poverty, a heavy burden of external debt, severe weather patterns, and conflicts strain many African countries. Of the 52 countries identified by the Jubilee 2000 campaign as needing immediate debt relief,[5] 36 are located in sub-Saharan Africa. Twenty-three percent of the world's hungry people, some 186 million, live in sub-Saharan Africa.[6] Unlike most other regions, hunger in Africa has increased in the past decade.

In East Africa, political conflict and war have exacerbated hunger in Rwanda, Burundi, Eritrea, Ethiopia, Somalia, and Kenya. Sudan suffers the long-term effects of a 15-year civil war. A border war between Ethiopia and Eritrea further complicates the effect of the two-year drought cycle ravaging these countries. The drought is creating hunger in Somalia and northern Kenya as well. The people of East Africa will continue to require food aid targeting children and the elderly in rural areas.

In Central Africa, people in the Democratic Republic of Congo suffer from the intensification of civil war. The resulting disruption of agricultural production is most serious for over 1 million internally displaced people. Access to these internally displaced persons continues to challenge

When the Fighting Stops: Sowing Seeds of Hope in Sierra Leone

BY DAVIDSON JONAH

Sierra Leone's farmers managed to cultivate some rice despite ongoing civil war, only to lose every bit of it to systematic looting by soldiers who prematurely harvested rice, cassava, and potato from community farms and recklessly left cassava sticks and vines to dry up. Even the seeds the farmers had stored were stolen or burned. Sierra Leone's agriculture was destroyed by the wanton chaos of war.

Even in periods of relative stability, food security is tenuous. The reasons: inadequate supplies of seed rice, poor produce management, and large households that consume seed rice meant for the next farming season.

To reactivate farming, Christian Children's Fund (CCF) formed food security committees in 17 communities. The committees identified and registered farmers, and distributed tools, seeds, and planting materials. Rebel activity had forced people to flee, disrupting relief activities. However, in the relatively stable Mile 91 zone, the effort to reestablish agriculture is going according to plan.

CCF furnished 200 bushels of rice and 100 bushels of groundnuts in five communities in Mile 91 zone, which were augmented by 100 bushels of rice and 100 bushels of groundnuts from Sierra Leone's National Commission for Resettlement, Rehabilitation, and Reconstruction. Each community received food, 100 hoes, 50 machetes, cassava cuttings, and potato vines. In the end, 2,500 farmers benefited in 11 communities.

The farmers have planted their seeds and are looking forward to a good harvest next year. They are especially gratified by the creation of seed and tool banks, which never existed before, and a livestock management program. As the farmers of Sierra Leone return to work their fields, agriculture will provide not only food and income for this war-torn country, but also a harvest of hope for the future.

Mr. Jonah, an agriculture education specialist, is CCF program manager in Sierra Leone.

humanitarian aid agencies. The sheer size and difficult terrain of the country and the ongoing hostilities complicate the distribution of emergency aid.

In West Africa, the primary hunger hotspots remain the tiny countries of Liberia and Sierra Leone. Sierra Leone is attempting to recover and rebuild from a brutal eight-year civil war, but the U.N. peacekeeping mission in Sierra Leone has yet to ensure a countrywide peace. Emergency food aid is required for the eastern and northern parts of the country, where rebels of the Revolutionary United Front still hold power. The rebels have blocked humanitarian assistance missions. Poor road conditions and the arrival of a rainy season will exacerbate this hunger hotspot in 2001.

In southern Africa, Botswana, Lesotho, Malawi, South Africa, and Zambia will have adequate supplies of locally grown cereals and crops in 2001. But Madagascar and Mozambique face major food shortages due to devastating floods caused by tropical storms. One million people are expected to require emergency food assistance in these two countries during 2001. Hunger also increased in Zimbabwe due to political violence and in Angola due to civil war. In Zimbabwe, a major maize and tobacco exporting country, poor landless farmers have seized commercial farms in actions orchestrated by President Mugabe's government. Commercial farmers are abandoning their land and livestock and fleeing to urban areas for safety, lowering Zimbabwe's cereal output in 2001.

In Angola, renewed civil conflict and massive population displacement are putting over 2.6 million people at risk in 2001. Media coverage of this emergency has waned over the past decade due to "compassion fatigue" and the emergence of other hotspots in politically strategic regions such as the Balkans. During the second half of 2000, peacebuilding efforts led by NGOs and faith-based institutions sought a permanent peace in Angola; if these efforts fail, millions of Angolans will continue to endure lives of misery and wasted potential.

Floods in Southern Africa

BY KATHLEEN BULGER

In February 2000, heavy rains and cyclones swept southern Africa, destroying homes and schools. Three thousand miles of main road and acres of cropland disappeared under waves of muddy water. One-third of all cattle and a quarter of all crops were lost. In Mozambique and surrounding countries, more than 1 million people were stranded without food or potable water. Illness and hunger spread rapidly, threatening to increase an already alarming death toll. By the end of March, the devastation seemed as endless as the rain.

Continuous destruction of wetlands, overgrazing of grasslands, and rapid urbanization had decreased the region's ability to absorb water and to mediate the flooding. Too quickly, large volumes of water flowed out of the river basins in South Africa and Zimbabwe, swelled with heavy rains farther south, and poured into the Limpopo, Save, and Buzi Rivers of Mozambique. These factors combined to cause the worst flooding ever recorded in the region, leaving hundreds dead and thousands homeless.

© Alfredo Mazieve

© Alfredo Mazieve

Relief agencies scrambled to respond. African, European, and North American aid teams began to rescue the more than 14,000 people marooned atop trees, roofs, and utility poles. United Nations agencies and nongovernmental organizations delivered food and medical supplies to stop the spread of malaria and cholera. Foreign aid supplied drinking water, fuel, shelter, and medical care to more than 650,000 displaced people who had traveled to refugee camps. Such immediate assistance was essential to the survival of these families while they waited for the floods to subside.

Now that the waters have receded and displaced families have returned to their communities, a different kind of assistance is necessary. Mozambique must rebuild roads and schools, assist farmers, and counter the health problems caused by disruptions to medical services and water sources. Recovery will be slow and costly. Continued foreign aid is needed to support reconstruction through programs such as debt relief, agricultural development, medical aid, and basic construction projects. Environmental protection and land management assistance can help prevent future floods.

Humanitarian organizations, governments, and southern Africans stood up to the raging floodwaters and saved the lives of thousands. Working together, they continue the struggle to return Mozambique to dry land.

Ms. Bulger, a Mickey Leland Hunger Fellow with the Congressional Hunger Center, was a research assistant at BFW Institute in 2000.

Asia: Drought Hurts Millions

In 1999 and 2000, Asia faced the worst drought in decades. Natural disaster, endemic poverty, and the financial crisis of 1997 stretch Asia's hunger hotspots across a wide swath of the region.

Over one-third of the world's chronically hungry people live in South Asia. India, Bangladesh, Nepal, Pakistan, and Sri Lanka together have 294 million hungry persons. Half of all South Asian children are underweight, the highest percentage in any world region. Another 221 million chronically hungry people live in East Asia, Oceania, and Southeast Asia.

In India, long-term drought affected 50 million people in the states of Rajasthan, Gujarat, Orissa, Andhra Pradesh, and Madhya Pradesh. Water for irrigation and human consumption is unavailable, prompting millions of farmers to migrate in search of work. Production of coarse grains, groundnuts, and lentils declined by 50 percent. Ironically, in the second half of 2000, massive monsoon rainstorms began a pattern of flooding across India, pounding the states of Assam, Bihar, West Bengal, Gujarat, Andhra Pradesh, Kerala, and Uttar Pradesh.

Bangladesh, a low-lying country at the confluence of the Brahmaputra, Ganges, and Meghna rivers, receives the runoff from the Indian floods, which are the result of heavy monsoon rains and river erosion from poor land management in the Himalayas and northern India. With the highest population density in the world, some 1.2 million poor farmers in Bangladesh are struggling to rebuild their homes and find work in their flooded country.

The drought of 1999-2000 has posed a serious challenge to China's recent impressive gains in food production. Wheat, maize, and rice production fell. Locusts have destroyed 1 million hectares of farmland. In Mongolia, farmers face a second severe winter after the sub-zero temperatures of 1999-2000 killed close to 3 million animals. Almost one-third of Mongolia's 2.4 million inhabitants are pastoralists who depend on their herds for livelihood. The drought of 1999-2000 is weakening the remaining herds, and if the winter of 2000-2001 is as severe as the previous year, a catastrophe looms.

In Pakistan, almost 2 million people in the province of Baluchistan have been affected by

School feeding program in China.

drought and 2 million livestock have perished. In nearby Sindh province, an estimated 700,000 people and 5 million livestock have been affected. Livestock prices have declined tenfold, depriving many people of the income to buy food, even when it is available. The U.N. is working with the government of Pakistan to set up disaster management committees composed of local people,

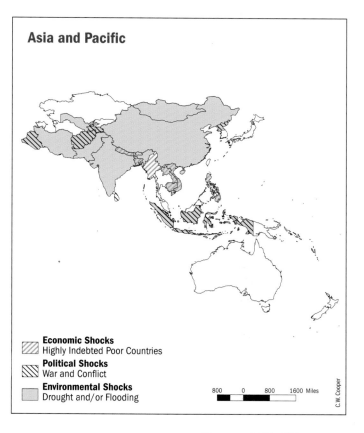

Asia and Pacific

Economic Shocks
Highly Indebted Poor Countries

Political Shocks
War and Conflict

Environmental Shocks
Drought and/or Flooding

800   0   800   1600 Miles

C.W. Cooper

along with representatives from UNICEF, WFP, FAO, and the World Health Organization.

Indonesia, an archipelago of thousands of islands, poses a unique dilemma in 2001. With the end of the Suharto regime, the nation must democratize and decentralize without losing territory and people to separatist movements. East Timor's 1999 vote to secede from Indonesia unleashed violent militia attacks from Indonesian loyalists that triggered an armed intervention by Australian military to prevent mass murder. Ongoing attacks by former militias and paramilitaries operating from West Timor have prevented reconstruction and rehabilitation of the agricultural sector, keeping East Timor dependent on some food assistance during 2001.

North Korea continues to experience food shortages due to floods and a centrally planned economy that has not modernized and reformed its agriculture sector. North Korea needs massive food aid for almost 5 million vulnerable children, pregnant and lactating women, and the elderly. An estimated 2 million North Koreans have died due to malnutrition and disease since 1994. Twenty-two percent of North Korea's 22 million people are now receiving supplemental rations. Recently, North Korea has engaged in talks with the U.S., Japan, Italy, and South Korea. These steps will likely ensure more food aid in 2001, but the need for ongoing structural reforms and trade is paramount in achieving a greater degree of food security for the people of North Korea.

The Near East and North Africa: Pockets of Hunger

Afghanistan, Iran, Iraq, and Yemen face serious hunger problems while the other countries of the Near East and North Africa have adequate food supplies or can purchase food. These four countries account for 78 percent of the 36 million chronically hungry people in the region. Afghanistan has the least ability to cope with drought. Two decades of civil war and the oppressive restrictions of the Taliban government have made life nothing short of misery for women and children. Women who once fed their families are no longer allowed to work outside the home. In 2000, drought caused the Afghan wheat and barley crop to fail and rice and maize

Afghan girl outside a refugee camp in Takhar Province.

yields to be much lower than in prior years. The WFP is reaching over 1.2 million beneficiaries in Afghanistan with food-for-work and food-for-seed projects, and relief feeding of pregnant women and children.

In Iran, farmers had lost more than 800,000 cattle by the second half of 2000, prompting nomadic herders to migrate to cities in search of work, swelling the ranks of the urban poor. Iran also suffered from a 25 percent reduction in its wheat crop in 2000. Eighteen of Iran's 28 provinces have been hit hard by drought.

Iraq has been under international economic sanctions for 10 years. The U.N. developed an oil-for-food program to allow Iraq to sell some of its oil in order to purchase medicine and food. But two directors of the U.N. program have quit in protest over the increasing cost of the sanctions in human lives. To make matters worse, a three-year drought has reduced domestic cereal yields.

Egypt, Jordan, and Syria, all low-income, food-deficit countries, faced serious food shortages in 2000. In the occupied territories of Gaza and the West Bank, long-term unemployment and lack of external investment have prevented Palestinians from achieving their full economic potential. Supplemental community food programs and improvements in agricultural productivity have provided a safety net for woman-headed households, the most impoverished residents of Palestine.

In Yemen, one of the region's least developed low-income food-deficit countries, a large gender gap in nutritional status and literacy contributes to high rates of infant and maternal mortality. Yemen and Morocco both need debt relief to improve food security.

Eastern Europe and the Commonwealth of Independent States (CIS): Pockets of Conflict

The former Yugoslavia and the Chechen Republic remain the primary hunger hotspots in Eastern Europe and the CIS, though the entire region suffers from drought. In Kosovo, a province of Serbia, the agricultural system was disrupted in the spring of 1999 when the Serbian army and paramilitary groups began a campaign of terror against the ethnic Albanian population. In just a few months, close to 1 million refugees fled Kosovo to neighboring Albania and Macedonia, then repatriated rapidly beginning in June 1999. While Kosovo's emergency food supplies remain adequate, the rehabilitation of agriculture and livestock will take time.

In Serbia itself, sanctions resulting from former President Slobodan Milosevic's aggression created hardship for almost 2 million civilians. The NATO bombing of power plants and transportation facilities in Serbia set the country back decades in economic development and agricultural production. According to a joint FAO and WFP assessment, food supplies will decrease in 2001 and prices for food will rise, increasing dependency on outside humanitarian food assistance. Displaced Serbs from Kosovo and from the earlier wars in Bosnia and Croatia require special assistance within Serbia.

The CIS has abundant natural resources and the potential for adequate agricultural production. But chronic structural poverty, decades of mismanagement, and the collapse of the centrally planned economy have compromised food security for the majority of Russians. Since the Soviet Union ended in 1991, land reform and market liberalization have proceeded slowly, with under- and unemployment rendering millions food insecure.

Russia has waged a multi-year war against Chechnya, using heavy weapons and a scorched-earth policy. More than 500,000 civilians in Chechnya have been displaced and need urgent humanitarian assistance. Until the second half of 2000, most civilians inside Chechnya proper could not be reached by humanitarian organizations. The devastation of the economy and agricultural sector is so complete that the capital and surrounding region may take decades to recover. Unlike Kosovo, where the response of the international community was swift and massive, Chechen civilians remain underserved because of their location within the Russian Federation and the Russian government's refusal to allow access.

Tajikistan, making a difficult transition from a centrally planned Soviet state to a market economy, was hard hit by the regional drought. With a shortage of capital and inputs such as irrigation methods, fertilizer, and equipment, the farming sector has been unable to increase yields. Over 1 million people will require emergency humanitarian assistance through the WFP in 2001.

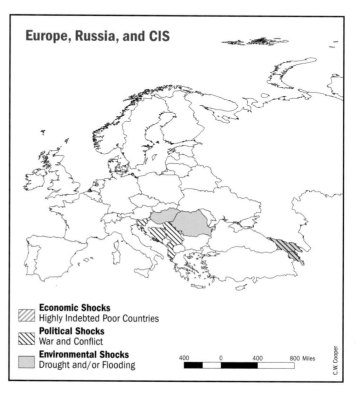

Europe, Russia, and CIS

Economic Shocks
Highly Indebted Poor Countries

Political Shocks
War and Conflict

Environmental Shocks
Drought and/or Flooding

400   0   400   800 Miles

C.W. Cooper

South America: The Gap Widens Between Rich and Poor

Many countries in South America that made economic gains over the past 30 years now face an economic crisis, with low growth rates again after 1997. Throughout Latin America, long-standing inequities between the poorest of the poor and the wealthy elite have increased.

Venezuela, Bolivia, Peru, Brazil, and Colombia stand out as hunger hotspots. In Venezuela, where over 16 percent of the population is chronically hungry, torrential rains and landslides inflicted over $3.2 billion in damage. Venezuela is an oil-exporting country and has the potential to reduce chronic poverty, yet income distribution is grossly unequal.

The 1.8 million poor citizens of Bolivia have not seen the steady economic growth of their country translate into improved living standards for their communities: 23 percent of Bolivians are chronically undernourished. Bolivia is the top recipient of development assistance in Latin America and is highly indebted to the World Bank and the IMF.[7] With a legacy of chronic poverty, Bolivia will remain a hunger hotspot in 2001, even with debt relief imminent under the Highly Indebted Poor Country (HIPC-II) program.[8]

In Peru, 4.4 million people (about 18 percent of the population) are chronically undernourished.[9] The economic recovery of the early 1990s, after years of civil war against the Marxist Shining Path guerilla movement, is slowing. While Peru produces most of its food, future El Niño events may require disaster relief and humanitarian food aid.

In Brazil, the financial crisis of 1997 rolled back the progress that it had made in the fight against poverty during the 1980s and early 1990s. Sixteen million people, over 10 percent of the population, suffer from chronic undernourishment and poverty.[10] Agrarian reform is much needed and could help millions of landless families (see *Hunger for Land*, p. 76). Federal and state laws have established procedures for redistribution of idle land, but they have not been enforced.

Colombia's food crisis is the worst in the Western Hemisphere. The 30-year civil war has pushed 1 million poor peasants from their homes into urban areas in the northern part of the country. The conflict will escalate with the introduction of a multi-billion dollar U.S.-funded military package to defeat the Armed Revolutionary Forces of Colombia. The potential exists for a "spillover effect" into Ecuador, Peru, Brazil, and Venezuela, where displaced persons may migrate. Unfortunately, in comparison with the billions of dollars being spent for military equipment and training, the international community has provided very little humanitarian aid for displaced persons in Colombia. The international emergency food operation in Colombia has received only 25 percent of the total needed to serve the most vulnerable displaced persons.[11]

South America

Economic Shocks
Highly Indebted
Poor Countries

Political Shocks
War and Conflict

Environmental Shocks
Drought and/or Flooding

400 0 400 800 Miles

C.W. Cooper

Central America and the Caribbean: Natural Disasters and Grinding Poverty

Central America saw a brief period of recovery after decades of civil wars ended in the late 1980s. But in 1998 Hurricane Mitch reversed much of that progress. Over 7 million people (25 percent of the Central American population) were affected by Hurricane Mitch and 3 million were left homeless.[12] Fields of beans, maize, and sorghum were completely destroyed, along with coffee and other export crops. The countries with the highest incidence of chronic hunger (Honduras, Nicaragua, Guatemala, and El Salvador) were most affected. Despite huge flows of emergency assistance, these countries will require decades to rebuild their economies.

While 20 percent of people in Central America and 10 percent of people in South America are hungry, Caribbean nations are the most food insecure. The FAO found that 31 percent of Caribbean people were undernourished during 1996-98. In Haiti, 62 percent of the population (4.8 million persons) face chronic hunger. In the Dominican Republic, 28 percent of the population (2.2 million persons) are hungry. And in Cuba, close to 19 percent of the population (2.1 million persons) are malnourished.

Central America and the Caribbean

200 0 200 400 Miles

C.W. Cooper

Economic Shocks
Highly Indebted Poor Countries

Political Shocks
War and Conflict

Environmental Shocks
Drought and/or Flooding

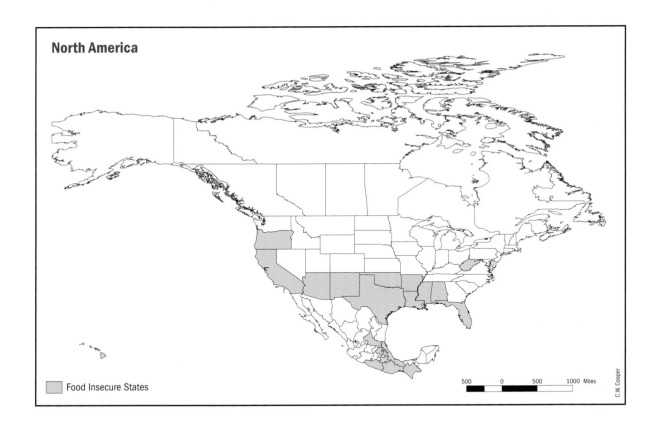

North America

Food Insecure States

500 0 500 1000 Miles

C.W. Cooper

North America: Hunger in Lands of Plenty

The landmass of North America, encompassing Mexico, the United States, and Canada, produces much of the world's maize, soybean, wheat, and other staple foods for export and domestic consumption. In Canada, as in the United States, pockets of poverty exist in marginal rural areas and in major urban centers, although severe undernourishment is rare. Despite economic progress and growth during most of the 1990s, Mexico still has over 5 million chronically hungry people concentrated in rural Chiapas and in large urban areas.

In the United States, close to 31 million Americans live in households that are food insecure, meaning they resort to emergency food banks each month or skip meals to pay for rent.[13]

Alabama, Arizona, Arkansas, California, the District of Columbia, Florida, Hawaii, Louisiana, Mississippi, New Mexico, Oklahoma, Oregon, Texas, and West Virginia have the greatest food insecurity – over 10 percent of total households.

The Food Research and Action Center asserts that a combination of low wages and declining participation in the federal food stamp program keeps people "on the edge." The aggregate percentage decline in food stamp participation for 1996-1999 in the U.S was 27 percent, with Washington declining 41 percent and Texas dropping 38 percent.[14] Increased food stamp program participation would dramatically reduce hunger in the United States.

Dr. Zeigler is the Deputy Director of the Congressional Hunger Center in Washington, DC.

The Hunger Index

BY DOUGLAS A. HICKS

Experts and citizens disagree about how best to measure the severity of hunger within a population. Difficulties include both conceptual issues (What is hunger?) and data issues (Are these figures reliable?). The Hunger Index (HI), ranging from 0 to 1, is a simple but theoretically sound way to assess the level of a country's hunger problem and measure progress to overcome it. Two aspects of the HI make it distinctive and innovative. First, unlike other indices discussed below, it focuses directly on hunger and not on other aspects of human development. Second, it combines in a single index data related to different aspects of hunger (availability of and access to food and the way food is "converted" into healthy bodies and lives).

Background and Concepts[1]

Over the past decade, nongovernmental organizations, policymakers, and scholars have conducted an international discussion about the meaning of human development, including pathbreaking indices that set precedents for the HI. The United Nations Development Programme (UNDP) helped create public concern through its publication of an annual *Human Development Report*, beginning in 1990. One of the most significant elements of these reports has been a Human Development Index (HDI) calculated for each country. The HDI was a breakthrough in helping citizens and leaders to measure and understand development as broader than economic indicators such as gross national product per capita. Rather than seeing development in terms of economic growth alone, the UNDP asked what really mattered in the development process, and put people at its center.[2] The three components of its index reflect the UNDP's answer: income to purchase basic goods and services, educational enrollment and literacy, and health (as reflected in life expectancy).[3]

More recently, three other UNDP indices have been used to highlight particular dimensions of development. The Human Poverty Index focuses on severe forms of deprivation related to education and health. A Gender-related Development Index accounts for inequalities between men's and women's conditions, and a Gender Empowerment Measure reflects women's participation in government and the professions.[4] The World Health Organization (WHO) has presented indices that indicate the ability to live disease-free and to access one's health system.[5] The Fordham Institute for Innovation in Social Policy features an Index of Social Health within the United States,[6] and the think tank Redefining Progress presents an index that incorporates concern for the environment and various aspects of people's social and economic situation.[7] These indices highlight important dimensions of development, but none considers hunger directly.[8]

Scholars and policymakers in international bodies such as the Food and Agriculture Organization (FAO) and WHO have offered various methods to estimate levels and trends of *hunger* and *undernutrition*. Two principal approaches have emerged. The first uses a "food balance sheet." It estimates the number of undernourished people, based on total available kilocalories as well as the inequality in people's consumption of those kilocalories. FAO uses this method to estimate the total number of people in each country who are undernourished. The FAO's recent "depth of hunger" measure also derives from the food supply approach.[9] The second method uses medical examination of sample groups to determine the number of children in a population who are underweight (low weight for age), stunted (low height for age), or wasted (low weight for height).

A fundamental question about the very definition of hunger is at stake. Is hunger measured by whether food is available and accessible to all people? Or is it also about how that food is converted into healthy lives? To avoid being underweight, stunted, or wasted requires taking in calories, but it also requires nutritionally balanced food, clean water, and avoiding disease. These aspects of hunger are described by the FAO's Inter-Agency Working Group on Food Insecurity Vulnerability Information Mapping System (IAWG-FIVIMS) as three elements of food security: *availability*, *access*, and *utilization*.[10]

Nobel-winning economist and leading expert on hunger Amartya Sen argues for a "capability approach" to hunger that treats calories as a means to the more important ends of "being well-fed" and "being in good health." We are only interested in food availability, Sen argues, as it enables persons to function well within their societies. Sen's capability framework reminds us that we are most interested in how food is converted into human functioning and capability; a measure of hunger must look beyond availability and access to utilization. A broad understanding of hunger, then, entails more than simply looking at the calorie supply, though this remains important. We must also account for how food is used and balanced to avoid malnutrition and to promote well-being.[11]

Constructing the Hunger Index

The Hunger Index presents a single measure that reflects the overall hunger situation in countries of the world.[12] The HI combines indicators related to availability, access, and utilization. (See the Technical Note, in Appendices, for a full description of the HI methodology.) The three components included in the HI are:

Availability of food: The most recent FAO estimates of dietary energy supply (calories per person per day) are employed.[13] To be sure, there are ways to measure

The Hunger Index

Country	Calories/ Capita/Day	Gini for Consumption Expenditures	Proportion of Children Who Are Stunted	HI = Hunger Index
Ethiopia	1,805	40.0	64.2	0.32
Burundi	1,579	33.3	47.4	0.38
Madagascar	2,001	46.0	48.3	0.41
Bangladesh	2,050	33.6	54.6	0.42
Lesotho	2,210	56.0	44.0	0.42
Yemen	2,087	39.5	51.7	0.42
Zambia	1,950	49.8	42.4	0.42
Niger	1,966	50.5	41.1	0.43
Sierra Leone	2,045	62.9	34.7	0.43
Papua New Guinea	2,168	50.9	43.2	0.43
Nepal	2,170	36.7	48.4	0.45
United Rep. of Tanzania	1,999	38.2	43.4	0.45
Rwanda	2,036	28.9	48.7	0.46
India	2,466	37.8	51.8	0.46
Central African Republic	2,056	61.3	28.4	0.47
Mozambique	1,911	39.6	35.9	0.48
Laos	2,175	30.4	47.3	0.48
Kenya	1,968	44.5	33.6	0.48
Burkina Faso	2,149	48.2	33.3	0.49
Pakistan	2,447	31.2	49.6	0.49
Mali	2,118	50.5	30.1	0.50
Uganda	2,216	39.2	38.3	0.50
Mauritania	2,640	38.9	44.0	0.51
Nigeria	2,882	50.6	37.7	0.51
Philippines	2,288	46.2	32.7	0.51
Zimbabwe	2,153	56.8	21.4	0.52
Nicaragua	2,208	50.3	24.9	0.53
Gambia	2,559	47.8	30.1	0.54
Vietnam	2,422	36.1	35.9	0.54
Ecuador	2,725	43.7	34.0	0.55
South Africa	2,909	59.3	22.8	0.55
Mongolia	2,010	33.2	26.4	0.55
Senegal	2,277	41.3	22.9	0.58
Sri Lanka	2,314	34.4	23.8	0.60
Thailand	2,462	41.4	21.5	0.60
Guyana	2,476	40.2	20.7	0.61
Cote d'Ivoire	2,695	36.7	24.4	0.62
Ghana	2,684	32.7	25.9	0.63
Panama	2,476	48.5	9.9	0.63
Morocco	3,165	39.5	24.2	0.64
Russian Federation	2,835	48.7	12.7	0.64
Kazakhstan	2,517	35.4	15.8	0.65
Tunisia	3,297	40.2	22.5	0.65
Turkey	3,554	41.5	20.5	0.67
Algeria	3,020	35.3	18.3	0.68
Egypt	3,282	28.9	24.9	0.69
Jamaica	2,711	36.4	9.6	0.70
Jordan	2,791	36.4	7.8	0.71
Croatia	2,479	26.8	0.8	0.75

Sources: see Technical Note, Appendices.

food availability besides calories; in particular, attention to the availability of protein and micronutrients is also an important part of assessing the hunger situation. The availability component of the HI focuses on calorie supply principally because of the difficulty in obtaining reliable data on these other components.

Access to food: For hunger to be alleviated, food must be available in a country and people must be able to gain physical and economic *access* to it. There is no ideal way to measure access to food. The indicator used here is a measure of the inequality of consumption (based on how much different people spend on goods and services). The more equal the consumption, in general terms, the more access vulnerable persons have to food, and thus the higher the value of this part of the index. This indicator gives a good general idea of a person's *relative* access to food supply.

Utilization of food: People require nutritional and micronutrient balance and availability, access to safe water, and decent basic health care. These are complementary factors that make it possible for people to convert food into good nutrition. Here the measures of children's physical health are important, as indicated in the prevalence of underweight, stunting, and wasting. The figure for wasting gives vital information on severe, emergency forms of hunger but it does not reflect more chronic forms of hunger. Underweight and stunting each capture effects of more persistent, if less extreme, hunger. Consistent with the most current U.N. research, the best indicator of chronic undernutrition is stunting rather than underweight.[14] Thus, the HI employs the proportion of the population that is free from stunting as a basic indicator of food utilization.

The HI combines all of these indicators to create a good overall picture of the hunger situation in a particular country. The HI is weighted to consider availability and access to food as 50 percent of the index; the other half of the index is obtained from the figures on child stunting. Consistent with other indices of human development, the HI ranges from 0 to 1, with lower scores reflecting more dire hunger situations. A country's movement over time towards a score of 1 indicates progress in the fight against hunger.

The HI has been calculated for a set of 49 countries, for which the necessary data were available, as indicated in the HI table. Countries are listed from least to most favorable HI. For this set of countries, Burundi and Ethiopia have the most dire hunger situation (with HI below .40). Croatia, Jordan, and Jamaica fare best (above .70).

In its present form, the HI can be used as an assessment tool to determine how countries are succeeding, or failing, in their efforts to reduce hunger. People can draw on this table to determine how much the food supply must be increased, or inequality decreased, or child

stunting reduced, in order to make progress against hunger. The HI shows more directly than any other index the hunger-related challenges to human survival and well-being. It points leaders and citizens toward the specific problems of food availability, access, and utilization that contribute to hunger. Following a country's HI value can monitor results of national and international efforts to fight hunger. The HI and more careful analysis of its component parts can highlight countries and specific aspects of hunger that deserve particular attention and effort. Finally, progress can be encouraged by presenting higher HI values as targets to pursue in the battle against hunger.

Dr. Hicks is Assistant Professor of Leadership Studies and Religion at the University of Richmond, VA.

[1] I would like to thank Liza Stutts for her research assistance in completing this project and Jonathan Wight for helpful comments on the construction of the Hunger Index.

[2] The human development approach is refined in each issue of the UNDP's *Report*. The most recent one is *Human Development Report 2000*, (New York: Oxford University Press, 2000).

[3] See *Human Development Report 2000*, "Technical Note. Computing the Indices," 269-270.

[4] Each of these is included in the *Human Development Report 2000*. See Tables 1-5 (157-177) as well as "Technical Note. Computing the Indices," 269-273.

[5] See the World Health Organization, *World Health Report 2000*, (Geneva: WHO, 2000), Statistical Annex, 143-151, and various tables. The *Report* notes the innovative nature of its health indices and calls for constructive feedback and refinement.

[6] The Index of Social Health and many other measures for assessing social health in the United States are discussed in Marc Miringoff and Marque-Luisa Miringoff, *The Social Health of the Nation: How America is Really Doing*, (New York: Oxford University Press, 1999).

[7] See "Why Bigger Isn't Better: The Genuine Progress Indicator – 1999 Update," http://www.rprogress.org/pubs/gpi1999/gpi1999.html [accessed August 7, 2000].

[8] Overall, the HI has a relatively high correlation with other indicators of hunger, malnutrition, and human development. The correlation between HI and the FAO estimates for proportion of the population that is undernourished is –0.77; that between HI and the proportion of the population that is underweight is –0.71; and that between HI and the Human Development Index is 0.70. These correlation figures run in the expected direction and indicate significant, but not complete, overlap of aspects of hunger and human development.

[9] Food and Agriculture Organization, The State of Food Insecurity in the World, (Rome: FAO, 2000), 3.

[10] http://www.fivims.net/defn.htm [accessed August 3, 2000].

[11] For a discussion, see Amartya Sen, "Family and Food: Sex Bias in Poverty," in *Resources, Values and Development*, Amartya Sen, ed., (Cambridge, MA: Harvard University Press, 1983), especially 347-352.

[12] *Hunger 2001* calculates the HI for 49 countries for which the relevant and reliable data could be obtained.

[13] These data are the most widely employed and reliable estimates based on total food supply and population of a given country.

[14] The Administrative Committee on Coordination's Sub-Committee on Nutrition (ACC/SCN) employs stunting instead of underweight in its most recent nutritional reports. T. J. Cole, "Methods to Estimate Trends in Undernutrition Prevalence: A Review," *4th Report of the World Nutrition Situation: Nutrition Throughout the Life Cycle*, (Appendix 3), United Nations Administrative Committee on Coordination, Sub-Committee on Nutrition (ACC/SCN) in collaboration with International Food Policy Research Institute (IFPRI), Geneva, January 2000, 87.

CHAPTER 8

What You Can Do

BY JOANNA BERKMAN

In this year's annual report, Bread for the World Institute shares a simple message: poverty-focused development assistance helps hungry people help themselves. Successful foreign aid starts with listening respectfully to poor people. They often know what they need to create their own well-being, and it isn't just technical expertise in agriculture or education. Hungry people need others to stand in solidarity with them against unjust and unwise policies and to speak up for them when their voices are not heard.

But how do affluent people become activists on behalf of hungry people in their midst and around the world? Most people in the United States have never faced food insecurity and never will. In fact, we are chronically overfed. "In the United States, 55 percent of adults are overweight by international standards. A whopping 23 percent of American adults are considered obese. . . [O]ne in five American [children is]. . .overweight."[1]

In poor developing countries, hungry people struggle for an adequate diet that provides the minimum nutrition required to maintain productive, active, and healthy lives. By contrast, in the United States the term "diet" is universally understood to apply to weight loss. For the amount of money Americans spend to lose weight, we could end hunger in the world in short order.

According to Marketdata Enterprises, the annual revenue for the diet industry was over $30 billion dollars in 1990. This figure includes money spent on diet centers and programs; group and individual weight loss; diet camps; prepackaged foods; over-the-counter and prescription diet drugs; weight-loss books and magazines; physicians, nurses, nutritionists, and other health professionals specializing in weight loss; commercial and residential exercise clubs with weight-loss programs; sugar-free, fat-free, and reduced calorie (lite) food products; and imitation fats and sugar substitutes.[3]

We are inundated with food. We are bombarded with advertisements urging us to eat. Our relationship to food is so distorted that we are constantly waging the battle of the bulge. Despite our self-indulgence and frequent excess, we idealize skeletal fashion models and celebrities. We believe that you can't be too thin or too rich. We believe that thin is beautiful. Four percent of adolescent girls and young women in America have eating disorders, a conservative estimate that does not include those with serious borderline symptoms of anorexia nervosa and bulimia.[4]

How could we explain this to the world's poorest people? For them, hunger itself is *the* eating disorder. How could we explain to the African mother who sends her children to glean kernels of maize that had fallen off passing trucks from the side of the road (*Sex for Food*, p. 90) that there are children of plenty who starve themselves until they are as emaciated as famine victims?

What makes hungry people in developing countries different from you and me is their relationship to food. They do not have enough to eat. We have too much. We struggle with surfeit, not starvation. How can affluent people, blessed with comfort and security, begin to bridge the "dinner table" divide? Coming to terms with food, as individuals and as a nation, might reveal the connection we need to make with hungry people. They are obsessed with food and so are we, but in very different circumstances. By raising our own consciousness about food, we can move toward compassion for the millions who go hungry every day. Equally important, a change in our own consciousness could lead to a change in the politics of hunger.

Some people understand their relationship to food through fasting, the voluntary refusal of food, not for weight loss but for religious, spiritual, and political reasons. Fasting is an important element of worship in many faiths. It has also been used successfully in social change movements throughout the world. For Mahatma Gandhi, fasting was a powerful political tool against British rule in India. Both American and British Suffragists used fasting effectively to win the vote for women.

Rockstar Bono speaks at a press conference on debt relief.

This is a prescription for political involvement as well as the title of a study guide produced by Bread for the World Institute and the Christian Reformed World Relief Committee. It educates people about complex issues such as:

- The role of sustainable development programs in bringing hope to poor and hungry people, reducing conflict, encouraging economic growth, protecting the environment, and building democracy
- The role of public and private international development organizations in shaping activities around the globe that bring permanent, positive change
- The need for a well-informed public that understands how development assistance helps people in the developing world and supports the World Food Summit goal
- The value of listening to and maintaining relationships with international grassroots leaders in order to learn about and act on international policy issues that concern to them.

Next Steps[8]

Bread for the World Institute believes that knowledge about world hunger is a first step to taking action. Many people want to do something to help, but they don't know how. Below, we suggest steps that individuals and organizations can take. Individual actions count. "William Wilberforce succeeded in getting the British Parliament to abolish the slave trade in 1806. It took 27 additional years of struggle. . . [but] the efforts of Wilberforce and his cohorts, together with the rising support of public opinion, finally paid off. Parliament brought the scandal of slavery to an end throughout the British Empire."[8]

"James P. Grant, head of UNICEF from 1980 until his death in 1995, . . . relentlessly promoted child survival programs to grassroots groups, Washington politicians, and heads of state."[9] In every case where great social change has occurred, visionary individuals joined with networks of committed people working toward justice. Ending hunger requires this kind of effort.

In 2000, Reverend David Duncombe, then 71, explained why he fasted as part of the Jubilee 2000 campaign:

> [I]t's very difficult for me to avoid the knowledge in my own life that there are millions of starving people and to go about my life as though there were not. I find it very undesirable to eat when other people can't. And to take advantage of their poverty because I live in the 'first world.' I intend to symbolize starvation. I want to do that because a lot of people in Congress – through no fault of their own – have never seen a starving person. . .In a very abstract way, they know that. . .many people are starving, but they have never seen it. They have never looked upon it. They have never touched it. So I will go. . .to each [congressional] office and let my starving body talk for itself. I hope that my message will get through and lift their consciences.[5]

Throughout the nation, Bread for the World members participated in a "rolling fast" in support of Jubilee 2000.

Education is another way we can connect with hungry people. *Foreign Aid to End Hunger* is part of Bread for the World Institute's ongoing mission to inform our members, our elected officials, and the general public about hunger and how to fight it. Reading this year's report is a start. The next step: *Listen, Learn, and Act!*[6]

Ms. Berkman is the editor of *Foreign Aid to End Hunger*.

Individuals can:

- Work with others in churches, civic, and grassroots organizations to press governments to implement the 1996 World Food Summit goal.
- Call, write, and e-mail elected officials urging them to support policies that help poor and hungry people, locally, nationally, and internationally.
- Get involved in party politics at the local, state, and national levels.
- Register and vote! As the U.S. national election in 2000 clearly proved, every vote matters. Cast your vote for candidates who take a stand against hunger. Hold your elected officials accountable for their positions on hunger issues.
- Stay informed about national and international events that create food emergencies and chronic hunger. Demand that U.S. media cover world events adequately. Watch news programs with an international perspective, such as the BBC and the ITN (both broadcast on PBS stations) and CNN International.
- Learn more about hunger in your own community or region and what is being done about it.
- Volunteer at food pantries and feeding programs; get to know and listen to people who don't have enough to eat.
- Contribute financially to organizations that help hungry people.

Media can:

- Move beyond stories of pity and charity to explain the causes of hunger.
- Listen to what poor people say. They are real experts on poverty. Give them a voice so that policymakers and the public can hear them — and respond.

Governments can:

- Set out a strategy, with time-specific benchmarks, to implement the World Food Summit commitment.
- Increase support for research on sustainable agricultural practices, especially in Africa, that protect genetic diversity and provide livelihoods for small and medium producers.
- Support programs that empower women and girls, especially education, training, extension services, and health care.
- Establish and implement policies that encourage the creation of jobs and livelihoods in rural areas.
- Increase poverty-focused foreign aid.

Nongovernmental and Private Voluntary Organizations can:

- Participate in World Food Day events.
- Support research projects on sustainable agriculture that minimize chemical inputs and preserves genetic diversity in local and regional ecosystems.
- Strengthen anti-hunger advocacy groups and low-income people's organizations that influence government policies.

Businesses can:

- Invest in developing countries where foreign aid is helping to create basic infrastructure and public goods.
- Pay a fair price to workers and agricultural producers. Recognize their right to organize to promote fair labor practices.
- Ensure that local populations receive a fair return from the sale of seed varieties based on local genetic material.

Consumers can:

- Boycott companies that engage in unfair labor practices or environmentally unsustainable activities.
- Buy from companies and fair trade organizations that pay workers a living wage and practice sustainable agricultural techniques in the growth and manufacture of their products.

Dieters can:

- Pledge $5 or $10 for each pound you lose to an organization that works on behalf of hungry people, at home or abroad. Ask your friends and support group members to do the same.
- Write to the companies who gain from your weight loss efforts and insist that they donate a percentage of their profits to organizations and programs that help poor and hungry people.

How to Get Involved

Bread for the World collaborates with hundreds of other organizations to build a movement to win the changes needed to end widespread hunger. Many of these groups become sponsors or co-sponsors of Bread for the World. They are described at the end of this volume. Contact them to learn about their pro-poor relief and development projects. They can help you get involved by referring you to state and local affiliates where you can join in the fight against hunger.

Advocacy and Community Organizing

Bread for the World

Bread for the World is a lively grassroots presence in hundreds of local communities. There are four ways you can take part: become a member of BFW, contribute financially, join or form a BFW group in your church or community, and become an activist yourself. BFW members learn and draw strength from each other. Some BFW groups meet monthly for worship, study, or action. Others meet just a few times a year to take specific action – to see their member of Congress, for example, or to plan a workshop for local congregations on BFW's Offering of Letters, our main campaign for the year. Contact your regional organizer to find out about groups in your area. In most congressional districts, volunteers have organized telephone trees at key points in the legislative process.

National office:

Bread for the World
50 F Street NW, Suite 500
Washington, DC 20001
(202)-639-9400 or (800) 82-BREAD
E-mail: bread@bread.org
Web site: www.bread.org

Regional offices:

Pasadena, CA
Phone: (625) 568-3233
E-mail: breadca@igc.org

Charleston, SC
Phone: (843) 579-9900
E-mail: breadsouth@igc.org

Chicago, IL
Phone: (312) 629-9529
E-mail: breadchicago@igc.org

Minneapolis, MN
Phone: (612) 871-9084
E-mail: breadmn@igc.org

Transforming Anti-Hunger Leadership is a Bread for the World Institute initiative with programs in many communities and 14 states. These programs bring together leaders from various organizations that deal with hunger and poverty for leadership training, collective planning, and coalition building. TAHL has improved the racial and income diversity of leadership in the anti-hunger movement. It is also helping to build state and local coalitions that speak for hungry people.

Transforming Anti-Hunger
Leadership Program
Bread for the World Institute
50 F Street NW, Suite 500
Washington, DC 20001
(202)-639-9400 or (800) 82-BREAD
E-mail: transforming.leadership@bread.org
Web site: www.bread.org

The Community Food Security Coalition is a nonprofit, membership-based national coalition of over 600 organizations and individuals that focus on food and agriculture issues. Its mission is to bring about lasting social change by promoting community-based solutions to hunger, poor nutrition, and the globalization of the food system.

Community Food Security Coalition
P.O. Box 209
Venice, CA 90294
Phone: (310) 822-5410
Fax: (310) 822-1440

The Food Research and Action Center (FRAC) is a national organization working to improve public policies to eradicate hunger and undernutrition in the United States. Founded in 1970 as a public interest law firm, FRAC is a nonprofit and nonpartisan research and public policy center and hub of an anti-hunger network of thousands of individuals and agencies across the country. FRAC engages in a variety of activities at the national, state, and local levels as part of a comprehensive strategy for reducing hunger.

Food Research and Action Center
1875 Connecticut Ave., NW Suite 540
Washington, DC 20009
Phone: (202) 986-2200
Fax: (202) 986-2525
E-mail: webmaster@frac.org

Industrial Areas Foundation (IAF) builds on the work of the renowned community organizer Saul Alinsky. The IAF empowers volunteers in communities to have an impact on local issues that affect the quality of life. Volunteers are trained in the nuts and bolts of community organizing, including relationship-building, influencing legislators, and media work. IAF stresses building powerful local organizations that include faith-based groups representing a diverse cross-section of the community.

IAF has affiliated organizations in metropolitan areas throughout the United States. For example, BUILD, an IAF affiliate in Baltimore, successfully lobbied for a requirement that contractors for the city government pay workers a living wage.

Industrial Areas Foundation
220 West Kinzie, 5th floor
Chicago, IL 60610
Phone: (312) 245-9211

Workers' Rights

National Labor Committee (NLC) strives to end labor and human rights violations, ensure a living wage, and help workers and their families live and work with dignity. Working with a strong network of local, national, and international groups, the NLC builds coalitions to promote labor rights and pressure companies to adhere to national and international labor and human rights standards. The NLC exposed the appalling working conditions in the factories that made clothing for the Kathie Lee label, which prompted Kathie Lee Gifford to oppose the exploitation and abuse of workers.

National Labor Committee
275 7th Avenue, 15th floor
New York, NY 10001
Phone: (212) 242-3002
E-mail: nlc@nlcnet.org
Web site: www.nlcnet.org

Student Groups

Student Campaign Against Hunger and Homelessness works through education, service, and action. Started by the student Public Interest Research Groups (PIRGs), the campaign has become the largest student network fighting hunger and homelessness in the United States, with more than 600 participating campuses in all 50 states. During the week prior to Thanksgiving each year, the campaign sponsors an awareness week featuring sleep-outs, fasts, educational programs, food-waste surveys, and letter-writing efforts. During the Annual Hunger Clean-up, student volunteers repaint local shelters, plant community gardens, repair food banks, and raise funds. Student leaders establish food rescue programs to salvage unused food from campus dining facilities for local food banks and soup kitchens. SPLASH (Students Pushing Legislative Action to Stop Hunger and Homelessness) is an action alert network that calls, writes, and e-mails members of Congress on relevant issues.

National Office
233 N. Pleasant Street
Amherst, MA 01002.
Phone: (413) 253-6417
Fax: (413) 256-6435
E-mail: nscah@aol.com
Web site: www.nscahh.org

United Students Against Sweatshops (USAS)

With activities on over 200 university campuses nationwide, United Students Against Sweatshops has sparked student activism. USAS targets companies that produce clothing for colleges and universities. Students pressure their schools to purchase college gear only from companies that abide by codes of conduct guaranteeing the protection of the basic human rights of workers. Students advocate full public disclosure, enforcement of the rights of women, independent monitoring, and a living wage.

United Students Against Sweatshops (USAS)
1413 K Street, NW 9th floor
Washington, DC 20005
Phone: (202) 667-9328 or (800) NO SWEAT

Socially Responsible Investing/Shopping

Ethicalshopper.com sells socially and environmentally responsible products. The company carefully screens all products to ensure that the manufacturing processes, working conditions, and environmental impact of the products conform to its mandate. Consumers who use EthicalShopper.com contribute to good causes and to companies committed to preventing environmental or social harm and pollution.

Founded in 1999, this on-line location for one-stop shopping sells clothing and products for baby care, children, body and spa, travel, the kitchen, and the garden. It also offers an Eco-supermarket that includes environmentally safe cleaners and insecticides, pet care products, and food. The site provides detailed information on each product.

> Ethicalshopper.com
> 2130 Sawtelle Blvd., Suite 308
> Los Angeles, CA 90025
> Phone: (310) 213-0421 or (877) 4-e-ethic
> (877)- 433-8442
> Web site: www.ethicalshopper.com

SocialFunds.com helps socially responsible investors make informed decisions regarding their investments. The web site provides financial education, investment research, investment analysis and recommendations, professional financial services, and industry news.

SocialFunds.com, together with the Interfaith Center on Corporate Responsibility, have developed the Shareholder Activism Center. This interactive web-based tool provides extensive coverage of shareholder resolutions pertaining to the environment, corporate governance, global finance, human rights, militarism, health, and equality. The Shareholder Activism Center can assist stockholders in the process of voting. It provides all the information needed to quickly and easily contact the company and tell management how you feel about a particular issue, policy, or behavior.

> SocialFunds.com /SRI World Group, Inc.
> 74 Cotton Mill Hill
> Brattleboro, VT 05301
> Web site: www.socialfunds.com

Calvert Social Investment Foundation

Investors can choose development programs that assist impoverished communities. A Community Investment Note in the amount of $1,000 or higher earns a rate of return of up to 4 percent.

Through microcredit programs, investors help start or strengthen small businesses. Investor money also builds and refurbishes affordable housing for sale or rent. Community development loan programs create more jobs, provide good day care, and reinforce locally owned businesses in troubled communities. Investors can target funds to specific geographic areas or development programs. The Calvert Social Investment Foundation is a nonprofit organization, not to be confused with the Calvert Group's socially responsible mutual funds.

> Calvert Social Investment Foundation
> 4550 Montgomery Avenue
> Bethesda, MD 20814
> Phone: (800) 248-0337
> E-mail: foundation@calvert.com
> Web site: www.calvertfoundation.org

Campaign Finance Reform

Common Cause is a nonprofit, nonpartisan citizen's lobbying organization that promotes open, honest, and accountable government and the right of all citizens to shape public policies.

The organization has been a leader in developing support for legislation to ban the use of soft money, donations to political parties that indirectly support candidates for national office. Political fundraisers use soft money to get around limits on the size of donations that can legally be given to individual candidates, allowing corporations, unions, and wealthy individuals to make substantial contributions to political parties.

Common Cause lobbies for passage of bills that would end the soft money system by prohibiting candidates and national political parties from raising soft money and state political parties from spending soft money on activities that affect federal elections.

> Common Cause
> 1250 Connecticut Avenue, NW, #600
> Washington, DC 20036
> Phone: (202) 833-1200
> Web site: www.commoncause.org

Student Leaders Organize for Social Change

BY STEPHANIE SEIDEL

Students have always been at the forefront of movements for social change. Whether protesting against the Vietnam War, marching for civil rights, or demonstrating against university investment in apartheid South Africa, young people have forged a more just world. Some believe that the current generation of young people is apolitical. But in Bread for the World's experience, many talented student leaders are mobilizing around today's important justice struggles.

Get Out the Vote

The highest voter turnout in 35 years elected Selma, Alabama's first African-American mayor, the first change in municipal administration since the 1965 Voting Rights Act. The victory occurred because local teens and young adults joined with community organizers and elders to initiate a nonpartisan project that galvanized voters.

Many people had not voted in years. They didn't believe their vote would change the city leadership. But the campaigners convinced townspeople that their vote would make a difference. Going door to door on "street crusades," young organizers talked to citizens and heard the community's needs. Hip-hop artists and actors went to Selma to lead weekly rallies and make radio announcements urging young people to vote.

These efforts energized the town. "People were moved to vote," organizer Malika Sanders said. "Even before the polls closed on election night, everyone gathered in the streets to celebrate. We knew we were a part of a new day in Selma." *Contact: Malika Sanders, 21st Century Youth Leadership Movement, (334) 874-0065 or youth421c@aol.com.*

Men Against Violence

"Rape and sexual assault are not women's issues," according to Christopher Watson. "They are everyone's issue." That's why Watson organized a chapter of Men Against Violence (MAV) at Southwest Texas State University. Since MAV's inception in 1995, young leaders on university campuses have been making educational presentations, conducting awareness campaigns, and initiating community actions to end violence against women.

Men Against Violence seeks to change traditional norms of masculinity – the ways that men are taught to behave. MAV challenges young men to redefine male-female relationships in an equitable manner, to resolve conflicts effectively, to develop meaningful friendships with other men, and to manage anger and fear without violence.

Men perpetrate more than 90 percent of violence in the U.S. "Males are conditioned to instigate violence in our culture through media, peer pressure, tradition, and inadequate role models," Watson said. This reality is heightened on college campuses. Daily, universities across the country deal with violence in the form of date and acquaintance rape, drunk driving incidents, and binge drinking.

At Southwest Texas State University, MAV members conduct workshops and rap sessions for male students at fraternities and residence halls on violence against women

and sexual assault. Working with the university's women's center, MAV leaders also co-facilitate violence prevention groups at junior and senior high schools and make referrals to community centers for victims and perpetrators. Watson and other MAV activists testified before the Texas House Subcommittee on Higher Education to urge passage of a bill that would require a mandatory acquaintance rape workshop during orientation for all first-year students at state universities. The measure got stuck in committee, but Watson says MAV will continue to urge passage of the bill in the next legislative session. *Contact: Alcohol and Drug Resource Center, Southwest Texas State University, (512) 245-3601.*

Ending Sweatshop Labor

Laura McSpedon organized Georgetown University students to demand that products bearing the university logo not be made by exploited workers. Students organized a fashion show of clothing made in sweatshops. As students modeled the clothes, the announcer described in detail the conditions of the garment workers who made them. After months of educating the campus about the issue, McSpedon organized a sit-in at President O'Donovan's office, during which other students held a demonstration outside the administration building. Local television stations and two national newspapers covered the event.

"We won full public disclosure," McSpedon said. "We know the locations of the factories that make Georgetown apparel. We also created a code of conduct that all vendors must agree to follow." Factories must be open for random monitoring, pay just wages, and provide decent working conditions. Georgetown students worked with United Students Against Sweatshops (USAS), a national network of more than 200 campuses. More than 60 campuses have achieved gains similar to those won at Georgetown. *Contact: United Students Against Sweatshops, www.usasnet.org.*

Ms. Seidel is the campus organizer at Bread for the World.

Public Campaign provides support and technical assistance to grassroots organizations who advocate Clean Money Clean Elections campaign finance reform. Public Campaign's Clean Money Clean Election model legislation offers local, state and federal candidates an optional publicly financed campaign without the influence of special interest money. In return, the candidates receive a set amount of public funds to run for office. In addition to public funds, federal candidates would receive a prescribed amount of free and discounted TV and radio time. Clean Money Clean Elections campaign reform has been implemented in Arizona and Maine and will be implemented this year in Massachusetts.

Public Campaign
1320 19th Street, NW, Suite M-1
Washington, D.C. 20036
Phone: (202) 293-0222 phone
E-mail: info@publicampaign.org
Web site: www.publicampaign.org

Sustainable Agriculture and Community Gardening

The Community Food Security Coalition's mission is to promote comprehensive community-based solutions to the nation's food, farming, and nutrition problems. Community members work together to find local solutions to the problem of hunger.

The Community Food Security Coalition
P.O. Box 209
Venice, CA 90294
Phone: (310) 822-5410
E-mail: asfisher@aol.com

Endnotes

Introduction

1 Bread for the World Institute, *A Program to End Hunger: Hunger 2000*, Silver Spring, MD. See also J. Dirck Stryker and Jeffrey C. Metzel, *Meeting the Food Summit Target: The United States Contribution – Global Strategy, Agricultural Policy Analysis Project, Phase III*, Research Report No. 1039, prepared for the Office of Economic Growth and Agricultural Development, Global Bureau, U.S. Agency for International Development (Cambridge, MA: Associates for International Resources and Development, September 1998).

2 Our analysis is based on numbers published in 1998, which assume that interventions were already underway. Thus, we have had to include an additional sum because of steps that could have been taken in 1998-2000, but were not.

3 Fr. J. Bryan Hehir, "Foreign Aid In the Framework of Development and Globalization," transcript from a Catholic Relief Services meeting on foreign aid, February 2000, 23-35.

4 Robert G. Kaiser, "Foreign Disservice," *Washington Post*, April 16, 2000, B01.

5 Emmanuel Dabou, Balancing Act News Update 18, August 2000, www.balancingact-africa.com/balancing-act18.html.

6 John Lewis with Michael D'Orso, *Walking With the Wind*, (New York: Simon & Schuster, 1998), 12-13.

Chapter 1

1 United States Government General Accounting Office, *Food Security: Factors That Could Affect Progress Toward Meeting World Food Summit Goals* (Washington, DC: March 1999) GAO/NSIAD-99-15, 16, 32 et seq.

2 Jeffrey Sachs, "A New Map of the World," *Economist*, June 14, 2000, 81-83.

3 *Foreign Aid: What Counts Toward Sustainable Development and Humanitarian Relief?* (Washington, DC: Bread for the World Institute, 1993), 1-2.

4 *At the Crossroads: The Future of Foreign Aid,* Occasional Paper No. 4 (Silver Spring, MD: Bread for the World Institute, 1995), 14-18.

5 Ibid, 12.

6 Indra de Soysa and Nils Petter Gleditsch, "Summary," of *To Cultivate Peace: Agriculture in a World of Conflict* (Oslo, Norway: Peace Research Institute, 1999), www.futureharvest.org.

7 United States National Intelligence Council (NIC), *Global Humanitarian Emergencies: Trends and Projections, 1999-2000*, (Washington, DC, August 1999), 10-11.

8 NIC, *Global Humanitarian Emergencies*, 13.

9 Donald Snow, *Uncivil Wars: Internal Security and the New Internal Conflicts* (Boulder, CO: Lynne Reinner, 1996), 98.

10 The number of "manmade emergencies" (humanitarian crises that result from war or conflict) rose from an average of five per year in the 1980s to 23 per year in the 1990s, and the number of displaced persons tripled in the same period [*Global Humanitarian Emergencies: Trends and Projections, 1999-2000*, (Washington, DC, United States National Intelligence Council, August 1999)].

11 Jonathan Mermin, "Television News and American Intervention in Somalia: The Myth of Media-Driven Foreign Policy," *Political Science Quarterly* 112 (3, Fall 1997): 385-403. Mermin demonstrates in detail how the "CNN effect" took place, and indeed was used for this purpose, by groups seeking a U.S. response to the humanitarian and food crisis in Somalia in 1992.

12 Ibid, 385-403.

13 Michael O'Hanlon and Carol Graham, *A Half Penny on the Federal Dollar: The Future of Development Aid* (Washington, DC: Brookings Institution Press, 1999), 15; NIC, *Global Humanitarian Emergencies*, 16.

14 The U.S. agricultural community, which 15 years ago vehemently opposed U.S. assistance for agriculture in developing countries (out of concern that U.S. assistance could underwrite new competitors against U.S. farm exports), now recognizes the need to help poor developing countries improve their agricultural productivity. The U.S. farm community recognizes that agriculture is crucial to increasing prosperity in those countries, and that only such prosperity will increase U.S. agricultural commodity exports since the developing world is the only growth market for agricultural commodities. The fewer hungry and poor people overseas, and the more countries that cut hunger and poverty in half, the bigger the market for U.S. exports. The U.S. agricultural community also recognizes that the benefits to U.S. farmers of new genetic material from research to help developing country farmers has yielded tremendous returns, a rate of 140 to 1 in terms of benefits to costs to the U.S.

15 See testimony by small business in United States Government Printing Office, "The Benefits of Foreign Aid to the United States Economy," Hearing Before a Subcommittee of the Committee on Appropriations, United States Senate, 104th Congress, Special Hearing, 1996.

16 Business Alliance for International Economic Development, "Protecting America's Future: The Role of Foreign Assistance," March 2000.

17 Representative Tony P. Hall, "The Critical Role of U.S. Leadership," in *A Program to End Hunger: Hunger 2000*, Tenth Annual Report on the State of World Hunger (Silver Spring, MD: Bread for the World Institute, 2000), 20-21.

Chapter 2

1 "Nationwide Poll Finds Majority of American Women Concerned About U.S. Foreign Policy," press release, A Women's Lens on Global Issues, June 5, 2000, New York.

2 Steven Kull, *Americans on Globalization: A Study of U.S. Public Attitudes* (Washington, DC: Program on International Policy Attitudes, 2000), 35.

3 Ibid.

4 John E. Rielly, ed., *American Public Opinion and U.S. Foreign Policy 1998* (Chicago: Chicago Council on Foreign Relations, 1999).

5 "Post-Cold War Era Looks Better: America's Place in the World II," (Washington DC: Pew Research Center for the People and the Press, October 1997).

6 Kull, Steven, I.M. Destler and Clay Ramsay, *The Foreign Policy Gap: How Policymakers Misread the Public*, (Washington, DC: Program on International Policy Attitudes, 1997), 107.

7 Kull, Steven, *Americans on Foreign Aid*, (College Park, MD: Program on International Policy Attitudes, 1995).

8 Kull, Steven, *An Emerging Consensus: A Study of American Public Attitudes on America's Role in the World* (College Park, MD: Program on International Policy Attitudes, 1996) as cited in Kull et al., *The Foreign Policy Gap*, 101.

9 Kull et al., *The Foreign Policy Gap*, 163-168.

10 Belden, Russonello, and Stewart Research and Communications, *Connecting Women in the U.S. and Global Issues: A Report of Survey Research for A Women's Lens on Global Issues (*Washington, DC: A Women's Lens on Global Issues, 2000), 11.

11 Ibid, 4.

12 Margaret Bostrom, *Public Attitudes Toward Foreign Affairs: An Overview of the Current State of Public Opinion,* commissioned by the Benton Foundation for the Global Interdependence Initiative (Washington, DC: Aspen Institute, 1999), 3.

13 Kull, *Americans on Globalization*, 22-24.

14 Joseph Grady and Axel Aubrun, *Ten Differences between Public and Expert Understandings of International Affairs: Findings From the Mainstream American Press*, commissioned by the FrameWorks Institute for the Global Interdependence Initiative. (Washington, DC: Cultural Logic, November 1999), 6.

15 Bostrom, *Public Attitudes Toward Foreign Affairs*, 17.

16 Ibid, 12.

17 ABC News/*Washington Post* Poll, 1526 adults nationwide, August 30-September 2, 1999. (Washington, DC, September 1999).

18 Kull et al., *The Foreign Policy Gap*, 179.

19 Ibid, 179.

20 Daniel Amundson, Linda Lichter, and Robert Lichter, *The Myopic Neighbor: Local and National Network Television Coverage of the World*, commissioned by the FrameWorks Institute for the Global Interdependence Initiative (Washington, DC: Center for Media and Public Affairs, 2000), 35.

21 Susan Bales, *Veterans of Perception: GII Antecedents in the Literature of Media and Foreign Policy*, commissioned by the Aspen Institute for the Global Interdependence Initiative (Washington, DC: FrameWorks Institute, 2000), 16.

22 Richard Burt, in *The Media and Foreign Policy*. S. Serfaty, ed., (New York: St. Martin's Press, 1991).

23 Kull et al., *The Foreign Policy Gap*, 179.

24 Ibid, 179.

25 Susan Bales, *Communicating Global Interdependence: A FrameWorks Message Memo*, commissioned by the Aspen Institute for the Global Interdependence Initiative (Washington, DC: FrameWorks Institute, 2000), 8.

26 Eric Alterman, *Who Speaks for America? Why Democracy Matters in Foreign Policy* (Ithaca, NY: Cornell University Press, 1998), 7.

27 Ethel Klein, *Becoming Global Citizens: How Americans View the World at the Beginning of the 21st Century* (New York: EDK Associates, 1999), 11.

28 Bales, *Communicating Global Interdependence*, 11.

29 *Washington Post*. July 31, 1998, A20.

30 Grady and Aubrun, *Ten Differences Between Public and Expert Understandings*, 2.

31 Kull, Steven and I.M. Destler. *Misreading the Public: The Myth of a New Isolationism* (Washington, DC: Brookings Institution Press, 1999).

32 Bostrom, *Public Attitudes Toward Foreign Affairs*.

33 Bales, *Communicating Global Interdependence*, 11.

34 Axel Aubrun and Joseph Grady, *American Understandings of the United States' Role in the World: Findings from Cognitive Interviews,* commissioned by the Benton Foundation for the Global Interdependence Initiative (Washington, DC: Aspen Institute, 1999), 7.

35 Ibid, 3.

36 Grady and Aubrun, *Ten Differences Between Public and Expert Understandings*, 4.

37 Belden Russonello, and Stewart Research and Communications, *Connecting Women in the U.S. and Global Issues,* 31.

38 Bales, *Communicating Global Interdependence*, 11.

39 Amundson et al., *The Myopic Neighbor*, 41.

40 Ibid, 22.

41 Grady and Aubrun, *Ten Differences Between Public and Expert Understandings*, 3.

42 Bales, *Communicating Global Interdependence*, 13.

43 Eric Alterman, *Who Speaks for America?*, 198.

44 Ethel Klein, *Becoming Global Citizens,* 11.

45 "America's Place in the World II," based on telephone survey conducted between September 4 and 11, 1997. (Washington, DC: Pew Research Center for the People and the Press, 1998).

46 Margaret Bostrom, *Primed and Suspect: How the Public Responds to Different Frames on Global Issues*, commissioned by the FrameWorks Institute for the Global Interdependence Initiative (Washington, DC: FrameWorks Institute, 2000), 9.

Chapter 3

1 David A. Atwood, *Cutting Hunger and Poverty in Half: Interest Groups and a Renewed U.S. Commitment in the Post-Cold War World*, Unpublished paper, [Washington, DC] 2000.

2 The World Bank website, *What is IDA*, http://www.worldbank.org/ida/idao.html [accessed November 21, 2000].

3 Denis J. Sullivan, "The Failure of U.S. Foreign Aid: An Examination of Causes and a Call for Reform," In *Global Governance* 2 (1996), 404.

4 Atwood, *Cutting Hunger and Poverty in Half*, 12.

5 Carol Lancaster, *Transforming Foreign Aid: United States Assistance in the 21st Century* (Washington, DC: Institute for International Economics, 2000).

6 Organisation for Economic Cooperation and Development, *Development Co-operation 1999 Report: International Development* Vol. 1, No. 1 (Paris: OECD, 2000), 173.

7 Isaac Shapiro, *Trends in U.S. Development Aid and the Current Budget Debate* (Washington, DC: Center for Budget and Policy Priorities, 2000).

8 OECD Development Assistance Committee, *OECD News Release: Attachment 2 form Press Statement by the DAC Chairman DAC High Level Meeting, 11-12 May 2000*, http://www.oecd.org/dac/htm/hlm2000stats.htm [accessed October 5, 2000].

9 *Making Appropriations for Foreign Operations, Export Financing, and Other Related Programs for Fiscal Year Ending September 30, 2001*, 106th Congress Report House of Representatives Conference, October 24, 2000.

10 State Department Website, *International Affairs (Function 150) Fiscal Year 2001 Budget Request* http://www.state.gov/www/budget/fy2001/fn150/fn150_fy2001_cmtes.html [accessed February 18, 2001] and USAID Website, *Budget Justification FY 2001*, http://www.usaid.gov/pubs/bj2001 [accessed November 6, 2000].

11 Sullivan, "The Failure of U.S. Foreign Aid," 401-415.

12 M.R. Auer, "Agency Reform as Decision Process: The Reengineering of the Agency for International Development," *Policy Sciences* 31 (1998): 101.

13 World Bank. *International Bank for Reconstruction and Development Subscriptions and Voting Power of Member Countries.* www.worldbank.org/html/extdr/about/voting/kibrd.htm [accessed January 8, 2001] and IMF, *IMF Members' Quotas and Voting Poser and IMF Governors, December 22, 2000.* www.imf.org/external/np/sec/memdir/members.htm [accessed January 8, 2001].

[14] DAC, *Development Co-operation Review Series: United States*. No. 28, (Paris: OECD, 1998).

[15] Overseas Development Institute, *Reforming Food Aid: Time to Grasp the Nettle?*, Briefing Paper No. 1, January 2000, 6.

[16] OECD *Development Co-operation Report 1999: International Development*, 1 (1, 2000) 243, 253.

[17] OECD, *Development Co-operation Report 1999: International Development*, 1 (1, 2000) 48.

[18] The following section has been excerpted and adapted with permission from Isaac Shapiro, *Trends in U.S. Development Aid and the Current Budget Debate* (Washington, DC: Center for Budget and Policy Priorities, 2000). The data combines and averages two years to help smooth out yearly fluctuations.

[19] A very small part of this percentage decline reflects the addition of new donor countries to the list for which OECD compiles data. For example, in the 1977-1978 period, the OECD did not examine contributions from Luxembourg, Portugal or Spain. These countries are included in the 1987-88 and 1997-98 data, and account for only a tiny fraction of ODA. Had these countries not been included in the OECD list in recent years, the U.S. share of total ODA would have been 15.9 percent in 1997-1998 instead of 15.6 percent.

[20] The U.S. "Gross National Product" (used by OECD) and the U.S. "Gross Domestic Product" are virtually identical. In 1998, U.S. GNP and GDP differed by only one-tenth of one percent.

[21] The U.S. dedicated 0.21 percent of GDP to ODA in the 1987-1988 period.

[22] OECD, *Development Co-operation 1999 Report* 234, 242-3.

[23] Carol Lancaster, *Aid to Africa: So Much to Do, So Little Done* (Chicago: The University of Chicago Press, 1999), 77.

[24] Aidan Cox and John Healey, "Poverty Reduction: A Review of Donor Strategies and Practices," In *Waging the Global War on Poverty: Strategies and Case Studies,* Halvorsen-Quevedo, Raundi and Hartmut Schneider eds., (Paris: OECD, 2000), 26.

[25] The following has been excerpted and adapted with permission from Isaac Shapiro, *Trends in U.S. Development Aid and the Current Budget Debate* (Washington, DC: Center for Budget and Policy Priorities, 2000).

[26] World Bank, *World Development Report 1999/2000: Entering the 21st Century* (New York: Oxford University Press, 1999), and World Bank, *Can Anyone Hear Us? Voices of the Poor* (New York: Oxford University Press, 1999).

[27] United Nations Development Program, *Human Development Report 1999* (New York: Oxford University Press, 1999).

Chapter 4

[1] See Hansen, Henrik and Finn Tarp, "Aid Effectiveness Disputed," in *Foreign Aid and Development: Lessons Learnt and Directions for the Future,* Finn Tarp, ed., (London: Routledge, 2000), 103-128; for a survey of a number of empirical studies on the impact of aid on savings, investment and growth, Robert H. Cassen and Associates. 1994. *Does Aid Work?* (Oxford: Clarendon Press, 1994).

[2] World Bank. *Assessing Aid*, (New York: Oxford University Press, 1998).

[3] Ibid, 105-108.

[4] Ibid, 30.

[5] David Atwood, *Cutting Hunger and Poverty in Half: Interest Groups and a Renewed U.S. Commitment in the Post-Cold War World.* Unpublished paper, Washington, DC, 2000, 2.

[6] Atwood, *Cutting Hunger and Poverty in Half*, 2.

[7] World Bank, *World Development Report 2000/2001: Attacking Poverty.* (New York: Oxford University Press, 2000), 182.; Marco Ferroni, *Reforming Foreign Aid: The Role of International Public Goods*. OED Working Paper Series, no. 4. (Washington, DC: World Bank Operations Evaluation Department, 2000), 17.

[8] Atwood, *Cutting Hunger and Poverty in Half*, 2.

[9] Cassen & Associates, *Does Aid Work?*, 98.

[10] Ibid, 99.

[11] Ibid, 99.

[12] International Fund for Agricultural Development, *Drylands: A Call to Action, Building on IFAD's Experience: Lessons from Sub-Saharan Africa.* (Rome: IFAD, 1998).

[13] World Bank, *World Development Report 2000/2001*, 200.

[14] Carol Lancaster, *Aid to Africa* (The University of Chicago Press: 1999), 56-59; Deborah Brautigam, "State Capacity and Effective Governance," In *Agenda for Africa's Economic Renewal,* Benno J. Ndulu and Nicolas van de Walle, eds., ODC Policy Perspective No. 21, (New Brunswick: Transaction Publishers, 1996), 97-98, and Stephen Browne, *Beyond Aid: From Patronage to Partnership* (Aldershot: Ashgate Publishing Ltd., 1999), 49.

[15] World Bank, *Assessing Aid*, 41-42.

[16] World Bank, *World Development Report 2000/2001*, 23.

[17] World Bank, 2000a. *World Development Indicators* (Washington, DC: The World Bank), 344.

[18] World Bank, *World Development Report 2000/2001*, 200.

[19] "Gifts with Strings Attached," *The Economist*. June 17, 2000, 21.

[20] Browne, *Beyond Aid*, 48.

[21] World Bank, *World Development Report 2000/2001*, 200; Browne, *Beyond Aid*, 48.

[22] World Bank Listserve, devnews@lists.worldbank.org, Development News Wednesday, December 13, 2000.

[23] World Bank, *World Development Report 2000/2001*, 193.

[24] R. Kanbur and Todd Sandler with Kevin Morrison, *The Future of Development Assistance: Common Pools and International Public Goods* (Washington: Overseas Development Council, 1999), 27; World Bank, *World Development Report 2000/2001*, 197.

[25] World Bank, *Assessing Aid*, 70-74.

[26] Browne, *Beyond Aid*, 45-47.

[27] Overseas Development Institute, *Reforming Food Aid: Time to Grasp the Nettle,* Briefing Paper, No. 1, (London: ODI), January 2000; Browne, *Beyond Aid*, 46; "Gifts with Strings Attached," 21.

[28] World Bank, *Assessing Aid*.

[29] Ibid, 23.

[30] Browne, *Beyond Aid*, 173.

[31] Tony Addison, "Aid and Conflict." In *Foreign Aid and Development: Lessons Learnt and Directions for the Future*. Finn Tarp, ed., (London: Routledge, 2000), 404-405.

[32] Oxfam, *Growth With Equity is Good for the Poor* (Oxford: Oxfam, 2000), 4.

[33] United Nations Development Programme, *Poverty Report 2000: Overcoming Human Poverty* (New York: UNDP, 2000), 94.

[34] Per Pinstrup-Andersen, Rajul Pandya-Lorch, and Mark W. Rosengrant, *World Food Prospects: Critical Issues for the Early Twenty-First Century,* 2020 Food Policy Report (Washington, DC: International Food Policy Research Institute, October 1999), 9.

[35] IFAD, *Assessment of Rural Poverty in the Eastern and Southern Africa Region: Supporting the Livelihood Strategies of the Rural Poor in East and Southern Africa*, Main Report and Working Papers of Workshop on Rural Poverty, 24-25, January 2000, (Rome: Draft Report, IFAD, 1999), 75-77.

36 Deepa Narayan et al., *Voices of the Poor: Crying for Change*. New York: Oxford University Press for the World Bank, 2000, 75

37 IFAD, *Assessment*, 73-87.

38 Ibid, 72-73.

39 Deepa Narayan et al., *Voices of the Poor: Crying for Change*. New York: Oxford University Press for the World Bank, 2000, 98.

40 World Bank, *World Development Report 2000/2001*, 2000, table 7, 286-287.

41 David Dollar and Roberta Gatti. *Gender Inequality, Income and Growth: Are Good Times Good to Women?* World Bank Policy Research Report on Gender and Development, Working Paper Series, No. 1, Washington, DC, May 1999, 3.

42 Lawrence Haddad and Lisa C. Smith, *Explaining Child Malnutrition in Developing Countries: A Cross-Country Analysis,* International Food Policy Research Institute Research, Report 111, 2000, (Washington, DC: IFPRI, 2000).

43 Lawrence Haddad and Lisa C. Smith, *Overcoming Child Malnutrition in Developing Countries: Past Achievements and Future Choices*. IFPRI 2020 Brief 64 (Washington, DC, February 2000).

44 Kanbur et al., 35-36.

45 Ibid, 39.

46 World Bank website, http://www.worldbank.org/cdf, [accessed December 14, 2000].

47 Kanbur et al., 41.

48 Kanbur et al., *The Future of Development Assistance,* 41-51; World Bank, *World Development Report 2000/2001*, 97.

Chapter 5

1 Thomas L. Friedman, *The Lexus and the Olive Tree: Understanding Globalization* (New York: Farrar, Straus and Giroux, 1999), 352.

2 *Global Development Finance 1999* (Washington, DC: The World Bank, 1999), 24.

3 Ibid, 51.

4 D, A. McGrew Held., D. Goldblatt, and J. Perraton, "Rethinking Globalization" in D. Held and A. McGrew, eds., *The Global Transformations Reader* (Cambridge, UK: Polity Press, 2000), 54.

5 Carol Lancaster, "Transforming U.S. Foreign Aid," in *Foreign Affairs*, July/August 2000, and Marco Ferroni, *Reforming Foreign Aid: The Role of International Public Goods*, World Bank Operations Evaluation Department Working Paper Series No. 4, Spring 2000, 5.

6 Paul Hirst and Grahame Thompson, "Globalization – A Necessary Myth?" in D. Held and A. McGrew, eds., *The Global Transformations Reader* (Cambridge, UK: Polity Press, 2000), 69.

7 World Bank, *World Development Report 2000/2001: Attacking Poverty* (New York: Oxford University Press, 2000), 3.

8 Jeffrey D. Sachs, "New Approaches to Helping the Poorest of the Poor in the Global Economy," lecture at the Nobel Conference XXXVI, Gustavus Adolphus University, Minnesota, October 3-4, 2000.

9 A. Lateef, *Linking up with the Global Economy: A Case Study of the Bangalore Software Industry,* International Institute for Labour Studies Discussion Paper Series DP/96/1997, (Geneva: IILS, 1997).

10 World Bank, *World Development Report 2000/2001*, 46

11 Friedman, 273-274.

12 *State of the World's Children, 1988,* (United Nations Children's Fund, New York: Oxford University Press, 1988); *Human Development Report 1996* (United Nations Development Programme, New York: Oxford University Press, 1996).

13 The decline was from 41% to 16% in East and Southeast Asia from 1961 to 1992; in South Asia, the decline was from 33% to 22%. *What Governments Can Do: Hunger 1997*, Bread for the World Institute, Silver Spring, MD, 1997, 17.

14 Michael Lipton and Richard Longhurst, *New Seeds and Poor People* (London: Unwin Hyman, 1989).

15 Jeffrey D. Sachs and Andrew Warner, "Economic Reform and the Process of Global Integration," *Brookings Papers on Economic Activity,* No.1, 1995.

16 World Bank, *World Development Report 2000/2001*, 180.

17 Alvin Toffler and Heidi Toffler, *War and Anti-war: Making Sense of Today's Global Chaos* (New York: Time Warner, 1995), 25.

18 Friedman, 272–273.

19 Allen Hammond, *Which World: Scenarios for the 21st Century,* http://mars3.gps.caltech.edu/whichworld/explore/scenarios/scenfw_top.html. [accessed 4/25/00].

20 Marco Ferroni, *Reforming Foreign Aid: The Role of International Public Goods*, World Bank Operations Evaluation Department Working Paper Series No. 4, Spring 2000, 6.

21 World Bank. *World Development Report 2000/2001*, 181.

22 Ibid, 183.

23 Global Alliance for Vaccines and Immunization http://www.vaccinealliance.org/newsletter/nov2000/briefing.html.

24 Carol Lancaster, *Transforming Foreign Aid: U.S. Assistance in the 21st Century* (Washington, DC: Institute for International Economics, 2000), 82–87.

Chapter 6

1 "In 46 percent of the countries [of sub-Saharan Africa], the undernourished have an average deficit of more than 300 kilocalories per person per day. By contrast, in only 16 percent of the countries in Asia and the Pacific do the undernourished suffer from average food deficits this high." Food and Agriculture Organization, *State of Food Insecurity in the World 2000* (Rome, Italy: FAO, 2000), 1.

2 Ibid, 3.

3 United Nations Conference on Trade and Development, http://www.unctad.org/en/subsites/ldcs/aboutldc.htm [accessed December 21, 2000].

4 FAO, *State of Food Insecurity*, 27.

5 Ibid, 29.

6 World Bank, *Can Africa Claim the 21st Century?* (Washington, DC: World Bank, 2000), 124.

7 William Dhlamini, *Africa: Moving Away From Dependence on Agriculture* (Johannesburg: Inter Press Service, November 14, 2000); and Southern African Development Community Website, *SADC Objectives,* http://www.sadc.int/sadcmain/docs6_4/overview/objectiv.htm, [accessed December 20, 2000].

8 World Bank, *Can Africa Claim the 21st Century?*, 15.

9 J. Dirck Stryker and Jeffrey Metzel, *Meeting the Food Summit Target: The United States Contribution,* APAP III Research Report 1039 (Washington, DC: U.S. Agency for International Development, 1998).

10 Raymond W. Copson, *Africa: U.S. Foreign Assistance Issues,* Congressional Research Service Issue Brief for Congress, IB95052, Washington, DC, November 21, 2000, 4.

11 Ibid, 3.

12 USAID, *Budget Justification FY 2001*, http://www.usaid.gov/pubs/bj2001, 6, [accessed December 22, 2000].

13 Copson, *Africa*, 13.

[14] The African Development Foundation website, http://www.adf.gov, [accessed December 21, 2000].

[15] International Fund for Agricultural Development, *Drylands: A Call to Action* (Rome: IFAD, 1998), 9-15.

[16] Tamanda Chidzanja, Vice President of Program Operations, National Association of Smallholder Farmers of Malawi, private communication.

[17] Deepa Narayan, et al., *Voices of the Poor: Can Anyone Hear Us?* New York: Oxford University Press for the World Bank, 2000, 29.

[18] UNICEF, *State of the World's Children 2001* (New York: United Nations, 2001), 93.

[19] Jerker Carlsson, Gloria Somolekae and Nicolas van de Walle, *Foreign Aid in Africa: Learning from Country Experiences* (Uppsala: Nordiska Afrikaininstitutet, 1997), 27-28.

[20] UNICEF, State of the World's Children 2000 (New York: United Nations, 2000), 87.

[21] World Bank, *Can Africa Claim the 21st Century?*, 109.

[22] UNAIDS, "Report on the Global HIV/AIDS Epidemic, June 2000" (Geneva: UNAIDS, 2000), 124.

[23] Ibid, 9.

[24] African Development Forum 2000, "AIDS: The Greatest Leadership Challenge," Daily Report for December 7, 2000.

[25] World Bank, *Can Africa Claim the 21st Century?*, 140.

[26] Deepa Narayan et al., *Voices of the Poor: Crying Out for Change.* New York: Oxford University Press for the World Bank, 2000, 73.

[27] World Bank, *Can Africa Claim the 21st Century?*, 140.

[28] USAID, *A New Day in Africa, the Food Security Initiative: Progress Toward Implementing the Africa: Seeds of Hope Act* (New York: United Nations, October 2000).

Chapter 7

[1] UN World Food Programme data, http://www.wfp.org, [accessed August 16, 2000].

[2] Reliefweb, http://www.reliefweb.org, [accessed August 16, 2000].

[3] Complex humanitarian emergencies are caused by intra-state political conflicts between groups competing for resources or control of the economy. Refugees and internally displaced persons require massive amounts of humanitarian assistance from international agencies to survive.

[4] The primary sources of information in the following sections include Reliefweb and the websites of the UN Food and Agriculture Organization and the UN World Food Program.

[5] Forty-one are Highly Indebted Poor Countries (HIPC), and another 11 are countries considered by the Jubilee 2000 campaign to require debt relief due to their poverty and inability to pay their external debt. See http://www.jubilee2000uk.org.

[6] "The State of Food Insecurity in the World, 2000," Food and Agriculture Organization of the United Nations, http://www.fao.org.

[7] "Bolivia in the Struggle Against Poverty: Is the International Debt Relief Initiative Working?" Bread for the World Institute Debt and Development Dossier, August 2000, Issue #4.

[8] Countries that undertake consultations to enhance structural adjustment of the economy may qualify for debt reduction or debt forgiveness under the Highly Indebted Poor Countries Initiative (HIPC). But many countries were dissatisfied with IMF and World Bank conditionality, and negotiated more favorable conditions under HIPC II.

[9] "The State of Food Insecurity in the World, 2000."

[10] Ibid.

[11] News Release, UNWFP, Rome, Italy, August 30, 2000.

[12] "The Reality of Aid – 2000," (London: Earthscan, 2000), 179.

[13] "State of the States: A Profile of Food and Nutrition Programs Across the Nation," Food Research and Action Center (FRAC), December 1999.

[14] Ibid, 72.

Chapter 8

[1] Worldwatch, "Chronic Hunger and Obesity Epidemic Eroding Global Progress," news release, March 4, 2000, www.worldwatch.org/alerts/000304.html, [accessed July 7,2000].

[2] Paul Rogat Loeb, *Soul of a Citizen: Living with Conviction in a Cynical Time,* New York: St. Martin's Press, 1999, Reprinted in *Utne Reader,* July-August, 1999, 46-53.

[3] National Association to Advance Fat Acceptance (NAAFA), "NAAFA Policy on Dieting and the Diet Industry," www.naafa.org/documents/policies/dieting.html, [accessed August 5, 2000].

[4] Claudia Kalb, "When Weight Loss Goes Awry," *Newsweek,* (July 3, 2000): 46.

[5] Jubilee 2000/USA. "Pastor and Activist from Washington State Starts Water-only, Open-ended 'Fast for Life' on Capitol Hill!" www.j2000usa.org/updates/fast.html, [accessed July 20, 2000].

[6] Bread for the World Institute and Christian Reformed World Relief Committee. *Listen, Learn, Act!,* Washington, DC, 1997.

[7] Adapted from "In Common: Global Action Against Poverty. What We Can Do: A 10-Point Agenda for Global Action Against Poverty." www.incommon.web.ca/anglais/agenda/menu.html, [accessed January 4, 2001].

[8] David Beckmann and Arthur Simon, *Grace at the Table*, Downers Grove, IL: Intervarsity Press, 1999, 193.

[9] Ibid, 39.

Appendices
Development and Empowerment Outcomes

BY MICHAEL KUCHINSKY AND ASMA LATEEF

Development empowers individuals and communities. Development policies and programs, which aim to foster economic and human development, must provide poor people with skills, opportunities and choices, empowering them to improve their lives. Therefore, evaluating poverty-reduction strategies in terms of outcomes that empower people holds development partners accountable to poor people.

By targeting sectors and activities that are a part of poor and hungry people's daily lives, development partners can reduce hunger and poverty. An agricultural development strategy that does not improve the economic, social, political, and institutional capacities of people cannot be considered development and would not end chronic hunger. If people are politically empowered, this is reflected in all their activities. Political empowerment ensures that poor and hungry people are heard and that their needs are addressed. This, in turn, leads to development.

This matrix summarizes the interrelationship of sectoral development strategies and empowerment. Each cell contains outcomes in four sectors that can help alleviate hunger and empower poor people. For example, if access to primary and secondary education is the outcome of development policy, poor people are socially empowered. With the ability to read and write, poor people can access information, protect their rights, and compete. If development partners invest in institutions so that poor people have safety nets and livelihood security, access to improved communications, and a sense of ownership of the transparent and accountable institutions upon which they depend, poor people are empowered. They benefit from and have control over the institutions that they need to succeed. The economic empowerment of smallholder farmers suggests that they have improved access to markets, credit, information and other supports necessary to increase productivity. Integrating gender equity into all aspects policymaking empowers poor women politically. Development strategies and projects can be evaluated to ensure that each development investment yields outcomes that empower.

Development and Empowerment Outcomes Matrix

Sectors	Forms of Empowerment			
	Economic Empowerment/ Livelihood Strategies	Social Empowerment/ Investment	Political Empowerment/ Policy	Institutional Empowerment/ Capacity Building
Agriculture	▪ Market development ▪ Infrastructure ▪ Knowledge management ▪ Information technology ▪ Microcredit ▪ Sustainable practices	▪ Demand-driven agricultural extension, training, and research ▪ Policies to attract investment	▪ Land reform ▪ Commodity pricing policies ▪ Land titles ▪ Investment regulatory framework	▪ Producer organizations ▪ Local financial infrastructure
Health	▪ HIV/AIDS education ▪ Prevention and treatment of infectious diseases ▪ Training health care professionals	▪ Nutrition training ▪ Community-based primary health care facilities	▪ Public health promotion ▪ Recognition of HIV/AIDS threat	▪ National oversight of health care system (through Ministry of Health)
Education	▪ Grants and exchanges for university students ▪ Vocational training	▪ Primary and secondary education	▪ Universal primary education ▪ Literacy and numeracy	▪ National oversight of education curriculum (through Ministry of Education) ▪ Communications
Gender	▪ Microcredit ▪ Access to information ▪ Training	▪ Primary girls' education ▪ Nutrition and reproductive health training for women	▪ Inheritance rights ▪ Gender lens on policy: focus on participation	▪ Women's associations ▪ Developing women's leadership
Institutions	▪ Access to credit ▪ Entrepreneurial and market training ▪ Private sector/enterprise development ▪ Debt cancellation	▪ Capacity building of civil society organizations	▪ Governance ▪ Democratization ▪ Anti-corruption ▪ Participatory approaches ▪ Peace/conflict resolution ▪ Fair labor practices	▪ Safety net ▪ Livelihood security ▪ Communications ▪ Transparency ▪ Accountability ▪ Ownership

Hunger Index Technical Note

BY DOUGLAS A. HICKS

The Hunger Index (HI) is calculated based on information taken from the most reliable and updated sources available at the time of publication.

Components of the Hunger Index

The HI contains three component parts that represent availability of food, access to food, and utilization of food. Values for dietary energy supply, or calories per capita per day, are taken from the "food balance sheets" of the FAO, as found in their FAOSTAT database.[1] The most recent available data is for the year 1998. Clearly, an important indicator for assessing how the physiological needs of a population are met is a country's supply of food. As the FAO has emphasized, the minimal daily energy supply of particular persons vary by age, gender, and other factors. Since national populations have different demographic compositions (by age and gender distribution, for instance), the daily energy needs of an "average" or "representative" person in a particular population vary. The HI could be further refined by making some adjustment to calorie supply per person that accounts for the population's particular demographic composition. As a general indicator, though, the HI does not incorporate this difference.

Access to food reflects the distributional component of hunger. As Amartya Sen has definitively shown, starvation among a segment of the population has frequently occurred in times of adequate food supply; conversely, even the worst famines have not affected the entirety – or even the majority – of the population.[2] Data on the distribution of food consumption within a country are difficult to obtain. Indeed, one of the most problematic aspects of the FAO's method to estimate the number of undernourished persons worldwide – and recently, to measure the "depth of hunger" – is its calculation of the distribution of dietary energy supply among national popula-

tions.[3] The HI avoids this particular problem by using more reliable measures of inequality in the consumption of all goods. The HI uses the Gini coefficient, a standard relative measure of inequality for consumption of all goods. The data come from the *World Bank Atlas 2000*.[4] Only countries for which there is a Gini coefficient for consumption, and not income, are included. Distributions of consumption are less disparate than are distributions of income; they are also more reflective of the distribution of the consumption of food. To be sure, the consumption of all goods is more disparate than is the consumption of food. Thus, the figure used is higher than the figure for inequality of food intake. More important, the difference in the two figures can vary across countries (since there is variability among countries in the distribution of the consumption of nonfood items). Nonetheless, this World Bank data set is a reasonable indicator of the inequality of access to food and provides a reliable data set for 49 countries.

The component indicating "utilization" of food uses the WHO *Global Database on Child Growth and Malnutrition's* most recent estimates for stunting among children under age 5. These estimates appear in the *4th Report on the World Nutrition Situation,* published by the United Nations.[5]

Calculating the Hunger Index

The Hunger Index combines these data into a single scalar index that runs from 0 (most dire hunger problem) to 1 (no significant hunger problem).

Step one. The figure for food availability per capita per day – dietary energy supply (DES) – is first converted into an indicator (FAvail) within the 0 to 1 range for each country, according to the following formula: **FAvail = log [(.00321 × DES) − 2.86]** This formula is devised so that the

DES values that correspond to 0 and 1, respectively, are 1,200 and 4,000 calories per capita per day, levels that are below the lowest national figure and above the highest national figure. The value of 1,200 thus serves as the fixed minimum value for national DES, and the value of 4,000 serves as the fixed maximum value. Since the normative interest is first in removing the severe levels of hunger, this figure gives more "reward" to a country that moves its DES from, say, 1,600 to 1,800 Kcal/capita/day than it does to a country that moves its DES from 2,000 to 2,200 Kcal/capita/day. This method of valuing more basic progress over more advanced progress by giving more weight to changes closer to the lower end of the range was employed to determine the income component of the Human Development Index – both in its earlier form and its present form.[6]

Step two. The availability indicator, FAvail, is adjusted or reduced according to the level of consumption inequality to obtain an AccessAdjustedFAvail. The Gini of consumption (ConsumGini) is subtracted from 1 in order to have the adjustment work in the proper direction. There is significant precedent for this exercise, in the income sphere and in determinations of levels of well-being or development.[7] In this case, the combined indicator (AccessAdjustedFAvail) for availability and access takes into account both the absolute amount of food that is available to a population and a measure (Gini coefficient) of the relative access to food and other goods within that population. Among countries with equivalent daily energy supplies per capita, those with more egalitarian distributions of consumption receive a higher value. While the weighting of, and method of combining, indicators for the absolute supply and the distributional concerns can be refined in the future, attention to both factors remains a vital part of assessing hunger: **AccessAdjustedFAvail = (1 – ConsumGini) × FAvail**

Step three: The utilization indicator, Utiliz, is simply the proportion of the youth-under-age-five population that is free from stunting (Stunting = proportion of stunted children), as follows: **Utiliz = 1 – Stunting**

Step four: The access-adjusted availability figure and the utilization figure are combined in an unweighted or, more precisely, an equally weighted manner to obtain the Hunger Index.

$$HI = \frac{AccessAdjustedFAvail + Utiliz}{2}$$

---

[1] The URL for the FAOSTAT is http://apps.fao.org. The FAO calculates the total food supply that is available for human consumption though not all of this food is actually consumed, due to waste of food within the household. Food supplies devoted to livestock and other uses are not counted. The per capita figure is determined by dividing total human supply by the best estimate of people actually living within a geographic area. See http://www.fao.org/waicent/faostat//agricult/fs-e.htm.

[2] Amartya Sen, *Poverty and Famines: An Essay on Entitlement and Deprivation* (Oxford: Clarendon Press, 1981).

[3] The methodology that the FAO uses for estimating distribution of food intake is explained in Food and Agricultural Organization of the United Nations, *The Sixth World Food Survey* (Rome: FAO, 1996), 132-137. A coefficient of variation is estimated for each country using different indirect methods, depending on the data that are available for particular countries. The methodology, the FAO notes, is problematic, and for many countries, there "was virtually no satisfactory basis for estimating the distribution parameter" (FAO, 135). In contrast, the distributional factor in the HI is admittedly less complex, but it employs the same data item (Gini coefficient of consumption) for each country as a general indicator of the inequality of access to food.

[4] *World Bank Atlas* CD-ROM (Washington: World Bank, 2000), Table 2.8, "Distribution of Income or Consumption."

[5] World Health Organization, Global Database on Child Growth and Malnutrition (Geneva: WHO, 2000); as reported in "Latest National Prevalence of Stunting and Underweight in Preschool Children," *4th Report of the World Nutrition Situation: Nutrition Throughout the Life Cycle*, (Appendix 5), United Nations Administrative Committee on Coordination, Sub-Committee on Nutrition (ACC/SCN) in collaboration with International Food Policy Research Institute (IFPRI), Geneva, January 2000, 94-96. The percentage of children who are "stunted" is the percentage estimated to fall, after a method of standardization, more than two standard deviations below the mean of a "normal" reference group of children. See http://www.who.int/nutgrowthdb/intro_text.htm#mainsum.

[6] This method is used with the HDI in both its original and revised forms. See *Human Development Report 1999*, "Technical Note. Computing the Indices," 159.

[7] These precedents are discussed fully in Douglas A. Hicks, *Inequality and Christian Ethics*, (Cambridge, UK: Cambridge University Press, 2000), Chapter 10 (especially 222-223 and 226-229) and Appendix C (especially 259-260).

Table 1: Global Hunger – Life and Death Indicators

	Total (millions) 2000	Projected (millions) 2025	Projected growth rate (%) 1995-2000	Total fertility rate 1995-2000	% population under age 15 1999	% population urban 1998	Life expectancy at birth Male	Life expectancy at birth Female	Infant mortality rate per 1,000 live births 1998	% of low birth weight infants 1990-1998y	% of 1-year-old children immunized (measles) 1995-98y	Under-5 mortality rate per 1,000 live births 1960	Under-5 mortality rate per 1,000 live births 1998	Maternal mortality rate per 100,000 live births 1980-98y	Refugees as of December 31, 1999 Country of origin	Refugees as of December 31, 1999 Country of asylum
Developing Countries	..	..	..	..	..	..	..	..	64	18	72	216	95	..	..	..
Africa (Sub-Saharan)		..		..	..	32.7m	..	..	107e	15e	48e	261e	173e	..	..	..
Angola	12.9	25.1	3.2	6.80	48	32.9	44.9	48.1	170	19	65	345	292	..	339,300	15,000
Benin	6.1	11.1	2.7	5.80	46	40.7	51.7	55.2	101	..	82	300	165	500	..	3,000
Botswana	1.6	2.2	1.9	4.35	42	68.8	46.2	48.4	38	11	80	170	48	330	..	1,000
Burkina Faso	11.9	23.3	2.7	6.57	47	17.4	43.6	45.2	109	21	46	315	165	..	..	..
Burundi	6.7	11.6	1.7	6.28	47	8.4	41.0	43.8	106	..	44	255	176	..	311,000	2,000
Cameroon	15.1	26.5	2.7	5.30	44	47.3	53.4	56.0	94	13	44	255	153	430	..	10,000
Cape Verde	0.4	0.7		3.56	40	59.3	65.5	71.3	54	9	66	164	73	55	..	..
Central African Republic	3.6	5.7	1.9	4.90	43	40.3	42.9	46.9	113	15	39	327	173	1,100	..	55,000
Chad	7.7	13.9	2.6	6.07	46	23.1	45.7	48.7	118	..	30	325	198	830	13,000	20,000
Comoros	0.7	1.2		4.80	43	32.1	57.4	60.2	67	8	67	265	90	500	..	..
Congo, Dem. Rep. of	51.7	104.8	2.6	6.43	48	29.6	49.2	52.3	128	15	10	302	207	..	229,000	235,000
Congo, Republic of	2.9	5.7	2.8	6.06	46	61.0	46.3	50.8	81	16	18	220	108	..	25,000	40,000
Côte d'Ivoire	14.8	23.3	1.8	5.10	44	45.3	46.2	47.3	90	12	66	300	150	600	..	135,000
Djibouti	0.6	1.0		5.30	41	82.9	48.7	52.0	111	11	21	289	156	..	1,000	23,000
Equatorial Guinea	0.5	0.8		5.58	43	45.9	48.4	51.6	108	..	82	316	171	..	..	..
Eritrea	3.9	6.7	3.8	5.70	44	18.0	49.3	52.4	70	13	52	250	112	1,000	323,100	2,000
Ethiopia	62.6	115.4	2.5	6.30	46	16.7	42.4	44.3	110	16	46	280	173	..	53,300	246,000
Gabon	1.2	2.0	2.6	5.40	40	53.2	51.1	53.8	85	..	32	287	144	600	..	15,000
Gambia	1.3	2.2		5.20	40	31.1	45.4	48.6	64	..	91	364	82	..	..	25,000
Ghana	20.2	36.9	2.7	5.15	44	37.3	58.3	61.8	67	8	62	215	105	210	10,000	12,000
Guinea	7.4	12.5	0.8	5.51	44	31.3	46.0	47.0	124	13	58	380	197	670	..	453,000
Guinea-Bissau	1.2	1.9	2.2	5.75	43	22.9	43.5	46.5	130	20	51	336	205	910	5,300	5,000
Kenya	30.1	41.8	2.0	4.45	44	31.3	51.1	53.0	75	16	71	205	117	590	5,000	254,000
Lesotho	2.2	3.5	2.2	4.75	40	26.4	54.7	57.3	94	11	43	203	136	..	..	..
Liberia	3.2	6.6	8.2	6.31	44		46.1	48.5	157	..	31	288	235	..	249,000	90,000
Madagascar	15.9	29.0	3.0	5.40	44	28.3	56.0	59.0	95	5	65	364	157	490	..	..
Malawi	10.9	20.0	2.4	6.75	47	14.6	38.9	39.6	134	20	90	361	213	620	..	..
Mali	11.2	21.3	2.4	6.60	46	28.7	52.0	54.6	144	16	57	517	237	580	2,000	7,000
Mauritania	2.7	4.8	2.7	5.50	44	55.3	51.9	55.1	120	11	20	310	183	550	45,000	25,000
Mauritius	1.2	1.4	0.8	1.91	26	40.9	67.9	75.1	19	13	85	92	23	50	..	..
Mozambique	19.7	30.6	2.5	6.25	45	37.8	43.9	46.6	129	20	87	313	206	1,100	..	1,000
Namibia	1.7	2.3	2.2	4.90	42	38.9	51.8	53.0	57	16	63	206	74	230	1,000	8,000
Niger	10.7	21.5	3.2	6.84	48	19.6	46.9	50.1	166	12	27	354	280	590	..	2,000
Nigeria	111.5	183.0	2.4	5.15	43	42.2	48.7	51.5	112	16	26	207	187	..	..	7,000
Rwanda	7.7	12.4	7.7	6.20	46	5.9	39.4	41.7	105	17	66	210	170	..	37,000	36,000
Senegal	9.5	16.7	2.6	5.57	45	45.7	50.5	54.2	70	4	65	300	121	560	10,000	42,000
Sierra Leone	4.9	8.1	3.0	6.06	44	35.3	35.8	38.7	182	11	68	390	316	..	454,000	7,000
Somalia	10.1	21.2	4.2	7.25	48		45.4	48.6	125	16	47	294	211	..	415,600	..
South Africa	40.4	46.0	1.5	3.25	35	49.9	51.5	58.1	60	..	76	130	83	..	..	40,000
Sudan	29.5	46.3	2.1	4.61	40	34.2	53.6	56.4	73	15	63	210	115	550	423,200	363,000
Swaziland	1.0	1.8		4.70	43	33.9	57.9	62.5	64	10	62	233	90	230	..	..
Tanzania	33.5	57.9	2.3	5.48	46	26.4	46.8	49.1	91	14	72	240	142	530	..	413,000
Togo	4.6	8.5	2.6	6.05	46	32.2	47.6	50.1	81	20	32	267	144	480	3,000	10,000
Uganda	21.8	44.4	2.8	7.10	50	13.5	38.9	40.4	84	13	30	224	134	510	15,000	197,000
Zambia	9.2	15.6	2.3	5.55	47	43.9	39.5	40.6	112	13	69	213	202	650	..	205,000
Zimbabwe	11.7	15.1	1.4	3.80	42	33.9	43.6	44.7	59	10	65	159	89	400	..	1,000
South Asia		2,049.9j		3.36j		..			76	33	64	239	114	..	..	..
Afghanistan	22.7	44.9	2.9	6.90	43		45.0	46.0	165	20	36	360	257	..	2,561,050	..
Bangladesh	129.2	178.8	1.7	3.11	36	20.0	58.1	58.2	79	50	62	247	106	440	..	53,100
Bhutan	2.1	3.9	2.8	5.50	43	6.7	59.5	62.0	84	..	71	300	116	380	125,000	..
India	1013.7	1,330.4	1.6	3.13	34	27.7	62.3	62.9	69	33	66	236	105	410	15,000	292,000
Maldives	0.3	0.5		5.40	43	27.7	65.7	63.3	62	13	98	300	87	350	..	..
Nepal	23.9	38.0	2.4	4.45	41	11.2	57.6	57.1	72	..	73	297	100	540	..	130,000
Pakistan	156.5	263.0	2.8	5.03	42	35.9	62.9	65.1	95	25	55	226	136	..	..	1,217,000
Sri Lanka	18.8	23.5	1.0	2.10	27	22.9	70.9	75.4	17	25	91	133	19	60	110,000	..

Table 1: Global Hunger – Life and Death Indicators

| | Population | | | | | | Life expectancy at birth | | Infant mortality rate per 1,000 live births 1998 | % of low birth weight infants 1990-1998[y] | % of 1-year-old children immunized (measles) 1995-98[y] | Under-5 mortality rate per 1,000 live births | | Maternal mortality rate per 100,000 live births 1980-98[y] | Refugees as of December 31, 1999 | |
	Total (millions) 2000	Projected (millions) 2025	Projected growth rate (%) 1995-2000	Total fertility rate 1995-2000	% population under age 15 1999	% population urban 1998	Male	Female				1960	1998		Country of origin	Country of asylum
East Asia and the Pacific		..		..					38[f]	10[f]	87[f]	201[f]	50[f]	..	..	..
Brunei	0.3	.5		2.80	33	71.1	73.4	78.1	8	..	100	87	9	0	..	..
Cambodia	11.2	16.5	2.3	4.60	41	22.2	51.5	55.0	104	..	63	217	163	470	15,100	100
China	1,277.6	1,480.4	0.9	1.80	25	32.7	67.9	72.0	38	9	97	209	47	65	130,000	292,800
Hong Kong[a]	6.9	7.7	2.1	1.32	18	95.4	75.8	81.4	..	..	..	..	..	..	..	..
Fiji	0.8	1.1		2.73	32	41.6	70.6	74.9	19	12	75	97	23	38	..	..
Indonesia	212.1	273.4	1.4	2.58	31	38.3	63.3	67.0	40	8	60	216	56	450	8,000	120,000
Korea, DPR (North)	24.0	29.4	1.6	2.05	28		68.9	75.1	23	..	34	120	30	110	..	..
Korea, Rep. of (South)	46.8	52.5	0.8	1.65	22	84.5	68.8	76.0	5	9	85	127	5	20	..	..
Laos, PDR	5.4	9.7	2.6	5.75	44	22.3	52.0	54.5	96	18	71	235	116	650	13,900	..
Malaysia	22.2	31.0	2.0	3.18	34	55.8	69.9	74.3	9	8	86	105	10	39	..	45,400
Mongolia	2.7	3.7	1.7	2.60	36	62.4	64.4	67.3	105	7	93	185	150	150	..	..
Myanmar (Burma)	45.6	58.1	1.2	2.40	29	26.9	58.5	61.8	80	24	85	252	113	230	240,100	..
Papua New Guinea	4.8	7.5	2.2	4.60	39	16.8	57.2	58.7	79	23	59	204	112	370	..	8,000
Philippines	76.0	108.3	2.1	3.62	37	56.9	66.5	70.2	32	9	71	110	44	170	45,000	200
Singapore	3.6	4.2	1.4	1.68	22	100.0	74.9	79.3	4	7	96	40	5	6	..	..
Solomon Islands	0.4	0.8		4.85	43	18.6	69.7	73.9	22	20	64	185	26	550	..	..
Thailand	61.4	72.7	0.9	1.74	26	20.9	65.8	72.0	30	6	91	148	37	44	..	158,400
Vietnam	79.8	108.0	1.6	2.60	34	19.5	64.9	69.6	31	17	89	219	42	160	292,000	15,000
Latin America and the Caribbean		696.7[k]		2.70[k]		..	66.1	72.6	32[g]	9[g]	89[g]	154[g]	39[g]	..	..	..
Argentina	37.0	47.2	1.3	2.62	28	88.9	69.7	76.8	19	7	99	72	22	38	..	3,300
Belize	0.2	0.4	2.4	3.66	40	46.4	73.4	76.1	35	4	84	104	43	140	..	3,000
Bolivia	8.3	13.1	2.3	4.36	40	63.2	59.8	63.2	66	5	51	255	85	390	..	400
Brazil	170.1	217.9	1.3	2.27	29	80.2	63.1	71.0	36	8	96	177	42	160	..	2,300
Chile	15.2	19.5	1.4	2.44	29	84.3	72.3	78.3	11	5	93	138	12	23	..	300
Colombia	42.3	59.8	1.9	2.80	33	74.1	67.3	74.3	25	9	75	130	30	80	..	250
Costa Rica	4.0	5.9	2.5	2.83	33	50.8	74.3	78.9	14	7	86	112	16	29	..	22,900
Cuba	11.2	11.8	0.4	1.55	22	77.1	74.2	78.0	7	7	99	54	8	27	850	1,000
Dominican Republic	8.5	11.2	1.7	2.80	34	63.9	69.0	73.1	43	13	95	149	51	230	..	650
Ecuador	12.6	17.8	2.0	3.10	34	61.1	67.3	72.5	30	13	88	180	39	160	..	350
El Salvador	6.3	9.1	2.0	3.17	36	45.9	66.5	72.5	30	11	98	210	34	160	253,000	..
Guatemala	11.4	19.8	2.6	4.93	44	39.7	61.4	67.2	41	15	81	202	52	190	146,000	750
Guyana	0.9	1.0		2.32	30	37.0	61.1	67.9	58	15	93	126	79	190	..	..
Haiti	8.2	12.0	1.7	4.38	41	33.6	51.4	56.2	91	15	22	253	130	..	23,000	..
Honduras	6.5	10.7	2.8	4.30	42	45.7	67.5	72.3	33	9	99	204	44	220	..	..
Jamaica	2.6	3.2	0.9	2.50	31	55.1	72.9	76.8	10	10	88	76	11	120	..	50
Mexico	98.9	130.2	1.6	2.75	34	74.0	69.5	75.5	28	7	89	134	34	48	..	8,500
Nicaragua	5.1	8.7	2.7	4.42	43	63.7	65.8	70.6	39	9	71	193	48	150	18,000	500
Panama	2.9	3.8	1.6	2.63	32	56.9	71.8	76.4	18	8	96	104	20	85	..	600
Paraguay	5.5	9.4	2.6	4.17	40	54.6	67.5	72.0	27	5	..	90	33	190	..	..
Peru	25.7	35.5	1.7	2.98	34	72.0	65.9	70.9	43	11	90	234	54	270	1,700	700
Suriname	0.4	0.5		2.21	31	51.0	67.5	72.7	28	13	82	98	35	110	..	..
Trinidad and Tobago	1.3	1.5	0.5	1.65	26	73.2	71.5	76.2	16	10	90	73	18	..	..	..
Uruguay	3.3	3.9	0.7	2.40	25	90.9	70.5	78.0	16	8	92	56	19	21	..	150
Venezuela	24.2	34.8	2.0	2.98	35	86.8	70.0	75.7	21	9	94	75	25	65	..	200
Middle East and North Africa		..		..					51[h]	11[h]	87[h]	241[h]	66[h]	..	..	..
Algeria	31.5	46.6	2.3	3.81	37	57.9	67.5	70.3	35	9	75	255	40	220	5,000	84,000
Bahrain	0.6	0.9		2.90	30	91.6	71.1	75.3	16	6	100	203	20	46	..	..
Cyprus	0.8	0.9		2.03	24	55.7	75.5	80.0	8	..	90	36	9	0	..	300
Egypt	68.5	95.6	1.9	3.40	36	45.3	64.7	67.9	51	10	98	282	69	170	3,000	47,000
Iran	67.7	94.5	1.7	2.80	37	60.6	68.5	70.0	29	10	100	233	33	37	31,200	1,835,000
Iraq	23.1	41.0	2.8	5.25	42	75.9	60.9	63.9	103	15	79	171	125	..	534,450	129,400
Jordan	6.7	12.1	3.0	4.86	42	73.1	68.9	71.5	30	10	86	139	36	41	..	1,518,000
Kuwait	2.0	3.0	3.1	2.89	35	97.4	74.1	78.2	12	7	100	128	13	5	..	52,000
Lebanon	3.3	4.4	1.7	2.69	33	88.9	68.1	71.7	29	10	91	85	35	100	..	378,100

Table 1: Global Hunger – Life and Death Indicators

	Population						Life expectancy at birth		Infant mortality rate per 1,000 live births 1998	% of low birth weight infants 1990-1998[y]	% of 1-year-old children immunized (measles) 1995-98[y]	Under-5 mortality rate per 1,000 live births		Maternal mortality rate per 100,000 live births 1980-98[y]	Refugees as of December 31, 1999	
	Total (millions) 2000	Projected (millions) 2025	Projected growth rate (%) 1995-2000	Total fertility rate 1995-2000	% population under age 15 1999	% population urban 1998	Male	Female				1960	1998		Country of origin	Country of asylum
Libya	5.6	8.6	2.4	3.80	38	86.8	68.3	72.2	20	7	92	270	24	75	..	11,000
Morocco	28.4	38.7	1.8	3.10	33	54.0	64.8	68.5	57	9	91	220	70	230	..	..
Oman	2.5	5.4	3.3	5.85	45	81.2	68.9	73.3	15	8	98	280	18	19	..	..
Qatar	0.6	0.8		3.74	26	92.1	70.0	75.4	15	..	90	239	18	10	..	..
Saudi Arabia	21.6	40.0	3.4	5.80	41	84.7	69.9	73.4	22	7	93	292	26	..	..	128,600
Syria	16.1	26.3	2.5	4.00	42	53.5	66.7	71.2	26	7	97	201	32	110	..	379,200
Tunisia	9.6	12.8	1.4	2.55	31	64.1	68.4	70.7	25	8	94	254	32	70	..	..
Turkey	66.6	87.9	1.7	2.50	29	73.1	66.5	71.7	37	8	76	219	42	130	11,800	9,100
United Arab Emirates	2.4	3.3	2.0	3.42	29	85.2	73.9	76.5	9	6	95	223	10	3	..	..
West Bank and Gazaa	18.1	..		..	..		..	..	..	..	..	..	..	..	3,931,400	1,368,100
Yemen	18.1	39.0	3.7	7.60	48	36.2	57.4	58.4	87	19	66	340	121	350	..	60,000
Countries in Transition[b]		..		..	..	67.0			29[i]	7[i]	92[i]	101[i]	35[i]	..	..	..
Albania	3.1	3.8	-0.4	2.50	30	38.3	69.9	75.9	30	7	89	151	37	..	..	5,000
Armenia	3.5	3.9	-0.3	1.70	25	69.4	67.2	73.6	25	7	94	48	30	35	188,400	240,000
Azerbaijan	7.7	9.4	0.5	1.99	29	56.6	65.5	74.1	36	6	98	74	46	37	230,000	222,000
Belarus	10.2	9.5	-0.3	1.36	19	73.2	62.2	73.9	22	..	98	47	27	22	..	2,900
Bosnia and Herzegovina	4.0	4.3	3.0	1.35	19		70.5	75.9	16	..	80	160	19	10	260,350	60,000
Bulgaria	8.2	7.0	-0.7	1.23	17	69.4	67.6	74.7	14	6	95	70	17	15	..	2,800
Croatia	4.5	4.2	-0.1	1.56	17	56.9	68.8	76.5	8	..	91	98	9	12	336,000	24,000
Czech Republic	10.2	9.5	-0.2	1.19	17	65.9	70.3	77.4	5	6	95	25	6	9	..	1,800
Estonia	1.4	1.1	-1.2	1.29	18	73.8	63.0	74.5	18	..	89	52	22	50	..	..
Georgia	5.0	5.2	-1.1	1.92	22	59.7	68.5	76.8	19	..	90	70	23	70	2,800	5,200
Hungary	10.0	8.9	-0.4	1.37	17	66.0	66.8	74.9	10	9	100	57	11	15	..	6,000
Kazakhstan	16.2	17.7	-0.4	2.30	28	60.8	62.8	72.5	36	9	100	74	43	70	..	14,800
Kyrgyzstan	4.7	6.1	0.6	3.21	35	39.5	63.3	71.9	56	6	98	180	66	65	..	10,900
Latvia	2.4	1.9	-1.5	1.25	18	73.7	62.5	74.4	18	..	97	44	22	45	..	..
Lithuania	3.7	3.4	-0.3	1.43	20	73.6	64.3	75.6	19	..	97	70	23	18	..	100
Macedonia, FYR	2.0	2.3	0.6	2.06	23	61.1	70.9	75.3	23	..	98	177	27	11	..	17,400
Moldova	4.4	4.5	0.0	1.76	24	53.8	63.5	71.5	28	4	99	88	35	42	..	..
Poland	38.8	39.1	0.1	1.53	20	64.8	68.2	76.9	10	..	91[x]	70	11	8	..	1,300
Romania	22.3	19.9	-0.4	1.17	18	57.3	66.2	73.9	21	7	97	82	24	41	..	900
Russian Federation	146.9	137.9	-0.2	1.35	19	77.0	60.6	72.8	21	6	98	64	25	50	12,350	104,300
Slovakia	5.4	5.4	0.1	1.39	20	60.2	69.2	76.7	9	..	99	40	10	9	..	400
Slovenia	2.0	1.8	-0.1	1.26	16	52.0	70.6	78.2	5	..	93	45	5	11	..	5,000
Tajikistan	6.2	8.9	1.5	4.15	41	32.5	64.2	70.2	55	..	95	140	74	65	62,500	4,700
Turkmenistan	4.5	6.3	1.8	3.60	38	45.2	61.9	68.9	53	5	99	150	72	110	..	18,500
Ukraine	50.5	45.7	-0.4	1.38	18	71.6	63.8	73.7	18	..	96	53	22	25	..	5,800
Uzbekistan	24.3	33.4	1.6	3.45	38	41.8	64.3	70.7	45	..	96	120	58	21	33,200	38,000
Yugoslavia, FR	10.6	10.8	0.1	1.84	20		70.2	75.5	18	..	94	120	21	10	376,400	476,000
Industrial Countries		..		..	..		6	6	89	37	6	..		..	..	..
Australia	18.9	23.1	1.0	1.79	21	84.7	75.5	81.1	5	6	86	24	5	..	..	17,000
Austria	8.2	8.2	0.5	1.41	17	64.5	73.7	80.2	5	6	90	43	5	..	..	16,600
Belgium	10.2	9.9	0.1	1.55	17	97.2	73.8	80.6	6	6	64	35	6	..	..	42,000
Canada	31.1	37.9	1.0	1.55	19	76.9	76.1	81.8	6	6	96	33	6	..	..	53,000
Denmark	5.3	5.2	0.3	1.72	18	85.5	73.0	78.3	5	6	84	25	5	10	..	8,500
Finland	5.2	5.3	0.3	1.73	18	64.3	73.0	80.6	4	4	98	28	5	6	..	3,800
France	59.1	61.7	0.4	1.71	19	75.2	74.2	82.0	5	5	97	34	5	10	..	30,000
Germany	82.2	80.2	0.1	1.30	16	87.1	73.9	80.2	5	..	88	40	5	8	..	285,000
Greece	10.6	9.9	0.3	1.28	15	59.7	75.6	80.7	6	6	90	64	7	1	..	7,500
Ireland	3.7	4.4	0.7	1.90	22	58.1	73.6	79.2	6	4	..	36	7	6	..	8,500
Israel	6.2	8.3	2.2	2.68	28	91.0	75.7	79.7	6	7	94	39	6	5	..	400
Italy	57.3	51.3	0.0	1.20	14	66.8	75.0	81.2	6	5	55	50	6	7	..	24,900
Japan	126.7	121.2	0.2	1.43	15	78.5	76.8	82.9	4	7	94	40	4	8	..	400
Luxembourg	0.4	0.5		1.67	18	90.4	73.3	79.9	5	..	91	41	5	0	..	..

Table 1: Global Hunger – Life and Death Indicators

| | Population | | | | | | Life expectancy at birth | | Infant mortality rate per 1,000 live births 1998 | % of low birth weight infants 1990-1998[y] | % of 1-year-old children immunized (measles) 1995-98[y] | Under-5 mortality rate per 1,000 live births | | Maternal mortality rate per 100,000 live births 1980-98[y] | Refugees as of December 31, 1999 | |
	Total (millions) 2000	Projected (millions) 2025	Projected growth rate (%) 1995-2000	Total fertility rate 1995-2000	% population under age 15 1999	% population urban 1998	Male	Female				1960	1998		Country of origin	Country of asylum
Netherlands	15.8	15.8	0.4	1.50	18	89.2	75.0	80.7	5	..	96	22	5	7	..	40,000
New Zealand	3.9	4.7	1.0	2.01	23	86.5	74.1	79.7	5	6	81	26	6	15	..	..
Norway	4.5	4.8	0.5	1.85	20	73.8	75.2	81.1	4	4	93[x]	23	4	6	..	9,500
Portugal	9.9	9.3	0.0	1.37	17	37.0	71.8	78.9	8	5	96	112	9	8	..	1,700
Spain	39.6	36.7	0.0	1.15	15	77.1	74.5	81.5	6	4	78[x]	57	6	6	..	4,500
Sweden	8.9	9.1	0.3	1.57	18	83.2	76.3	80.8	4	5	96[x]	20	4	5	..	20,200
Switzerland	7.4	7.6	0.7	1.47	18	61.9	75.4	81.8	5	5	..	27	5	5	..	104,000
United Kingdom	58.8	60.0	0.2	1.72	19	89.4	74.5	79.8	6	7	95	27	6	7	..	112,000
United States	278.4	325.6	0.8	1.99	22	76.8	73.4	80.1	7	7	89[x]	30	8	8	..	638,000
World	**6,055.0**	**7,823.7**	**1.3**	**2.71**	**..**	**46.6**	**63.3**	**67.6**	**59**	**17**	**74**	**193**	**86**	**..**	**..**	**14,078,000**

.. Data not available.

a Territory.

b Central and Eastern European countries and the newly independent states of the former Soviet Union.

c Special administrative region, data exclude China.

e Data include São Tomé and Principe and Seychelles. Data exclude Djibouti and Sudan.

f Data include Cook Islands, Kiribati, Marshall Islands, Micronesia, Nauru, Nieu, Palau, Samoa, Tonga, Tuvalu, and Vanautu. Data exclude Hong Kong.

g Data include Antigua and Barbuda, Bahamas, Barbados, Dominica, Grenada, St. Kitts and Nevis, St. Lucia, and St. Vincent and the Grenadines.

h Data include Djibouti and Sudan. Data exclude Turkey and the West Bank and Gaza.

i Data include Turkey. Data exclude Slovenia.

j Data include Iran. Data exclude Maldives.

k Data include Anguilla, Antigua and Barbuda, Aruba, British Virgin Islands, Cayman Islands, Dominica, Grenada, Montserrat, Netherlands Antilles, Saint Kitts and Nevis, Saint Lucia, Saint Vincent and the Grenadines, Turks and Caicos Islands, the U.S. Virgin Islands, the Falkland Islands, and French Guyana.

m Data exclude Djibouti, Liberia, Somalia, and Sudan.

n Data include Iran.

p Data exclude China, Hong Kong, and Mongolia.

q Data include Antigua and Barbuda, Bahamas, Barbados, Dominica, Grenada, St. Kitts and Nevis, St. Lucia, and St. Vincent and the Grenadines.

r Data include Djibouti, Sudan, and Tunisia. Data exclude Turkey, Iran, and the West Bank and Gaza.

x Data refer to a period other than the one specified in the column heading.

y Data refer to most recent year available.

Table 2: Global Food, Nutrition, and Education

	Food supply				Adult literacy rate (% age 15 and above) 1998			Total primary school (net) 1997	Educational enrollment (% of relevant age group)			
	Per capita dietary energy supply (DES) (calories/day) 1998	Food production per capita 1980=100 1999	Food expenditures (% of household consumption) 1998	Vitamin A supplementation coverage rate (6 to 59 months) 1998	Total	Female	Male		Primary school (net) 1997 Female	Primary school (net) 1997 Male	Combined primary, secondary, tertiary (gross) 1997 Female	Combined primary, secondary, tertiary (gross) 1997 Male
Developing Countries	**2,663.0**	..	..	48	72.3	64.5	80.3	85.7	..	..	55	63
Africa (Sub-Saharan)	**2221.2[r]**	**101.8[r]**	..	68[k]	58.5[e]	51.6[e]	68.0[e]	56.2[e]	..	..	37[e]	46[e]
Angola	1,920.0	104.6	..	..	42.0[x]	..	..	34.7	34	35	23	28
Benin	2,571.2	133.2	52	100	37.7	22.6	53.8	67.6	50	85	31	53
Botswana	2,159.2	78.8	24	..	75.6	78.2	72.8	80.1	83	78	71	70
Burkina Faso	2,149.3	106.2	..	97	22.2	12.6	32.0	32.3	25	39	16	25
Burundi	1,578.5	76.1	..	15	45.8	37.5	54.8	35.6	33	38	20	25
Cameroon	2,209.2	97.6	33	..	73.6	67.1	80.3	61.7	59	64	41	52
Cape Verde	3,098.8	113.2	..	..	72.9	64.6	83.7	99.9	..	..	76	79
Central African Republic	2,056.0	111.6	..	..	44.0	31.7	57.5	46.2	38	55	20	33
Chad	2,170.9	122.6	..	0	39.4	..	..	47.9	35	61	20	41
Comoros	1,857.6	91.6	..	..	58.5	51.6	65.5	50.1	..	..	35	42
Congo, Dem. Rep. of	1,701.0	68.1	..	46	58.9	47.1	71.3	58.2	48	69	27	38
Congo, Republic of	2,241.1	92.2	34	93	78.4	71.5	85.7	78.3	76	81	58	71
Côte d'Ivoire	2,694.9	103.9	30	..	44.5	35.7	52.8	58.3	50	66	32	48
Djibouti	2,074.2	71.4	..	41	62.3	51.4	74.0	31.9	..	..	17	24
Equatorial Guinea	..	80.0	..	..	81.1	71.5	91.4	79.3	..	..	60	69
Eritrea	1,744.3	..	..	86	51.7	38.2	65.7	29.3	28	31	24	30
Ethiopia	1,805.1	..	..	83	36.3	30.5	42.1	35.2	27	44	19	32
Gabon	2,560.4	89.7	40	..	63.0[x]	..	..	..	..	..	..	..
Gambia	2,558.6	93.0	..	..	34.6	27.5	41.9	65.9	58	74	35	48
Ghana	2,683.8	128.2	..	90	69.1	59.9	78.5	43.4	..	..	38	48
Guinea	2,314.5	112.4	29	97	36.0[x]	..	..	45.6	33	58	19	36
Guinea-Bissau	2,410.5	98.3	..	..	36.7	17.3	57.1	52.3	39	66	24	43
Kenya	1,967.6	82.7	31	10	80.5	73.5	87.6	65.0	67	63	49	50
Lesotho	2,210.4	82.6	..	..	82.4	92.9	71.0	68.6	74	63	61	53
Liberia	1,978.6	87.8	..	..	51.0	..	..	..	..	..	..	..
Madagascar	2,001.4	85.5	61	100	64.9	57.8	72.2	58.7	62[x]	60[x]	39	39
Malawi	2,226.0	114.1	50	34	58.2	44.1	73.2	98.5	100	97	70	79
Mali	2,117.8	95.6	53	93	38.2	31.1	45.8	38.1	31	45	20	31
Mauritania	2,640.1	82.7	..	80	41.2	31.0	51.7	62.9	53[x]	61[x]	36	45
Mauritius	2,944.3	77.2	21	0	83.8	80.3	87.3	96.5	97	96	63	62
Mozambique	1,911.3	104.3	..	..	42.3	27.0	58.4	39.6	34	45	20	29
Namibia	2,096.0	77.4	..	83	80.8	79.7	81.9	91.4	94	89	84	80
Niger	1,965.7	103.4	..	82	14.7	7.4	22.4	24.4	19	30	11	19
Nigeria	2,882.4	126.1	51	..	61.1	52.5	70.1	..	..	..	38	48
Rwanda	2,035.5	85.6	..	75	64.0	56.8	71.5	78.3	75	76	42	44
Senegal	2,276.9	95.5	46	0	35.5	25.8	45.4	59.5	54	65	31	40
Sierra Leone	2,045.2	68.5	47	..	31.0[x]	..	..	44.0	..	..	..	..
Somalia	1,530.6	74.8	..	90	24.0[x]	..	..	..	..	..	..	..
South Africa	2,909.3	87.6	..	..	84.6	83.9	85.4	99.9	100	100	94	93
Sudan	2,443.8	128.3	..	80	55.7	43.4	68.0	..	..	..	31	37
Swaziland	2,502.8	63.3	25	..	78.3	77.3	79.5	94.6	..	..	70	74
Tanzania	1,999.4	82.5	67	80	73.6	64.3	83.3	47.4	49	48	32	33
Togo	2,512.5	104.1	..	..	55.2	38.4	72.5	82.3	70	94	47	75
Uganda	2,215.9	93.0	..	95	65.0	54.2	76.1	..	..	..	36	44
Zambia	1,950.4	82.5	52	91	76.3	69.1	84.0	72.4	72	73	46	53
Zimbabwe	2,153.2	86.8	20	..	87.2	82.9	91.7	93.1	92	94	66	71
South Asia	**2,416.5[s]**	**107.7[s]**	..	30	54.3[f]	42.3[f]	65.7[f]	78.0[f]	70	83	44[f]	59[f]
Afghanistan	1,774.3	76.8	..	..	35.0	..	..	..	..	..	..	..
Bangladesh	2,050.1	99.9	49	95	40.1	28.6	51.1	75.1	70	80	30	40
Bhutan	..	88.0	..	87	42.0[x]	..	..	13.2	..	..	..	..
India	2,466.1	107.8	..	25	55.7	43.5	67.1	77.2	71	83	46	61
Maldives	2,450.6	89.5	..	..	96.0	96.0	96.0	..	..	..	75	74
Nepal	2,170.0	98.0	44	90	39.2	21.7	56.9	78.4	63	93	49	69
Pakistan	2,446.8	111.9	45	1	44.0	28.9	58.0	..	..	..	28	56
Sri Lanka	2,314.2	103.6	43	..	91.1	88.3	94.1	99.9	100	100	67	65

Table 2: Global Food, Nutrition, and Education

	Food supply				Adult literacy rate (% age 15 and above) 1998			Educational enrollment (% of relevant age group)				
	Per capita dietary energy supply (DES) (calories/day) 1998	Food production per capita 1980=100 1999	Food expenditures (% of household consumption) 1998	Vitamin A supplementation coverage rate (6 to 59 months) 1998	Total	Female	Male	Total primary school (net) 1997	Primary school (net) 1997 Female	Male	Combined primary, secondary, tertiary (gross) 1997 Female	Male
East Asia and the Pacific	..	106.5[t]	..	70[l]	88.2[z]	85.0[z]	92.4[z]	87.9[z]	99[h]	99[h]	63[z]	66[z]
Brunei	2,851.2	122.1	..	..	90.7	86.7	94.1	87.9	..	..	73	71
Cambodia	2,078.0	108.9	..	80	65.0[x]	..	..	99.9	100	100	54	68
China	2,972.2	151.3	..	..	82.8	74.6	90.7	99.9	100	100	67	71
Hong Kong[a]	3,200.1	48.6	10	..	92.9	89.1	96.3	91.3	93	90	67	64
Fiji	2,851.8	96.4	35	..	92.2	89.9	94.4	99.9	..	..	79	81
Indonesia	2,849.6	102.5	47	66	85.7	80.5	91.1	99.2	99	100	61	68
Korea, DPR (North)	1,899.1	69.6	..	..	..	..	..	..	..	..	..	..
Korea, Rep. of (South)	3,069.2	93.2	18	..	97.5	95.9	99.0	99.9	100	100	84	94
Laos, PDR	2,174.9	122.1	..	39	46.1	30.2	61.9	73.0	69	77	48	62
Malaysia	2,900.6	115.4	..	..	86.4	82.0	90.7	99.9	100	100	66	64
Mongolia	2,010.0	75.5	56	87	83.0[x]	..	..	85.1	88	83	62	50
Myanmar (Burma)	2,832.1	130.1	..	91	84.1	79.5	88.7	99.3	99	100	54	55
Papua New Guinea	2,168.2	92.3	..	..	63.2	55.1	70.9	78.9	..	..	33	40
Philippines	2,288.1	106.6	37	80	94.8	94.6	95.1	99.9	100	100	85	80
Singapore	..	29.8	15	..	91.8	87.6	96.0	91.4	91	92	71	74
Solomon Islands	2,129.8	91.2	..	..	62.0[x]	..	..	..	..	..	44	48
Thailand	2,462.4	104.2	23	4	95.0	93.2	96.9	88.0	89	87	59	58
Vietnam	2,422.1	132.4	49	98	92.9	90.6	95.3	99.9	100	100	59	64
Latin America and Caribbean	..	..	..	52	87.7[p]	86.7	88.7	93.3	93	95	73	72
Argentina	3,143.6	121.4	30	..	96.7	96.6	96.7	99.9	100	100	82	77
Belize	2,922.1	122.4	27	..	92.7	92.5	92.9	99.9	..	..	72	72
Bolivia	2,214.1	106.2	37	73	84.4	77.8	91.3	97.4	95	100	64	75
Brazil	2,925.5	122.3	22	20	84.5	84.5	84.5	97.1	94	100	82	78
Chile	2,843.8	115.2	17	..	95.4	95.2	95.6	90.4	89	92	76	78
Colombia	2,559.4	99.0	..	..	91.2	91.2	91.3	89.4	89	89	71	70
Costa Rica	2,780.8	102.0	..	..	95.3	95.4	95.3	91.8	89	89	65	66
Cuba	2,473.4	57.4	..	..	96.4	96.3	96.5	99.9	100	100	73	70
Dominican Republic	2,277.3	87.6	..	16	82.8	82.8	82.9	91.3	94	89	72	68
Ecuador	2,724.5	109.2	26	69	90.6	88.7	92.5	99.9	100	100	72	75
El Salvador	2,522.0	102.1	..	..	77.8	75.0	80.8	89.1	89	89	63	64
Guatemala	2,159.5	95.7	..	57	67.3	59.7	74.9	73.8	70	77	43	51
Guyana	2,475.8	180.6	..	..	98.3	97.8	98.8	92.8	..	..	66	65
Haiti	1,876.2	81.7	..	60	47.8	45.6	50.1	19.4	..	..	24	25
Honduras	2,343.5	85.4	..	58	73.4	73.5	73.4	87.5	89	86	59	57
Jamaica	2,711.0	110.1	24	..	86.0	89.9	81.9	95.6	96	96	63	62
Mexico	3,144.3	109.4	30	93	90.8	88.7	92.9	99.9	100	100	69	71
Nicaragua	2,207.8	95.9	..	63	67.9	69.3	66.3	78.6	80	77	65	61
Panama	2,476.4	86.5	22	..	91.4	90.8	92.1	89.9	90	90	74	72
Paraguay	2,577.4	108.5	..	..	92.8	91.5	94.0	96.3	97	96	64	65
Peru	2,420.0	140.8	26	..	89.2	84.3	94.2	93.8	93	94	77	79
Suriname	2,633.2	73.4	..	..	93.0[x]	..	..	99.9	..	..	82	76
Trinidad and Tobago	2,711.3	88.8	20	..	93.4	91.5	95.3	99.9	100	100	66	67
Uruguay	2,866.0	130.8	22	..	97.6	98.0	97.2	94.3	95	94	81	74
Venezuela	2,357.8	96.5	30	..	92.0	91.4	92.6	82.5	84	81	68	66
Middle East and North Africa	..	..	..	69[m]	59.7[q]	47.3[q]	71.5[q]	86.4[l]	84[n]	91[n]	54[l]	65[l]
Algeria	3,020.4	110.1	..	..	65.5	54.3	76.5	96.0	93	99	64	71
Bahrain	..	94.9	32	..	86.5	81.2	90.2	98.2	..	..	82	78
Cyprus	3,473.8	102.2	..	..	96.6	94.7	98.6	..	..	..	81	79
Egypt	3,282.3	128.1	44	..	53.7	41.8	65.5	95.2	91	100	66	77
Iran	2,822.5	128.3	20	35	74.6	67.4	81.7	90.0	89	91	67	73
Iraq	2,419.1	70.2	..	89	53.7	43.2	63.9	74.6	70	80	44	57
Jordan	2,791.3	93.2	32	..	88.6	82.6	94.2	..	68[x]	67[x]	..	..
Kuwait	3,059.4	216.8	..	..	80.9	78.5	83.2	65.2	64	66	59	56
Lebanon	3,285.0	110.9	31	..	85.1	79.1	91.5	76.1	..	..	77	76
Libya	3,267.4	132.0	..	..	78.1	65.4	89.6	99.9	100	100	92	92

Table 2: Global Food, Nutrition, and Education

| | Food supply | | Food expenditures (% of household consumption) 1998 | Vitamin A supplementation coverage rate (6 to 59 months) 1998 | Adult literacy rate (% age 15 and above) 1998 | | | Total primary school (net) 1997 | Primary school (net) 1997 | | Combined primary, secondary, tertiary (gross) 1997 | |
	Per capita dietary energy supply (DES) (calories/day) 1998	Food production per capita 1980=100 1999			Total	Female	Male		Female	Male	Female	Male
Morocco	3,165.0	82.7	33	75	47.1	34.0	60.3	76.6	67	86	43	56
Oman	..	83.2	22	98	68.8	57.5	78.0	67.7	67	69	57	60
Qatar	..	153.8	22	..	80.4	81.7	79.8	83.3	..	..	75	72
Saudi Arabia	2,888.1	68.1	..	..	75.2	64.4	82.8	60.1	58	62	54	58
Syria	3,378.0	104.3	..	..	72.7	58.1	87.2	94.7	91	99	56	63
Tunisia	3,296.8	110.4	28	..	68.7	57.9	79.4	99.9	100	100	68	74
Turkey	3,554.1	97.6	45	..	84.0	75.0	92.9	99.9	98	100	54	67
United Arab Emirates	3,371.7	200.3	..	..	74.6	77.1	73.4	82.0	81	83	72	66
Yemen	2,087.0	86.1	25	100	44.1	22.7	65.7	..	..	..	27	70
Countries in Transition[b]	**2,883.4**	..	..	25	**98.6**	**98.2**	**99.1**	..	..	..	**78**	**74**
Albania	2,976.4	134.3	62	..	83.5	76.2	90.5	..	..	..	68	67
Armenia	2,355.8	..	52	..	98.2	97.3	99.2	..	..	..	68	75
Azerbaijan	2,190.6	..	51	..	99.0	..	..	..	..	..	71	71
Belarus	3,136.1	..	36	..	99.5	99.4	99.7	..	84[x]	87[x]	83	79
Bosnia and Herzegovina	2,801.4	..	..	..	..	..	..	..	..	..	..	..
Bulgaria	2,739.8	76.2	30	..	98.2	97.6	98.9	97.9	99	97	75	69
Croatia	2,479.0	..	24	..	98.0	96.9	99.3	99.9	100	100	69	68
Czech Republic	3,292.3	..	24	..	99.0	99.0	99.0	99.9	100	100	74	73
Estonia	3,058.0	..	41	..	99.0	99.0	99.0	99.9	100	100	87	82
Georgia	2,251.6	..	33	..	99.0[x]	..	..	89.0	89	89	71	70
Hungary	3,407.6	77.9	25	..	99.3	99.1	99.4	97.5	97	98	75	73
Kazakhstan	2,517.2	..	37	..	99.0	..	..	..	..	..	79	73
Kyrgyzstan	2,535.0	..	33	..	97.0[x]	..	..	99.5	99	100	71	68
Latvia	2,994.0	..	30	..	99.8	99.8	99.8	99.9	100	100	76	73
Lithuania	3,103.8	..	33	..	99.5	99.4	99.6	..	..	..	78	74
Macedonia, FYR	2,938.4	..	33	..	94.6[x]	..	..	..	95[x]	96[x]	68	69
Moldova	2,762.5	..	31	..	98.6	97.9	99.5	..	..	..	71	69
Poland	3,351.0	86.8	28	..	99.7	99.7	99.7	99.4	99	100	79	78
Romania	3,263.4	101.7	36	..	97.9	96.9	98.9	99.9	100	100	69	69
Russian Federation	2,835.0	..	28	..	99.5	99.3	99.7	99.9	100	100	81	75
Slovakia	2,953.3	..	26	..	99.0	99.0	99.0	..	..	..	75	73
Slovenia	2,949.8	..	27	..	99.6	99.6	99.7	..	94	95	82	77
Tajikistan	2,176.2	..	48	..	99.0	98.6	99.5	..	..	..	65	73
Turkmenistan	2,684.1	..	32	..	98.0[x]	..	..	..	..	..	..	..
Ukraine	2,878.4	..	34	..	99.6	99.4	99.7	..	..	..	80	74
Uzbekistan	2,564.0	..	34	..	88.0	83.4	92.7	..	..	..	74	78
Yugoslavia, FR	2,963.2	..	..	25	98.0[x]	..	..	..	70	69	..	..
Industrial Countries	**3,415.6**	..	..	..	..	..	..	..	..	..	..	..
Australia	3,190.5	121.5	24	..	99.0	99.0	99.0	99.9	100	100	114[j]	111[j]
Austria	3,530.8	99.8	20	..	99.0	99.0	99.0	99.9	100	100	85	86
Belgium	3,606.3[y]	94.4[y]	17	..	99.0	99.0	99.0	99.9	100	100	107[j]	104[j]
Canada	3,167.4	117.6	14	..	99.0	99.0	99.0	99.9	100	100	101[j]	98
Denmark	3,433.3	104.2	16	..	99.0	99.0	99.0	99.9	100	100	95	90
Finland	3,179.7	86.6	17	..	99.0	99.0	99.0	99.9	100	100	104[j]	95
France	3,541.2	103.8	22	..	99.0	99.0	99.0	99.9	100	100	94	91
Germany	3,402.4	91.4	14	..	99.0	99.0	99.0	99.9	100	100	88	90
Greece	3,629.9	92.3	32	..	96.9	95.5	98.4	99.9	100	100	80	80
Ireland	3,622.0	103.8	21	..	99.0	99.0	99.0	99.9	100	100	92	87
Israel	3,465.8	86.5	23	..	95.7	93.7	97.7	..	..	..	81	79
Italy	3,608.3	105.3	23	..	98.3	97.9	98.8	99.9	100	100	83	80
Japan	2,874.1	90.8	12	..	99.0	99.0	99.0	99.9	100	100	83	86
Luxembourg	..	..	17	..	99.0	99.0	99.0	..	..	..	70	68
Netherlands	3,282.1	96.2	17	..	99.0	99.0	99.0	99.9	100	100	96	99

Table 2: Global Food, Nutrition, and Education

| | Food supply | | | | Adult literacy rate (% age 15 and above) 1998 | | | Educational enrollment (% of relevant age group) | | | | |
	Per capita dietary energy supply (DES) (calories/day) 1998	Food production per capita 1980=100 1999	Food expenditures (% of household consumption) 1998	Vitamin A supplementation coverage rate (6 to 59 months) 1998	Total	Female	Male	Total primary school (net) 1997	Primary school (net) 1997 Female	Male	Combined primary, secondary, tertiary (gross) 1997 Female	Male
New Zealand	3,315.0	107.6	21	..	99.0	99.0	99.0	99.9	100	100	99	92
Norway	3,424.8	93.2	16	..	99.0	99.0	99.0	99.9	100	100	98	93
Portugal	3,691.1	96.3	29	..	91.4	89.0	94.2	99.9	100	100	94	88
Spain	3,347.9	107.4	33	..	97.4	96.5	98.4	99.9	100	100	96	90
Sweden	3,113.6	94.3	17	..	99.0	99.0	99.0	99.9	100	100	108ʲ	95
Switzerland	3,221.6	88.0	19	..	99.0	99.0	99.0	99.9	100	100	76	83
United Kingdom	3,256.7	96.7	14	..	99.0	99.0	99.0	99.9	100	100	109ʲ	99
United States	3,756.8	111.4	13	..	99.0	99.0	99.0	99.9	100	100	97	91
World	**2,791.8**	**106.4**	**..**	**48**	**78.8**	**73.1**	**84.6**	**87.6**	**88**	**92**	**60**	**67**

.. Data not available.

a Special administrative region, data exclude China.

b Central and Eastern European countries and newly independent states of the former Soviet Union.

c Data include Luxembourg.

d Data exclude Papua New Guinea.

e Data exclude Djibouti, Liberia, Somalia, and Sudan.

f Data include Iran. Data exclude Afghanistan.

g BFWI average.

h Data exclude Hong Kong and Singapore.

i Data include Djibouti and Sudan. Data exclude Kuwait, Qatar, Turkey, and the United Arab Emirates.

j For purposes of calculating the GDI, a value of 100.0% was applied.

k Data include São Tomé and Principe and Seychelles. Data exclude Djibouti and Sudan.

l Data include Kiribati, Marshall Islands, and Micronesia.

m Data include Djibouti and Sudan. Data exclude Turkey and the West Bank and Gaza.

n Data exclude Kuwait, Turkey, and the United Arab Emirates.

p Data include Antigua and Barbuda, Bahamas, Barbados, Dominica, Grenada, St. Kitts and Nevis, St. Lucia, and St. Vincent and the Grenadines.

q Data include Djibouti and Sudan. Data exclude Cyprus, Iran, and Turkey.

r Data include São Tomé and Principe. Data exclude South Africa.

s Data exclude Afghanistan and Bhutan.

t Data exclude Fiji and Solomon Islands.

x Data refer to a period other than the one specified in the column heading.

y Data include Luxembourg.

z Data exclude China, Hong Kong, Rep. of Korea, and Mongolia.

The number '0' (zero) means zero or less than half the unit shown.

Table 3: Hunger, Malnutrition, and Poverty

	Undernourished population		% under-5 (1990-1998ᵖ) suffering from:				Population with access to safe water % 1990-1998ᵖ			Population in Poverty (%)			
			Underweight		Wasting	Stunting				Below national poverty line 1984-1998ᵖ			Population below $1 a day 1989-1999ᵖᑫ
	% 1996-1998	Number (millions) 1996-1998	Moderate & severe	Severe	Moderate & severe	Moderate & severe	Total	Urban	Rural	National	Urban	Rural	
Developing Countries	**18**	**791.9**	**31.0**	**12.0**	**11.0**	**39.0**	**72**	**89**	**62**	..	..	..	..
Africa (Sub-Saharan)	**34**	**185.9**	**32.0ʰ**	**10.0ʰ**	**9.0ʰ**	**41.0ʰ**	**50ʰ**	**77ʰ**	**39ʰ**	..	..	..	..
Angola	43	5.0	42.0	14.0	6.0	53.0	31	46	22	..	..	..	..
Benin	14	0.8	29.0	7.0	14.0	25.0	56	71	46	33.0	..	..	..
Botswana	27	0.4	17.0	5.0	11.0	29.0	90	100	88	..	..	..	33.3ˣ
Burkina Faso	32	3.5	30.0	8.0	13.0	29.0	42	66	37	..	..	..	61.2
Burundi	68	4.3	37.0	11.0	9.0	43.0	52	92	49	36.2	..	..	..
Cameroon	29	4.1	22.0	5.0	6.0	29.0	54	81	41	40.0	44.4	32.4	..
Cape Verde	..	..	14.0	2.0	6.0	16.0	65	84	44	..	..	..	..
Central African Republic	41	1.4	27.0	8.0	7.0	34.0	38	55	21	..	..	..	66.6
Chad	38	2.7	39.0	14.0	14.0	40.0	54	48	56	64.0	63.0	67.0	..
Comoros	..	..	26.0	8.0	8.0	34.0	53	76	45	..	..	..	..
Congo, Dem. Rep. of	61	29.3	34.0	10.0	10.0	45.0	42	89	26	..	..	..	..
Congo, Rep. of	32	0.9	17.0ˣ	3.0ˣ	4.0ˣ	21.0ˣ	34	53	7	..	..	..	..
Côte d'Ivoire	14	1.9	24.0	6.0	8.0	24.0	42	56	32	..	..	..	12.3
Djibouti	..	..	18.0	6.0	13.0	26.0	90	77	100	..	..	..	..
Equatorial Guinea	..	..	..	..	..	..	95	88	100	..	..	..	..
Eritrea	65	2.2	44.0	17.0	16.0	38.0	22	60	8	..	..	..	..
Ethiopia	49	28.4	48.0	16.0	8.0	64.0	25	91	19	..	..	..	31.3
Gabon	8	0.1	..	..	..	..	67	80	30	..	..	..	..
Gambia	16	0.2	26.0	5.0	..	30.0	69	80	65	64.0	..	..	53.7
Ghana	10	1.9	27.0	8.0	11.0	26.0	65	88	52	31.4	26.7	34.3	..
Guinea	29	2.1	..	..	12.0	29.0	46	69	36	40.0	..	..	..
Guinea-Bissau	..	..	23.0ˣ	..	..	..	43	..	..	..	..	..	..
Kenya	43	12.2	22.0	5.0	6.0	33.0	44	87	30	42.0	29.3	46.4	26.5
Lesotho	29	0.6	16.0	4.0	5.0	44.0	62	91	57	49.2	27.8	53.9	43.1
Liberia	46	1.1	..	..	..	..	46	79	13	..	..	..	..
Madagascar	40	5.8	40.0	13.0	7.0	48.0	40	71	30	70.0	47.0	77.0	60.2
Malawi	32	3.2	30.0	9.0	7.0	48.0	47	95	40	54.0	..	..	..
Mali	32	3.4	40.0	17.0	23.0	30.0	66	87	55	..	..	..	72.8
Mauritania	13	0.3	23.0	9.0	7.0	44.0	37	34	40	57.0	..	..	3.8
Mauritius	6	0.1	16.0	2.0	15.0	10.0	98	95	100	10.6	..	..	..
Mozambique	58	10.7	26.0	9.0	8.0	36.0	46	85	37	..	..	..	37.9
Namibia	31	0.5	26.0	6.0	9.0	28.0	83	100	71	..	..	..	34.9
Niger	46	4.5	50.0	20.0	21.0	41.0	61	70	59	63.0	52.0	66.0	61.4
Nigeria	8	8.6	36.0	12.0	9.0	43.0	49	58	40	34.1	30.4	36.4	70.2
Rwanda	39	2.3	27.0	11.0	9.0	42.0	..	..	79	51.2	..	..	35.7ˣ
Senegal	23	2.0	22.0	..	7.0	23.0	81	96	70	..	..	..	26.3
Sierra Leone	43	1.9	29.0	..	9.0	35.0	34	58	21	68.0	53.0	76.0	57.0
Somalia	75	6.6	..	..	..	..	31	46	28	..	..	..	..
South Africa	..	..	9.0	1.0	3.0	23.0	87	99	70	..	..	..	11.5
Sudan	18	5.1	34.0	11.0	13.0	33.0	73	..	..	..	..	..	..
Swaziland	14	0.1	10.0ˣ	..	1.0ˣ	30.0ˣ	50	..	..	..	..	..	..
Tanzania	41	12.7	27.0	8.0	6.0	42.0	66	92	58	51.1	..	..	19.9
Togo	18	0.8	25.0	7.0	12.0	22.0	55	84	40	32.3	..	..	..
Uganda	30	6.0	26.0	7.0	5.0	38.0	46	77	41	55.0	..	..	36.7
Zambia	45	3.9	24.0	5.0	4.0	42.0	38	84	10	86.0	..	..	72.6
Zimbabwe	37	4.2	15.0	3.0	6.0	32.0	79	99	69	25.5	10.0	31.0	36.0
South Asia	**23ʸ**	**294.2ʸ**	**51.0**	**19.0**	**18.0**	**52.0**	**80**	**86**	**78**	..	..	..	..
Afghanistan	70	14.6	48.0	..	25.0	52.0	6	16	3	..	..	..	..
Bangladesh	38	46.8	56.0	21.0	18.0	55.0	95	99	95	35.6	14.3	39.8	29.1
Bhutan	..	..	38.0ˣ	..	4.0ˣ	56.0ˣ	58	75	54	..	..	..	..
India	21	207.6	53.0	21.0	18.0	52.0	81	85	79	35.0	30.5	36.7	44.2
Maldives	..	..	43.0	10.0	17.0	27.0	60	98	50	..	..	..	..
Nepal	28	6.2	47.0	16.0	11.0	48.0	71	93	68	42.0	23.0	44.0	37.7
Pakistan	20	28.9	38.0	13.0	..	..	79	89	73	34.0	28.0	36.9	31.0
Sri Lanka	25	4.5	34.0	..	14.0	18.0	57	88	52	35.3	28.4	38.1	6.6

Table 3: Hunger, Malnutrition, and Poverty

	Undernourished population % 1996-1998	Undernourished population Number (millions) 1996-1998	% under-5 (1990-1998[p]) suffering from: Underweight Moderate & severe	Underweight Severe	Wasting Moderate & severe	Stunting Moderate & severe	Population with access to safe water % 1990-1998[p] Total	Urban	Rural	Population in Poverty (%) Below national poverty line 1984-1998[p] National	Urban	Rural	Population below $1 a day 1989-1999[pq]
East Asia and the Pacific	..	..	22.0[i]	..	..	36.0[i]	69[i]	95[i]	58[i]	..	..	..	..
Brunei	..	..	..	..	..	..	..	..	..	..	..	..	..
Cambodia	33	3.4	52.0	18.0	13.0	56.0	30	53	25	36.1	21.1	40.1	..
China	11	140.1	16.0	..	..	34.0	67	97	56	4.6	<2	4.6	18.5
Hong Kong[a]	..	0.1	..	..	..	..	..	..	..	..	..	..	..
Fiji	..	..	8.0	1.0	8.0	3.0	77	..	..	..	..	..	..
Indonesia	6	12.3	34.0	8.0	13.0	42.0	74	92	67	20.3	17.8	22.0	15.2
Korea, DPR (North)	57	13.2	60.0	..	19.0	60.0	100	100	100	..	..	..	..
Korea, Rep. of (South)	..	0.5	..	..	..	..	93	100	76	..	..	..	<2.0
Laos, PDR	29	1.5	40.0	12.0	11.0	47.0	44	..	..	46.1	24.0	53.0	..
Malaysia	..	0.5	19.0	1.0	..	..	78	96	66	15.5	..	..	..
Mongolia	45	1.1	10.0	..	2.0	22.0	45	67	22	36.3	38.5	33.1	13.9
Myanmar (Burma)	7	3.1	39.0	13.0	..	..	60	78	50	..	..	..	..
Papua New Guinea	29	1.3	30.0[x]	6.0[x]	6.0[x]	43.0[x]	41	88	32	..	..	..	..
Philippines	21	15.2	28.0	..	6.0	30.0	85	92	79	40.6	22.5	51.2	..
Singapore	..	..	..	..	..	..	100[x]	100[x]	..	..	..	..	..
Solomon Islands	..	..	21.0[x]	4.0[x]	7.0[x]	27.0[x]	..	80	62	..	..	..	..
Thailand	21	12.2	19.0	..	6.0	16.0	81	88	73	13.1	10.2	15.5	<2.0
Vietnam	22	16.5	41.0	9.0	14.0	44.0	45	61	39	50.9	25.9	57.2	..
Latin America and the Caribbean	**11**	**54.9**	10.0[j]	1.0[j]	3.0[j]	18.0[j]	78[k]	88[k]	42[k]	..	..	..	..
Argentina	..	0.4	..	..	..	..	71	77	29	17.6	..	..	..
Belize	..	..	6.0	1.0	..	..	83	100	69	..	..	..	..
Bolivia	23	1.8	10.0	2.0	2.0	26.0	80	95	56	..	..	79.1	11.3
Brazil	10	15.9	6.0	1.0	2.0	11.0	76	88	25	17.4	13.1	32.6	5.1
Chile	4	0.6	1.0	..	0.0	2.0	91	99	41	20.5	..	..	4.2
Colombia	13	5.2	8.0	1.0	1.0	15.0	85	97	56	17.7	8.0	31.2[x]	11.0
Costa Rica	6	0.2	2.0	..	..	..	96	100	92	..	..	..	9.6
Cuba	19	2.1	9.0	..	3.0	..	93	96	85	..	..	..	..
Dominican Republic	28	2.2	6.0	1.0	1.0	11.0	79	95	54	20.6	10.9	29.8	3.2
Ecuador	5	0.5	17.0[x]	0.0[x]	2.0[x]	34.0[x]	68	80	49	35.0	25.0	47.0	20.2
El Salvador	11	0.6	11.0	1.0	1.0	23.0	66	84	40	48.3	43.1	55.7	25.3
Guatemala	24	2.5	27.0	6.0	3.0	50.0	68	92	54	57.9	33.7	71.9	39.8
Guyana	18	0.2	12.0	..	12.0	10.0	91	96	85	..	..	..	..
Haiti	62	4.8	28.0	8.0	8.0	32.0	37	50	28	..	..	66.0	..
Honduras	22	1.3	18.0	3.0	2.0	40.0	78	95	65	53.0	57.0	51.0	40.5
Jamaica	10	0.2	10.0	1.0	4.0	6.0	86	..	..	34.2	..	..	3.2
Mexico	5	5.1	14.0[x]	..	6.0[x]	22.0[x]	85	..	..	10.1	..	..	17.9
Nicaragua	31	1.5	12.0	2.0	2.0	25.0	78	94	52	50.3	31.9	76.1	3.0
Panama	16	0.4	7.0	1.0	1.0	9.0	93	..	..	37.3	15.3	64.9	10.3
Paraguay	13	0.7	4.0	1.0	0.0	17.0	60	..	..	21.8	19.7	28.5	19.4
Peru	18	4.4	8.0	1.0	1.0	26.0	67	84	33	49.0	40.4	64.7	15.5
Suriname	10	0.0	..	..	..	..	..	..	..	..	..	..	..
Trinidad and Tobago	13	0.2	7.0[x]	0.0[x]	4.0[x]	5.0[x]	97	99	91	21.0	24.0	20.0	12.4
Uruguay	4	0.1	5.0	1.0	1.0	8.0	..	95	..	..	..	..	<2.0
Venezuela	16	3.7	5.0	1.0	3.0	13.0	79	80	75	31.3	..	..	14.7
Middle East and North Africa	**10[z]**	**35.9[z]**	18.0[m]	5.0[m]	8.0[m]	25.0[m]	85[m]	97[m]	72[m]	..	..	..	..
Algeria	5	1.4	13.0	3.0	9.0	18.0	90	98	79	22.6	14.7	30.3	<2.0
Bahrain	..	..	9.0	2.0	5.0	10.0	94	94	..	..	..	..	..
Cyprus	..	..	..	..	..	..	100	100	100	..	..	..	..
Egypt	4	2.6	12.0	3.0	6.0	25.0	87	97	77	22.9	22.5	23.3	3.1
Iran	6	4.1	16.0	3.0	7.0	19.0	95	99	86	..	..	..	..
Iraq	17	3.5	23.0	6.0	10.0	31.0	81	96	48	..	..	..	..
Jordan	5	0.2	5.0	1.0	2.0	8.0	97	98	88	11.7	..	..	<2.0
Kuwait	4	0.1	6.0[x]	..	3.0[x]	12.0[x]	..	..	..	..	..	..	..
Lebanon	..	0.1	3.0	..	3.0	12.0	94	96	88	..	..	..	..
Libya	..	0.0	5.0	..	3.0	15.0	97	97	97	..	..	..	..

Table 3: Hunger, Malnutrition, and Poverty

| | Undernourished population | | % under-5 (1990-1998p) suffering from: | | | | Population with access to safe water % 1990-1998p | | | Population in Poverty (%) | | | |
| | | | Underweight | | Wasting | Stunting | | | | Below national poverty line 1984-1998p | | | Population below $1 a day 1989-1999pq |
	% 1996-1998	Number (millions) 1996-1998	Moderate & severe	Severe	Moderate & severe	Moderate & severe	Total	Urban	Rural	National	Urban	Rural	
Morocco	5	1.4	9.0	2.0	2.0	23.0	65	98	34	19.0	12.0	27.2	<2.0
Oman	..	..	23.0	3.0	13.0	23.0	85	..	..	..	..	..	..
Qatar	..	..	6.0	..	2.0	8.0		100		..	..	..	..
Saudi Arabia	3	0.6	..	..	..	..	95x	100x	74x	..	..	..	..
Syria	..	0.2	13.0	4.0	9.0	21.0	86	95	77	..	..	..	..
Tunisia	..	0.1	9.0	..	4.0	23.0	98	100	95	14.1	8.9	21.6	<2.0
Turkey	..	1.2	10.0	3.0	..	..	49	66	25	..	..	..	2.4
United Arab Emirates	..	0.0	14.0	3.0	15.0	17.0	97	..	..	..	..	..	..
Yemen	35	5.7	46.0	15.0	13.0	52.0	61	72	57	19.1	18.6	19.2	5.1
Countries in Transitionb	**6**	**26.4**	**8.0n**	**2.0n**	**5.0n**	**16.0n**	..	..	..	..	..	..	..
Albania	3	0.1	..	..	..	..	..	..	..	..	..	..	..
Armenia	21	0.7	..	..	..	..	..	..	..	..	..	..	..
Azerbaijan	32	2.4	10.0	2.0	3.0	22.0	..	..	..	68.1	..	..	..
Belarus	..	0.1	..	..	..	..	..	..	..	22.5	..	..	<2.0
Bosnia and Herzegovina	10	0.4	..	..	..	..	..	..	..	..	..	..	..
Bulgaria	13	1.1	..	..	..	..	..	..	..	..	..	..	<2.0
Croatia	12	0.5	1.0	..	1.0	1.0	..	..	..	..	..	..	..
Czech Republic	..	0.1	1.0	0.0	2.0	2.0	..	..	..	..	..	..	<2.0
Estonia	6	0.1	..	..	..	..	..	..	..	8.9	6.8	14.7	4.9
Georgia	23	1.2	..	..	..	..	..	..	..	11.1	12.1	9.9	..
Hungary	..	0.1	2.0x	0.0x	2.0x	3.0x	..	..	..	8.6	..	..	<2.0
Kazakhstan	5	0.7	8.0	2.0	3.0	16.0	93	99	84	34.6	30.0	39.0	1.5
Kyrgyzstan	17	0.8	11.0	2.0	3.0	25.0	79	98	66	51.0	28.5	64.5	..
Latvia	4	0.1	..	..	..	..	..	..	..	..	..	..	<2.0
Lithuania	..	0.1	..	..	..	..	..	..	..	..	..	..	<2.0
Macedonia	7	0.1	..	..	..	..	..	..	..	..	..	..	..
Moldova	11	0.5	..	..	..	..	55	98	18	23.3	..	26.7	7.3
Poland	..	0.3	..	..	..	..	..	..	..	23.8	..	..	5.4
Romania	..	0.3	6.0	1.0	3.0	8.0	..	..	..	21.5	20.4	27.9	2.8
Russia	6	8.6	3.0	1.0	4.0	13.0	..	..	..	30.9	..	..	7.1
Slovakia	4	0.2	..	..	..	..	..	..	..	..	..	..	<2.0
Slovenia	3	0.1	..	..	..	..	..	..	..	..	..	..	<2.0
Tajikistan	32	1.9	..	..	..	..	60	82	49	..	..	..	..
Turkmenistan	10	0.4	..	..	..	..	74	..	..	..	..	..	20.9
Ukraine	5	2.6	..	..	..	..	..	..	..	31.7	..	..	<2.0
Uzbekistan	11	2.6	19.0	5.0	12.0	31.0	90	99	88	..	..	..	3.3
Yugoslavia	3	0.3	2.0	0.0	2.0	7.0	76	98	57	..	..	..	..

Table 3: Hunger, Malnutrition, and Poverty

| | Undernourished population | | % under-5 (1990-1998p) suffering from: | | | | Population with access to safe water % 1990-1998p | | | Population in Poverty (%) | | | |
| | | | Underweight | | Wasting | Stunting | | | | Below national poverty line 1984-1998p | | | Population below |
	% 1996-1998	Number (millions) 1996-1998	Moderate & severe	Severe	Moderate & severe	Moderate & severe	Total	Urban	Rural	National	Urban	Rural	$1 a day 1989-1999pq
Industrial Countries	..	..	..	..	..	..	..	..	..	..	..	..	..
Japan	..	..	..	..	..	..	97	100	85	..	..	..	..
New Zealand	..	..	..	..	..	..	97	100	82	..	..	..	..
United States	..	..	1.0	0.0	1.0	2.0	..	..	..	..	..	..	..
Data not available for other Industrial Countries													
World	..	..	**30.0**	**11.0**	**11.0**	**37.0**	**72**	**90**	**62**	..	..	..	..

..   *Data not available.*

a   *Special Administrative Region, data exclude China.*

b   *Central and Eastern European countries and the newly independent states of the former Soviet Union.*

c   *Poverty line is $14.40 (1985 PPP$) per person per day.*

d   *Poverty line is $4.00 (1990 PPP$) per person per day.*

e   *BFWI estimate.*

f   *Data included as part of China.*

g   *Djibouti, Somalia, and Sudan are included in Middle East and North Africa.*

h   *Data include São Tomé and Principe and Seychelles. Data exclude Djibouti and Sudan.*

i   *Data include the Cook Islands, Kiribati, Marshall Islands, Micronesia, Nauru, Nieu, Palau, Samoa, Tonga, Tuvalu and Vanuatu. Data exclude Hong Kong.*

j   *Data include Antigua and Barbuda, Bahamas, Barbados, and Dominica.*

k   *Data include Bahamas, Barbados, Dominica, St. Kitts and Nevis, St. Lucia, and St. Vincent and the Grenadines.*

m   *Data inlude Djibouti and Sudan. Data exclude Turkey and the West Bank and Gaza.*

n   *Data include Turkey.*

p   *Data refer to the most recent year available during the period specified in the column heading.*

q   *Measured in 1985 international prices and adjusted to local currency using purchasing power parities.*

x   *Indicates data that refer to years or periods other than those specified in the column heading, differ from the standard definition, or refer to only part of a country.*

y   *Data exclude Afghanistan.*

z   *Data include Afghanistan.*

The number '0' (zero) means zero or less than half the unit of measure.

Table 4: Economic and Development Indicators

| | GNP per capita | | | Human Development Index (HDI) rank 2000 | Distribution of income or consumption by quintiles[k] 1986-1996 | | | | | | Central government expenditure (% of GDP) 1998 | Public education expenditure (% of total government expenditure) 1995-1997[t] | Military expenditure (% of central government expenditure) 1997 | Per capita energy consumption (kg. of oil equivalent) 1997 | Annual deforestation[m] (% of total forest) 1990-1995 |
	US$ 1998	Purchasing Power Parity (PPP), $ 1998	Average annual growth % 1997-98		Lowest 20%	Second quintile	Third quintile	Fourth quintile	Highest 20%	Ratio of highest 20% to lowest 20%[e]					
Developing Countries	..	..	..		..	..	..	..	..	..	..	..	..	..	..
Africa (Sub-Saharan)	510[p]	1,140[p]	-0.4[p]		..	..	..	..	..	..	..	..	9.8[p]	695[p]	..
Angola	380	999[c]	16.3	160	..	..	..	..	..	..	..	..	36.3	587	1.0
Benin	380	857	1.9	157	..	..	..	..	..	..	..	15.2	6.8	377	1.2
Botswana	3,070	5,796	1.8	122	..	..	..	..	..	..	35.3[x]	20.6	13.4	..	0.5
Burkina Faso	240	866[c]	3.8	172	5.5	8.7	12.0	18.7	55.0	10.00	..	11.1	12.3	..	0.7
Burundi	140	561[c]	2.6	170	7.9	12.1	16.3	22.1	41.6	5.27	24.0[x]	18.3	25.8	..	0.4
Cameroon	610	1,395	3.8	134	..	..	..	..	..	..	12.7[x]	..	17.7	413	0.6
Cape Verde	1,200	3,192[c]	2.2	105	..	..	..	..	..	..	..	..	..	..	-24.0
Central African Republic	300	1,098[c]	2.6	166	2.0	4.9	9.6	18.5	65.0	32.50	..	..	27.7	..	0.4
Chad	230	843[c]	5.5	167	..	..	..	..	..	..	..	..	12.6	..	0.8
Comoros	370	1,400[c]	-2.5	137	..	..	..	..	..	..	..	..	..	..	5.6
Congo, Dem. Rep. of	110	733[c]	0.7	152	..	..	..	..	..	..	10.4[x]	..	41.4	311	0.7
Congo, Republic of	680	846	8.4	139	..	..	..	..	..	..	38.4[x]	14.7	12.3	459	0.2
Côte d'Ivoire	700	1,484	3.9	154	7.1	11.2	15.6	21.9	44.3	6.24	24.0	24.9	4.0	394	0.6
Djibouti	g	..	..	149	..	..	..	..	..	..	..	..	..	..	0.0
Equatorial Guinea	1,110	..	31.2	131	..	..	..	..	..	..	..	5.6[x]	..	..	0.5
Eritrea	200	984[c]	-6.7	159	..	..	..	..	..	..	..	..	18.1	..	0.0
Ethiopia	100	566[c]	-4.2	171	7.1	10.9	14.5	19.8	47.7	6.72	..	13.7	7.9	287	0.5
Gabon	4,170	5,615	3.2	123	..	..	..	..	..	..	..	..	7.0	1,419	0.5
Gambia	340	1,428[c]	2.0	161	4.4	9.0	13.5	20.4	52.8	12.00	..	21.2	15.0	..	0.9
Ghana	390	1,735[c]	1.9	129	8.4	12.2	15.8	21.9	41.7	4.96	..	19.9	2.4	383	1.3
Guinea	530	1,722	1.5	162	6.4	10.4	14.8	21.2	47.2	7.38	16.9	26.8	8.0	..	1.1
Guinea-Bissau	160	573[c]	-30.4	169	2.1	6.5	12.0	20.6	58.9	28.05	..	..	13.0	..	0.4
Kenya	350	964	0.3	138	5.0	9.7	14.2	20.9	50.2	10.04	29.0[x]	16.7	7.2	494	0.3
Lesotho	570	2,194	-5.3	127	2.8	6.5	11.2	19.4	60.1	21.46	55.8	..	6.1	..	0.0
Liberia	f	..	..	..	..	..	..	..	..	..	..	..	..	..	0.6
Madagascar	260	741	1.7	141	5.1	9.4	13.3	20.1	52.1	10.22	17.3	16.1	8.5	..	0.8
Malawi	210	551	-1.0	163	..	..	..	..	..	..	..	18.3	2.9	..	1.6
Mali	250	673	1.3	165	4.6	8.0	11.9	19.3	56.2	12.22	..	..	7.2	..	1.0
Mauritania	410	1,500[c]	1.5	147	6.2	10.8	15.4	22.0	45.6	7.35	..	16.2[v]	9.8	..	0.0
Mauritius	3,730	8,236	4.0	71	..	..	..	..	..	..	22.4	17.4	1.2	..	0.0
Mozambique	210	740[c]	9.7	168	6.5	10.8	15.1	21.1	46.5	7.15	..	..	9.2	461	0.7
Namibia	1,940	5,280[c]	-1.2	115	..	..	..	..	..	..	..	25.6	7.3	..	0.3
Niger	200	729[c]	4.8	173	2.6	7.1	13.9	23.1	53.3	20.50	..	12.8[w]	6.9	..	0.0
Nigeria	300	740	-1.5	151	4.4	8.2	12.5	19.3	55.7	12.66	..	11.5	12.3	753	0.9
Rwanda	230	..	7.1	164	9.7	13.2	16.5	21.6	39.1	4.03	..	..	22.2	..	0.2
Senegal	520	1,297	3.8	155	6.4	10.3	14.5	20.6	48.2	7.53	..	33.1	8.5	315	0.7
Sierra Leone	140	445	-2.9	174	1.1	2.0	9.8	23.7	63.4	57.64	17.7[x]	..	33.0	..	3.0
Somalia	f	..	..	..	..	..	..	..	..	..	..	..	..	..	0.2
South Africa	3,310	8,296[c]	-1.3	103	2.9	5.5	9.2	17.7	64.8	22.34	29.7	23.9	5.6	2,636	0.2
Sudan	290	1,240[c]	2.7	143	..	..	..	..	..	..	..	..	53.8	414	0.8
Swaziland	1,400	4,195	-1.3	112	2.7	5.8	10.0	17.1	64.4	23.85	..	18.1	..	..	0.0
Tanzania	220[n]	483	3.8	156	6.8	11.0	15.1	21.6	45.5	6.69	..	..	10.7	455	1.0
Togo	330	1,352[c]	-3.5	145	..	..	..	..	..	..	..	24.7	11.6	..	1.4
Uganda	310	1,072[c]	2.8	158	6.6	10.9	15.2	21.3	46.1	6.98	..	21.4	23.9	..	0.9
Zambia	330	678	-4.1	153	4.2	8.2	12.8	20.1	54.8	13.05	..	7.1	3.9	634	0.8
Zimbabwe	620	2,489	-1.4	130	4.0	6.3	10.0	17.4	62.3	15.58	35.7[x]	..	11.9	866	0.6
South Asia	430	1,940	3.7		..	..	..	..	..	..	17.6s	..	15.6	443	..
Afghanistan	f	..	..	..	..	..	..	..	..	..	..	..	..	..	6.8
Bangladesh	350	1,407	4.2	146	8.7	12.0	15.7	20.8	42.8	4.92	..	..	10.7	197	0.8
Bhutan	470	1,438c	2.4	142	..	..	..	..	..	..	36.9	7.0	..	..	0.3
India	440	2,060c	4.3	128	8.1	11.6	15.0	19.3	46.1	5.69	14.4	11.6	14.3	479	0.0
Maldives	1,130	3,436c	4.4	89	..	..	..	..	..	..	51.1	10.5	..	..	..
Nepal	210	1,181	0.3	144	7.6	11.5	15.1	21.0	44.8	5.89	17.5	13.5	5.1	321	1.1
Pakistan	470	1,652	0.5	135	9.5	12.9	16.0	20.5	41.1	4.32	21.4	7.1	24.2	442	2.9
Sri Lanka	810	2,945	3.3	84	8.0	11.8	15.8	21.5	42.8	5.35	25.0	8.9	21.2	386	1.1

Table 4: Economic and Development Indicators

	GNP per capita US$ 1998	GNP per capita Purchasing Power Parity (PPP), $ 1998	Average annual growth % 1997-98	Human Development Index (HDI) rank 2000	Distribution of income or consumption by quintiles[k] 1986-1996 Lowest 20%	Second quintile	Third quintile	Fourth quintile	Highest 20%	Ratio of highest 20% to lowest 20%[e]	Central government expenditure (% of GDP) 1998	Public education expenditure (% of total government expenditure) 1995-1997[i]	Military expenditure (% of central government expenditure) 1997	Per capita energy consumption (kg. of oil equivalent) 1997	Annual deforestation[m] (% of total forest) 1990-1995
East Asia and the Pacific	**990[q]**	**3,280[q]**	**-2.6[q]**		..	..	..	..	..	..	..	..	**15.1[q]**	**942[q]**	..
Brunei	i	24,886[c]	..	32	..	..	..	..	..	..	..	..	..	..	0.6
Cambodia	260	1,246[c]	-2.3	136	6.9	10.7	14.7	20.1	47.6	6.90	..	..	25.8	..	1.6
China	750	3,051	6.4	99	5.9	10.2	15.1	22.2	46.6	7.90	8.1[x]	12.2	17.6	907	0.1
Hong Kong[a]	23,660[j]	20,763	-7.8	26	..	..	..	..	..	..		17.0	..	2,172	..
Fiji	2,210	4,094	-5.2	66	..	..	..	..	..	..	29.6[x]	..	..	..	0.4
Indonesia	640	2,407	-18.0	109	8.0	11.3	15.1	20.8	44.9	5.61	17.9	7.9[y]	13.1	693	1.0
Korea, DPR (North)	f	..	..	..	..	..	..	..	..	..	..	..	..	..	0.0
Korea, Rep. of (South)	8,600	13,286	-7.5	31	7.5	12.9	17.4	22.9	39.3	5.24	17.4[x]	17.5	14.6	3,834	0.2
Laos, PDR	320	1,683	1.4	140	9.6	12.9	16.3	21.0	40.2	4.19	..	8.7	17.5	..	1.2
Malaysia	3,670	7,699	-8.0	61	4.5	8.3	13.0	20.4	53.8	11.96	19.7[x]	15.4	9.9	2,237	2.4
Mongolia	380	1,463	1.9	117	7.3	12.2	16.6	23.0	40.9	5.60	23.0	15.1	5.1	..	0.0
Myanmar (Burma)	f	..	..	125	..	..	..	..	..	..	8.9[x]	14.4[vx]	75.5[x]	296	1.4
Papua New Guinea	890	2,205[c]	0.0	133	4.5	7.9	11.9	19.2	56.5	12.56	..	..	4.1	..	0.4
Philippines	1,050	3,725	-2.1	77	5.4	8.8	13.2	20.3	52.3	9.69	19.3[x]	15.7	7.9	520	3.5
Singapore	30,170	25,295	-0.4	24	..	..	..	..	..	..	16.8[x]	23.4	19.4	8,661	0.0
Solomon Islands	760	1,904[c]	-9.8	121	..	..	..	..	..	..	..	..	..	..	0.2
Thailand	2,160	5,524	-8.6	76	6.4	9.8	14.2	21.2	48.4	7.56	18.6	20.1	12.1	1,319	2.6
Vietnam	350	1,689	4.3	108	8.0	11.4	15.2	20.9	44.5	5.56	20.1	7.4	11.1	521	1.4
Latin America and the Caribbean	**3,860**	**6,340**	**0.5**		..	..	..	..	..	..	..	..	**6.5[x]**	**1,181**	..
Argentina	8,030	11,728	2.6	35	..	..	..	..	..	..	15.3[x]	12.6	6.3	1,730	0.3
Belize	2,660	4,367	-0.9	58	..	..	..	..	..	..	..	19.5	..	..	0.3
Bolivia	1,010	2,205	2.7	114	5.6	9.7	14.5	22.0	48.2	8.61	21.9	11.1	6.7	548	1.2
Brazil	4,630	6,460	-1.4	74	2.5	5.5	10.0	18.3	63.8	25.52	..	..	3.9[x]	1,051	0.5
Chile	4,990	8,507	7.2	38	3.5	6.6	10.9	18.1	61.0	17.43	21.6	15.5	17.8	1,574	0.4
Colombia	2,470	5,861[c]	-2.4	68	3.0	6.6	11.1	18.4	60.9	20.30	16.0	19.0[v]	19.9	761	0.5
Costa Rica	2,770	5,812[c]	2.9	48	4.0	8.8	13.7	21.7	51.8	12.95	30.1[x]	22.8	3.1	769	3.0
Cuba	g	..	..	56	..	..	..	..	..	..	..	12.6	..	1,291	1.2
Dominican Republic	1,770	4,337[c]	4.9	87	4.3	8.3	13.1	20.6	53.7	12.49	16.7[x]	13.8	7.3	673	1.6
Ecuador	1,520	3,003	2.2	91	5.4	9.4	14.2	21.3	49.7	9.20	..	13.0	20.3	713	1.6
El Salvador	1,850	4,008[c]	1.1	104	3.4	7.5	12.5	20.2	56.5	16.62	..	16.0	6.7	691	3.3
Guatemala	1,640	3,474[c]	2.8	120	2.1	5.8	10.5	18.6	63.0	30.00	..	15.8[v]	15.0[x]	536	2.0
Guyana	780	3,139[c]	0.1	96	6.3	10.7	15.0	21.2	46.9	7.44	..	10.0	..	..	0.0
Haiti	410	1,379[c]	1.1	150	..	..	..	..	..	..	..	..	..	237	3.4
Honduras	740	2,338[c]	1.1	113	3.4	7.1	11.7	19.7	58.0	17.06	..	16.5	5.6[x]	532	2.3
Jamaica	1,740	3,344	0.1	83	7.0	11.5	15.8	21.8	43.9	6.27	..	12.9	2.4	1,552	7.2
Mexico	3,840	7,450	3.0	55	3.6	7.2	11.8	19.2	58.2	16.17	16.3[x]	23.0	6.2	1,501	0.9
Nicaragua	370	1,896[c]	3.3	116	4.2	8.0	12.6	20.0	55.2	13.14	33.2[x]	8.8[w]	4.5	551	2.5
Panama	2,990	4,925	0.9	59	3.6	8.1	13.6	21.9	52.8	14.67	27.0[x]	16.3	4.8	856	2.1
Paraguay	1,760	4,312[c]	-3.0	81	2.3	5.9	10.7	18.7	62.4	27.13	..	19.8[v]	10.5	824	2.6
Peru	2,440	4,180	-3.3	80	4.4	9.1	14.1	21.3	51.2	11.64	16.4	19.2	13.4	621	0.3
Suriname	1,660	..	2.5	67	..	..	..	..	..	..	..	..	..	..	0.1
Trinidad and Tobago	4,520	7,208	5.6	50	5.5	10.3	15.5	22.7	45.9	8.35	28.2[x]	..	5.4	6,414	1.5
Uruguay	6,070	8,541	3.2	39	5.4	10.0	14.8	21.5	48.3	8.94	33.3	15.5	4.4	883	0.0
Venezuela	3,530	5,706	-2.4	65	3.7	8.4	13.6	21.2	53.1	14.35	19.8	22.4[x]	9.8	2,526	1.1
Middle East and North Africa	**2,030[r]**	**4,630[r]**	**1.6[r]**		..	..	..	..	..	..	**29.6[r]**	..	**22.4[r]**	**1,353[r]**	..
Algeria	1,550	4,595[c]	3.6	107	7.0	11.6	16.1	22.7	42.6	6.09	29.2[x]	16.4	12.0	904	1.2
Bahrain	7,640	11,556	-1.5	41	..	..	..	..	..	..	32.0	12.0	..	..	0.0
Cyprus	11,920	17,599[c]	4.1	22	..	..	..	..	..	..	37.0[x]	13.2	..	..	0.0
Egypt	1,290	3,146	4.5	119	9.8	13.2	16.6	21.4	39.0	3.98	30.6[x]	14.9	11.0	656	0.0
Iran	1,650	5,121	-0.2	97	..	..	..	..	..	..	26.7	17.8	11.6	1,777	1.7
Iraq	g	..	..	126	..	..	..	..	..	..	..	..	..	1,240	0.0
Jordan	1,150	2,615	0.5	92	7.6	11.4	15.5	21.1	44.4	5.84	34.0[x]	19.8	25.0	1,081	2.5
Kuwait	i	..	..	36	..	..	..	..	..	..	50.9	14.0	26.8	8,936	0.0
Lebanon	3,560	4,144	1.4	82	..	..	..	..	..	..	32.1	8.2[v]	8.4	1,265	7.8
Libya	h	..	..	72	..	..	..	..	..	..	..	..	19.7[x]	2,909	0.0

Table 4: Economic and Development Indicators

| | GNP per capita | | | | Distribution of income or consumption by quintiles[k] 1986-1996 | | | | | | | | | | |
	US$ 1998	Purchasing Power Parity (PPP), $ 1998	Average annual growth % 1997-98	Human Development Index (HDI) rank 2000	Lowest 20%	Second quintile	Third quintile	Fourth quintile	Highest 20%	Ratio of highest 20% to lowest 20%[a]	Central government expenditure (% of GDP) 1998	Public education expenditure (% of total government expenditure) 1995-1997[t]	Military expenditure (% of central government expenditure) 1997	Per capita energy consumption (kg. of oil equivalent) 1997	Annual deforestation[m] (% of total forest) 1990-1995
Morocco	1,240	3,188	5.3	124	6.5	10.6	14.8	21.3	46.6	7.17	33.3[x]	24.9[v]	12.9	340	0.3
Oman	[h]	..	..	86	..	..	..	..	..	..	31.6	16.4	36.4	3,003	0.0
Qatar	[i]	..	..	42	..	..	..	..	..	..	..	..	..	..	0.0
Saudi Arabia	6,910	10,498[c]	-1.0	75	..	..	..	..	..	..	..	22.8	35.8	4,906	0.8
Syria	1,020	2,702	-2.3	111	..	..	..	..	..	..	24.6[x]	13.6[w]	26.2[x]	983	2.2
Tunisia	2,060	5,169	4.1	101	5.9	10.4	15.3	22.1	46.3	7.85	32.6[x]	19.9	5.3	738	0.5
Turkey	3,160	6,594	2.3	85	5.8	10.2	14.8	21.6	47.7	8.22	29.9[x]	14.7	14.7	1,140	0.0
United Arab Emirates	17,870	18,871	-10.6	45	..	..	..	..	..	..	11.0	16.7	46.5	11,967	0.0
Yemen	280	658	4.3	148	6.1	10.9	15.3	21.6	46.1	7.56	42.2	21.6	17.4	208	0.0
Countries in Transition[b]	..	..	..		..	..	..	..	..	..	..	..	..	..	..
Albania	810	2,864	6.8	94	..	..	..	..	..	..	29.8	..	4.9	317	0.0
Armenia	460	2,074	3.1	93	..	..	..	..	..	..	..	10.3	..	476	-2.7
Azerbaijan	480	2,168	8.9	90	..	..	..	..	..	..	25.1	18.8	10.8	1,529	0.0
Belarus	2,180	6,314	10.8	57	11.4	15.2	18.2	21.9	33.3	2.92	32.2	17.8	4.8	2,449	-1.0
Bosnia and Herzegovina	[f]	..	..	..	..	..	..	..	..	..	..	..	14.1	479	0.0
Bulgaria	1,220	4,683	5.1	60	8.5	13.8	17.9	22.7	37.0	4.35	0.0	7.0	9.2	2,480	0.0
Croatia	4,620	6,698	2.6	49	9.3	13.8	17.8	22.9	36.2	3.89	45.6	..	20.1	1,687	0.0
Czech Republic	5,150	12,197	-2.1	34	10.3	14.5	17.7	21.7	35.9	3.49	35.0	13.6	5.8	3,938	0.0
Estonia	3,360	7,563	6.4	46	6.2	12.0	17.0	23.1	41.8	6.74	32.9	25.5	4.5	3,811	-1.0
Georgia	970	3,429	2.5	70	..	..	..	..	..	..	8.6	6.9[x]	9.6	423	0.0
Hungary	4,510	9,832	4.6	43	8.8	12.5	16.6	22.3	39.9	4.53	43.4	6.9	4.3	2,492	-0.5
Kazakhstan	1,340	4,317	-1.2	73	6.7	11.5	16.4	23.1	42.3	6.31	..	17.6	4.4	2,439	-1.9
Kyrgyzstan	380	2,247	2.8	98	6.3	10.2	14.7	21.4	47.4	7.52	..	23.5	..	603	0.0
Latvia	2,420	5,777	4.3	63	7.6	12.9	17.1	22.1	40.3	5.30	33.0	14.1	..	1,806	-0.9
Lithuania	2,540	6,283	4.8	52	7.8	12.6	16.8	22.4	40.3	5.17	30.4	22.8	2.8	2,376	-0.6
Macedonia, FYR	1,290	4,224	2.4	69	..	..	..	..	..	..	..	20.0	10.2	..	0.0
Moldova	380	1,995	-9.2	102	6.9	11.9	16.7	23.1	41.5	6.01	..	28.1	1.9	1,029	0.0
Poland	3,910	7,543	4.4	44	7.7	12.6	16.7	22.1	40.9	5.31	37.7	24.8	5.6	2,721	-0.1
Romania	1,360	5,572	-8.1	64	8.9	13.6	17.6	22.6	37.3	4.19	31.9[x]	10.5	6.9	1,957	0.0
Russian Federation	2,260	6,180	-6.4	62	4.4	8.6	13.3	20.1	53.7	12.20	25.4[x]	9.6	30.9	4,019	..
Slovakia	3,700	9,624	4.1	40	11.9	15.8	18.8	22.2	31.4	2.64	..	..	8.0	3,198	-0.1
Slovenia	9,780	14,400	4.1	29	8.4	14.3	18.5	23.4	35.4	4.21	..	12.6	12.5	3,213	0.0
Tajikistan	370	1,041	13.3	110	..	..	..	..	..	..	..	11.5	10.6	562	0.0
Turkmenistan	[f]	..	..	100	6.1	10.2	14.7	21.5	47.5	7.79	..	..	15.6	2,615	0.0
Ukraine	980	3,130	-1.6	78	8.6	12.0	16.2	22.0	41.2	4.79	..	15.7	8.4	2,960	-0.1
Uzbekistan	950	2,044	3.6	106	..	..	..	..	..	..	..	21.1	6.1[x]	1,798	-2.7
Yugoslavia, FR	[g]	..	..	..	..	..	..	..	..	..	..	..	..	..	0.0
Industrial Countries	..	..	..		..	..	..	..	..	..	..	..	..	..	..
Australia	20,640	21,795	4.4	4	5.9	12.0	17.2	23.6	41.3	7.00	24.5	13.5	8.6	5,484	0.0
Austria	26,830	23,145	3.2	16	10.4	14.8	18.5	22.9	33.3	3.20	40.5[x]	10.4	1.9	3,439	0.0
Belgium	25,380	23,622	2.8	7	9.5	14.6	18.4	23.0	34.5	3.63	46.6[x]	6.0[u]	3.2	5,611	0.0
Canada	19,170	22,814	2.0	1	7.5	12.9	17.2	23.0	39.3	5.24	24.7[x]	12.9[x]	..	7,930	-0.1
Denmark	33,040	23,855	2.4	15	9.6	14.9	18.3	22.7	34.5	3.59	41.4[x]	13.1	3.9	3,994	0.0
Finland	24,280	20,641	6.5	11	10.0	14.2	17.6	22.3	35.8	3.58	35.3[x]	12.2	4.3[x]	6,435	0.1
France	24,210[x]	21,214	2.8	12	7.2	12.6	17.2	22.8	40.2	5.58	46.6[x]	10.9	6.4	4,224	-1.1
Germany	26,570	22,026	2.8	14	8.2	13.2	17.5	22.7	38.5	4.70	32.9	9.6	4.7	4,231	0.0
Greece	11,740	13,994	3.1	25	7.5	12.4	16.9	22.8	40.3	5.37	34.0[x]	8.2	13.8	2,435	-2.3
Ireland	18,710	17,991	7.9	18	6.7	11.6	16.4	22.4	42.9	6.40	35.5[x]	13.5	3.3	3,412	-2.7
Israel	16,180	16,861	1.2	23	6.9	11.4	16.3	22.9	42.5	6.16	49.0	12.3[x]	20.9	3,014	0.0
Italy	20,090	20,365	1.3	19	8.7	14.0	18.1	22.9	36.3	4.17	44.6	9.1	4.1	2,839	-0.1
Japan	32,350	23,592	-2.9	9	10.6	14.2	17.6	22.0	35.7	3.36	..	9.9[x]	6.6	4,084	0.1
Luxembourg	45,100	36,703	3.9	17	9.4	13.8	17.7	22.6	36.5	3.88	41.0[x]	15.1	..	..	0.0
Netherlands	24,780	22,325	2.7	8	7.3	12.7	17.2	22.8	40.1	5.49	47.6[x]	9.8	6.4	4,800	0.0

Table 4: Economic and Development Indicators

| | GNP per capita | | | Human Development Index (HDI) rank 2000 | Distribution of income or consumption by quintiles[k] 1986-1996 | | | | | Ratio of highest 20% to lowest 20%[e] | Central government expenditure (% of GDP) 1998 | Public education expenditure (% of total government expenditure) 1995-1997[t] | Military expenditure (% of central government expenditure) 1997 | Per capita energy consumption (kg. of oil equivalent) 1997 | Annual deforestation[m] (% of total forest) 1990-1995 |
	US$ 1998	Purchasing Power Parity (PPP), $ 1998	Average annual growth % 1997-98		Lowest 20%	Second quintile	Third quintile	Fourth quintile	Highest 20%						
New Zealand	14,600	16,084	-1.5	20	2.7	10.0	16.3	24.1	46.9	17.37	33.4	17.1	3.9	4,435	-0.6
Norway	34,310	26,196	1.7	2	9.7	14.3	17.9	22.2	35.8	3.69	35.7[x]	15.8	4.8	5,501	-0.3
Portugal	10,670	14,569	3.7	28	7.3	11.6	15.9	21.8	43.4	5.95	40.8[x]	11.7	5.9	2,051	-0.9
Spain	14,100	15,960	3.6	21	7.5	12.6	17.0	22.6	40.3	5.37	36.1[x]	11.0	6.0	2,729	0.0
Sweden	25,580	19,848	2.8	6	9.6	14.5	18.1	23.2	34.5	3.59	42.7	12.2	5.4	5,869	0.0
Switzerland	39,980	26,876	1.5	13	6.9	12.7	17.3	22.9	40.3	5.84	27.9[x]	15.4	5.8[x]	3,699	0.0
United Kingdom	21,410	20,314	2.0	10	6.6	11.5	16.3	22.7	43.0	6.52	37.9	11.6	7.1	3,863	-0.5
United States	29,240	29,240	1.5	3	5.2	10.5	15.6	22.4	46.4	8.92	21.1	14.4[x]	16.3	8,076	-0.3
World	**4,890**	**6,300**	**1.5[aa]**	..	..	..	..	..	..	..	..	..	**11.0**	**1,692**	..

.. Data not available.

a Special administrative region, data exclude China.

b Central and Eastern European countries and the newly independent states of former the Soviet Union.

c Estimate based on regression; others are extrapolated from the latest International Comparison Programme benchmark estimates.

d Data from the World Development Report 1999/2000, World Bank.

f Estimated to be low income ($760 or less)

g Estimated to be lower-middle income ($761 to $3,030)

h Estimated to be upper-middle income($3,031 to $9,360).

i Estimated to be high income ($9,361 or more).

j GDP data.

k Income shares by percentiles of population, ranked by per capita income, except as noted.

m Positive data indicate loss of forest; negative data indicate gain in forest.

n Mainland Tanzania only.

p Data include São Tomé and Principe and Seychelles. Data exclude Djibouti.

q Data exclude Hong Kong, Sinapore, and Brunei.

r Data include Djibouti, Cyprus, and the West Bank and Gaza. Data exclude Kuwait, Qatar, Turkey, and the United Arab Emirates.

s Data include Iran.

t Data refers to most recent year available during the period specified in the column heading.

u Data refer to the Flemish community only.

v Data refer to expenditures by the ministry of education only.

w Not including expenditure on tertiary education.

x Data refer to a period other than the one specified in the column heading.

y Data refer to the central government only.

z Includes the French overseas departments of French Guyana, Guadeloupe, Martinique, and Réunion.

The number '0' (zero) means zero or less than half the unit of measure.

Table 5: Economic Globalization

	Trade 1998						Investment 1998						Debt 1998	
	Exports of goods and services (% of GDP)		Manufactured exports (% of merchandise exports)	Food Trade		Imports of goods and services (% of GDP)	Gross domestic investment (GDI) (% of GDP)	Net private capital flows[c] (US $ millions)	Foreign direct investment (US $ millions)	Aid (% of GDI)	Foreign direct investment net inflows (% of GDI)	Foreign direct investment net inflows (% of GDP)	Total External debt (US $ billions)	Debt service (% of exports of goods and services)
	1980	1998		Food exports (% of merchandise exports)	Food imports (% of merchandise imports)									
Developing Countries	..	..	..	..	..	..	..	..	..	..	..	..	..	..
Africa (sub-Saharan)	**32**	**28**	..	**7.63**	**7.99**	**31**	**17**	**3,452**	**4,394**	**22.3**	**7.0**	**1.3**	**230.13**	**14.7**
Angola	..	52	..	..	13.73	42	20	40	360	22.2	23.8	4.8	12.17	34.4
Benin	23	23	..	6.62	17.15	32	17	34	34	53.4	8.5	1.5	1.65	10.6
Botswana	50	35	..	5.13	11.15	34	21	91	95	10.6	9.4	1.9	1.40	2.7
Burkina Faso	10	14	..	11.51	14.77	30	29	0	0	53.8	0.0	0.0	1.12	40.0
Burundi	9	8	..	0.69	18.01	20	9	2	1	95.9	1.3	0.1	9.83	22.3
Cameroon	28	26	..	16.66	9.47	25	18	1	50	26.5	3.1	0.6	..	..
Cape Verde	..	..	..	0.10	23.65	..	..	..	..	..	..	..	0.92	20.9
Central African Republic	25	16	..	1.18	9.51	25	14	5	5	83.8	3.5	0.5	1.09	10.6
Chad	17	19	..	12.85	12.68	32	15	16	16	65.9	6.3	0.9	..	..
Comoros	..	..	..	24.61	42.44	..	..	..	..	..	..	..	12.93	1.2
Congo, Dem. Rep. of	16	24[x]	..	1.12	39.14	22[x]	8	1	1	22.3	0.1	0.0	5.12	3.3
Congo, Republic of	60	63	..	1.07	24.40	72	35	4	4	9.4	0.6	0.2	14.85	26.1
Côte d'Ivoire	35	44	..	44.56	13.24	38	18	181	435	39.9	21.7	4.0	..	..
Djibouti	..	..	..	34.67	23.85	..	..	..	..	..	..	..	0.15	1.5
Equatorial Guinea	..	..	..	9.73	10.50	..	..	..	..	..	..	..	10.35	11.3
Eritrea	..	20	..	2.59	13.03	90	41	0	0	59.6	0.0	0.0	4.43	12.0
Ethiopia	11[x]	16	..	8.95	11.37	28	18	6	4	54.4	0.3	0.1	0.48	9.7
Gabon	65	51	..	0.13	13.29	40	32	-57	-50	2.5	-2.8	-0.9	6.88	28.4
Gambia	43	51	..	21.56	36.16	62	18	13	13	49.5	17.0	3.1	3.55	19.5
Ghana	8	27	..	41.57	13.84	36	23	42	56	40.8	3.3	0.7	0.96	25.6
Guinea	..	22	..	2.29	14.42	23	21	-9	1	47.3	0.1	0.0	7.01	18.8
Guinea-Bissau	13	15	..	76.68	54.80	35	11	1	1	410.5	2.1	0.2	0.69	8.4
Kenya	28	25	24	15.65	15.03	32	14	-57	11	28.3	0.7	0.1	..	..
Lesotho	20	33	..	0.94	15.40	125	49	281	265	17.2	68.8	33.4	4.39	14.7
Liberia	..	..	..	0.44	17.74	..	..	..	..	..	..	..	2.44	14.7
Madagascar	13	21	28[x]	12.93	13.86	29	13	15	16	99.0	3.2	0.4	3.20	12.6
Malawi	25	31	..	10.53	9.84	44	14	24	1	187.8	0.4	0.1	2.59	27.7
Mali	15	24	..	19.96	10.33	34	21	17	17	62.0	3.0	0.6	2.48	11.3
Mauritania	32	41	..	8.81	101.10	54	21	3	5	82.3	2.4	0.5	8.21	18.0
Mauritius	51	65	73	23.27	10.58	65	24	-79	12	3.9	1.2	0.3	..	..
Mozambique	11	12	17[x]	11.02	16.95	30	20	209	213	130.7	26.8	5.5	1.66	18.4
Namibia	76	63	..	10.82	5.10	63	19	..	..	30.7	..	..	30.32	11.2
Niger	25	16	..	13.57	18.96	23	10	-23	1	136.4	0.5	0.0	1.23	16.9
Nigeria	29	23	..	0.67	3.82	32	20	1,028	1,051	2.5	12.7	2.5	3.86	23.2
Rwanda	14	5	..	0.56	29.84	23	16	7	7	110.1	2.2	0.3	1.24	18.2
Senegal	27	33	..	6.33	31.70	38	20	24	40	54.7	4.4	0.9	..	..
Sierra Leone	18	22	..	4.07	87.71	31	8	5	5	202.3	9.5	0.8	24.71	12.2
Somalia	..	..	..	48.93	54.40	..	..	..	..	..	..	..	16.84	9.8
South Africa	35	26	54[d]	6.60	3.93	25	16	783	550	2.5	2.6	0.4	..	..
Sudan	11	..	3[x]	48.05	11.39	..	..	371	371	..	..	3.6	7.60	20.8
Swaziland	..	..	..	37.82	14.12	..	..	..	..	..	..	..	1.45	5.7
Tanzania	..	18	10[x]	23.24	16.41	25	15	157	172	82.8	14.3	2.1	3.94	23.6
Togo	51	34	..	9.12	10.95	40	14	0	0	60.0	0.0	0.0	6.87	17.7
Uganda	19	10	..	7.79	7.58	20	15	198	200	46.0	19.5	3.0	4.72	38.2
Zambia	41	29	..	4.38	21.73	38	14	40	72	72.6	15.0	2.1		
Zimbabwe	23	46	..	9.98	4.71	48	17	-217	76	25.7	7.0	1.2		
South Asia	**8**	**13**	**78[x]**	**8.54**	**9.39**	**16**	**23**	**7,580**	**3,659**	**3.8**	**2.9**	**0.7**	**163.78**	**18.9**
Afghanistan	..	..	..	27.29	16.60	..	..	..	..	..	..	..	..	..
Bangladesh	4	14	91	0.49	13.91	19	22	288	308	13.2	3.3	0.7	16.38	9.1
Bhutan	..	..	..	9.30	11.90	..	..	..	..	..	..	..	..	..
India	6	11	74[x]	9.34	6.84	14	24	6,151	2,635	1.6	2.6	0.6	98.23	20.6
Maldives	..	..	..	..	11.84	..	..	..	..	..	..	..	..	..
Nepal	12	23	77[x]	15.47	7.82	34	22	-1	12	39.0	1.2	0.3	2.65	7.0
Pakistan	12	16	84	12.54	16.00	20	17	806	500	9.7	4.6	0.8	32.23	23.6
Sri Lanka	32	36	..	3.93	11.50	42	25	325	193	12.3	4.8	1.2	8.53	6.6

Table 5: Economic Globalization

	Trade 1998						Investment 1998						Debt 1998	
	Exports of goods and services (% of GDP)		Manufactured exports (% of merchandise exports)	Food Trade		Imports of goods and services (% of GDP)	Gross domestic investment (GDI) (% of GDP)	Net private capital flows[c] (US $ millions)	Foreign direct investment (US $ millions)	Aid (% of GDI)	Foreign direct investment net inflows (% of GDI)	Foreign direct investment net inflows (% of GDP)	Total External debt (US $ billions)	Debt service (% of exports of goods and services)
				Food exports (% of merchandise exports)	Food imports (% of merchandise imports)									
	1980	1998												
East Asia and the Pacific	22[g]	42[g]	82[g]	3.26	3.75	33[g]	28[g]	67,249[g]	64,162[g]	..	12.4[g]	3.9[g]	667.52[g]	13.3[g]
Brunei	..	42[g]	..	0.96	7.73	..	..	..	..	..	..	..	..	..
Cambodia	..	34	..	1.37	10.45	44	15	118	121	78.3	28.1	4.2	2.21	1.5
China	8	22	87	2.73	3.05	17	38	42,676	43,751	0.6	11.9	4.6	154.60	8.6
Hong Kong[a]	90	125	95	1.50	3.64	125	30	..	..	0.0	..	..	..	..
Fiji	..	..	..	20.65	9.79	..	..	..	..	..	..	..	..	..
Indonesia	34	54	45	4.88	8.98	44	14	-3,759	-356	9.6	-2.7	-0.4	150.88	33.0
Korea, DPR (North)	..	..	..	4.63	21.93	..	..	..	..	..	..	..	..	..
Korea, Rep. of (South)	33	49	91	0.86	4.27	36	21	7,644	5,415	-0.1	8.1	1.7	139.10	12.9
Laos, PDR	..	4	..	11.72	9.10	5	25	46	46	89.6	14.7	3.6	2.44	6.3
Malaysia	58	114	79	8.52	4.38	93	27	8,295	5,000	1.0	25.8	6.9	44.77	8.7
Mongolia	21[x]	50	10[x]	5.21	11.03	55	26	7	19	75.7	7.1	1.8	0.74	6.3
Myanmar (Burma)	9	1[x]	..	16.54	7.03	1[x]	12[x]	153	70	..	..	..	5.68	5.3
Papua New Guinea	43	68	..	14.68	19.85	70	30	230	110	31.8	9.7	2.9	2.69	8.6
Philippines	24	56	90	5.32	6.88	60	21	2,587	1,713	4.5	12.8	2.6	47.82	11.8
Singapore	215	153	86[f]	1.32	2.44	135	34	..	7,218	0.0	25.5	8.6	..	..
Solomon Islands	..	..	..	17.71	10.63	..	..	..	..	..	..	..	..	..
Thailand	24	59	71[x]	8.72	2.23	42	25	7,825	6,941	2.5	24.7	6.2	86.17	19.2
Vietnam	..	44[x]	..	15.21	3.43	52[x]	29	832	1,200	14.9	15.4	4.4	22.36	8.9
Latin America and the Caribbean	12	15	49	15.95	7.87	18	22	126,854	69,323	1.0	16.1	3.5	786.02	33.6
Argentina	5	10	35	36.78	3.72	13	20	18,899	6,150	0.1	10.4	2.1	144.05	58.2
Belize	..	..	..	66.10	12.74	..	..	..	..	..	..	..	..	..
Bolivia	25	20	30	19.45	8.26	29	20	860	872	36.6	50.9	10.2	6.08	30.2
Brazil	9	7	55	17.29	7.64	10	21	54,385	31,913	0.2	19.3	4.1	232.00	74.1
Chile	23	28	17	13.19	5.23	29	27	9,252	4,638	0.5	22.2	5.9	36.30	22.3
Colombia	16	14	32	10.41	9.14	20	20	3,629	3,038	0.8	15.1	3.0	33.26	30.7
Costa Rica	26	49	56	35.05	6.41	51	29	800	559	0.9	18.6	5.3	3.97	7.6
Cuba	..	..	..	36.83	12.93	..	..	..	..	..	..	..	..	..
Dominican Republic	19	31	8	34.76	8.67	40	26	771	691	2.9	16.9	4.4	4.45	4.2
Ecuador	25	27	10	31.00	9.77	34	26	584	831	3.6	17.1	4.5	15.14	28.8
El Salvador	34	23	47	8.92	12.67	36	17	242	12	9.1	0.1	0.1	3.63	10.4
Guatemala	22	19	33	34.27	10.54	27	16	621	673	7.7	22.2	3.6	4.57	9.8
Guyana	..	..	..	43.78	7.78	..	..	..	..	..	..	..	..	..
Haiti	22	11	84[x]	6.51	32.35	29	11	11	11	98.3	2.7	0.3	1.05	8.2
Honduras	36	46	17	17.36	8.91	52	30	193	84	20.0	5.3	1.6	5.00	18.7
Jamaica	51	49	70[x]	15.39	11.71	62	31	586	369	0.9	18.3	5.7	4.00	12.8
Mexico	11	31	85	7.33	7.80	33	24	23,188	10,238	0.0	10.7	2.6	159.96	20.8
Nicaragua	24	39	8	23.66	13.46	71	33	171	184	83.8	27.4	9.2	5.97	25.5
Panama	51	34	17	35.45	8.97	43	33	1,459	1,206	0.7	40.2	13.2	6.69	7.6
Paraguay	15	45	15[x]	57.31	9.26	49	21	236	256	4.2	14.2	3.0	2.30	5.3
Peru	22	12	24	4.82	14.44	17	24	2,724	1,930	3.3	12.7	3.1	32.40	28.3
Suriname	..	..	..	6.50	16.81	..	..	..	..	..	..	..	..	..
Trinidad and Tobago	50	41	44	6.05	9.13	56	22	761	730	1.0	51.7	11.4	2.19	10.2
Uruguay	15	22	39	44.74	7.43	22	16	496	164	0.7	5.0	0.8	7.60	23.5
Venezuela	29	20	19	1.68	8.57	20	20	6,866	4,435	0.2	23.8	4.7	37.00	27.4
Middle East and North Africa	42[h]	25[h]	17[x]	4.45	12.03	28[h]	22[h]	9,223[h]	5,054[h]	4.7[h]	3.2[h]	.7[h]	208.06[h]	14.0[h]
Algeria	34	23	..	0.29	27.88	23	27	-1,321	5	3.0	0.0	0.0	30.67	42.0
Bahrain	..	..	..	1.63	8.59	..	..	..	..	..	..	..	..	..
Cyprus	..	..	..	11.22	7.05	..	..	..	..	..	..	..	..	..
Egypt	31	17	44	11.87	18.87	23	22	1,385	1,076	10.4	5.8	1.3	31.96	9.5
Iran	13	13	..	5.36	20.59	15	16	588	24	0.9	0.1	0.0	14.39	20.2
Iraq	..	..	..	0.14	36.27	..	..	..	..	..	..	..	..	..
Jordan	40	49	..	8.87	16.76	70	25	207	310	22.1	16.8	4.2	8.48	16.4
Kuwait	78	45	14[x]	0.39	12.50	47	14	..	59	0.2	1.6	0.2	..	..
Lebanon	..	11	..	13.60	10.51	51	28	1,740	200	5.0	4.2	1.2	6.73	18.7
Libya	66	..	..	0.41	15.86	..	..	..	..	..	..	..	..	..

Table 5: Economic Globalization

	Trade 1998						Investment 1998						Debt 1998	
	Exports of goods and services (% of GDP)		Manufactured exports (% of merchandise exports)	Food Trade		Imports of goods and services (% of GDP)	Gross domestic investment (GDI) (% of GDP)	Net private capital flows[c] (US $ millions)	Foreign direct investment (US $ millions)	Aid (% of GDI)	Foreign direct investment net inflows (% of GDI)	Foreign direct investment net inflows (% of GDP)	Total External debt (US $ billions)	Debt service (% of exports of goods and services)
	1980	1998		Food exports (% of merchandise exports)	Food imports (% of merchandise imports)									
Morocco	15	18	49[x]	15.27	12.69	26	23	965	322	6.6	4.0	0.9	20.69	23.0
Oman	63	..	..	2.61	10.62	..	..	-214	106	..	..	0.7	3.63	..
Qatar	..	..	..	0.39	5.98	..	..	..	..	..	..	..	..	..
Saudi Arabia	71	36	9[x]	0.69	15.80	31	21	..	..	0.1	..	..	..	..
Syria	18	29	10[x]	22.33	15.58	40	29	76	80	3.0	1.6	0.5	22.44	6.4
Tunisia	40	42	82	6.32	7.97	46	28	694	650	2.7	11.8	3.3	11.08	15.1
Turkey	5	25	77	14.11	3.52	28	25	1,641	940	0.0	1.9	0.5	102.07	21.2
United Arab Emirates	78	..	..	1.57	6.18	..	..	..	..	..	..	..	..	..
Yemen	..	34	..	0.28	39.75	54	22	-210	-210	33.4	-22.6	-4.9	4.14	4.2
Countries in Transition[b]	..	..	..	**5.16**	**7.69**	..	..	..	..	..	..	..	..	..
Albania	23	9	68	2.05	24.71	32	16	42	45	49.7	9.2	1.5	0.82	4.5
Armenia	..	19	54[x]	1.75	24.78	52	19	232	232	38.4	64.4	12.2	0.80	8.9
Azerbaijan	..	25	..	3.84	24.78	59	39	1,081	1,023	5.8	66.5	26.1	0.69	2.3
Belarus	..	62	76	3.94	6.62	68	26	122	149	0.5	2.5	0.7	1.12	2.0
Bosnia and Herzegovina	..	..	..	..	..	..	..	..	..	..	..	..	..	..
Bulgaria	36	45	61[x]	8.56	5.05	46	15	498	401	12.9	22.2	3.3	9.91	22.1
Croatia	..	40	76	6.28	4.52	49	23	1,666	873	0.8	17.3	4.0	8.30	8.9
Czech Republic	..	60	88	2.96	3.91	61	30	3,331	2,554	2.7	15.1	4.5	25.30	15.2
Estonia	..	80	66[x]	18.29	16.97	89	29	714	581	5.9	38.1	11.2	0.78	2.1
Georgia	..	14	..	4.74	15.48	28	8	57	50	40.5	12.5	1.0	1.67	7.6
Hungary	39	50	82	10.00	2.28	52	31	4,683	1,936	1.4	13.1	4.0	28.58	27.3
Kazakhstan	..	31	23	7.52	7.87	35	17	1,983	1,158	5.4	30.5	5.3	5.71	13.0
Kyrgyzstan	..	35	38[x]	12.49	10.84	51	18	108	109	69.3	35.0	6.4	1.15	9.4
Latvia	..	48	58	5.54	8.27	61	23	366	357	6.6	24.3	5.6	0.76	2.5
Lithuania	..	47	61	9.92	6.11	59	24	982	926	4.9	35.7	8.6	1.95	3.3
Macedonia, FYR	..	41	..	9.95	16.99	57	23	190	118	16.2	20.8	4.7	2.39	13.0
Moldova	..	47	25	38.13	5.63	75	26	62	85	8.0	20.3	5.3	1.04	18.5
Poland	28	26[x]	77	8.75	4.37	30[x]	26	9,653	6,365	2.1	15.2	4.0	47.71	9.7
Romania	35	26	81	4.13	5.84	34	18	1,826	2,031	5.3	30.1	5.3	9.51	23.5
Russian Federation	..	32	28	0.97	15.73	27	16	19,346	2,764	2.3	6.1	1.0	183.60	12.1
Slovakia	..	64	84	3.66	4.56	75	39	1,480	562	1.9	7.0	2.8	9.89	15.9
Slovenia	..	57	90	2.33	5.03	58	25	..	165	0.8	3.4	0.8	..	..
Tajikistan	..	..	..	2.53	22.98	..	17	-3	18	..	5.1	0.8	1.07	13.7
Turkmenistan	..	..	..	3.69	28.34	..	..	473	130	..	..	5.5	2.27	42.0
Ukraine	..	40	..	11.12	3.81	43	21	2,087	743	4.2	8.2	1.7	12.72	11.4
Uzbekistan	..	22	..	4.47	24.06	22	19	592	200	3.7	5.1	1.0	3.16	13.2
Yugoslavia, FR	..	..	..	10.32	9.62	..	..	0	0	..	..	..	13.74	..
Industrial Countries	**20[l]**	**22[lx]**	..	**5.33**	**5.16**	..	..	..	..	..	..	..	..	..
Australia	16	21[x]	29	18.03	2.96	21[x]	22[x]	..	6,165	n/a	8.5[x]	1.7	..	..
Austria	36	42[x]	83	3.53	4.25	43[x]	25[x]	..	6,034	n/a	5.0[x]	2.8	..	..
Belgium	57	73[x]	..	8.30[j]	7.36[j]	68[x]	18[x]	..	..	n/a	..	..	..	..
Canada	28	41[x]	66	5.68	3.73	39[x]	20[x]	..	16,514	n/a	9.6[x]	2.8	..	..
Denmark	33	36[x]	65	15.33	5.73	33[x]	21[x]	..	6,373	n/a	8.0[x]	3.6	..	..
Finland	33	40[x]	86	1.70	4.14	31[x]	17[x]	..	12,029	n/a	10.3[x]	9.7	..	..
France	22	27[x]	80	8.08	5.74	23[x]	17[x]	..	27,998	n/a	9.8[x]	2.0	..	..
Germany	..	27[x]	86	3.20	5.98	25[x]	21[x]	..	18,712	n/a	2.3[x]	0.9	..	..
Greece	16	16[x]	..	19.70	10.61	24[x]	20[x]	..	..	n/a	4.1[x]	0.8[x]	..	..
Ireland	48	80[x]	84	7.51	5.05	62[x]	20[x]	..	2,920	n/a	18.1[x]	3.6	..	..
Israel	44	32	92	3.55	5.47	43	20	..	1,850	5.2	9.1	1.8	..	..
Italy	22	27[x]	89	4.69	7.22	23[x]	18[x]	..	2,635	n/a	1.8[x]	0.2	..	..
Japan	14	11[x]	94	0.22	8.23	10[x]	29[x]	..	3,268	n/a	0.3	0.1	..	..
Luxembourg	..	..	..	..	..	..	..	..	..	n/a	..	..	..	..
Netherlands	51	56[x]	70	9.30	6.46	49[x]	20[x]	..	33,346	n/a	17.3[x]	8.7	..	..

Table 5: Economic Globalization

	Trade 1998						Investment 1998						Debt 1998	
	Exports of goods and services (% of GDP)		Manufactured exports (% of merchandise exports)	Food Trade		Imports of goods and services (% of GDP)	Gross domestic investment (GDI) (% of GDP)	Net private capital flows[c] (US $ millions)	Foreign direct investment (US $ millions)	Aid (% of GDI)	Foreign direct investment net inflows (% of GDI)	Foreign direct investment net inflows (% of GDP)	Total External debt (US $ billions)	Debt service (% of exports of goods and services)
				Food exports (% of merchandise exports)	Food imports (% of merchandise imports)									
	1980	1998												
New Zealand	30	29ˣ	32	38.05	5.42	28ˣ	21ˣ	..	..	n/a	19.7ˣ	4.1ˣ	..	..
Norway	43	41ˣ	30	0.55	3.40	34ˣ	25ˣ	..	3,597	n/a	9.2ˣ	2.5	..	..
Portugal	25	31ˣ	87	3.22	7.66	40ˣ	26ˣ	..	1,783	n/a	9.8ˣ	1.7	..	..
Spain	16	28ˣ	78	11.51	6.17	27ˣ	21ˣ	..	11,392	n/a	5.1ˣ	2.1	..	..
Sweden	29	44ˣ	82	1.58	4.09	37ˣ	14ˣ	..	19,413	n/a	32.0ˣ	8.6	..	..
Switzerland	35	40ˣ	93	1.83	3.74	35ˣ	20ˣ	..	5,488	n/a	11.0	2.1	..	..
United Kingdom	27	29ˣ	85	3.05	6.10	29ˣ	16ˣ	..	67,481	n/a	18.2ˣ	5.0	..	..
United States	10	12ˣ	82	5.63	2.59	13ˣ	19ˣ	..	193,373	n/a	7.5	2.3	..	..
World	**20**	**23**	**80**	**5.42**	**5.60**	**22**	**22**	**..**	**619,258**	**..**	**7.1**	**2.2**	**..**	**..**

.. Data not available.

a Special administrative region, data exclude China.

b Central and Eastern European countries and the newly independent states of the former Soviet Union.

c Net private capital flows consist of private debt flows (commercial bank lending, bonds and other private credits) and nondebt private flows (foreign direct investment and portfolio equity investment).

d Data on export commodity shares refer to the South African Customs Union, which comprises Botswana, Lesotho, Namibia, and South Africa.

e BFWI estimate.

f Data include re-exports.

g Data exclude Hong Kong and Singapore.

h Data exclude Kuwait, Turkey, and the United Arab Emirates.

i Data include Iceland. Data exclude Israel.

j Data include Luxembourg.

x Data refer to a year other than the one specified.

y OECD data from 1996.

The number '0' (zero) means zero or less than half the unit of measure.

n/a Not applicable

Table 6: United States – National Hunger and Poverty Trends

	1970	1980	1985	1990	1991	1992	1993	1994	1995	1996	1997	1998	1999
Total population (millions)	**205.1**	**227.8**	**239.3**	**249.4**	**252.1**	**255.0**	**257.8**	**260.4**	**262.9**	**265.3**	**267.63**	**270.30**	**272.7**
Food insecurity prevalence estimates													
All U.S. households—food insecure (%)	..	..	..	..	..	..	..	..	10.3	10.4	8.7	10.2	10.1
Without hunger	..	..	..	..	..	..	..	..	6.4	6.3	5.6	6.6	7.1
With hunger	..	..	..	..	..	..	..	..	3.9	4.1	3.1	3.6	3.0
Adult members (total)—food insecure (%)	..	..	..	..	..	..	..	..	9.5	9.6	8.1	9.5	9.5
Without hunger	..	..	..	..	..	..	..	..	6.1	6.0	5.4	6.4	7.0
With hunger	..	..	..	..	..	..	..	..	3.4	3.6	2.6	3.1	2.5
Child members (total)—food insecure (%)	..	..	..	..	..	..	..	..	17.4	18.2	14.6	17.3	16.9
Without hunger	..	..	..	..	..	..	..	..	11.6	12.0	10.5	12.8	13.1
With hunger	..	..	..	..	..	..	..	..	5.8	6.2	4.1	4.6	3.8
Percent of federal budget spent on food assistance[a]	**0.5**	**2.4**	**2.0**	**1.9**	**2.0**	**2.3**	**2.5**	**2.47**	**2.48**	**2.43**	**1.94**	**2.03**	**1.94**
Total infant mortality rate (per 1,000 live births)	**20.0**	**12.6**	**10.6**	**9.1**	**8.9**	**8.5**	**8.4**	**8.0**	**7.6**	**7.3**	**7.2**	**7.2**	**..**
White	17.8	11.0	9.3	7.7	7.3	6.9	6.8	6.6	6.3	6.1	6.0	6.0	..
African American	32.6	21.4	18.2	17.0	17.6	16.8	16.5	15.8	15.1	14.7	14.2	13.8	..
Hispanic	..	..	..	7.8	7.5	6.8	..	..	..	5.9	..	7.2	..
American Indian	..	..	..	..	..	..	..	..	..	..	..	9.3	..
Asian or Pacific Islander	..	..	..	..	..	..	..	..	..	..	..	5.5	..
Total poverty rate (%)	**12.6**	**13.0**	**14.0**	**13.5**	**14.2**	**14.8**	**15.1**	**14.5**	**13.8**	**13.7**	**13.3**	**12.7**	**11.8**
Northeast	..	..	..	10.2	11.3	12.6	13.3	12.9	12.5	12.7	12.6	12.3	10.9
Midwest	..	..	..	11.9	12.8	13.3	13.4	13.0	11.0	10.7	10.4	10.3	9.8
South	..	..	..	15.9	16.2	17.1	17.1	16.1	15.7	15.1	14.6	13.7	13.1
West	..	..	..	11.6	12.4	14.8	15.6	15.3	14.9	15.4	14.6	14.0	12.6
White	9.9	10.2	11.4	10.7	11.3	11.9	12.2	11.7	11.2	11.2	11.0	10.5	9.8
African American	33.5	32.5	31.1	31.9	32.7	33.4	33.1	30.6	29.3	28.4	26.5	26.1	23.6
Hispanic	..	25.7	29.0	28.1	28.7	29.6	30.6	30.7	30.3	29.4	27.1	25.6	22.8
American Indian/Alaskan Native[b]	..	..	..	..	..	..	..	..	..	..	..	..	25.9
Asian and Pacific Islander[b]	..	..	..	..	..	..	..	..	..	..	..	..	12.4
Elderly (65 years and older)	24.6	15.7	12.6	12.2	12.4	12.9	12.2	11.7	10.5	11.5	10.5	10.5	9.7
Female-headed households	38.1	36.7	37.6	33.4	39.7	39.0	38.7	34.6	32.4	32.6	31.6	29.9	27.8
Total child poverty rate (%) (18 years and under)	**15.1**	**18.3**	**20.7**	**20.6**	**21.1**	**22.3**	**22.7**	**21.8**	**20.8**	**20.5**	**19.9**	**18.9**	**16.9**
White	..	13.9	16.2	15.9	16.1	17.4	17.8	16.9	16.2	16.3	16.1	15.1	13.5
African American	..	42.3	43.6	44.8	45.6	46.6	46.1	43.8	41.9	39.9	37.2	36.7	33.1
Hispanic	..	33.2	40.3	38.4	39.8	40.0	40.9	41.5	40.0	40.3	36.8	34.4	30.3
Asian and Pacific Islander	..	..	..	17.6	17.5	16.4	18.2	18.3	19.5	19.5	20.3	18.0	11.8
Unemployment rate (%)	**4.9**	**7.1**	**7.2**	**5.6**	**6.8**	**7.5**	**6.9**	**6.1**	**5.6**	**5.4**	**4.9**	**4.5**	**4.2**
White	4.5	6.3	6.2	4.8	6.1	6.6	6.1	5.3	4.9	4.7	4.2	3.9	3.7
African American	..	14.3	15.1	11.4	12.5	14.2	13.0	11.5	10.4	10.5	10.0	8.9	8.0
Hispanic	..	10.1	10.5	8.2	10.0	11.6	10.8	9.9	9.3	8.9	7.7	7.2	6.4

Table 6: United States – National Hunger and Poverty Trends

	1970	1980	1985	1990	1991	1992	1993	1994	1995	1996	1997	1998	1999
Household income distribution (per quintile in %)													
All races													
Lowest 20 percent	4.1	4.2	3.9	3.9	3.8	3.8	3.6	3.6	3.7	3.7	3.6	3.6	3.6
Second quintile	10.8	10.2	9.8	9.6	9.6	9.4	9.0	8.9	9.1	9.0	8.9	9.0	8.9
Third quintile	17.4	16.8	16.2	15.9	15.9	15.8	15.1	15.0	15.2	15.1	15.0	15.0	14.9
Fourth quintile	24.5	24.8	24.4	24.0	24.2	24.2	23.5	23.4	23.3	23.3	23.2	23.2	23.2
Highest 20 percent	43.3	44.1	45.6	46.6	46.5	46.9	48.9	49.1	48.7	49.0	49.4	49.2	49.4
Ratio of highest 20 percent to lowest 20 percent[e]	10.6	10.5	11.7	11.9	12.2	12.3	13.6	13.6	13.2	13.2	13.7	13.7	13.7
White													
Lowest 20 percent	4.2	4.4	4.1	4.2	4.1	4.1	3.9	3.8	4.0	3.9	3.8	3.8	3.9
Second quintile	11.1	10.5	10.1	10.0	9.9	9.7	9.3	9.2	9.3	9.2	9.1	9.2	9.1
Third quintile	17.5	17.0	16.4	16.0	16.0	15.9	15.3	15.1	15.3	15.2	15.0	15.1	15.0
Fourth quintile	24.3	24.6	24.3	23.9	24.1	24.1	23.3	23.2	23.3	23.2	23.0	23.1	23.1
Highest 20 percent	42.9	43.5	45.1	46.0	45.8	46.2	48.2	48.6	48.1	48.4	49.1	48.8	49.0
Ratio of highest 20 percent to lowest 20 percent[e]	10.2	9.9	11.0	11.0	11.2	11.3	12.4	12.8	12.0	12.4	12.9	12.8	12.6
African American													
Lowest 20 percent	3.7	3.7	3.5	3.1	3.1	3.1	3.0	3.0	3.2	3.1	3.2	3.1	3.1
Second quintile	9.3	8.7	8.3	7.9	7.8	7.8	7.7	7.9	8.2	8.0	8.5	8.2	8.3
Third quintile	16.3	15.3	15.2	15.0	15.0	14.7	14.3	14.3	14.8	14.5	15.1	14.8	14.7
Fourth quintile	25.2	25.2	25.0	25.1	25.2	24.8	23.7	24.3	24.2	23.7	24.5	24.4	24.0
Highest 20 percent	45.5	47.1	48.0	49.0	48.9	49.7	51.3	50.5	49.6	50.7	48.7	49.5	50.0
Ratio of highest 20 percent to lowest 20 percent[e]	12.3	12.7	13.7	15.8	15.8	16.0	17.1	16.8	15.5	16.4	15.2	16.0	16.1
Hispanic origin													
Lowest 20 percent	..	4.3	4.1	4.0	4.0	4.0	3.9	3.7	3.8	3.8	3.6	3.6	4.1
Second quintile	..	10.1	9.4	9.5	9.4	9.4	9.1	8.7	8.9	9.0	8.9	8.9	9.5
Third quintile	..	16.4	16.1	15.9	15.8	15.7	15.1	14.8	14.8	14.7	14.9	14.8	15.2
Fourth quintile	..	24.8	24.8	24.3	24.3	24.1	23.1	23.3	23.3	23.1	23.1	22.9	23.4
Highest 20 percent	..	44.5	45.6	46.3	46.5	46.9	48.7	49.6	49.3	49.5	49.5	49.7	47.9
Ratio of highest 20 percent to lowest 20 percent[e]	..	10.3	11.1	11.6	11.6	11.7	12.5	13.4	13.0	13.0	13.8	13.8	11.7

.. Data not available.

a Data refer to fiscal year.

b 3-year average, 1997, 1998, and 1999.

e BFWI estimate.

Table 7: United States – State Hunger and Poverty Statistics

	Total population (millions) July 1999	Food insecure (% of households)	Food insecure with hunger (% of households)	Infant mortality rate 1998 (per 1,000 live births)			% population in poverty[a] 1998-99	Unemployment rate (%) 1999
				All Races	White	African American		
Alabama	4.37	11.3	3.2	10.2	7.7	15.5	14.8	4.8
Alaska	0.62	7.6	3.5	5.9	4.7	..	8.5	6.4
Arizona	4.78	12.8	4.2	7.5	6.9	20.0	14.3	4.4
Arkansas	2.55	12.6	4.6	8.9	7.6	14.0	14.7	4.5
California	33.15	11.4	4.1	5.8	5.3	13.7	14.6	5.2
Colorado	4.06	8.8	3.4	6.7	6.4	16.0	8.7	2.9
Connecticut	3.28	8.8	3.8	7.0	5.6	17.4	8.3	3.2
Delaware	0.75	6.8	2.6	9.6	6.9	18.7	10.3	3.5
District of Columbia	0.52	11.1	4.6	12.5	..	15.5	18.6	6.3
Florida	15.11	11.5	4.2	7.2	5.9	12.3	12.8	3.9
Georgia	7.79	9.7	3.2	8.5	6.0	13.4	13.2	4.0
Hawaii	1.19	10.4	2.8	6.9	5.3	..	10.9	5.6
Idaho	1.25	10.1	3.3	7.2	7.1	..	13.5	5.2
Illinois	12.13	8.2	3.1	8.4	6.4	17.2	10.0	4.3
Indiana	5.94	7.8	2.8	7.6	6.5	17.3	8.0	3.0
Iowa	2.87	7.0	2.5	6.6	6.2	18.3	8.3	2.5
Kansas	2.65	9.9	4.0	7.0	7.0	10.0	10.9	3.0
Kentucky	3.96	8.4	3.2	7.5	6.8	15.4	12.8	4.5
Louisiana	4.37	12.8	4.4	9.1	5.7	14.0	19.1	5.1
Maine	1.25	8.7	3.7	6.3	6.4	..	10.5	4.1
Maryland	5.17	7.1	3.0	8.6	5.2	15.3	7.2	3.5
Massachusetts	6.18	6.3	2.0	5.1	4.9	8.3	10.2	3.2
Michigan	9.86	8.1	2.9	8.2	6.3	16.8	10.3	3.8
Minnesota	4.78	6.9	2.9	5.9	5.1	13.4	8.8	2.8
Mississippi	2.77	14.0	4.2	10.1	6.3	14.8	16.9	5.1
Missouri	5.47	8.6	2.9	7.7	6.1	16.8	10.7	3.4
Montana	0.88	10.2	3.0	7.4	7.2	..	16.1	5.2
Nebraska	1.67	7.5	2.4	7.3	6.7	19.4	11.6	2.9
Nevada	1.81	8.6	3.7	7.0	6.0	17.3	10.9	4.4
New Hampshire	1.20	7.4	2.9	4.4	4.3	..	8.8	2.7
New Jersey	8.14	7.3	2.8	6.4	5.0	12.8	8.2	4.6
New Mexico	1.74	15.1	4.7	7.2	6.9	..	20.5	5.6
New York	18.20	10.0	3.9	6.3	5.3	10.9	15.4	5.2
North Carolina	7.65	8.8	2.6	9.3	6.5	17.6	13.8	3.2
North Dakota	0.63	4.6	1.4	8.6	8.2	..	14.1	3.4
Ohio	11.26	8.5	3.4	8.0	7.0	14.2	11.6	4.3
Oklahoma	3.36	11.9	4.2	8.5	8.1	13.5	13.4	3.4
Oregon	3.32	12.6	5.8	5.4	5.3	..	13.8	5.7
Pennsylvania	12.00	7.1	2.3	7.1	5.8	15.4	10.3	4.4
Rhode Island	0.99	8.7	2.6	7.0	6.2	..	10.7	4.1
South Carolina	3.89	10.2	3.4	9.6	6.0	16.2	12.7	4.5
South Dakota	0.73	6.4	2.1	9.1	7.5	..	9.3	2.9
Tennessee	5.48	10.9	4.3	8.2	6.3	15.0	12.7	4.0
Texas	20.04	12.9	5.0	6.4	5.8	11.6	15.0	4.6
Utah	2.13	8.8	3.1	5.6	5.7	..	7.3	3.7
Vermont	0.59	7.7	2.6	7.0	6.8	..	9.8	3.0
Virginia	6.87	8.3	2.9	7.7	5.7	14.9	8.4	2.8
Washington	5.76	11.9	4.6	5.7	5.2	13.5	9.2	4.7
West Virginia	1.81	9.0	3.1	8.0	8.0	..	16.8	6.6
Wisconsin	5.25	7.2	2.3	7.2	6.0	18.7	8.7	3.0
Wyoming	0.48	9.0	3.3	7.2	5.8	..	11.1	4.9
Puerto Rico		..	..	10.5	11.1	..	..	11.7
United States	**276.09**	**9.7**	**3.5**	**7.2**	**6.0**	**14.3**	**12.3**	**4.2**

.. Data not available.

a 1998-1999 average.

Table 8: United States – Federal Nutrition and Assistance Programs

	Food Stamp Participation: Monthly Average by State					
	1995[e]	1996[e]	1997[e]	1998[e]	1999[d,e]	2000[c,d]
Alabama	524,522	509,214	469,268	426,819	405,273	392,289
Alaska	45,448	46,233	45,234	42,451	41,262	41,224
Arizona	480,195	427,481	363,779	295,703	257,362	260,839
Arkansas	272,174	273,900	265,854	255,710	252,957	244,668
California	3,174,651	3,143,390	2,814,761	2,259,069	2,027,089	1,785,937
Colorado	251,880	243,692	216,748	191,015	173,497	151,562
Connecticut	226,061	222,758	209,529	195,866	178,168	162,233
Delaware	57,090	57,836	53,655	45,581	38,571	30,381
District of Columbia	93,993	92,751	90,391	85,396	84,082	78,763
Florida	1,395,296	1,371,352	1,191,664	990,571	933,435	864,429
Georgia	815,920	792,502	698,323	631,720	616,600	545,567
Hawaii	124,575	130,344	126,901	122,027	125,155	115,903
Idaho	80,255	79,855	70,413	62,393	57,201	58,007
Illinois	1,151,035	1,105,160	1,019,600	922,927	820,034	819,620
Indiana	469,647	389,537	347,772	313,116	298,213	300,653
Iowa	184,025	177,283	161,184	141,067	128,790	122,131
Kansas	184,241	171,831	148,734	119,218	114,875	116,281
Kentucky	520,088	485,628	444,422	412,028	396,440	399,990
Louisiana	710,597	670,034	575,411	536,834	516,285	490,088
Maine	131,955	130,872	123,767	115,099	108,749	100,513
Maryland	398,727	374,512	354,436	322,653	264,393	213,686
Massachusetts	409,870	373,599	339,505	292,997	261,021	223,875
Michigan	970,760	935,416	838,917	771,580	682,680	613,751
Minnesota	308,206	294,825	260,476	219,744	208,062	197,895
Mississippi	479,934	457,106	399,062	329,058	288,057	273,451
Missouri	575,882	553,930	477,703	410,966	408,331	418,450
Montana	70,873	70,754	66,605	62,328	60,898	59,673
Nebraska	105,133	101,625	97,176	94,944	92,404	80,448
Nevada	98,538	96,712	82,419	71,531	61,673	62,449
New Hampshire	58,353	52,809	46,000	39,578	37,438	36,021
New Jersey	550,628	540,452	491,337	424,738	384,888	332,888
New Mexico	238,854	235,060	204,644	174,699	178,439	166,612
New York	2,183,101	2,098,561	1,913,548	1,627,170	1,540,784	1,422,792
North Carolina	613,502	631,061	586,415	527,790	505,410	471,652
North Dakota	41,401	39,825	37,688	33,801	33,442	31,728
Ohio	115,490	1,045,066	873,562	733,565	639,786	610,635
Oklahoma	374,893	353,790	321,894	287,577	271,351	249,232
Oregon	288,687	287,607	258,615	238,446	223,978	236,111
Pennsylvania	1,173,420	1,123,541	1,008,864	906,735	834,898	764,794
Rhode Island	93,434	90,873	84,627	72,301	76,394	73,737
South Carolina	363,822	358,341	349,137	333,017	308,570	291,393
South Dakota	50,158	48,843	46,901	45,173	44,065	42,542
Tennessee	662,014	637,773	585,889	538,467	510,828	492,963
Texas	2,557,693	2,371,958	2,033,750	1,636,175	1,400,526	1,313,217
Utah	118,836	110,011	98,338	91,764	88,163	80,652
Vermont	59,292	56,459	53,005	45,702	44,287	39,887
Virginia	545,829	537,531	476,088	396,581	361,581	328,659
Washington	476,019	476,391	444,800	364,418	306,654	294,724
West Virginia	308,505	299,719	287,035	269,140	247,249	221,590
Wisconsin	320,142	283,255	232,103	192,887	182,206	197,081
Wyoming	35,579	33,013	28,584	25,452	23,477	22,367
Puerto Rico	n/a	n/a	n/a	n/a	n/a	n/a
United States	**26,618,773**	**25,540,331**	**22,854,273**	**19,788,115**	**18,182,595**	**16,984,005**

Table 8: United States – Federal Nutrition and Assistance Programs

	WIC[a] Annual Monthly Average Participation by State					
	1995[e]	1996[e]	1997[e]	1998[e]	1999[d,e]	2000[c,d]
Alabama	121,979	118,163	118,899	117,319	115,172	105,745
Alaska	19,235	22,410	23,537	23,829	26,131	24,553
Arizona	122,179	141,466	145,849	142,000	142,488	143,907
Arkansas	87,362	90,662	87,310	82,939	82,882	82,339
California	1,003,611	1,141,598	1,224,224	1,216,253	1,229,495	1,230,703
Colorado	70,617	70,523	75,068	74,679	74,801	71,092
Connecticut	63,625	62,520	59,368	60,267	58,299	55,882
Delaware	15,444	15,831	15,581	15,635	15,274	15,809
District of Columbia	17,368	16,116	16,747	16,593	16,406	15,064
Florida	317,095	332,130	354,971	345,150	337,559	294,581
Georgia	217,207	223,746	230,153	232,258	224,069	218,806
Hawaii	25,410	27,466	30,807	34,098	34,137	31,872
Idaho	31,120	31,085	31,475	31,678	31,543	31,028
Illinois	244,661	244,223	236,068	237,262	241,016	243,831
Indiana	132,621	132,532	132,700	131,099	128,269	122,011
Iowa	65,260	66,020	66,293	65,885	63,996	60,718
Kansas	55,890	54,377	54,754	52,896	52,345	52,440
Kentucky	118,198	119,457	122,948	122,910	122,056	110,811
Louisiana	133,992	139,603	139,223	136,866	135,430	131,757
Maine	26,905	26,300	26,663	25,786	24,646	21,700
Maryland	86,349	87,961	91,412	92,744	93,338	93,591
Massachusetts	113,605	115,942	118,818	117,681	115,042	115,100
Michigan	209,272	212,270	218,371	217,924	215,138	211,774
Minnesota	90,979	93,971	94,807	95,101	90,101	90,286
Mississippi	102,718	102,532	100,124	99,097	96,863	98,349
Missouri	127,005	129,245	131,638	128,176	126,640	122,256
Montana	20,889	22,155	21,679	21,428	21,346	21,305
Nebraska	35,715	36,101	33,041	31,770	33,047	33,000
Nevada	31,053	36,310	37,324	37,972	37,415	39,437
New Hampshire	19,423	19,342	19,179	18,678	18,100	16,831
New Jersey	141,962	137,988	141,514	140,732	129,603	128,043
New Mexico	53,816	56,131	54,040	56,183	56,494	58,429
New York	452,997	466,185	478,980	482,882	476,563	465,379
North Carolina	182,264	188,828	194,566	1,979,544	196,389	194,551
North Dakota	17,754	17,484	16,868	15,810	14,930	14,259
Ohio	259,121	258,400	254,668	250,815	245,994	243,370
Oklahoma	95,964	103,373	108,348	109,581	108,485	108,760
Oregon	82,212	86,048	89,299	31,341	92,831	89,074
Pennsylvania	260,544	262,111	257,018	246,337	235,526	230,858
Rhode Island	21,450	22,382	22,596	22,768	22,454	21,551
South Carolina	124,252	123,669	118,966	118,556	110,850	110,031
South Dakota	22,397	22,439	21,945	20,507	20,445	20,418
Tennessee	137,280	144,174	150,289	148,692	148,824	148,978
Texas	637,229	641,150	683,583	691,292	707,872	748,073
Utah	53,287	54,893	57,511	57,391	59,592	56,834
Vermont	16,140	16,061	16,133	16,308	16,051	16,285
Virginia	126,882	126,760	129,520	132,317	131,304	126,735
Washington	112,915	129,256	145,147	144,052	141,089	147,725
West Virginia	51,890	54,173	55,065	53,962	52,335	50,300
Wisconsin	109,151	109,712	108,886	108,352	104,041	99,264
Wyoming	11,745	11,965	12,447	11,789	11,583	10,678
Puerto Rico	182,795	204,717	211,454	206,968	205,228	217,613
United States	**6,894,413**	**7,187,831**	**7,406,866**	**7,367,397**	**7,311,206**	**7,232,459**

Table 8: United States – Federal Nutrition and Assistance Programs

	TANF[b] Individual Recipients: Monthly Average by State[f]				
	1995	1996	1997	1998	1999
Alabama	113,971	101,772	77,096	54,164	49,470
Alaska	36,257	36,532	34,434	29,599	25,221
Arizona	185,282	166,865	140,161	100,216	88,665
Arkansas	61,631	57,231	49,156	32,633	29,023
California	2,674,971	2,592,547	2,318,036	1,997,709	1,661,769
Colorado	105,921	95,858	71,088	53,089	35,207
Connecticut	169,358	159,736	151,801	115,941	77,947
Delaware	24,097	23,314	21,139	10,547	16,613
District of Columbia	71,950	69,668	64,663	55,949	50,035
Florida	606,490	540,667	403,838	252,257	184,486
Georgia	377,630	338,830	254,243	182,274	147,581
Hawaii	65,963	66,375	60,593	46,724	44,069
Idaho	23,967	22,173	12,277	4,059	2,545
Illinois	684,438	642,465	563,129	474,976	335,395
Indiana	176,939	140,514	119,429	109,114	107,688
Iowa	97,331	86,311	75,864	66,212	57,539
Kansas	77,030	65,201	49,463	34,718	33,912
Kentucky	184,482	172,003	150,900	119,161	95,488
Louisiana	250,865	229,097	166,395	134,370	101,257
Maine	58,746	54,801	46,944	39,537	33,757
Maryland	220,148	195,287	153,367	115,728	81,736
Massachusetts	262,646	229,777	199,403	167,315	121,784
Michigan	578,463	510,409	428,622	332,240	243,818
Minnesota	178,260	168,672	151,907	139,993	120,788
Mississippi	140,454	124,248	92,211	52,667	36,191
Missouri	249,254	224,880	186,396	147,035	128,703
Montana	33,376	30,214	24,326	17,727	13,618
Nebraska	41,496	38,966	37,439	35,657	31,838
Nevada	40,808	35,444	28,787	25,472	18,203
New Hampshire	26,859	23,306	19,248	16,045	15,203
New Jersey	309,556	279,515	242,285	189,418	155,753
New Mexico	103,051	99,119	71,573	75,237	79,183
New York	1,240,825	1,157,503	1,017,878	908,776	793,366
North Carolina	305,240	269,841	230,819	172,813	124,004
North Dakota	14,149	13,071	10,633	8,682	8,123
Ohio	591,659	538,597	466,524	340,179	262,806
Oklahoma	120,196	99,035	80,294	69,316	49,715
Oregon	100,680	80,946	57,672	46,395	46,761
Pennsylvania	582,160	527,214	437,898	357,684	278,036
Rhode Island	60,375	57,429	55,286	53,369	49,020
South Carolina	126,534	114,709	81,944	60,110	41,029
South Dakota	16,797	15,759	12,550	9,609	7,680
Tennessee	270,805	248,310	166,582	149,440	153,286
Texas	729,525	661,975	530,281	370,857	310,698
Utah	44,077	39,096	32,067	28,934	28,151
Vermont	26,777	24,764	21,086	19,644	17,585
Virginia	178,679	155,249	122,766	100,358	85,933
Washington	282,658	271,270	246,202	202,573	166,100
West Virginia	102,303	88,437	82,899	44,179	30,150
Wisconsin	202,448	158,581	98,732	41,651	41,984
Wyoming	14,120	12,180	5,679	2,586	1,576
Puerto Rico	164,317	152,242	140,344	121,402	102,806
United States	**13,418,386**	**12,320,970**	**10,376,224**	**8,347,041**	**6,836,093**

a   Special Supplemental Nutrition Program for Women, Infants and Children.

b   Temporary Assistance for Needy Families.

c   Data from January 1, 2000 to July 31, 2000.

d   Preliminary data, subject to change.

e   Data refer to fiscal year.

f   Data refer to calendar year.

Sources for Tables

Table 1: Global Hunger — Life and Death Indicators

Total population, projected population, projected growth rate, total fertility rate, life expectancy: United Nations Population Fund (UNFPA) *The State of the World's Population 2000* (New York: UNFPA, 2000).

Population under age 15: Statistics and Population Division of the United Nations Secretariat, "Indicators of Youth and Elderly Populations," data posted at: www.un.org/Depts/unsd/social/youth.htm.

Population urban: United Nations Development Programme, *Human Development Report, 2000* (HDR) (New York: Oxford University Press, 2000).

Infant mortality, low-birth weight infants, children immunized, under-5 mortality rate, maternal mortality rate: United Nations Children's Fund, *The State of the World's Children, 2000 (SWC)* (New York: UNICEF, 2000).

Refugees: U.S. Committee for Refugees, World Refugees Survey, 2000 (Washington, DC: Immigration and Refugee Services of America, 2000) data posted at www.refugees.org.

Table 2: Global Food, Nutrition, and Education

Per capita dietary energy supply, food production per capita: Food and Agriculture Organization of the United Nations (FAO), data posted at www.apps.fao.org.

Food expenditures, gender-related primary school enrollment: The World Bank, *2000 World Development Indicators (WDI)* (Washington DC: The World Bank, 2000).

Vitamin A supplementation coverage: *SWC, 2000.*

Adult literacy rate, total primary school enrollment, gender-related combined school enrollment: *HDR, 2000.*

Table 3: Hunger, Malnutrition, and Poverty

Undernourished population: FAO, *The State of Food Insecurity in the World, 2000* (Rome: FAO, 2000).

Underweight, wasting, stunting, safe water: *SWC, 2000.*

Population in poverty: *WDI, 2000.*

Table 4: Economic and Development Indicators

GNP per capita, distribution of income or consumption, per capita military expenditures, energy consumption: *WDI, 2000.*

HDI rank, central government expenditures, public education expenditures: *HDR, 2000.*

Table 5: Economic Globalization

Exports of goods and services, manufactured exports, imports of goods and services, investment, aid, debt: *WDI, 2000.*

Food exports, food imports: FAO, data posted at: www.apps.fao.org.

Table 6: United States — National Hunger and Poverty Trends

Total population: U.S. Bureau of the Census, data posted at: www.census.gov/population/www/popest.html.

Food insecurity prevalence: USDA, Household Food Insecurity in the U.S., 1999, posted at: www.ers.usda.gov.

Percent of the budget spent on food assistance: Congressional Budget Office,

U.S. Budget for fiscal year 2001, posted at: www.cbo.gov.

Infant mortality: Centers for Disease Control and Prevention, National Center for Health Statistics, "Deaths: Final Data for 1998," National Vital Statistics Report, Vol. 48, No. 12, data posted at: www.cdc.gov/nchswww.

Poverty: U.S. Bureau of the Census, data posted at: www.census.gov/hhes/www/poverty.html.

Unemployment: U.S. Department of Labor, Bureau of Labor Statistics, *Monthly Labor Review*, March 2000.

Income: U.S. Bureau of the Census, data posted at: www.census.gov/hhes/www.income.html.

Table 7: United States — State Hunger and Poverty Trends

Total population: U.S. Bureau of the Census, data posted at: www.census.gov/population/estimates/state/st-99-3.txt.

Poverty: U.S. Bureau of the Census, data posted at: www.census.gov/hhes/www/poverty.html.

Food insecurity prevalence: USDA, Prevalence of Food Insecurity and Hunger by State, 1996-98. Food Assistance and Research Nutrition Service, Report No. 2 (FANRR-2). Report posted at: www.ers.usda.gov.

Infant mortality: Centers for Disease Control and Prevention, National Center for Health Statistics, "Deaths: Final Data for 1998," National Vital Statistics Report, Vol. 48, No. 11, data posted at: www.cdc.gov/nchswww.

Unemployment rate: U.S. Bureau of Labor Statistics, data posted at: http://stats.bls.gov/laus/Lauastrk.htm.

Table 8: United States — Federal Nutrition and Assistance Programs

Food stamp participation, WIC participation: USDA, Food and Nutrition Service national databank.

TANF: U.S. Department of Health and Human Services, Administration for Children and Families, data posted at: www.acf.dhhs.gov/news/tables.htm.

Acronyms

AIDS	Acquired Immune Deficiency Syndrome	**MDB**	Multilateral Development Bank
BFW	Bread for the World	**NATO**	North Atlantic Treaty Organization
CGIAR	Consultative Group on International Agricultural Research	**NGO**	Nongovernmental organization
		OA	Official assistance
CSD	Child Survival and Development Fund	**ODA**	Official development assistance
CIS	Commonwealth of Independent States (former Soviet Union)	**OECD**	Organisation for Economic Co-operation and Development
CSO	Civil society organization	**OL**	Offering of Letters
DAC	OECD Development Assistance Committee	**OMB**	Office of Management and Budget
ESF	Economic Support Fund	**OPIC**	Overseas Private Investment Corporation
FAO	Food and Agriculture Organization of the United Nations	**PIPA**	Program on International Policy Attitudes, University of Maryland
FRAC	Food Research and Action Center	**PRSP**	Poverty Reduction Strategy Paper
FY	Fiscal year	**PVO**	Private Voluntary Organization
G7/G8	Group of Seven (United States, Great Britain, Germany, France, Canada, Japan, Italy); Group of Eight includes Russia.	**SEED**	Support for Eastern European Democracy
		TAHL	Transforming Anti-Hunger Leadership Program, BFW Institute
GAVI	Global Alliance for Vaccines and Immunization	**TANF**	Temporary Assistance for Needy Families
GDP	Gross Domestic Product	**TB**	Tuberculosis
GEF	Global Environment Facility	**UNCTAD**	U.N. Conference on Trade and Development
GNP	Gross National Product	**UNDP**	U.N. Development Programme
HIPC	Heavily or Highly Indebted Poor Country	**UNFPA**	U.N. Fund for Population Activities
HIV	Human Immunodeficiency Virus	**UNHCR**	U.N. High Commissioner for Refugees
IBRD	International Bank for Reconstruction and Development, commonly known as the World Bank	**UNICEF**	U.N. Children's Fund
		UNRISD	U.N. Research Institute for Social Development
IDA	International Development Association	**USAID**	U.S. Agency for International Development
IDB	Inter-American Development Bank	**USDA**	U.S. Department of Agriculture
IFAD	International Fund for Agricultural Development	**WFP**	World Food Programme
IFI	International financial institution	**WHO**	World Health Organization
IFPRI	International Food Policy Research Institute	**WTO**	World Trade Organization
IFST	International Food Security Treaty		
ILO	International Labour Organization		
IMF	International Monetary Fund		

Glossary

Absolute poverty – The income level below which a minimally adequate diet plus essential non-food requirements (e.g., housing, health care, education) are not affordable.

Agricultural extension – The process of disseminating knowledge and information from researchers to farmers.

Bilateral assistance – Funds provided by a donor-country government to a recipient-country government.

Civil society – The sphere of civic action outside government, comprised of citizens' groups, nongovernmental organizations, religious congregations, labor unions, and foundations.

Coalition – A set of actors (e.g., NGOs, public interest groups, foundations) that coordinate shared strategies and tactics to influence public policy and effect social change.

Cold War – The global state of tension and military rivalry that existed from 1945 to 1990 between the United States and the former Soviet Union and their respective allies.

Daily calorie requirement – The average number of calories needed per person per day (about 2,350) to sustain normal levels of activity and health, taking into account age, sex, body weight, and climate.

Debt relief – Measures to reduce the debt owed by developing-country governments to either private commercial lenders (e.g., Citibank), governments (e.g., the United States or Germany), or international financial institutions (e.g., the World Bank or IMF).

Democratization – The process by which political systems move toward democratic principles and practices, such as an open multi-party regime with regular and fair elections, universal suffrage, freedom of the press, and other civil liberties (freedom of expression, freedom of assembly).

Developed countries – Countries in which the annual per capita income is greater than $9,266, as defined by the World Bank. Also called the "industrialized countries" or the "North."

Developing countries – Countries in which the annual per capita income is below $755, as defined by the World Bank. Also known as the "Third World," the "South," and the "less-developed countries."

Development Assistance Committee (DAC) – A specialized group of OECD country representatives that coordinates and oversees the development assistance policies of member countries to increase resources and improve effectiveness. Member countries include: Australia, Austria, Belgium, Canada, Denmark, Finland, France, Germany, Greece, Ireland, Italy, Japan, Luxembourg, the Netherlands, New Zealand, Norway, Portugal, Spain, Sweden, Switzerland, the United Kingdom, the United States, and the Commission of European Communities.

Dietary energy supply (DES) – The total daily food supply, expressed in calories, available within a country for human consumption.

Empowerment – The process by which people gain greater economic and political voice and power over the decisions affecting their lives.

Famine – A situation of extreme food scarcity, potentially leading to widespread starvation.

Food security – Assured access for every person to enough nutritious food to sustain an active and healthy life with dignity.

Food self-sufficiency – The ability of countries, communities, or regions to rely exclusively on their own food production.

Foreign aid – See Official development assistance.

Foreign direct investment (FDI) – Investment from abroad in ownership and control of productive activities, as opposed to more passive stock and bond investment.

Free trade agreements – Agreements between two countries (bilateral) or among several countries (multilateral) to eliminate or reduce practices that restrict trade. These may include tariffs (taxes on traded goods and services) and/or non-tariff barriers such as quotas (limits on the amount traded).

Global communications revolution – The growing interconnection of people around the world through communications technologies such as television, satellites, cellular phones, computers, and the Internet.

Globalization – In economic terms, the process of increasing integration of national economies at the global level.

Gross domestic product (GDP) – The value of all goods and services produced within a nation during a specified period, usually a year.

Gross national product (GNP) – The value of all goods and services produced by a country's citizens, wherever they are located.

Human Development Index (HDI) – A measure of well-being based on economic growth, educational attainment, and health developed and used by the United Nations Development Programme.

Human rights – The basic rights and freedoms due all human beings, including the right to food and other basic necessities, the right to life and liberty, freedom of thought and expression, and equality before the law.

Hunger – A condition in which people do not get enough food to provide the nutrients (carbohydrates, fats, proteins, vitamins, minerals, and water) for active and healthy lives.

Infant mortality rate (IMR) – The annual number of deaths of infants under 1 year of age per 1,000 live births.

International financial institutions (IFIs) – International organizations supported by membership country contributions that provide financial assistance and credit to developing countries for economic development. IFIs are multilateral development banks such as the World Bank, the Asian Development Bank, the African Development Bank, the Inter-American Development Bank, the European Bank for Reconstruction and Development, and the International Monetary Fund.

International Monetary Fund (IMF) – An international organization that makes loans to countries with short-term foreign exchange and monetary problems. These loans are conditioned upon the borrowing country's willingness to adopt IMF-approved economic policies.

Internet – The global communication network formed by the interconnection of all the Internet Protocol computer networks.

Jubilee 2000 – A worldwide movement calling for cancellation of the foreign debt of heavily indebted poor countries by the year 2000.

Jubilee 2000/USA – A movement in the United States, working in collaboration with Jubilee 2000 that calls for cancellation of poor-country debt. Debt cancellation includes acknowledgment of responsibility by both lenders and borrowers, as well as mechanisms to prevent recurrence of such debts.

Least developed countries (LDCs) – These are the poorest countries in the world as designated by the United Nations based on criteria such as per capita GDP, share of manufacturing in total GDP, and the adult literacy rate. Currently there are 48 LDCs, which account for 10.5 percent of the world's population.

Livelihood security – The ability of a household to meet all its basic needs for food, shelter, water, sanitation, health care, and education.

Living wage – The wage level necessary for ensuring an adequate standard of living.

Macroeconomic policies – Policies related to general levels of production and income, and the relationship among economic sectors. Microeconomics refers to individual units of activity, such as a small business, a household, or prices for a specific product.

Malnutrition – A condition resulting from inadequate or excessive consumption of food or specific nutrients. Undernutrition can impair physical and mental health and can be the cause or result of infectious diseases. Overnutrition results in obesity and can lead to diabetes, heart disease, and other health problems.

Market economy – An economy in which prices for goods and services are set primarily by private markets rather than by government planning or regulation.

Microcredit – Small, short-term loans to people too poor to borrow from commercial banks to help them start their own businesses, generate income, and raise their standard of living.

Minimum caloric requirements – See "Daily calorie requirement."

Monetization – In the context of food aid, the sale of commodities to finance development activities.

Multilateral development assistance – Assistance provided through organizations such as the international financial institutions and United Nations.

Nongovernmental organizations (NGOs) – Voluntary, nonprofit organizations that support community development, provide social services, protect the environment, and promote the public interest.

Official development assistance (ODA) – ODA is the term used by the Organisation for Economic Co-operation and Development (OECD) for grants and loans to developing countries governments to pursue economic development at concessional financial terms.

Organisation for Economic Co-operation and Development (OECD) – The OECD is an association of industrialized countries. Its members are Australia, Austria, Belgium, Canada, the Czech Republic, Denmark, Finland, France, Germany, Greece, Hungary, Iceland, Ireland, Italy, Luxembourg, Mexico, the Netherlands, New Zealand, Norway, Poland, Portugal, the Republic of Korea, Spain, Sweden, Switzerland, Turkey, the United Kingdom, the United States, and the Commission of the European Communities.

Privatization – The transfer of company ownership and delivery of services from government to private firms or agencies.

Public policy advocacy – Citizen political action focused on the policies, programs, and practices of governments, international financial institutions, and corporations.

Social safety net – Government and private charitable programs to meet the basic human needs (health, education, nutrition) of low-income, disabled, and other vulnerable people.

Starvation – Suffering or death from extreme or prolonged lack of food.

Stunting – Failure to grow to normal height caused by chronic undernutrition during the formative years of childhood.

Sustainable development – The reduction of hunger and poverty and the pursuit of economic development in environmentally sound ways. It includes meeting basic human needs, expanding economic opportunities, protecting the environment, and promoting pluralism and democratic participation.

Trade deficit – The difference between the value of a country's imports and the value of its exports when imports are greater than exports.

Under-5 mortality rate – The annual number of deaths of children under 5 years of age per 1,000 live births. A high rate correlates closely with hunger and malnutrition.

United States Agency for International Development (USAID) – USAID is the primary federal government agency that provides assistance for economic development to governments and through NGOs.

Vulnerability to hunger – Individuals, households, communities, or nations that have enough to eat most of the time, but whose poverty makes them especially susceptible to hunger due to changes in the economy, climate, political conditions, or personal circumstances.

Wasting – A condition in which a person is seriously below the normal weight for her or his height due to acute undernutrition or a medical condition.

World Bank – A multilateral agency that makes long-term loans to the governments of developing nations for the purpose of economic development.

World Trade Organization (WTO) – An international organization, headquartered in Geneva, established in 1995 to enforce the Uruguay Round global trade agreement.

Sponsors

Bread for the World Institute seeks justice for hungry people by engaging in research and education on policies related to hunger and development. Based on policy analysis and consultation with poor people, the Institute develops educational resources and activities, including its annual report on the state of world hunger, policy briefs and study guides, together with workshops, seminars, briefings and an anti-hunger leadership development program. Contributions to the Institute are tax deductible. It works closely with Bread for the World, a Christian citizens' movement of 45,000 members and churches who advocate specific policy changes to help overcome hunger in the United States and overseas.

> 50 F Street NW, Suite 500
> Washington, D.C. 20001 USA
> Phone: (202) 639-9400
> Fax: (202) 639-9401
> E-mail: institute@bread.org
> Web site: www.bread.org

Brot für die Welt is an association of German Protestant churches that seeks to overcome poverty and hunger in developing countries, as an expression of their Christian faith and convictions, by funding programs of development, relief and advocacy. Founded in 1959, Brot has funded more than 20,000 programs in over 100 nations in Africa, Latin America and Asia. The emphasis of the programs that Brot funds has shifted from relief to development and empowerment. Brot's programs of education in Germany are intended to lead to changes in understanding and lifestyle at the personal level, and to policy changes at the national, European Community and international levels.

> Stafflenbergstrasse 76; Postfach 10 11 42
> D-70010 Stuttgart, Germany
> Phone: 011 49 7 11 2159 0
> Fax: 011 49 7 11 2159 110
> E-mail: bfdwinformation@brot-fuer-die-welt.org

Catholic Relief Services-USCC (CRS) is the overseas relief and development agency of the U.S. Catholic community. Founded in 1943, CRS provides over $400 million in development and relief assistance reaching 62 million persons in 87 countries and territories around the world. Assistance is given solely on the basis of need. Working in partnership with the Catholic Church and other local institutions in each country, CRS works to alleviate poverty, hunger and suffering, and supports peace-building and reconciliation initiatives. In the United States, CRS works for greater social justice abroad by engaging the public in the reform of legislation to better serve the interests of the poor overseas

and by educating and building awareness on issues of world poverty and hunger. Even while responding to emergencies, CRS supports over 2,000 development projects designed to build local self-sufficiency. CRS works in conjunction with Caritas Internationalis and CIDSE, worldwide associations of Catholic relief and development agencies. Together, these groups build the capacity of local nonprofit organizations to provide long-term solutions.

> 209 West Fayette Street
> Baltimore, MD 21201-3443 USA
> Phone: (410) 625-2220
> Fax: (410) 685-1635
> E-mail: webmaster@catholicrelief.org
> Web site: http://www.catholicrelief.org

Christian Children's Fund, recognized by *Consumers Digest* as one of the nation's most charitable charities, is a Richmond-based child development organization founded in 1938 to address the needs of children orphaned in the Sino-Japanese War. Regarded as one of the world's largest and most respected child development charities, Christian Children's Fund provides services to more than 2.5 million impoverished children regardless of race, religion, or gender. Christian Children's Fund works in 30 countries throughout Africa, Asia, Eastern and Central Europe, Latin America, the United States, and the Caribbean providing long-term, sustainable assistance to children in need.

> 2821 Emerywood Parkway, P.O. Box 26484
> Richmond, VA 23261-6484 USA
> Phone: (804) 756-2700
> Fax: (804) 756-2718
> Web site: www.christianchildrensfund.org

Episcopal Relief and Development (formerly the Presiding Bishop's Fund for World Relief) is the collective response of Episcopalians to help people in need in the United States and around the world. We work with churches in the Anglican Communion as well as with other denominations, local organizations and partner agencies. We send emergency relief funds in times of natural disasters and man-made catastrophes. We also provide long-term assistance for ongoing humanitarian and development programs around the world.

> The Episcopal Church Center
> 815 2nd Avenue
> New York, NY 10017

The **Evangelical Lutheran Church in America World Hunger Program** is a 26-year-old ministry that confronts hunger and poverty through emergency relief, long-term development, education, advocacy and stewardship of financial resources. Seventy-two percent of the program works internationally and 28 percent within the United States. Lutheran World Relief (Baltimore) and Lutheran World Federation (Geneva, Switzerland) are key implementing partners in international relief and development. Eleven percent is used for domestic relief and development, 10 percent for education and advocacy work in the United States and 7 percent for fundraising and administration.

> 8765 West Higgins Road
> Chicago, IL 60631-4190 USA
> Phone: (800) 638-3522, ext. 2709
> Fax: (773) 380-2707
> E-mail: jhalvors@elca.org

The **International Fund for Agricultural Development** (IFAD) is an international financial institution and Specialized Agency of the United Nations headquartered in Rome, Italy. Established as a result of the 1974 World Food Conference, IFAD has an exclusive mission: to work with the poorest populations in rural areas of developing countries to eliminate hunger and poverty, enhance food security, raise productivity and incomes, and improve the quality of lives. Throughout these efforts, IFAD adopts and advocates a targeted, community-based approach that emphasizes empowering the rural poor and promoting their access to productive resources. Between 1978 and 1999, IFAD committed $6.8 billion in loans and grants for 548 projects in 114 countries, mobilizing an additional $12.7 billion from beneficiary governments and cofinanciers. With 161 Member States, IFAD's governance and funding are the result of a unique partnership among developed and developing countries.

> Via del Serafico, 107
> 00142 Rome, Italy
> Phone: 39 6 54591
> Fax: 39 6 5043463
>
> 1775 K Street, NW, Suite 410
> Washington, DC 20006 USA
> Phone: (202) 331-9099
> Fax: (202) 331-9366
>
> E-mail: ifad@ifad.org
> Web site: www.ifad.org

LCMS World Relief (The Lutheran Church—Missouri Synod) provides emergency relief and sustainable development funding for domestic and international projects. Based under the Synod's Board for Human Care Ministries, LCMS World Relief provides grants for Lutheran congregations and social ministry organizations in the U.S. as well as other groups with Lutheran involvement which are engaged in ministries of human care. Domestic support is also provided to Lutheran

Disaster Response and Lutheran Immigration and Refugee Service. International relief and development assistance is channeled through the Synod's mission stations and partner churches as well as through Lutheran World Relief, Baltimore.

> 1333 So. Kirkwood Road
> St. Louis, MO 63122-7295 USA
> Phone: (800) 248-1930
> Fax: (314) 996-1128
> E-mail: lcms.worldrelief@lcms.org

Lutheran World Relief (LWR) acts on behalf of U.S. Lutherans in response to natural disasters, humanitarian crises and chronic poverty in some 50 countries of Asia, Africa, Latin America and the Middle East. In partnership with local organizations, LWR supports over 150 community projects to improve food production, health care, environment and employment, with special emphasis on training and gender. LWR monitors legislation on foreign aid and development, and advocates for public policies which address the root causes of hunger and poverty. LWR values the God-given gifts that each person can bring to the task of promoting peace, justice and human dignity. LWR began its work in 1945.

> Lutheran World Relief
> 700 Light Street
> Baltimore, MD 21230-3850 USA
> Phone: (410) 230-2700
> Resources: (800) LWR-LWR2
> E-mail: lwr@lwr.org
> Web site: www.lwr.org
>
> LWR/CWS Office on Public Policy
> 122 C Street, NW, Suite 125
> Washington, DC 20001 USA
> Phone: (202) 783-6887
> Fax: (202) 783-5328
> E-mail: jbowman@igc.org

For over 30 years, the **Presbyterian Hunger Program** has provided a channel for congregations to respond to hunger in the United States and around the world. With a commitment to the ecumenical sharing of human and financial resources, the program provides support for programs of direct food relief, sustainable development and public policy advocacy. A network of 100 Hunger Action Enablers leads the Presbyterian Church (USA) in the study of hunger issues, engagement with communities of need, advocacy for just public policies, and the movement toward simpler corporate and personal lifestyles.

> 100 Witherspoon Street
> Louisville, KY 40202-1396 USA
> Phone: (502) 569-5816
> Fax: (502) 569-8963
> Web site: www.pcusa.org/hunger

The **United Methodist Committee on Relief** (UMCOR) was formed in 1940 in response to the suffering of people during World War II. It was a "voice of conscience" expressing the concern of the church for the disrupted and devastated lives churned out by the war. UMCOR has expanded its ministry into more than 70 countries to minister with compassion to "persons in need, through programs and services which provide immediate relief and long-term attention to the root causes of their need." Focusing on refugee, hunger and disaster ministries, the work of UMCOR, a program department of the General Board of Global Ministries of the United Methodist Church, is carried out through direct services and a worldwide network of national and international church agencies that cooperate in the task of alleviating human suffering.

475 Riverside Drive, Room 330
New York, NY 10115 USA
Phone: (212) 870-3816
Hotline: (800) 841-1235
Fax: (212) 870-3624
E-mail: umcor@gbgm-umc.org

The United Nations Development Programme (UNDP) helps people in 174 countries and territories to help themselves, focusing on poverty eradication and democratic governance. In support of these goals, UNDP is frequently asked to help create and implement policies that are more responsive to the needs of ordinary people, and to help societies rebuild in the aftermath of war and humanitarian emergencies. UNDP is also an advocate for increased development assistance and a more inclusive global economy.

1 United Nations Plaza
New York, NY 10017 USA
Phone: (212) 906-5000
Fax: (212) 906-5001
E-mail: HQ@undp.org
Web site: www.undp.org

The **United Nations World Food Programme** (WFP) is the food aid arm of the United Nations system and the forefront UN Agency fighting to eradicate world hunger. WFP's mission is to provide: **Food for LIFE** to sustain victims of man-made and natural disasters; **Food for GROWTH** to improve the nutrition and quality of life of the most vulnerable people at critical times in their lives; and **Food for WORK** to help build assets and promote the self-reliance of poor people and communities, particularly through labour-intensive works programmes.

In carrying out its mandate, WFP focuses on those aspects of development where food-aid interventions are most useful. It will make all necessary efforts to forge a strong link between relief and development efforts through recovery activities and disaster mitigation efforts. WFP will continue to play a significant role in providing transport and logistics expertise and assistance to ensure rapid and efficient delivery of food aid.

WFP's commodities are provided primarily to least developed and low-income/food deficit countries and always with a focus on the most vulnerable: women, children and the elderly. In 1999, WFP purchased and transported 3.4 million tons of food, which was distributed to 89 million hungry and poor people in 82 countries.

The vision of WFP is a world in which every woman, man and child has access, at all times, to the food needed for an active and healthy life. Without food, there can be no sustainable peace, no democracy and no development.

Via Cesare Giulio Viola, 68/70
Parco de' Medici
00148 Rome, Italy
Phone: (39-06) 6513-1
Fax: (39-06) 6590-632/637
Web site: www.wfp.org

World Vision is one of the largest privately funded Christian humanitarian agencies in the world. Founded in 1950 to assist Korean War orphans, the organization has become internationally recognized for its relief and development programs. In its 50-year history World Vision has grown to annually year serve more than 70 million people in 89 countries in Africa, Asia, Latin America, Europe and North America. World Vision partners with people in need to empower individuals, families and whole communities, providing assistance regardless of ethnicity, religion, politics or economic status. Aid is based on a community's level of poverty and need. Staff members work alongside these communities to nurture both physical and spiritual transformation. Interventions include clean water, nutritious food, basic health care, education, economic opportunities and Christian witness. World Vision also advocates for public policies that address root causes of hunger, poverty and injustice through public awareness and education.

P O Box 9716
Federal Way, WA 98063
Phone: (253) 815-1000
Fax: (253) 815-3445
E-mail: info@worldvision.org
Web site: worldvision.org

220 "I" Street NE
Washington, DC 20002
Phone: (202) 547-3743
Fax: (202) 547-4834
E-mail: sduss@worldvision.org
Web site: worldvision.org

Co-Sponsors

The **Academy for Educational Development** (AED), founded in 1961, is an independent, nonprofit organization committed to solving critical social problems in the U.S. and throughout the world through education, social marketing, research, training, policy analysis and innovative program design. AED is dedicated to improving people's lives by increasing knowledge and promoting democratic and humanitarian ideals. AED is registered with the U.S. Agency for International Development as a private voluntary organization. AED is exempt from federal income taxes under Section 501(c)(3) of the Internal Revenue Code. Contributions to AED are tax deductible.

> 1825 Connecticut Avenue, NW
> Washington, DC 20009 USA
> Phone: (202) 884-8000
> Fax: (202) 884-8400
> E-mail: admin@aed.org
> Web site: www.aed.org

ACDI/VOCA is a U.S.-based private non-profit development organization that advances the pace of progress in emerging democracies and developing countries. Offering a comprehensive range of technical assistance services and strategies, ACDI/VOCA benefits small- and medium-scale enterprises—particularly agribusinesses, private and public associations, governmental agencies and others. ACDI/VOCA offers both long- and short-term assistance that focuses on economic growth at the grassroots level where long-lasting advancement begins and democratic traditions take hold. As appropriate, ACDI/VOCA provides a mix of volunteers and consultants, as well as methodologies honed through years of economic development success. This assistance is tailored to meet the unique needs of every ACDI/VOCA partner.

> 50 F Street, NW, Suite 1075
> Washington, DC 20001 USA
> Phone: (202) 383-4961
> Fax: (202) 783-7204
> Web site: www.acdivoca.org

Adventist Development and Relief Agency International (ADRA) is the worldwide agency of the Seventh-day Adventist church set up to alleviate poverty in developing countries and respond to disasters. ADRA works on behalf of the poor in more than 100 developing countries spanning Africa, Asia, the Middle East, and Central and South America, without regard to ethnic, political or religious association. ADRA's projects include working to improve the health of mothers and children, developing clean water resources, teaching agricultural techniques, building and supplying clinics, hospitals and schools training people in vocational skills, and feeding people in countries where hunger is a long-term problem. When disasters strike, ADRA sends emergency supplies and stays in the disaster area to help rebuild.

> 12501 Old Columbia Pike
> Silver Spring, MD 20904 USA
> Phone: (301) 680-6380
> Fax: (301) 680-6370
> Web site: www.adra.org

America's Second Harvest is the largest domestic charitable hunger-relief organization in the United States. Through a nationwide network of more than 200 food banks and food-rescue organizations, America's Second Harvest distributes more than 1.4 billion pounds of donated food and grocery product annually to nearly 50,000 local charitable agencies. These food pantries, soup kitchens, women's shelters, Kid's Cafes and other feeding programs serve more than 26 million hungry Americans each year, including 8 million children and four million seniors.

> 35 E. Wacker Drive, Suite 2000
> Chicago, IL 60601-2200 USA
> Phone: (312) 263-2303
> Fax: (312) 263-5626
> Web site: www.secondharvest.org

Baptist World Aid (BWAid) is a division of the Baptist World Alliance, a fellowship of almost 200 Baptist unions and conventions around the world, comprising a membership of over 43 million baptized believers. This represents a community of over 100 million Baptists ministering in more than 200 countries. For 80 years Baptists have been working in partnership to entrust, empower and enable the indigenous Baptist leadership to carry out programs of emergency relief, sustainable development and fellowship assistance.

> 6733 Curran Street
> McLean, VA 22101-6005 USA
> Phone: (703) 790-8980
> Fax: (703) 790-5719
> E-mail: bwaid@bwanet.org
> Web-site: www.bwanet.org/bwaid

The Board of World Mission of the Moravian Church (BWM) represents the Moravian Church in America in overseas ministries. BWM nourishes formal mission partnerships with Moravian Churches in Alaska, the eastern Caribbean, Guyana, Honduras, Labrador, Nicaragua and Tanzania, and with the Evangelical Church of the Dominican Republic. BWM supports medical clinics in Honduras and Nicaragua and has a long tradition of supporting educational efforts of all kinds. In addition, as a missionary sending agency, BWM is involved in evangelistic witness among people who have had little opportunity to hear the gospel. Offices are in Bethlehem, Pennsylvania and Winston-Salem, North Carolina.

Reverend Hampton Morgan Jr., Executive Director
1021 Center Street
Bethlehem, PA 18018 USA
Phone: (610) 868-1732
Fax: (610) 866-9223
E-mail: bwm@mcnp.org

Call to Action is a Catholic organization of 21,000 lay people, religious, priests and bishops working together to foster peace, justice and love in our world, our church and ourselves in the spirit of the Second Vatican Council and the U.S. Catholic Bishops' Call to Action (1976). Programs include publications each month (*CTA News*, *ChurchWatch* and *Spirituality/Justice Reprint*); annual *We Are Church* national conference, 40 local chapters, a *Church Renewal Directory* of 670 national and local faith groups committed to church and societal renewal; the Future of Priestly Ministry and Women in Church Leadership Dialogue Projects and a Focus on Sweatshops.

4419 N. Kedzie
Chicago, IL 60625 USA
Phone: (773) 604-0400
Fax: (773) 604-4719
E-mail: cta@cta-usa.org
Web site: www.cta-usa.org

Canadian Foodgrains Bank is a specialized food programming agency established and operated by 13 church-related relief and development organizations. It collects substantial amounts of foodgrain donations directly from Canadian farmers and from over 200 community groups that collectively grow crops for donation to the Canadian Foodgrains Bank. An extensive network of grain elevators across Canada facilitates this grain collection. The grain and cash donations, combined with matching support from the Canadian International Development Agency, is used to provide food assistance and food security support to food deficit countries and communities around the world. This assistance is provided through its 13 member agencies and their local partners. The Foodgrains Bank operates with a food security perspective seeking to ensure that all programming is contributing to both immediate food needs and to the longer-term ability of communities and households to feed themselves. Canadian Foodgrains Bank staff and its member agencies take an active interest in food security policy issues, produce discussion papers on food security programming and policy issues, engage in education activities regarding hunger, and actively seek to influence public policy and actions to reduce hunger globally.

Box 767, 400-280 Smith Street
Winnipeg, MB, Canada, R3C 2L4
Phone: (204) 944-1993
Fax: (204) 943-2597
E-mail: cfgb@foodgrainsbank.ca
Web site: www.foodgrainsbank.ca

The **Christian Reformed World Relief Committee** (CRWRC) is a ministry of the Christian Reformed Church in North America. CRWRC shows God's love to people in need through **development** working with families and communities in food production, income earning, health education, literacy learning, spiritual and leadership skills through **relief** working with disaster survivors by providing food, medicines, crisis counseling, rebuilding and volunteer assistance and through **education** working with people to develop and act on their Christian perspective of poverty, hunger and justice. CRWRC works with communities in North America and in over 30 countries worldwide to create permanent, positive change in Christ's name.

CRWRC U.S.
2850 Kalamazoo Avenue, SE
Grand Rapids, MI 49560-0600 USA
Phone: (800) 552-7972
Fax: (616) 246-0806

CRWRC CANADA
3475 Mainway
P.O. Box 5070 STN LCD1
Burlington, ON L7R 3Y8
Canada
Phone: (800) 730-3490
Fax: (905) 336-8344

E-mail for U.S. & Canada: CRWRC@crcna.org
Web site: www.crwrc.org

Church World Service (CWS) is a global relief, development and refugee-assistance ministry of the 35 Protestant and Orthodox communions that work together through the National Council of the Churches of Christ in the U.S.A. Founded in 1946, CWS works in partnership with local church organizations in more than 80 countries worldwide, supporting sustainable self-help development of people that respects the environment, meets emergency needs, and addresses root causes of poverty and powerlessness. Within the United States, CWS resettles refugees, assists communities in responding to disasters, advocates for justice in U.S. policies which relate to global issues, provides educational resources, and offers opportunities for communities to join a people-to-people network of global and local caring through participation in a CROP WALK.

475 Riverside Drive, Suite 678
New York, NY 10115-0050 USA
Phone: (800) 297-1516
Fax: (212) 870-3523
Web site: www.churchworldservice.org

The **Compton Foundation** was founded in 1973 to address community, national and international concerns in the fields of Peace and World Order, Population and the Environment. Other concerns of the Foundation include Equal Educational Opportunity, Community Welfare and Social Justice, and Culture and the Arts. The Foundation is concerned first and foremost with the prevention of war and the amelioration of world conditions that tend to cause conflict. Primary among these conditions are the increasing pressures and destabilizing effects of excessive population growth, the alarming depletion of the earth's natural resources, the steady deterioration of the earth's environment and the tenuous status of human rights. The Foundation believes that prevention is a more effective strategy than remediation, that research and activism should inform each other and that both perspectives are needed for a productive public debate. In order to demonstrate what can be done to bring about the necessary societal transformations, the Foundation seeks to encourage positive models of change. It actively encourages collaboration between agencies, institutions, and/or foundations, and projects that connect theory, research and practice.

> 545 Middlefield Road
> Suite 178
> Menlo Park, CA 94025 USA
> Phone: (650) 328-0101
> Web site: comptonfoundation.org

Congressional Hunger Center (CHC) was formed in 1993 by Democratic and Republican Members of Congress after the Select Committee on Hunger was eliminated. Now in its seventh year, CHC is training leaders at the community, national, and international levels in solutions to hunger and poverty. Our leaders work in locations as varied as the Mississippi Delta, rural Vermont, urban Washington, DC, and in the developing world to gain experience with food security efforts at the grassroots level. Then our Fellows return to Washington, DC, to help shape national and international food security policy at a broad spectrum of host sites. Our two programs are the *Mickey Leland-Bill Emerson National Fellows Program*, with a focus on domestic hunger, and the *Mickey Leland-Bill Emerson International Fellows Program*, with a focus on global hunger. We are proud to be fulfilling our mission: "To lead, speak and act on behalf of the poor, the hungry, and the victims of humanitarian crises by developing leaders at the community, national, and international levels."

> 229½ Pennsylvania Avenue, SE
> Washington, DC 20003 USA
> Phone: (202) 547-7022
> Fax: (202) 547-7575
> Web site: www.hungercenter.org

Covenant World Relief is the relief and development arm of The Evangelical Covenant Church. Dr. Timothy Ek is Director of Covenant World Relief. The Evangelical Covenant Church has its national offices in Chicago, IL. Covenant World Relief was formed in response to the Covenant's historic commitment to being actively involved in Christ's mission to respond to the spiritual and physical needs of others.

> 5101 North Francisco Avenue
> Chicago, IL 60625-3611 USA
> Phone: (773) 784-3000
> Fax: (773) 784-4366
> E-mail: 102167.1330@compuserve.com
> Web site: www.covchurch.org

EuronAid is a European association of non-governmental organizations (NGOs) which facilitates dialogue with the Commission of the European Union in the areas of food security and food aid. EuronAid cooperates with the Commission in programming and procuring food aid for the NGOs, arranging and accounting for delivery to NGOs in the development world for distribution. In recent years, local and triangular operations (purchases within the beneficiary country or in the region) have accounted for a growing proportion of EuronAid's food aid, which meets mainly development purposes. EuronAid assimilates the experiences of NGOs involved in food aid and food security and employs this knowledge in its dialogue with the Commission and the European Parliament to achieve improved management of food aid. EuronAid provides on-going and regular training to NGOs both in Europe and in the South, on Project Cycle Management, EC policies and EuronAid procedures, as well as specialised workshops on topics such as commodity management. EuronAid was created in 1980 by major European NGOs in cooperation with the Commission of the European Union. The association has at present 32 member agencies and provides services to more than 80 European and Southern non-member NGOs on a regular basis.

> P.O. Box 12
> NL-2501 CA Den Haag
> The Netherlands
> Phone: 31 70 330 57 57
> Fax: 31 70 362 17 39
> E-mail: euronaid@euronaid.nl
> Web site: www.euronaid.nl

Food for the Hungry (FH) is an international Christian relief and development organization of Christian motivation dedicated to helping the poor overcome hunger and poverty. Food for the Hungry works in 30 countries and maintains integrated self-development and relief programs to help those affected by natural disasters such as floods, famines, earthquakes, as well as those affected by war, hunger and poverty. FH programs include child sponsorship, emergency relief and rehabilitation, community- clean water projects, health education and intervention, agriculture development, income generation, skills training and education. Food for the Hungry also works with churches and indigenous organizations to help them better serve the needs of people in their own communities. Mission opportunities are offered through Team's Ministries and longer-term assignments through the Hunger Corps program.

Food for the Hungry's Vision of a Community (VOC) philosophy makes the organization uniquely effective. (Luke 2:52) The goal of VOC is that the community and its people are advancing towards their God given potential by: being equipped to progress beyond meeting basic needs; having a growing group of Christians; loving God and each other; manifesting the fruit of the Spirit; and serving others.

The international partnership of Food for the Hungry has more than 1,600 staff, about 65 of whom work at the headquarters in Arizona. About 90 percent are nationals working in their own country. Food for the Hungry has autonomous organizations raising funds in Japan, Korea, Canada, Norway, Sweden, the United Kingdom, Switzerland, and the United States. Support also comes from individuals, churches, foundations, businesses, and several government sources.

7729 E. Greenway Road
Scottsdale, AZ 85260 USA
Phone: (480) 998-3100
Fax: (480) 998-4806
E-mail: hunger@fh.org
Web site: www.fh.org

Founded in 1946, **Freedom from Hunger** fights chronic hunger with two of the most powerful and flexible resources ever created: money and information. Operating in rural regions of thirteen developing nations, our *Credit with Education* program builds on the success of village banking by integrating basic health, nutrition, family planning, and microenterprise management education into group meetings. Results from recent studies show beneficial impacts, not only on income and income-generating activities, but also on the health and nutrition of participants and their children. Freedom from Hunger's goal is to bring *Credit with Education* to one million women by the year 2003.

1644 DaVinci Court
Davis, CA 95616 USA
Phone: (800) 708-2555
Fax: (530) 758-6241
E-mail: info@freefromhunger.org

Heifer Project International. In response to God's love for all people, the mission of Heifer Project International is to alleviate hunger and poverty in all parts of the world. HPI does this by:

■ Providing food-producing animals, training and related assistance to families and communities.

■ Enabling those who receive animals to become givers by "passing on the gift" of training and offspring to others in need.

■ Educating people about the root causes of hunger.

Heifer Project International is supported by contributions from churches, individuals, corporations and foundations.

1015 Louisiana Street
Little Rock, AR 72202 USA
Phone: (800) 422-0474
Fax: (501) 376-8906
Web site: www.heifer.org

Helen Keller Worldwide Founded in 1915 with the help of deaf-blind crusader Helen Keller, Helen Keller Worldwide (HKW) is a non-profit international development organization that prevents blindness and works to improve the survival, health, and productivity of vulnerable populations. Through its operational divisions of Helen Keller International and ChildSight,® the agency is active in 29 countries throughout Asia, Africa, and the Americas.

90 West Street
New York, NY 10006 USA
Phone: (212) 766-5266
Fax: (212) 791-7590
Web site: www.hkworld.org

International Medical Corps (IMC) is a Los Angeles-based non-profit humanitarian organization dedicated to providing emergency medical relief and long-term training to local populations where war, civil strife, and other crises have crippled health care systems. Since it's founding in 1984, IMC has served in 32 countries on four continents. Current programs include Sierra Leone, Angola, East Timor, Kosovo, Southern Sudan, Kenya, Burundi, and Pakistan.

11500 West Olympic Boulevard
Suite 506
Los Angeles, CA 90064-1524
Phone: (310) 826-7800
Fax: (310) 442-6622
E-Mail: imc@imc-la.org
Web site: www.imc-la.org

MAZON: A Jewish Response to Hunger has granted more than $20 million since 1986 to nonprofit organizations confronting hunger in the United States and abroad. MAZON (the Hebrew word for "food") awards grants principally to programs working to prevent and alleviate hunger in the United States. Grantees include emergency and direct food assistance programs, food banks, multi-service organizations, anti-hunger advocacy/education and research projects, and international hunger-relief and agricultural development programs in Israel and impoverished countries. Although responsive to organizations serving impoverished Jews, in keeping with the best of Jewish tradition, MAZON responds to all who are in need.

12401 Wilshire Boulevard, Suite 303
Los Angeles, CA 90025-1015 USA
Phone: (310) 442-0020
Fax: (310) 442-0030
Web site: www.mazon.org

Mennonite Central Committee (MCC), founded in 1920 by the Mennonite and Brethren in Christ churches in North America, seeks to demonstrate God's love by working among people suffering from poverty, conflict, oppression and natural disaster. MCC serves as a channel of interchange by building relationships that are mutually transformative. MCC strives for peace, justice and dignity of all people by sharing our experiences, resources, and faith in Jesus Christ. MCC's priorities include disaster relief, capacity building (including Ten Thousand Villages), peace building, and connecting people.

21 South 12th Street
Box 500
Akron, PA 17501 USA
Phone: (717) 859-1151
Fax: (717) 859-2171
E-Mail: mailbox@mcc.org
Web site: www.mennonitecc.ca.mcc

The mission of the **National Association of WIC Directors** (NAWD) is to provide leadership to the WIC community to promote quality nutrition services, serve all eligible women, infants and children and assure sound and responsive management of the Special Supplemental Nutrition Program for Women, Infants and Children (WIC). The purpose of the association is to link state WIC directors, local WIC directors, nutrition services coordinators and others in a national forum to act collectively on behalf of the program to include the following functions: A) To promote the improved health, well-being and nutritional status of women, infants and children; B) To provide a national resource network through which ideas, materials and procedures can be communicated to persons working in the WIC community; C) To promote good management practices and to assist WIC program directors at the state and local levels; D) To act as a resource at the request of governmental bodies and individual legislators regarding issues particular to the health and nutrition of women, infants and children and to assist WIC clients; and E) To do whatever is necessary to promote and sustain the WIC program.

2001 S Street, NW, Suite 580
Washington, DC 20009-3355 USA
Phone: (202) 232-5492
Fax: (202) 387-5281
Web site: www.wicdirectors.org

Nazarene Compassionate Ministries (NCM) is dedicated to facilitating the practices of Christian compassion by responding to pressing human needs an addressing the root cause of problems confronting the poor and powerless. NCM is the vehicle through which the Nazarene church reaches out to needy people around the world. To accomplish its mission, NCM has a four-fold approach to ministering to those in need: child development, disaster response, development education and social transformation. In short, Nazarene Compassionate Ministries seeks to put "hands and feet" to Scriptural holiness and to transform darkness to light by providing a practical demonstration of the love of Jesus Christ for all mankind.

6401 The Paseo
Kansas City, MO 64131 USA
Phone: (816) 333-7000

Oxfam America is dedicated to creating lasting solutions to global poverty and hunger by working in partnership with grassroots organizations promoting sustainable development in Africa, Asia, the Caribbean and the Americas, including the United States. Our grant-making and advocacy work aims to challenge the structural barriers that foster conflict and human suffering and limit people from gaining the skills, resources, and power to become self-sufficient. Oxfam America envisions a world in which all people shall one day know freedom—freedom to achieve their fullest potential and to live secure from the dangers of hunger, deprivation and oppression—through the creation of a global movement for economic and social justice.

26 West Street
Boston, MA 02111 USA
Phone: (800) 77-OXFAM
Fax: (617) 728-2594
E-mail: oxfamusa@igc.apc.org
Web site: www.oxfamamerica.org

Pearl S. Buck International (PSBI) is a nonsectarian development and humanitarian assistance organization dedicated to improving the lives of children from ethnic and racial minorities, disabled children (including those affected by HIV/AIDS), orphans, and displaced and refugee children, principally in Asia. PSBI recognizes that female children in all these groups are especially vulnerable and merit particular support and attention.

PSBI works in four program areas: community development, child and family services, adoption, and intercultural education. Through sustainable development initiatives and the institutional development of community-based partners, PSBI serves more than 100,000 children and their families each year. PSBI's mission is to serve children who, as a result of circumstances of their birth, have been denied access to educational, social, economic and civil rights. By building the capacity of families and local agencies to provide direct services and by promoting understanding and appreciation of different cultures, PSBI helps these children succeed.

520 Dublin Road
P.O. Box 181
Perkasie, PA 18944-0181
Phone: (800) 220-9657
Fax: (215) 249-9657
Web site: www.pearl-s-buck.org
Bringing Hope to Children Worldwide!

Reformed Church World Service (RCWS) is the relief and development program for the Reformed Church in America. RCWS works through mission personnel and partners around the world to provide emergency relief to disaster survivors, to offer rehabilitation for those who have lost their homes and jobs, to encourage development on long-term solutions to overcome hunger and poverty, and to seek justice on behalf of poor and disadvantaged people.

4500 60th Street SE
Grand Rapids, MI 49512 USA
Phone: (616) 698-7071
Fax: (616) 698-6606

RESULTS is a 501(c)(4) grassroots citizens lobby whose mission is to generate the political will to end hunger and the worst aspects of poverty in the US and around the world. We believe that hunger has a cure, but without political action, it will continue to deepen silently within our midst.

Inherent in our mission is the empowerment and active engagement of average citizens. As citizens in a democracy, we have both the right and the responsibility to a voice in the policies our government makes. We believe that the political will to end hunger and poverty will only be created if citizens are engaged in the issues and take action on them.

RESULTS' network of 900 volunteers lobby their local elected officials on issues and policies concerning hunger and poverty. Our volunteers are average citizens who have a deep concern for the state of the world and are willing to work to change it. In 2000, we have successfully lobbied for international tuberculosis control, World Bank and International Monetary Fund reform, for the Hunger Relief Act and increased funding for Head Start.

Our lobbying efforts are complemented by the educational and awareness-raising activities of RESULTS Educational Fund, a 501(c)(3) organization. The Ed Fund concentrates on public education through research, media coverage and events, which highlight the reality and severity of hunger and poverty in the world and promote effective poverty-fighting strategies. We organize, train and empower our volunteers how to speak and write powerfully about these issues. Their actions help bring these issues to the forefront of public concern,

influence the national policy-making process and create the foundation for social change.

RESULTS/RESULTS Educational Fund
440 First Street, NW, Suite 450
Washington, DC 20001 USA
Phone: (202) 783-7100
Fax: (202) 783-2818
E-mail: results@resultsusa.org
Web site: www.resultsusa.org

The RLDS World Hunger Committee was established in 1979 to engage the membership of the Reorganized Church of Jesus Christ of Latter Day Saints in a corporate response to the needs of hungry persons throughout the world. Included in the charge to the committee is a three-fold purpose: to provide assistance for those who are suffering from hunger, to advocate for the hungry, and to educate about the causes and alleviation of hunger in the world. The committee meets several times a year to consider applications for funding. The majority of the proposals considered by the committee originate with Outreach International and World Accord, both of which are recognized by the church as agencies engaged in comprehensive human development on a global scale. Projects that support food production or storage, economic development, the providing of potable water, nutrition or food preparation information, the providing of animals for transportation or cultivation are among those that receive favorable consideration by the committee.

P.O. Box 1059
Independence, MO 64051-0559 USA
Phone: (816) 833-1000
Fax: (816) 521-3096
E-mail: kschnell@rlds.org
Web site: www.rlds.org

Save the Children Federation/U.S. works to make lasting, positive change in the lives of children in need in the United States and in more than 40 countries around the world. International programs in health, education, economic opportunities and humanitarian response place children at the center of activities and focus on women as key decision makers and participants. Key principles are child centeredness, women focus, participation and empowerment, sustainability, and maximizing impact. Programs in the United States emphasize youth and community service.

54 Wilton Road
Westport, CT 06880 USA
Phone: (203) 221-4000
Fax: (203) 454-3914
Web site: www.savethechildren.org

Share Our Strength works toward ending hunger and poverty in the United States and abroad. By supporting food assistance, treating malnutrition and other consequences of hunger, and promoting economic independence among people in need, Share Our Strength meets immediate demands for food while investing in long-term solutions to hunger and poverty. To meet its goals, Share Our Strength both mobilizes industries and individuals to contribute their talents to its anti-hunger efforts and creates community wealth to promote lasting change. Since 1984, Share Our Strength has distributed more than $60 million in grants to more than 1,000 anti-hunger, anti-poverty organizations worldwide. Share Our Strength's Operation Frontline is a food and nutrition education program that trains culinary professionals and financial planners who volunteer to teach six-week cooking, nutrition, food budgeting and financial planning classes to low-income individuals in 90 communities nationwide. Share Our Strength's Taste of the Nation, presented by American Express, is the nation's largest culinary benefit to fight hunger, with more than 100 events taking place each spring. Share Our Strength's Writers Harvest: The National Reading, is the nation's largest literary benefit. Each fall, hundreds of writers read in bookstores and on college campuses to fight hunger and poverty. Corporate partnerships and publishing ventures provide substantial support for the organization's anti-hunger, anti-poverty efforts.

733 15th Street, NW, Suite 640
Washington, DC 20005 USA
Phone: (202) 393-2925
Fax: (202) 347-5868
E-mail: info@strength.org
Web site: www.strength.org

United Church of Christ Justice and Witness Ministries Office for Poverty and Hunger coordinates and stimulates all UCC hunger and hunger-related ministries; increases awareness and understanding of world hunger and related issues; and promotes, interprets and administrates the Hunger Action Fund of the United Church of Christ.

700 Prospect Avenue
Cleveland, OH 44115 USA
Phone: (216) 736-3290
Fax: (216) 736-33293
E-mail: millers@ucc.org

U.S. Committee for UNICEF works for the survival, protection and development of children worldwide through education, advocacy and fundraising. UNICEF works in over 160 countries and territories providing needed assistance in the areas of health, nutrition, safe water and sanitation, education, child protection and emergency relief.

U.S. Committee for UNICEF
333 East 38th Street, 6th Floor
New York, NY 10016 USA
Phone: (212) 686-5522
Fax: (212) 779-1679
E-mail: information@unicefusa.org
Web site: www.unicefusa.org

World Hope International, Inc. seeks to mobilize individuals and organizations to exercise their specific gifts and abilities (personally and fiscally) by working in active partnership with persons around the world for the purpose of relief, economic and social development. World Hope is currently active in 27 countries around the world as well as communities in North America.

P.O. Box 2815
Springfield, VA 22152 USA
Phone: (888) 466-4673
Fax: (703) 923-9418
E-mail: whi@worldhope.net
Web site: www.worldhope.net

World Relief is the disaster response, refugee assistance and community development arm of the National Association of Evangelicals. World Relief's mandate, as stated in its mission statement, is "to work with the church in alleviating human suffering worldwide in the name of Christ." Founded in 1944, World Relief helps U.S. churches help churches around the world help the poor in their communities.

P.O. Box WRC
Wheaton, IL 60189-8004 USA
Phone: (800) 535-LIFE
Fax: (630) 665-0129
E-mail: worldrelief@wr.org
Web site: www.worldrelief.org